‖‖ ‖‖‖‖‖‖‖ ‖ ‖‖ ‖‖‖‖‖‖‖‖‖‖ ‖‖‖ ‖ ‖‖
W9-BYU-774

SPORTS PUBLICITY

Effective communications skills are essential for any organization. In this fully revised and updated edition of his groundbreaking guide to communications in sports, Joe Favorito introduces the skills, knowledge, and techniques needed to become a successful communicator. Drawing on nearly 30 years of professional experience, including work with the International Baseball Federation, New York Knicks, Philadelphia 76ers, Bloomberg Sports, and the US Tennis Association, as well as projects with the NFL, USOC, NASCAR, MLB, MLS, and many other elite groups and brands in sports and entertainment, Favorito outlines the history of sports communications, explores all the most important professional themes, topics, and issues, and highlights exciting opportunities for future growth and development.

With a strong emphasis on professional practice and the day-to-day realities of working in sports and entertainment, the book covers all the core functional areas such as:

- Effective writing and speaking
- Building and marketing brands
- Developing contacts and networks
- Social and digital media strategy
- Gaining experience and internships
- Crisis management
- Successful pitching
- Press conferences
- Working with individual athletes, teams, and league organizations
- Agents and agency
- Understanding the global sports market.

The second edition includes brand new material on using social media, gaming, and brand integration, as well as extended real-world case studies and interviews with trailblazing PR professionals.

No other book offers such a valuable insider's view of the sports communications industry or the importance of PR and media relations in building successful sports organizations. *Sports Publicity* is essential reading for all students working in sport business, marketing, or communications, and any PR practitioner looking to improve their professional skills and technique.

Joe Favorito is a leading consultant in strategic communications, marketing, social media, and public relations, and an instructor at Columbia University, USA. Joe runs a widely respected blog on sports marketing and publicity (joefavorito.com), and publishes a weekly industry newsletter with 28,000 members in over 25 countries.

SPORTS PUBLICITY
A Practical Approach

Second Edition

Joe Favorito

Routledge
Taylor & Francis Group

LONDON AND NEW YORK

First published 2007
by Butterworth-Heinemann

This edition published 2013
by Routledge
2 Park Square, Milton Park, Abingdon, Oxon OX14 4RN

Simultaneously published in the USA and Canada
by Routledge
711 Third Avenue, New York, NY 10017

Routledge is an imprint of the Taylor & Francis Group, an informa business

© 2013 Joe Favorito

The right of Joe Favorito to be identified as author of this work has been
asserted by him in accordance with sections 77 and 78 of the Copyright,
Designs and Patents Act 1988.

All rights reserved. No part of this book may be reprinted or reproduced or
utilised in any form or by any electronic, mechanical, or other means, now
known or hereafter invented, including photocopying and recording, or in
any information storage or retrieval system, without permission in writing
from the publishers.

Trademark notice: Product or corporate names may be trademarks or
registered trademarks, and are used only for identification and explanation
without intent to infringe.

British Library Cataloguing in Publication Data
A catalogue record for this book is available from the British Library

Library of Congress Cataloging in Publication Data
Favorito, Joseph.
Sports publicity : a practical approach / Joe Favorito. – 2nd ed.
p. cm.
Includes bibliographical references.
1. Sports–Public relations. I. Title.
GV174.F38 2012
659.2'9796–dc23
2012020498

ISBN: 978-0-415-63500-4 (hbk)
ISBN: 978-0-415-63501-1 (pbk)
ISBN: 978-0-203-08472-4 (ebk)

Typeset in Bembo
by GreenGate Publishing Services, Tonbridge, Kent

CONTENTS

ACKNOWLEDGMENTS

There are many who have given guidance and input in this updated edition, as the world has changed so much since its first printing just a few short years ago.

First special thanks to contributors Melissa Murphy, Rikki Massand, Terry Lyons, Peter Titlebaum, and Jon Long for taking the time to research and author some of the pieces included in the updates. Also a great debt of gratitude is owed to Lucas Rubin at Columbia and Jennifer Karpf at the National Sports Marketing Network for their assistance and support.

I would also like to thank all those who helped with ideas and best practices. They include: Gary Abbott, Silvia Alvarez, Harrie Bakst, Mike Bass, Barry Baum, Mark Beal, Art Berke, Chris Botta, Matt Bourne, Chris Brienza, Mike Broeker, David Brody, Kevin Byrne, Peter Casey, Rick Cerrone, Vernon Cheek, John Cirillo, Sean Clancy, Wayne Coffey, Ron Cohen, Ron Colangelo, Dan Courtemarche, Rosie Crews, Tim Curry, Matt Cutler, John Dato, Chris DeMaria, Sean Dennison, Carlo DeVito, Mindy Diamond, Bob DiBiaso, Greg Elkin, Jake Fehling, Meredith Geisler, Eric Gelfand, John Genzale, Andrew Giangola, Bobby Goldwater, Jim Hague, Eric Handler, Pat Hanlon, Brendan Hannan, Bryan Harris, David Higdon, Derrick Heggans, Ron Howard, Greg Hughes, John Humenik, Peter Hurley, Bob Ibach, Fran Kirmser, Barb Kowal, Pete Kowalski, Chris LaPlaca, Dan Lauria, Dennis Lee, Chris Lencheski, Sofia Lombardo, Shawn McBride, Abe Madkour, Veronique Marchal, Ed Markey, John Maroon, Beth Marshall, Karen Menez, Jerry Milani, Craig Miller, Scott Miranda, John Mooney, Patrick Nally, David Newman, Scott Novak, Jeff Nyweide, John Paquette, Tony Ponturo, Aaron Popkey, Don Povia, Josh Rawitch, Tom Richardson, Ray Ridder, Katherine Romaine, Josh Rosenfeld, Chris Russo, Dr Harvey Schiller, Eric Schuster, Jon Schwartz, Mary Scott, Gareb Shamus, Gail Sideman, Ira Silverman, Dave Siroty, Bob Sommer, Bill Squadron, Lee Stacey, Sammy Steinlight, Ben Sturner, Bart Swain, Seth Sylvan, Cara Taback, Dave Torromeo, Brian Walker, Randy Walker, Barry Watkins,

Jay Williams, "Q" Williams, Ethan Wilson, Vince Wladika, Ann Wool, and Ian Young for their professional help, stories, and support.

As with the original project, I owe my biggest thanks to those who continue to show me such great support in all I do. My parents, my mother-in-law, my brothers, brother-in-law and sisters-in-law, aunts, uncles, nieces, and nephews, as well as my friends from OLHC, Xaverian, Fordham, and now Columbia as well, thank you. The biggest thank you remains of course for Laura, Christine, and Andrew. You all make me a better person than I ever thought I could be.

Joe Favorito (@Joefav) (joefavorito.com)
River Vale, NJ, August 2012

INTRODUCTION

We are still the appetizer, not the entrée but there is so much more on the menu now

"We now are 360 degree communicators"

Chris LaPlaca, head of Global Communications, ESPN

When the idea for this book first came about in 2006, the worlds of sports and entertainment and marketing were intertwined, but not to the level that they are today. In looking back after the first edition was published in 2007, the predictions we made have come true, but no one could have envisioned the explosion of social media, or how quickly sport on a global scale would be adapted, or how fast gaming has become part of the culture. Evolutionary moves in sport that used to take weeks or months or years now take place in minutes; heroes are crowned, careers changed, new ideas brought to market faster than ever before, hopefully with additional practices to come.

For those of you who enjoyed the first edition of the book, thank you. For those who are new, welcome. For those who provided more input in best practices, your help is appreciated.

This new updated edition won't really break that much with the best practices of the past. It is aimed more to take the new trends in social and digital media, expanded crisis management, the increased global look at sport (especially with the role of women), and bring those pieces to light, combined with even more best practices seen over the past few years.

As you may also know, when we finished the first edition of this book, I was encouraged to start a blog, which I did, and it was hoped that the blog would be a living and breathing update to the text. I hope that the site joefavorito.com has done that and will continue to do so.

The scariest part is updating this book is that I know, in the 24/7 world we live in, that no matter how quickly you are reading this after publication, the world has changed again. Shortly after finishing the first edition, I had to deal with the suicide of a young mixed martial arts (MMA) fighter, who took his life without warning. The lessons learned on how to dignify not glorify that event missed the cut in the first edition, but were included in my blog and will be in Chapter 11 here.

We also talked lightly about the rise of MMA and the Ultimate Fighting Championship (UFC) in the first edition, but here that business will be a big part of several chapters. Other than Dana White, few could have predicted the rise of the UFC brand to where it stands today. We have also gone through an Olympic cycle, a world-altering World Cup, the tragedy of the loss of a Kontinental Hockey League (KHL) team in a plane crash, the rise and fall of sports business like the United Football League (UFL) and Women's Professional Soccer (WPS), the re-birth of the National Hockey League (NHL), crisis in the Serie A, two lockouts, and so many other issues. We hope that this text in its updated form is even more reflective and informative of where the world of sport business is today, and provides additional helpful best practices missed in the first edition.

So on we go …

The business of sports has exploded in the past 25 years and some might argue that sport and its ancillary offshoots may touch more people than any industry the world over. What was once viewed as an industry that folks got involved with because of their love of a game, or a team, or an athlete, or university, has now become a multibillion-dollar international phenomenon that is as well recognized and has gained as much respect as being a doctor, lawyer, or teacher in many cases. Years ago, parents would send their kids to university and worry for their future when they heard that their child was talking about sports as a career. What did that mean? He or she wanted to be a gym teacher or a coach? He or she wanted to be a professional athlete? Was there any money in that? Was there a future? Were there jobs? I have many colleagues whose parents asked them to make sure they had some sort of business background as a fallback in case this "sports" thing didn't work. I myself took a good number of economics classes as a fallback. We all know about the rise of *Moneyball* and how analytics have played a bigger role in sport. Shiraz Rehman, assistant general manager of the Chicago Cubs, was a stock trader before going back to his passion of baseball; my classmate and friend Bob Papa—now the voice of the New York Giants—was an accounting major in case his career choice as a broadcaster didn't work out. None of those moves were that long ago.

Now much of that has changed. Over 300 global universities are now offering a steady diet of sports administration degrees, in both undergraduate and graduate levels, online, and in traditional settings. There are summer "camps" where young people can go to learn how to be an announcer, or improve their writing and reporting skills. High schools have tailored their programs to a sports business curriculum to study, much like anyone would study for a science career or a career in mechanical or automotive engineering. We are all touched every day by aspects of the sports marketing and publicity field in areas such as consumer marketing and brand awareness. The opportunities seem endless.

This growth as a whole has spawned a whole list of opportunities of smaller, more concentrated but still very valuable and lucrative fields. Areas like athletic training and sports medicine, sports marketing, sports law, and sports publicity have all emerged as specialties where they were considered more general years ago. The explosion of the digital space and growth of areas like gaming, fantasy sports, and social media management have also added opportunities. In addition, the opportunities outside the borders of North America have also come crashing down, as the business of sports becomes more of a reality in countries around the world with the growth of television, the web, and all the digital platforms that sports fits so naturally into.

There are some great stories to be told on every level, and ways to get consumers and enthusiasts interested in all these growth areas. So with that, there is a need for professionals to figure out how to effectively:

- identify and tell those stories to a broad audience
- maximize the spending that is taking place in the industry
- handle crisis and effectively manage media opportunities
- come up with creative and unique ways to cut through the clutter.

That is where the sports publicity field comes in, and that is what we will talk about in this book. The book will look at the field of sports publicity from many angles. They will include:

- how you can get started in the industry and where to look for positions no matter where you live or what your interests are
- developing strong writing and speaking techniques to strengthen your position in the industry
- going over effective ways to actually get media coverage—called "the pitch"
- the difference in and the nuances of working in the collegiate setting as opposed to the professional team setting
- the differences between working with individual athletes
- what it's like to work in a league office or for a sport governing body
- how women's athletics has changed the publicity field
- how to properly run event publicity
- the difference in global sports publicity
- the differences in working in a major market as opposed to a smaller market

- the value of crisis management and media training
- the difference between working at an agency or on the media side of the business
- the evolution, opportunities, and pratfalls of the social media landscape
- what the future holds for the business.

The book will provide a series of case studies for the industry, as well as some valuable tips for what you will need to be successful in this field. It will also give many examples of effective campaigns and ideas, and some checklists and forms that can provide the basis for effective publicity campaigns. It will give you a basic guide, with examples from some of the best in the business, as to what you can expect and how you can effectively negotiate this very exciting and fast-growing business.

There are also a few other thoughts to consider and understand before we move forward. They are themes that will be interwoven into many of the chapters in this book. The book will show how these thoughts will apply to most areas of the sports publicity industry. They are as follows.

This is not rocket science, nor are there life-savings skills involved. The business of sports communications and management is really designed to help tell stories or to grow interest in products. It will also help document history. Like most areas of publicity, this is not about saving lives or curing the common cold. However, what communications does is take stories and put them in a light that makes the subject larger than life. We help create heroes and celebrities, build brand and product loyalty, enhance charity relationships, solve problems, sell advertising, grow interest in healthy lifestyles, increase television viewership and internet traffic, grow awareness of universities, and help sell magazines, photography, memorabilia, and newspapers. I have personally seen how good publicity efforts can help children get better, make people smile, and increase the value of products and services. Are we achieving world peace? No. But we are helping people feel better about their daily lives, increasing the value of their lifestyle and workplace and assisting in telling some good stories that need to be told.

The whole world is only two blocks long. My friend and former boss Scott Layden, now assistant coach for the Utah Jazz of the National Basketball Association (NBA), used this expression all the time. The business of sports is growing. However, it is also a very insular business, and especially on the publicity side you do not have to look far to know someone who knows someone. Therefore your reputation is key with both the media and those on the business side. It is a business of networking and referrals, and those contacts you make from day one will help you grow as you move up the ladder. You need to always think about that reputation, and how it can be enhanced or damaged with regard to what you offer up in the social world. LinkedIn, Facebook, Twitter, Foursquare are all great tools for communication, but even more so today, the whole world can watch. Be smart, be careful, and always think about how your actions on a keyboard can benefit or hurt you as a professional.

Be able to sing and dance. Versatility will be touched on a great deal. The more assets you have the better off you will be and the more appealing you will be to a client. Basic business skills—knowledge of financial matters, the ability to speak a second language, strong writing and speaking skills, the ability to implement new technology—will all help you grow as a communicator.

It is the games, but it's about business too. Like anything you choose as a career, passion is essential. I would bet that the reason you are interested in sports, or sports business, as a career is because you have followed sports or played sports in your life. That is different from say, accounting or many sales positions or maybe even the financial sector. Many people grow up with a love of sports or entertainment or the arts. Being able to translate that love into a career is special. However, always remember that this is a multibillion-dollar industry and the return on the investment that those are making in you and your skills is key. Loving your job is very important. However, translating that love into success on the business end is even more important.

Communication skills are essential in every field. The great thing about the communications industry is that the skills you acquire are skills that can translate into all other areas of your professional career. Learning good writing and notetaking, learning how to deal with people and products, and selling ideas are all essential skills that you can use in another area. Sports is a passion. Many other areas of business are not. You have a very good opportunity to use your passion in business, whereas others who enter this industry to make it a business and don't understand the passion may not succeed.

You may say it's not about the money, but it is OK to think about it. The entry-level jobs in this industry are all about acquiring skills and making contacts. They are not about making money. However, what this industry has now done is show a return on investment through publicity that makes the publicity vehicle very lucrative as you grow. There are some areas of the business that are about lifestyle, and a comfortable lifestyle. The college world is one of those where you may never get rich, but there are growing areas of the sports publicity area that have become much more lucrative as the years grow and the skills I mentioned above increase. Finding that niche and marketing yourself as a professional is the key.

Incorporate the marketing side and the buzz words that go with it. Communications at the end of the day is all about networking, selling, and merchandising your subject. It does not matter whether that subject is a goalkeeper for Manchester United or the manager of the Brooklyn Cyclones or the NBA on ESPN. You are not just a "PR guy or gal." You provide an integral marketing element with some very strong brands that help to grow a business. If you look at yourself in that light, and explain that to those who you are talking to in business, then your role as a communicator will grow in value.

Always look to learn. There is a great amount of experience in this field that comes only from being involved. Therefore the more areas you work in, the more events you attend, the more people you meet, the more you learn. Hands-on experience is best. The communications industry is one that is evolving very quickly, and many times it is the entry-level people who can teach "the pros" a thing or two about new areas of technology and media. So no matter how long you are in this industry, it is important to ask questions and find the new areas that will give you and your clients an edge.

Have fun. You are going to be in, or are already in, an industry that you are passionate about. The people you meet, the places you will go, and the opportunities you will create put you worlds ahead of many people. Will you need to commit long hours, deal with a skeptical and cynical media corps, find unruly fans, unrealistic business partners, and unappreciative subjects? Yes you will. However, at the end of the day, the sports publicity field gives you an opportunity to work as a professional in an area that many people would love to be in. Always take time to reflect and consider the options and enjoy the moments that make this field special.

You are a professional, so act like one. This is a highly competitive and professional field, with millions of dollars changing hands every day. It is one you are passionate about. Always remember that you represent a subject and an industry that is always under the public eye. Therefore you are usually the first face, the first voice, the first contact that many people have. That is a great deal of responsibility. Therefore always treat it as a profession. Dress appropriately, speak appropriately, use social media correctly, always be aware of where you are and who you represent, and most importantly, act appropriately. As the saying goes, you never get a second chance to make a first impression.

Also along those lines, *pick up the phone*—or handwrite a note. I am a slave to technology, especially my Blackberry, which I do refer to as my "second wife." Technology has made us closer on a global level, but do remember to call people as well. The sound of the human voice has a great nuance, one that is lost in text and tweets and email, and one that can solve more issues than it creates. Hand-written notes also go a long way. Maybe we have lost the art of penmanship, but a note in one's own writing has a personal effect that a few hundred emails never have. It is the little things that make a big difference in a business based on people, but one that has become more and more impersonal.

Lastly, there is one major principle to always remember as a communicator. We will expound upon it later, but it is very important to keep in top of mind at all times. Unfortunately, as the industry has grown, there are people who have gotten in it to make the story about them. Now it is important to be well respected and well networked in the business. It is a profession, and like every other profession, the goal is to acquire skills and grow. It should not be about just survival or repetition. It should be about growth and success, and you should both be appreciated and valued in this very unique skill that you bring to your organization.

That being said, the media, the fans, the sponsors, the athletes are all interested in what we can do for them, but not necessarily about what our story is. You must never confuse whom the focus should be on or what it takes to get that story out there.

At the end of the day, we are not the entrée … we are the appetizer.

This is what the trailblazers of this industry had in mind when it really began early in the twentieth century. We will talk about those people in just a bit. However, the first press agents, many of whom came to sports from the entertainment industry, were all about getting ink for their clients. Their reputations sold the stories to the media, and the larger-than-life images were created. That is one of the reasons why the founders of this field are pretty much unknown. They worked the backrooms, made the phone calls, wrote and delivered the press releases, covered up and created profound images for their clients through the media. They rarely sought to get attention for themselves. They helped open the doors to the media that their clients either did not have the time to do or did not know how to do. They provided the taste for what was the main meal to come.

So remember the following—we whet the whistle of the media and the consumer with tales of unbelievable human kindness, terrific (or in some cases horrific) athletic events, or just plain sponsor recognition that makes the mundane somehow special. We do not play the games, we help chronicle them. We make sure that every athlete, sponsor, event, nonprofit foundation, National Governing Body, entourage member, announcer, official, CEO, and human interest story gets their due. It ain't about us. It is about the story. We open the doors, inflame the egos, get those to do a double take, get the insignificant mentioned in the agate, find the hometown paper, take care of the little guy and the national columnist. That's what we do. Will it get us rich? Maybe. Will it be fulfilling? Sometimes. It is it going to cure cancer or solve the issues with conflict in Saharan Africa? Well … maybe not. But sports communications, and the publicity industry in general, provide an entry point into an escape of the greater good of the soul, and not just the soul of the sports fan.

Examples

In June 2011, the Peres Center, in partnership with the Al Quds Association for Democracy and Dialogue, held a Mini World Cup tournament for girls—called "I Can Kick Too." The tournament was held in cooperation with Athena—an organization that promotes sport amongst women—and the Israel Football Association. Each team—many made up of Israeli and Palestinian girls who have been playing together throughout the year—represented one of 16 countries that competed in that summer's World Cup in Germany. After the tournament all the girls went together to watch the final match of the Israeli Women's Cup—a unique chance to learn from their idols.

Every year, the New York Yankees, as powerful a brand as there is in sports, put all their efforts into community service for "Hope Week." From veterans aid to sick kids to adults with disabilities to the homeless, every member of the organization participates in a 24/7 community service blanket that literally assist thousands. It is not a "stunt," it is carefully thought out and from the heart. It also doesn't mean that the Yankees don't do acts of service all year round. What it becomes is a platform to showcase all the good works that are done in one week, and gives the media a large slice of success for the Yankees brand. Since its inception in 2009, Hope Week has been replicated by other organizations in other cities as a best practice on how to use effective Public Relations For Community Relations, or "PR For CR." They extend the brand and create multiple levels of good will.

So is the story about all the great PR efforts that went into making these events? Will anyone remember the names of Chris Brienza, Larry Wahl, Donna Turner, or Dan Schoenberg? No. But they will remember the moment. And that is what PR is all about. Finding the way to capitalize on what the late Whitney Houston created in song as "The One Moment in Time." The moment that a publicist has a hand in and plans out for months or for just a second, that consumers harken back to when they are older and wiser, or what they share with their friends and spouses forever. When sports touched their lives, and we helped to make it special and memorable … that is the payoff.

Lastly, one thing to think about as you read this book: What are your reasons for wanting to be involved in sports commuications?

To paraphrase the great sportswriting character Oscar Madison, "Is it to be Joe Namath or own Joe Namath?" Is it because you are a fan and want to get closer to those who have been your heroes? Is it because you have always played a sport and now wanted to make it a career? Is it for the money?

Well there is no right or wrong answer to the question. As the late actor Jack Pallance said to Billy Crystal in the movie "City Slickers," it is all about one thing … and that one thing is different for everyone. It is up to you to figure it out. And by the way, you don't have to know it right now, and may not know it five years from now. But somehow, sometime, you will figure it out. Hopefully it will make the business as self-fulfilling as it has been for so many.

Where is the business today? It is all about convergence. The skills that were once in a silo that made you a good writer now have to make you a blogger, a speaker, a videographer, a photographer, and a manager. It is all as one, and it is all part of being a 24/7 communicator, with skills that apply for the business of people, as much as the business of sport.

We hope you find the new edition useful.

1

HOW IT ALL GOT STARTED

This chapter looks at the background and the history of the sports communications publicity industry, and the wide range of people who have assisted in its growth, and have gone on to other things in very successful careers. Given the amount of time and effort that goes into the field in this era, it is hard to imagine that the business really is less than 70 years old. We will take a look at some of the pioneers of the business in some of the key areas where we spend a great deal of time—collegiate sports, television, and general sport publicity—and pull some lessons that they have passed to us as industry to apply today. There are many valuable areas that the sports publicity field continues to apply today in order to make the business viable. Those lessons which we will talk about going forward remain the base for the sports publicity field. They include:

- pitching
- relationship building
- note taking and writing
- historical accuracy.

So that's where this chapter will go. Taking a look back at what has become a multibillion-dollar industry in a very short time, it was a passion for them and remains a passion for all of us. Who knew that learning how to keep score with your mom or dad, or watching hoops on TV could turn into a lucrative career? Well some folks did, and that's who we will look at as we start off.

The Hall of Fame sports writer, Leonard Kopett, in his must-read *The Rise and Fall of The Press Box*, gives a clue as to where all this started:

Keep in mind, this is when the press was much more genteel, traveled with the team on trains and planes, and was very guarded about the way sports superstars were portrayed to the general public. Sports heroes had no feet of clay at that time. They were the Greek statues that we all knew and loved. Therefore the first jobs of publicists were to cater to the media. Most in fact were not full-time positions. They were side jobs handled also by the traveling secretary. The difference was:

> For the writer or broadcaster, good relations with the field manager or head coach remain a must. He must rely on your honest reporting, and you have to rely on him steering you straight, In old days, the publicity man was the beat writer's colleague and facilitator, but not the "gatekeeper" of access to the manager; the press credential assured that. (Originally, publicity was a side duty of the road secretary; after World War II, P.R. became professionalized but was vested in one man, an assistant and a secretary.)[1]

Today's PR departments have many functions; servicing the press box is only one but is not the most important. Whoever heads it doesn't have the time or opportunity to be a buddy of the writers the way it was in the 1940s, 1950s, or 1960s, but the ability to build those relationships and call on them remains as important.

The first publicists in sports were the press agents. Many of them came from the entertainment side, where they worked with actors and actresses trying to place notes and stories which would grow interest and keep them top of mind with a media-hungry fan base. This was in an era where the newspaper and the gossip column was key. The city of New York had as many as 12 dailies at one time, each with their own form of celebrity coverage. The same held true for many large cities, and the syndicated columnists like Walter Winchell and others had their stories sent to hundreds of other newspapers throughout the country. It was a time where the stars of stage and screen were not accessible to everyday folks. The only thing that people learned was what was in the papers or heard on the radio.

Sports soon became no different. Baseball, college football and then boxing were the first sports to use full-time press agents. These agents worked with the print media to help fill the stories, and sometimes create the stories, of these heroic athletes and what went on both on and off the playing field. The two worked in tandem to grow the athlete image. They also worked together to shield the athlete from negativity. The public was thirsty for heroes, and were not interested in the "feet of clay" of the everyday man. The press agent worked to fill that need.

The other reason this chapter needs to take a look back is to understand that we are not talking about very ancient history for the most part either. The business did not really start to change drastically until the mid-1980s. This was a very short time ago when elements like the web, cell phones, ESPN, fantasy sports, the Women's National Basketball Association (WNBA), and even laptop computers were not part of the sports publicity lexicon. It was the telecopier, a huge, loud, smelly fax machine (for those of you who even know what a fax machine is), which literally burned text over a regular phone line onto pages of coated paper at about three pages per minute. It was also the phone on your desk and a typewriter that was used to get the information out. There were also very few universities at the time that saw sports management as a career choice. It was mostly volunteering, internships, and journalism that got the publicist started, many areas of which we will cover going forward. Those who got into the business may have been touched by those that we will mention very shortly, or if they were not, chances are there were others like them who affected them.

The news cycle, the press, and the image of athletes have changed over the years, but the basic premise of the publicist has hopefully remained the same. The ability to garner positive press is one of the key messages. Here is the story of how some of the "legends" were able to do it.

So here now is a "brief history of sports PR time" (my apologies to the great mathematician Stephen Hawking for stealing some of his words as a title).

OK, now that we have had a chance to give you some nice trivia for the next "future sports publicist of America" meeting you attend, let's get on to the book itself. As we do that, I implore you to always think of folks like Joey Goldstein and "Unswerving Irving" in your reading and then your careers. Always think, "What would they have done?" … "Does my presser have a memorable hook?"… "Did I make friends and follow up?"

The sports publicity "Haul" of fame

Ernie Accorsi

Now retired, Ernie Accorsi may best be known for laying the blueprint to trade for Eli Manning as General Manager of the New York Giants. However, his true genius is in being a respectful student of the sport, and that started in his younger days in Hershey, Pennsylvania, and then as assistant sports information director at Penn State University. He also served as general manager of both the Baltimore Colts and Cleveland Browns, but his true passion was in maintaining the integrity of the game and the loyalty of those around him as he rose through the ranks.

What we can learn from Ernie Accorsi: Loyalty and a deep sense of history can lead to opportunity. Accorsi began in sport as a volunteer and found ways to work his way into positions of authority over time. It was those positions—long nights, volunteering, doing whatever he could to get a start—that led to his breaks with the Colts organization and eventually helped him lead the Giants to a world championship.

Marty Appel

Yet another veteran of the baseball wars in the Bronx, Marty Appel has spent his entire career in communications, public relations, and writing. Marty has won an Emmy Award, a Gold Record, and written award-winning books, has seen it all, working on events ranging from the New York Yankees to Olympic Games. He was the youngest public relations director ever selected to lead a major league baseball team and was George Steinbrenner's first hire in that position with the New York Yankees. After nine years with the Yankees, under both CBS and Steinbrenner ownership, Appel went on to direct public relations for Tribune Broadcasting's WPIX in New York and to serve as the Yankees Executive Producer concurrently. He later directed public relations for the Atlanta Committee for the Olympic Games and the Topps Company before opening his own agency. He has also done public relations for World Team Tennis' New York Apples and for the Office of the Baseball Commissioner. His 17 books include collaborations with Larry King, Bowie Kuhn, Tom Seaver, Lee MacPhail, umpire Eric Gregg, Thurman Munson, the definitive collection of Hall of Fame biographies in Baseball's Best, and the award-winning biography *Slide, Kelly, Slide* about a nineteenth-century baseball star. His autobiography, *Now Pitching for the Yankees,* named best New York baseball book of 2001 by ESPN, was published in June 2001.

What we can learn from Marty Appel: Sometimes the sports publicity field is all about building relationships. The publicist needs to be able to build them and be able to tell the story of the client in order to be effective, and then grow a career. The people you meet when you just start out may also be the same people you will work with later on.

Joyce Aschenbrenner

One of the trailblazers for women in the industry, Joyce Aschenbrenner made her first mark in the collegiate ranks at the University of Pittsburgh, having a hand in the publicity and promotion of future National Football League (NFL) stars Dan Marino and Tony Dorsett in a time when very few women were full-time in the industry, especially on a major college level. A graduate of the University of West Virginia and a Pittsburgh native, Joyce moved on to the

University of Nevada, Las Vegas from 1982 through 1990. It was while she was with the Runnin Rebels that college basketball became an even bigger showpiece than in the past, and her work fine-tuning the pre-game excitement at Rebels basketball for Jerry Tarkanian's squad—including light shows, red-carpet entrances, and indoor fireworks—became an industry trend. She took college basketball and helped make it into showtime in the showiest city in the world.

Aschenbrenner then moved on to the University of Colorado, where she was the associate athletics director for external affairs and senior women's administrator. During that time, she also worked as a liaison to the National Collegiate Athletic Association (NCAA) Women's Basketball Tournament. Following her time in Boulder, she served a three-year term on the Defense Advisory Commission for Women in the Services for the Department of Defense. She then left collegiate athletics and moved on to The V Foundation for Cancer Research in November 2001 as the director of marketing and communications and now works on various consulting projects. She is also a cancer survivor, and role model to the many women now entering the industry at record rates.

What we can learn from Joyce Aschenbrenner: The skills that are learned as publicists can translate to many different fields, including the not-for-profit area. There are many ways to help grow the area where charities and sports intermix these days, and make that area into a very worthwhile part of sports publicity as well.

Tim Cohane

Tim Cohane was the sports editor of *Look* magazine from 1944 until it ceased publication in 1965. As publicity director for Fordham University for five years after his graduation, he wrote about Fordham's excellent football teams and coined the phrase, "The Seven Blocks of Granite," in describing the Rams' famous line of the 1930s, which included Vince Lombardi. Tim then joined The New York World Telegram in 1940 and wrote a nationally syndicated column, "Frothy Facts," until 1944 when he moved to *Look*. There he wrote more than 500 articles, many dealing with college football. Cohane taught writing at Boston University's School of Public Communications from 1968 until his retirement in 1978.

What we can learn from Tim Cohane: Good writing skills and the ability to use publicity as a toll will open many doors for you. Whether you choose to stay in the industry as a publicist or not, the skills you refine and acquire will translate to other areas.

Mike Cohen

His nickname was "inky" and throughout his career that is what Mike Cohen got for his clients. Whether he was a Jewish publicist for a Catholic university

(Manhattan College) or if he was pioneering the part of the publicity industry that dealt with announcers, directors, and TV shows (when he was head of publicity for NBC Sports), there was no one better than Mike Cohen.

Cohen's life was based on the relationships he had in the media, and how he was able to take those relationships and make "name clients" bigger or rising clients important. He always found publicity angles for the athletes at Manhattan to put the university on a national stage in sports ranging from baseball and basketball to track and field, even when the teams did not warrant national coverage for their on-field exploits. His time at NBC saw the birth of what is today the area of TV sports publicity, with most major markets devoting time and coverage to that industry alone. Cohen had the ability to talk to those in front of and behind the camera (from people like Bob Costas, Marty Glickman, and Marv Albert to directors like Michael Weisman) and come up with unique human elements about their style that he could take and work his relationships with the media to make them into stories themselves. He also had a flair for the underdog, working with jockeys and trainers at places like Yonkers Raceway, as well as baseball scouts, also finding media opportunities for them. Mike was the quintessential relationship builder, and his legacy lives on today in the form of some of the great sports publicists in this country who worked for and under him. His company, Mike Cohen Communications, became part of industry leader Alan Taylor Communications following his untimely passing in 1988.

What we can learn from Mike Cohen: One of the greatest assets in sports publicity is the ability to see a story and then formulate a plan and match it with the right media outlet. By doing this, the publicist is able to tell his subject's story in an impactful way and thus be able to grow the image of the subject beyond what one thought was its normal boundaries.

John Condon

He is probably best known as the legendary "voice" of Madison Square Garden, but John Condon's work as a boxing publicist throughout a lifelong career was really his hallmark. He arranged some of the classic fights not only in Madison Square Garden, but around the world, and was arguably the best fight promoter and publicist during the sport's glory days of the 1950s and 1960s. John also had a great love for children, and New York's Kid Gloves program, founded by him when he was president of Madison Square Garden Boxing, was a trailblazing way to reach inner-city kids and get them off the streets for nine weeks each summer. Boxers such as Mike Tyson, Mark Breland, and Hector (Macho) Camacho all went through the Kid Gloves Program in their youth. As a symbol of his outstanding achievement in publicity and promotion, the current Madison Square Garden press room is named in his honor, as is the John F.X. Condon Award, given out annually by the Professional Boxing Writers Association to its top writer.

What we can learn from John Condon: Publicists have the ability to wield a great deal of influence with both the media and the client. That does not differ no matter what the market size or the interest in the sport or the product. Remembering that publicity has the ability to help tell stories and influence public opinion is always important.

Bob Cornell

One of the profession's biggest advocates and strongest mentors has now been plying his trade in upstate New York for over 30 years. Bob has been at Colgate University since May 1976, and his dedication to writing and teaching excellence, as well as molding the lives of young professionals entering the business, is unparalleled. In July 2001, Cornell was inducted into the College Sports Information Directors Association Hall of Fame. On September 19, 2003 he was inducted into the SUNY-Cobleskill Athletic Hall of Fame and on December 4, 2003 he received the Scoop Hudgins Outstanding Sports Information Director Award from the All-American Football Foundation. During his career in the sports information field, he has served as a press liaison for numerous NCAA and Eastern College Athletic Conference (ECAC) championships and regional events, including Media Coordinator of the NCAA Division I Golf Championships in 1977. He served on the press liaison staff for the US Olympic Committee at the 1984 Olympic Summer Games in Los Angeles and the 1988 Olympic Winter Games in Calgary. In addition, he was on the press liaison staff at four Olympic Festivals (1981, 1982, 1983, 1987). He has served on the Site Selection, Post-Graduate Scholarship, and Ethics Committees of the College Sports Information Directors of America. Cornell is a past president of the Eastern College Athletic Conference Sports Information Directors Association, and the 1992 recipient of the Irving T. Marsh Service Bureau Award, presented annually to the sports information director who has contributed the most to the work of the Bureau during the year and throughout his or her career.

What we can learn from Bob Cornell: If we choose the sports publicity field not just as a career but as a lifestyle, we can do great things. Mentoring and helping to mold young men and women, both as student athletes and as rising journalists and publicists, are very important in making the industry grow.

Bob Fishel

Bob Fishel was legendary baseball owner Bill Veeck's publicist for both the Cleveland Indians and the St. Louis Browns (now the Baltimore Orioles), and was the man who signed midget Eddie Gaedel to a Browns contract. In the classic book, *Veeck as in Wreck*, Veeck recalls Fishel's involvement in perhaps the greatest baseball publicity stunt of all time.

Instead of bringing the contract up to his room, Bob Fishel set up a meeting at a corner a block or two away from his hotel. Bob drove up in his Packard, Eddie slid into the front seat and scribbled his name onto two contracts and jumped out. One of the contracts was mailed to league headquarters on Saturday night, which meant it would not arrive til Monday morning. The other was given to (manager) Zack Taylor, in case our prized rookie was challenged by the umpires. The morning of the game I wired headquarters that Eddie Gaedel was put on our active list.[2]

Fishel arranged all the pre-game publicity, made sure that the photograph made the wires, and came up with the number (1/8) Gaedel wore on his back. He spent many years with Veeck, the man who is arguably the greatest promoter in the history of baseball. After leaving, he moved on to the Yankees, spending 20 years in the Bronx in an era that saw some of the greatest and toughest years for the Bronx Bombers. At the time of his death, he was the American League (AL) vice-president for public relations. As a symbol of his outstanding work, an award named in his honor is given to the outstanding baseball publicist each year. He also devoted a great amount of time to his alma mater, Hiram College, which has its baseball complex named in his honor.

What we can learn from Bob Fishel: The "stunt" still remains a key part of sports publicity. No matter how outrageous an idea is, it is the job of the publicist to weigh the options, determine the course of action, and figure out the best plan to get coverage. We can also learn that the "stunt" is also one part of our job. Dealing with the media before and after that event in a professional manner is also very important.

Rosa Gatti

Rosa Gatti joined ESPN in its first year of operation in 1980 and now serves as an advisor for ESPN Communications and oversees all of ESPN's corporate outreach initiatives, including The V Foundation for Cancer Research, corporate giving, cause marketing, and volunteerism.

Gatti joined ESPN in July 1980 as Director, Communications, and, together with her staff, built the communications department, establishing policies and procedures pertaining to media relations and viewer response. A year later she became a Vice President, and in July 1988 she was promoted to Senior Vice President, Communications. In 2003, she was promoted and given additional responsibilities as the corporate information liaison to The Walt Disney Company, parent company of ESPN. Gatti was responsible for all public relations efforts, including ESPN's Investor Relations matters.

Prior to joining ESPN, Gatti spent four years as the Sports Information Director at Brown University (1976–1980). Before Brown, Gatti was employed by her alma mater, Villanova University, starting as a secretary in the university's sports information office in 1973. Gatti was promoted to Assistant Director within a year, and shortly thereafter (December 1974) became the first female Sports Information Director (SID) in the NCAA's major university division.

During her career as a Sports Information Director, Gatti was selected as President of the ECAC SIDs and served as Vice President of CoSIDA (the national organization of College Sports Information Directors of America).

Gatti has received numerous awards for her contributions in communications and the industry including the Association of Cable Communicators Achievement Award in 2005, a Wonder Women of the year by Women in Cable and Multichannel News, and CableFax's Community Service Award, both in 2008.

What we can learn from Rosa Gatti: Being in the right place at the right time and surrounding yourself with competent people who share your vision will help you expand your career. You have the ability to grow in a start-up situation as long as you are flexible and put yourself in a position to learn from those around you as much as they will learn from you.

Joey Goldstein

For over 45 years, New York based publicist Joey Goldestein trafficked his wares in the national sports scene. His clients over the years included Bob Hope, corporations such as Mobil Oil, the New York Road Runners Club, the New York City Marathon, the Millrose Games, manufacturers Hanover and RJR Nabisco, and for years, the entire sport of harness racing. He wrote for newspapers, handled publicity for Madison Square Garden college basketball, and worked more fights for people like Joe Frazier than most people can remember. He worked every sport, including the Saudi Arabian Olympic soccer team, which is the ultimate irony for a Jewish boy from Conway, South Carolina.

His closest friends were three gentleman who hated each other, New York Post columnist Dick Young, New York Times columnist Red Smith, and the legendary Howard Cosell, but they all worked with Joey. Until his passing in 2009, he remained one of the true Runyonesque characters in the sports PR business, always wearing raincoats, carrying little note cards and a very clean linen handkerchief.

Harness racing was Joey's biggest success. Goldstein started working full-time for Roosevelt Raceway on Long Island in 1954, and later took over PR for the entire sport; until he gave it up in 1980, he generated attention far beyond the public's interest. His best story involved a French trotter named Jamin which came to the US for the International at Roosevelt Raceway. Goldstein created the myth that Jamin had to have artichokes to survive. Since there were no artichokes on Long Island at that time of year, they had to be found and flown in from California and then helicoptered to the track so that the race could take place. Jamin won the race amidst publicity, befitting the

Kentucky Derby. The real story was that the artichokes were used by the horse as a laxative.

Unlike other mainstream publicists, Goldstein worked every holiday and eve, believing that it was easier to get stories in on slow news days—and he is probably right, albeit with less circulation. His Rolodex or connections in New York for restaurants and theater tickets were unparalleled for the longest time.

What we can learn from Joey Goldstein: Even in a large market with a great amount of competition, the publicist can find ways to make stories compelling and unusual, and find ways to get their subject coverage. It may not always be the perfect kind of coverage, but the potential for solid exposure is always there, especially when the publicist has strong media connections.

Mary Jo Haverbeck

Another female trailblazer is former Penn State Associate Sports Information Director Mary Jo Haverbeck. The Wilmington, Delaware, native began her sports information career at the University of Delaware on a volunteer basis in the late 1960s, introducing the then three-sport Blue Hen women's program to the media while working full-time in the university's Public Information Office.

Haverbeck's interest in sports journalism led her to graduate school at Penn State where she wrote her master's degree thesis on media coverage of women's sports. Women's athletic director Della Durant had been lobbying for coverage of Penn State's then nine-sport womens program and sports information director John Morris hired Haverbeck on a part-time basis to write releases.

Haverbeck began a relentless campaign to place stories about Lady Lion coaches and athletes. Her persistence paid off as Penn State's women's program was featured on ABC's Wide World of Sports and in an extensive profile in *Sports Illustrated*. A photo of a Penn State Lady Lion lacrosse player also appeared on the cover of *Time* magazine.

Her efforts have not gone unnoticed, as she was the first woman to ever receive the Arch Ward Award for outstanding work in the college sports information field.

What we can learn from Mary Jo Haverbeck: The opportunity for women in sports publicity is growing very quickly. The advent of Title IX, as well as the added interest in women's professional sports, has opened career opportunities like never before. The need for quality publicists of any gender is greater today than ever before.

Gladys Heldman

The late Gladys Heldman—publisher, promoter, and modern matriarch of women's tennis—was honored by the Women's Tennis Association (WTA) with the 2012 Georgina Clark award.

She was ranked No. 1 in Texas as an amateur and played at the US National Championships and Wimbledon. In 1953, she became the founder, publisher, and editor of *World Tennis* magazine. When she sold the magazine in 1972, she liked to say she "was replaced by seven men." Before starting the Virigina Slims tour, her most successful promotion was the 1962 US Championships at Forest Hills, New York, the precursor to the US Open. The field was weak because top tennis players were competing in Europe for bigger under-the-table money. Gladys and her friends put up enough money to jet in the players from Europe and the tournament "was a huge success." However, that achievement came at a price.

Insulted by huge gender pay disparities at tournaments and rebuffed by the USLTA about forming a tour, the players turned to Heldman. The Original 9 signed $1 contracts with Heldman to start a women's tour and she rallied the support of her friend Joe Cullman at Philip Morris to land tour sponsorship. The Virginia Slims cigarette brand featured a logo of a 1920s flapper and the slogan "You've Come a Long Way, Baby."

Heldman helped organize the first tournament in Houston with prize money totaling $7,500. She often attracted advertisers by cold-calling the CEOs of companies and contacting anyone capable of promoting or sponsoring a women's pro tournament. The male leaders of US tennis threatened to suspend anyone who competed in Houston, but later realized that they should acknowledge those players after they figured out Philip Morris had more money. The WTA was formed in 1973, uniting all of women's pro tennis in one tour, and the US Open offered equal prize money that year for the first time.

In 1979, Gladys Heldman was inducted into the International Tennis Hall of Fame. The WTA celebrated the 40th anniversary of women's professional tennis in 2010, and the tour offered $85 million in worldwide prize money. Serena Williams leads the way with $35 million in career earnings.

What we can learn from Gladys Heldman: Promotion of a strong idea and attention to detail, along with linking key brands to the cause, will overcome a great amount of adversity.

Irv Kaze

Irv Kaze was the only man who can claim to have won a World Series ring working for Yankees owner George Steinbrenner and Super Bowl ring working for Raiders managing partner Al Davis. He also was the Hollywood Stars publicist when they played the final PCL game in Los Angeles on September 15, 1957. While attending New York University he worked for the *New York Post*. Upon graduation he began his baseball career with the Hollywood Stars of the Pacific Coast League, moving up to the parent Pittsburgh Pirates when the Dodgers moved from Brooklyn. Irv was the first public relations director of the Los Angeles (now Anaheim) Angels. When Al Davis became commissioner of the Arena Football League (AFL), Irv joined his staff and later became business manager and assistant to the president of the San Diego Chargers for seven years. Irv has been recognized on six occasions as the Best Radio Talk Show host by South Carolina Sports Broadcasters.

What we can learn from Irv Kaze: Sometimes we will work for very difficult subjects who may be neither media favorites nor have a full understanding of how sports publicity is done correctly. Being able to balance and educate while maintaining your credibility is difficult but doable, and is essential in today's world where sports and entertainment are mixed and the coverage of sports is so extensive.

Ramiro Martinez

One of the great Hispanic sports publicists was Cuban Ramiro Martinez, who oversaw the publicity for much of Cuban baseball and the AAA Havana Sugar Kings in the late 1950s. Martinez's gregarious personality and flamboyant publicity stunts made the Sugar Kings one of baseball's most storied franchises, as the International League grew in stature as the premier minor league before major league baseball expansion.

Martinez used his talents to help owner Bobby Maduro lure some of the top Hispanic players of the era to the team on their way to the major leagues, including Luis Arroyo, Tony Gonzalez, Cookie Rojas, Leo Cardenas, and Mike Cuellar. He also developed a strong friendship with rising Puerto Rican star Roberto Clemente, and stayed friends with Clemente throughout his life. Martinez also worked on a promotion to have new Cuban leader Fidel Castro pitch for the team shortly after he assumed power in 1959. The Sugar Kings went on to capture their first and only title. Martinez worked hard to keep the Sugar Kings in the sports eye as Castro's power grew, but unfortunately the team was forced to leave the island in 1960 after the United States implemented sanctions against the Island nation. Martinez went with the team to Jersey City, New Jersey, where it folded, despite his publicity efforts, after one season.

What we can learn from Ramiro Martinez: Sometimes, despite all the best intentions, great publicity stories, and hard work, forces outside can take control and make the job less than successful. Publicists always need to stay focused and do their job despite the outside forces which they cannot control. The publicist must expect the unexpected.

Harvey Pollock

The "Super Stat," as he was dubbed by Philadelphia Bulletin writer Bert Kiseda, has been involved with the NBA and sports in Philadelphia ... well ... since there has been an NBA in Philadelphia. One of only three employees to have worked for the league every day since it began operations, Pollock continues to go strong. The author of an annual NBA statistical guide, and now a member of the Naismith Hall of Fame as well as 11 others, is in a league by himself. He started as the assistant publicity director of the old Philadelphia Warriors (now Golden State) in 1946–1947 and midway through the 1952–1953 season, he became head of media relations for the Warriors. He maintained that post until the spring of 1962, when the franchise was sold to San Francisco. During the 1962–1963 season, when there was no team in Philadelphia, neutral court games were played here and he did the publicity to maintain his NBA connection. Then in 1963–1964, the Syracuse franchise was shifted to Philadelphia and the franchise was renamed the "76ers." He served as the media relations director for the 76ers until the 1987–1988 season, when he assumed the duties of Director of Statistical Information for the team, a position he still holds. Long before the league adopted the following categories, he kept them for Philadelphia home games: minutes played blocked shots, offensive and defensive rebounds, steals, and turnovers. At the same time, he began tabulating categories the league didn't do and the esoteric items and tables eventually became part of his widely read stat guide. In addition to his NBA duties, he also heads basketball stat crews at six major colleges in the Philadelphia area, and heads the crew at the Major Indoor Lacrosse League games of the Wings, and the Soul in the Arena Football League. His past includes 15 years as the head of the Baltimore Colts NFL stat crew and in football, also in Philadelphia, led the crew for the Philadelphia Stars, Bell and Bulldogs. He currently has been Temple University's football statistician since 1945. He is en route to *The Guinness Book of Records* by wearing a different t-shirt every day since June 29, 2003.

What we can learn from Harvey Pollock: Sports publicity remains a statistics driven business for the most part. By being able to create compelling stories via all the stats and figures that go into the games, and then being able to pitch those stats effectively, we can find new angles that have not been explored, even for the simplest of efforts.

Chuck Prophet

The amount of outstanding athletes that have come from the Southwestern Athletic Conference over the years is amazing. Football stars such as Walter Payton, Doug Williams, and Jerry Rice, and basketball hall of famers such as Willis Reed all track their roots to the schools that for many years had to toil in obscurity in the publicity world because of their largely African-American student body in the racially charged south. The push to bring these schools mainstream publicity and help get their stories told was led by longtime Mississippi Valley State sports information director Chuck Prophet.

Prophet worked with the Delta Devils for over 30 years before his retirement in 2001, and helped shape the publicity efforts of star athletes such as Jerry Rice, Willie Totten, Ashley Ambrose, Patricia Hoskins, and Eugene and Herman Sanders. He also publicized the exploits of such storied coaches as Archie Cooley and Lafayette Stribling.

As sports information director, Prophet received several honors, including selection as SWAC sports information director of the year and black college sports information director of the year. He also served on the College Sports Information Directors of America Board of Directors.

What we can learn from Chuck Prophet: There are always great stories to be told, even in the most rural of communities and in the smallest of sports efforts. Being able to uncover them, nurture them, and then promote them is a great challenge, but can be a very rewarding one.

Pete Rozelle

Perhaps the greatest leader in the history of modern sport, Alvin "Pete" Rozelle began his career at the University of San Francisco, working as a student publicist for the school's football team. He had already worked in public relations for the LA Rams' front office and while in the athletic office at the university he marketed the Don's national championship basketball season of 1949 into a national media event. He graduated from the University of San Francisco that year.

He held a series of public relations jobs in Southern California, marketing the 1956 Olympics in Melbourne, Australia for a Los Angeles based company. He joined the Los Angeles Rams as its public relations specialist. By 1957, Rozelle was offered the GM job with the Rams. He turned a disorganized, unprofitable team, lost in the growing LA market, into a business success and from there then went on to replace Bert Bell as NFL Commissioner.

What we can learn from Pete Rozelle: If we want to grow in the sports industry on the team or league side, the opportunity exists. The publicist is as essential part of the business of sports and many times is the link between the on and off field efforts of a team, a league, a sport, or an athlete. If we learn about all aspects of our business, it is possible to ascend to great heights.

Irving Rudd

"Unswerving Irving" was one of the greatest sports publicists not just of his era, but of all time. His ability to garner publicity for the most mundane harness race to the World Champion Brooklyn Dodgers made him the heavyweight in the sports publicity industry before anyone knew what the industry was. His tales (also contained in his book) from purposely misspelling the name of "Yonkers Raceway" to "Yonkers Racewya" were the stuff of creative genius. As was done before the days of billable hours, economies of scale, "column inches," and all the other terms that became publicity buzzwords and areas of measured growth as the public relations business expanded into the multibillion-dollar industry it is today.

Irving Rudd's career spanned the heyday of so many sports of a bygone era in New York. He began in the 1930s and 1940s in the world of boxing, working with some of the greats of the fight game from Beau Jack through Sugar

Ray Robinson, Rocky Graziano, Muhammad Ali, Ken Norton, and Sugar Ray Leonard. Along the way Unswerving Irving served as the chief publicist for the legendary Boys of Summer (the Brooklyn Dodgers, through their greatest days, including their only championship in 1955). He also was a key player in the sport of Kings, handling some of the biggest races, and publicity stunts, in the golden era of horse racing. One of the most beloved figures in professional sports, his legacy may be gone but it will never be forgotten.

What can we learn from Irving Rudd: No matter how big the event, how well recognizable the team is, we can always dig to find a story yet to be told. Creativity is also key, and presenting those opportunities in a unique light to the media will help us shape our story.

Don Smith

Another of the great publicists during the rise of the NFL was New York Giants impresario Don Smith. Smith oversaw the golden-boy era of Fran Gifford and Kyle Rote in the 1950s and stayed with the Giants through Fran Tarkenton and the darker days of the early 1970s, all the while working for the Mara family, protecting and promoting the image of the players and an organization always known for class. That resonated well with its top publicist. Smith was always known for his ability to turn a story, massage a player image, and, when needed, fire off "deep truthed" sarcasm which made him a favorite among New York scribes. One of his best lines came at the end of his run with the Giants, when the team struggled in the early 1970s: "You've heard about the Rubber Band Defense that bends but never breaks? Ours doesn't break either, but it stretches 101 yards." Through it all he remained fiercely loyal to the organization and to the Mara family. He is one of only a handful of top publicists ever to work for the Giants. The list includes Ed Croke and current Giants PR maven Pat Hanlon, all known for their ability to deal with the media, pitch stories, and preserve the tradition of the storied football franchise.

What can we learn from Don Smith: Being able to work in a professional atmosphere and represent the interests of your organization or subject as they would want you too are key. Also having some balance as the organization spokesperson will give you credibility with the media in good times and bad.

Roger Valdiserri

Notre Dame's former sports information director is universally regarded as the best ever at his profession. A 1954 graduate of Notre Dame, Valdiserri spent nearly 30 years overseeing sports publicity at his alma mater. He pioneered some of the publicity concepts that everyone uses today, such as having football coach Ara Parseghian record answers to questions for the media. The system dramatically reduced the time that Parseghian had to spend meeting enormous media demands. He was the king of balancing precious access time between the legendary football and basketball programs and the press. He maximized the effort both sides put in, and gave everyone the opportunity to do their jobs. Valdiserri may be best known for the changing of Joe Theismann's name from THEES-man to THEIS-man—which happened to rhyme with Heisman (awarded annually to the outstanding collegiate football player in the US). "Great" is an appropriate word to describe Valdiserri's contributions to Notre Dame. He's a member of the CoSIDA Hall of Fame, and was named one of the 100 most influential people in college football.

What can we learn from Roger Valdiserri: As sports publicists, sometimes we have to be the calming voice in the center of the storm. Many people will look to the publicist as the voice of reason when the media are swarming, and we have to be professional and calm enough to make judgments at a time when emotions may be running rampant. Finding the best way to deal with the media and creating a "win–win" situation for all involved is a big element of success in the field.

Christy Walsh

Walsh was a pioneer of sports licensing. His most frequent device was getting sports stars to put their names on ghostwritten articles in newspapers and magazines. Many a world series game was "analyzed" by a star who was nowhere near the scene of action. A 1911 graduate of St. Vincent's College in Los Angeles, Walsh first worked for the *Los Angeles Express*. In 1921, he started his own syndicate, creating a major industry for stars like Ruth, Gehrig, Rockne, among others. Walsh was sports director for the 1939–1940 New York World's Fair. His biggest success may have been working with Babe Ruth as his full-time publicist during the Babe's heyday. There were numerous philanthropic events with kids that the Babe took part in and assisted with from afar, all with Walsh as the master planner. He was one of the first to look to sports publicity as a solid industry, and he did very well with it.

What do we learn from Christy Walsh: Working with the individual athlete can have its merits as well. Helping grow the "image" as a publicist, no matter how well the athlete's career goes, can be very rewarding.

Conclusion

In conclusion, it is important for the publicist to know and understand the efforts of those who went before him or her, and be able to equate those efforts, especially those successes, to the business today. That is the best way that the publicist will be able to grow in the profession and have a better understanding of how the industry got to where it is today.

Notes

1 Koppett, Leonard. *The Rise and Fall of the Press Box*. Sport Classic Books, 2003.
2 Veeck, Bill with Linn, Ed. *Veeck as in Wreck*. University of Chicago Press, 1962.

2

GETTING STARTED AND BUILDING CONTACTS/VOLUNTEERISM

Being able to sing and dance

This chapter will examine all the ways a person can get started in communications, and how skills from other areas can help best prepare someone for a potential career. It will look at efforts such as volunteering, internships, blogging, and all the ways and skills you will need to try and get a foot in the door and begin your career. The chapter will also provide many examples of how some of the best in the industry have started their careers.

In any pursuit, motivation needs to be the key. The entry-level position needs to be filled by those with a passion and a desire to learn. Therefore it is extremely important to be also able to step out and ask for help. Network. Just like finding a job when unemployed, or gaining rungs on a social ladder, networking in sports is just as important for you as knowing which network the NHL plays on these days. But where to start?

Here are a few suggestions, both for the young person starting out and the person currently in a career but looking to make the jump.

Step 1: Volunteering

Until the last few years when there was a downturn in the economy, volunteering seemed to be a lost art. Getting dollars for any activity was tantamount. However, the influx of experienced people into the job market has now re-jigged the economy, and experience at every level is now the requirement. With that potential of experience comes fewer dollars. That's the bad news. The good news is that there is still a wealth of ways to get experience if you can fit it into your time and budget. The explosion of the digital space has also created the ability for virtual opportunities in writing, research, and design that never existed before, making the ability to find what you like, or what you don't like, even more available.

Sports and entertainment remain an industry that is still growing, especially on a global level, in terms of events, corporate sponsorship, and man-hours needed to pull off said events. There is no shortage of space for people to work. What there is, especially in smaller markets, is a shortage of quality people willing to put in the time investment to make events the success they can be, or even to make sure that those involved—athletes, organizers, corporate sponsors—get out of it what they are putting in. There is always the need for volunteers to fill that gap.

In the next few pages we will list just some of the organizations, events, and opportunities that you may be able to contact, not only where you live, work, or attend school now, but anywhere around the world. From Sochi 2014 to two events in Rio (World Cup 2014 and Olympics 2016) to local bike-a-thons, there remains a huge need for volunteers and all are *recruiting* quality volunteers now. In most major cities there are events that are constantly looking for volunteers. The New York City Marathon, the US Open, the White River Games in Indiana, the Rodeo in San Antonio, the Boston Marathon, even the Super Bowl organizing committee in New York for 2014 will take on hundreds of volunteers. The great thing if you are interested in working with the media, or even seeing how media operations work, is that there is a need with every mega-event to have quality, smart people work in the press room, press tent, what have you. For example, the US Open, which if you are not aware is the world's largest annual sporting event, is held every year at the beautiful Billie Jean King National Tennis Center in Flushing, New York. Every year, it is like handling the media crush for the Super Bowl every day for over two weeks. Over 1,500 journalists are accredited from around the world, and the level of volunteers in the media room was outstanding. They came not just from around the city, but from around the country and around the world to work the event, see and speak to journalists, and many actually went on to get credible jobs in sports and entertainment through the contacts they made in the press room. People every year from many professions take their two weeks of vacation just to work in the pressroom, in the hope that it opened some doors to ignite their career goal change. Is that a risk? Yes. But for some the risk paid off in great experience and the opportunity to find what they did or did not want to do.

Now taking two weeks to work the tennis US Open or flying to Russia for the Olympics is not for everyone. So what to do if you are not in a city that has a major event, or for that matter a major sports team? Even better. The ever-growing rage of sports statistics and coverage down to the little league level has created an even greater need for folks to do things like manage websites, volunteer to write game stories for websites and local newspapers, and in some cases, even create entire jobs built around selling sponsorships for leagues, creating coverage, and doing regular stats projects for websites.

Example

Dr Harvey W. Schiller is perhaps one of the most well-respected and accomplished professionals in the world of sport. Dr Schiller has headed the Southeastern Conference, the United States Olympic Committee, Turner Sports, YankeeNets, the International Baseball Federation, and several other high-profile public and private corporations. Yet for all his success, Dr Schiller did not start full time in athletics until he was almost 46. Prior to that his work was all volunteering—from running the rugby club at the University of Michigan (where he was getting his doctorate) to being on the athletic council for the Air Force Academy, among many other positions. Through his time in Colorado Springs, he met the people at the United States Olympic Committee (USOC) and he became the venue coordinator for boxing at the 1984 Los Angeles Summer Games. There he met more people involved in the Olympic movement and college athletics. When the Southeastern Conference was looking for a commissioner, they wanted a different background. Dr Schiller, a lifelong volunteer with a deep resume, got an interview and his first full-time job in sport.

Example

In the early 1990s, as the Atlanta Braves were beginning to make their legendary string of playoff runs, they realized that they needed to do a series of local events to promote both attendance and tune-in (getting people to watch the broadcasts) on WTBS. The Braves created a road show, which would go to local towns, set up autograph sessions, Q&A with former players, and give away items to create interest in the team. Peter Hurley, now the president of event management company Synergy Sports, was put in charge of creating the program and mapping out the events. It was a very daunting task since each small town throughout the south had to be identified and then he had to go in and locate space, deal with local politics, and drive interest in the coming event. However, what Peter found was that, in several towns, the local volunteers who ran the Little League or the softball league had their own mini publicity and sponsorship set up, all as volunteers. In particular was Marie Jordan from Alabaster, Alabama. Peter met this woman, she was able to identify local sponsors, people of influence, and generate interest in the event, all from her volunteering experience. She did it because of her passion to assist her local community and her interest in sports. It became both a regular stop and one of the most successful events the Braves ever did.

If the local Little League is not the opportunity you want, it is important to look to the collegiate ranks for a start. If you are a student or even working in a town where there are universities that offer athletics, it is important to look there to take advantage of the sports information office, the college newspaper, radio station, television station, or even website and start there as a volunteer. No matter what size the college, there is a huge need for volunteering and assisting in any way, shape, or form with those who get paid to assist student athletes on a day-to-day basis. It may not be covering football Saturdays at Michigan, but the sports communications office will probably need help with rowing, or softball, or another of the so-called Olympic sports that the Maize and Blue have. Those athletes are sometimes even more interesting to cover because they don't normally get the exposure and would probably be very open to assisting you in your needs to find ways to get them exposure (we will talk more about intercollegiate athletics later in the book). On top of that, you will probably come across other non-athletes, alumni, and university officials who will also be appreciative of your work in trying to gain life experience toward a full-time job. It does pay off sometimes to be a bigger fish in a small sea.

One other thing. If you want to work in sports, learn the audience you currently serve. If you are on the collegiate campus, *volunteer* to write for the school paper, radio station, website, or TV station. In many cases, these will not only open some doors for you into the sports PR side, but you will hone some very vital skills like reporting, note taking, public speaking, and even photography or layout and design. These basic skills are all very important in putting together the PR puzzle. They give you assets you may not have ever had the opportunity to add. Also, you may be able to use those press credentials, respectfully and honestly, to gain entry into covering some non-campus events. In New York, for example, many of the collegiate radio stations have the opportunity to cover the professional teams on a regular basis. That can be true in any market if you ask properly and act professionally. You may also, if you are lucky enough, be able to write or talk about alumni who have gone on to the professional ranks in one way or another through the guise of the school media outlets—another great opportunity gained through volunteering.

OK, let's move off the collegiate level to the pro level. Currently there are literally hundreds of minor league baseball teams, minor and junior hockey teams, minor league basketball teams, NASCAR events, United States Tennis Association (USTA) pro circuit events, and arena football clubs, in this country. That does not include all the mixed martial arts tournaments, professional wrestling, poker events, marathons, and Special Olympic and charity events. All of which suffer from a great amount of time needed to get the job done and not enough staff. It's simple, take a look in the local paper or website if you don't already know, and contact the media relations person. *Ask* them if you could volunteer to help them on a game night. My bet is there will be stunned silence, followed by a little laughter, and then you are in the door.

> **Important tip**
>
> If you don't get through on the first attempt or get turned down on the first try, try and try again. You may be catching someone who couldn't pay his stat crew, someone who lost all the popcorn sales money that night, someone who just got into a heated argument with the parking concessionaire and is having a bad day. Also, be cognicent of schedule and time. For example, do not call Raymond Ridder, head of communications for the Golden State Warriors, at 18:00 on a night when they have a home game. It shows that you don't really know their business. Think if you were in their shoes *when* would be a good time to call, and call then. Email is also a start, but follow up with a phone call as well.

So, to recap volunteering:

1 Locate the events in your community and campus.
2 Do your homework as to when and what to ask to help with—don't just show up and say "what can I do?"
3 Be prepared to put in long hours; treat the volunteering as your job.
4 Ask questions of the professionals there, both media members and staff.
5 Don't take volunteering for a lesser event or sport as a negative. Find ways to make the most out of it.
6 Make sure when you say you can do something that you have thought through the time commitment and stick to the plan. Worse than not volunteering is letting someone down.

Step 2: Internships

One of the great areas where a sense of pride develops for the publicity professional is selecting interns and watching them grow into professionals. Internships, other than volunteering, are probably the biggest advantage you as a student have over anyone else. The problem, of course, is for the graduate student, and how you find the time to properly find an internship. We will discuss that in a bit.

First, a few facts about internships. The role of the intern has become more competitive in the past 20 years than ever before. Due to changing labor laws, many public companies, which also own athletic teams, must have their interns receive college credit for their time invested. So many of the opportunities of using the intern as a volunteer on the pro level have gone by the boards. Also, due to the larger amount of folks interested in the sports field, the requests for internships have grown more demanding both younger and even older for folks looking to re-launch a career. Years ago, there would never be the thought of a high school or prep school senior, for example, coming in to take a summer internship unless he or she "knew" someone in the organization, and that usually amounted to filing papers or pulling clips and then leaving at the end of the day with the person who got them in the door. It was more of a favor. Nowadays, a growing number of seniors across the country can actually receive high school or college credit in advance of attending school with a jumpstart on their internship. It is not that uncommon to have blind calls to Human Resource departments these days from high school guidance counselors looking to place students at professional teams. Although, because of restrictions on child labor in some states, many organizations cannot accept high-school kids. That is however changing. For example, the city of New York and their sports group, The New York Sports Commission, actively accepts high-school students for a very competitive summer internship program. It is becoming more and more the norm.

So what's the answer to getting a good internship? *Don't wait.* One of the biggest crimes is when we get requests for interns in the fall of the person's senior year. Even if you are not sure what area of sports and entertainment you would like to go into, ask questions about opportunities as soon as you can with your career planning and placement office. If you are talking to younger friends and siblings about attending a university, make sure they ask about potential internships before enrolling. Internship placement should be a big part of the selection process for college bound students.

Also, fully understand the process before you start looking.

Some points for a checklist

1   Many places look for full-time interns, and a great deal of schools do not allow a semester just for an internship. Know that before you apply.
2   Can you put the time in? Especially on the team and league PR side, there will be many nights and weeks.
3   Can you *afford* to put the time in (so many of you have jobs to help defray tuition costs)? This is a critical question, but also may help clarify how and when you can volunteer for events.
4   What will your responsibilities be? Unfortunately many folks who get internships never ask the question and because folks are so busy with their daily schedules (especially in season), the internship has a great deal of downtime and is not beneficial.
5   When will the internship be? Think about that as well. If you are applying for an internship at BASS Fishing, it probably would be best to make sure that it is when fish are in season. Although the team side of PR is basically year-round these days, offseasons may not require the long nights as a regular season, which can either be helpful if you are limited in time or harmful if you want to learn about game operations.

6   Where have other interns who have done this gone? If you are talking to a team, ask them where interns who have gone through the program have ended up. If you talk to the New York Jets for example, it is good to know that NFL Commissioner Roger Goodell was a PR intern (true story). If the person in charge says "I don't know," you may want to think again.

7   Lastly, view the internship as a job. Your first one. What you put into it, you will get out of it.

Step 3: No one wants to talk just about sports

This will be a recurring theme in the book, but it is an important one. If you want to work in sports, know a little bit about everything. Here are three examples I have from personal experience.

Have a story to tell

Peter Guber, now the co-owner of the Golden State Warriors of the NBA but a legendary figure in the entertainment field, published a great book in 2011 called *Tell to Win*.[1] In it he went through many encounters he had with luminaries in business and entertainment and sport and what they all had in common—a way to relate to him through a common story they shared. Many times it was overcoming a hardship, or solving a business problem, or sharing a passion, or dealing with a family issue, but there was always some common ground which would make a connection. So before every interview, every encounter, think about what your story is, and how it can relate to the person you are speaking to. What is the one-on-one subtle connection you want to make, what is the leave-behind thought, what will make you the person that will be remembered?

What is your narrative, but more importantly, how does that narrative relate to the person you are speaking to. Everyone has a story that is common, but its uniqueness is how you present it—get your story straight and figure a way to make it relate.

Think like Tess

This is from the 1980s movie *Working Girl*. The lead character, Tess Magill, played by Melanie Griffith, is trying to make a career in the financial industry. However, she is being stunted in her growth by a number of factors, the least of which is she is not viewed as "executive material." However, Tess has a great trait that is very valuable in the PR field, especially in sports PR (although she didn't know it). She has the ability to take divergent topics and meld them together to find a pitchable story line. In the movie she makes her big play by taking a story from page six of the *New York Post* about a radio bigwig's daughter's wedding and putting it together with a story she saw in the business section about the sale of a southern radio network. It resulted in a merger that saw her get her job and Harrison Ford. What did she do? She was able to look outside what others saw as the conventional, take two divergent topics and make a story out of it. This is a great example of how one can get ahead in the sports industry. *Don't just read about sports.*

So think like Tess.

Maintain a casual working knowledge

One thing I firmly believe in is "never say never." Once again, I can relate this to life experience. I had always believed I would never meet my wife in a bar. But I did. Our first discussion was about women getting ahead in business. I maintained, and still do, that for women to get ahead in business, especially on an international level, that she has to have a casual working knowledge of sports (my future wife did to some extent, and I am proud to say has a little better one now). I believe that to get ahead in sports, you have to have a casual working knowledge of everything else.

The last thing a sports executive, especially one who has to deal with the media every day, wants to do is hear from a junior person about his or her daily team activity. Is it important to know what is going on? *Absolutely.* However, it is almost as important to be able to think and assimilate those thoughts into new, pitchable ideas. The more you can talk about the internet, multicultural programs, business, the theater, the more interesting and the more valuable you will be to the organization. You may also be able to open new areas of publicity from the start because of your varied background.

Therefore, to get started in this business, it is much more important to be the utility player than the strategic star. People say that a little knowledge is a dangerous thing. I think a little knowledge about a great deal of topics may be your most valuable asset in getting started in sports PR.

Step 4: Look left and right, build relationships

The ability to work in sports and get a start does not have to begin at a team, or a university, or at a league. As said before, the industry has continued to grow at such a fast rate that the ability to find your first opportunity could be on the sales side, or on the agency side with one of any number of small PR firms that have now emerged to assist companies in growing their exposure through sports and entertainment.

Make a list and check it twice. If you are using this book, chances are you know someone in business who can help you. It may be a teacher, a coach, a parent, a great aunt, a sales guy at the mall; someone can help you get started. The key is to make the list and then go down the list of who you know and who can help. It is all about the relationship.

One of my grandfathers was named Joe Sgro. Joe Sgro was the king of South Brooklyn, where I grew up. He was a master at building relationships, some of which only he understood as to how they related. However, he would bring people together, through the Knights of Columbus, through his work as an accountant, through contacts at the South Brooklyn Democratic Club, through his work with the church, Joe managed relationships. He may not have had a list all the time, but he always thought about who he knew where and kept a list of who all those people were.

So who is on your list? What can they help you with, and more importantly how can you help them? Developing those relationships, studying business cards, keeping a rolodex, and continuously updating your mental relationship file will be very important to getting started.

Many times you will not make that first connection yourself. It will be a friend of a friend who will refer you to a business opportunity, or a relative, or a coach who may ask you to read something or pass it along. However, if you are not constantly on the look or looking to expand that list, you may miss an opportunity. These days those lists are made easier by social networking—LinkedIn, Plaxo, and other sources that do some of that long-term linking for you. The common-sensical list of friends, relatives, and people who know you away from work will also be a huge benefit.

It might sound silly to you because it is overused at times, but *networking* is the key to success. It does not have to be overt or may not always be a push for a job, but having a working relationship with friends of friends and those in the industry is very important. The transparency between industries is also very important these days—the *Moneyball* era in baseball has made finance majors into sports executives—and can make applicable skills in other areas important more in sport. Using the proper networking tools—LinkedIn, Plaxo, social and fraternal organizations like UNICO or the Hibernians or the Knights of Pythias or the Kiwanis Club—are just, if not more, important now as they ever were. Why? Because in the past your network through these groups was just blocks long. Now in the digital age that network is global.

Make the list, check it twice.

Step 5: Ask for help

One of the things that is also vital as you begin your search for your first opportunity is to be aggressive and respectful in your outreach. Also—and this sounds simple but it's true—don't be too vague or too specific on your request.

Publicists will get many letters saying "I am interested in sports" or "I want to work in public relations." Now if you are just starting out and looking for a first opportunity, it would strike most people as a little bizarre (albeit flattering in some ways) that you always wanted to work in sports PR. It's not exactly the first area that folks think about. So take the time to look through a sports section, a website, a media guide, and jot down some names, phone numbers, and email addresses of folks you may want to talk to. Then think about some folks who may be able to get you to someone in that organization.

Important tip

It should be discouraged to send out blind résumés and notes to people without a personal follow-up. What you will get back is some really nice stationery from Human Resource folks. I would suggest personalizing each note you send. Make sure the person, no matter how high or low in the company, realizes that you took the time to find out something about them or their place of business that you would not normally know. That is impressive and will move you to the top of the list. No form letters. Be specific as much as you can. Ask for a few minutes of their time; you will be surprised at the results.

It is very important to follow up as well. Here is where you get the opportunity to use the other things we have outlined previously. Talk about your interests, ask folks about their interests, how they got started, what advice would they give you? Although the nature of PR is not to draw attention to yourself, you will be meeting with people who are successful in their field and they will love to talk about what it is they do in most instances. Take notes. Ask for them to think about how they can help. In most cases they will take an interest and an ownership in your interests, and away you go.

What do you bring to the table? You have many practical assets that those in the business every day maybe can't cultivate that well. You probably understand text messaging and how to motivate your friends better than the person you are talking to right now, so include a story or two about how you communicate with others, or something about what you have seen or read that is interesting. Have a dialogue and a conversation, not a dissertation.

You should also be aware that many industry publications give discount rates for students, and it is a great way to use tools like the *Sports Business Journal*, the *Sports Business Daily* and *PR Week* as a cost-efficient tool to find out about interesting opportunities, contact people, and start the ball rolling.

You will only find out if you ask.

How I got started

Always wondered how "so and so got started" in "the business"? Here is a list of a myriad of sports publicity professionals and how they got their first job. Some are traditional, some are funny, some are different, all are worth a read—and when you come across them now you have some fodder for a conversation. For example, did you know Rick Pitino's first job was as a graduate assistant at the University of Hawaii? Rush Limbaugh? How about in the sales and marketing office of the Kansas City Royals? Who knew? If today you watch the great success of the Arizona Diamondbacks, would you know their president, Derrick Hall, started as a PR intern with the Los Angeles Dodgers? Chris Simko, now the head of all sales for CBS Sports, had a great entry-level job at SportsChannel, the precursor to the regional sports networks of today. He had to take crayons and color a map of the United States as to where there was regional sports coverage of the NHL.

My personal experience: One of the most memorable was literally working for a hockey team on Staten Island that never really existed. I was doing some radio work for a sports service called "Sports Phone" (in those days before the internet and sports radio, this was how folks got scores!) and heard about a minor league hockey team starting in Staten Island. I did some of things mentioned in this chapter. Sent a note, called, followed up, showed up for a meeting, and talked about not just what I wanted to do but about what they wanted to do. The two day-to-day guys, sports veterans Charlie Cuttone and Norb Eksl, hired me to help sell tickets and sponsorships and do stats and PR as the team got going. Over the course of several weeks (without a car—walking the streets of Staten Island and taking the ferry) we started to sell signage and tickets (to an unbuilt arena), hired hockey legend Dave Schultz as a coach, and named the team the "Slapshots." I also got my first business card. Alas it was not meant to be. The building deal fell through, the team played in Newark for half a season, and then went out of business, but I loved the time there and actually landed a job as Sports Information Director at Iona College at the last minute. The rest, as they say, is history.

Here are some first jobs by a varied amount of sports professionals. It will show the first timer what you can do and where you can start

My first job in television was an internship at "The View" on ABC. I wanted to work in TV news, but the closest I could come was the daytime department. The first time I ever saw the show was my first day on the job. That first day, in the morning, the copy machine broke while some other interns were copying formats, and they sat around waiting for someone to come fix it. I decided to open it up and take a look, and successfully cleared the paper jam. One of the writers saw me do that, and took a liking to me. Soon, I was coming in at 7am every morning to "help him out"; i.e. watch him write jokes for the women to say on air. He insisted that I had to get off the show as soon as possible. A few weeks later, he was having lunch in the ABC cafeteria with a producer he'd worked with on a sports show. He told me to come to the cafeteria at precisely a certain time, and walk up to their table and he'd introduce me to the producer.

A few weeks after that, I was an intern on Monday Night Football and my career in sports television had begun.

Aaron Cohen, award winning writer for HBO Sports, the NFL and ESPN

I spent the first 23 years of my life in Italy and, even though my English is good enough to earn me a degree in a British university and a few articles published here and there, I was struggling to make in-roads. However, that worked just as a motivation for me to try harder: I approached the Welsh Gymnastics federation and offered myself as a volunteer media officer—with their limited budget, they were happy to take me onboard on a free. And then, miracle struck—ironically, *just* because I was an Italian mother tongue.

The Welsh Track & Field Federation, Welsh Athletics, had organized a Coaching Conference which some important Italian expert would attend, only for the professional translator to call ill the night before. A frantic round of calls to draft in *anyone* able to translate Italian among all of Wales's sports federation returned me as the only one, and I was duly called to take part. Once there, I tried to do my best in the job I was given and at the end of the day approached the CEO and offered myself for the position of Media Officer, which until then was non-existent at Welsh Athletics.

I have been working for them for four years and I have been lucky enough to attend the 2010 Commonwealth Games in Delhi, India, the 2011 Youth World Championships in France and will be part of the British teams at the 2012 World Junior Championships in Spain and the 2012 Olympic Games in London.

William Ponissi, Media & Publicity Officer, Welsh Athletics

As a middle school and high school mascot, I attended college, winning a spot on the cheer squad as a mascot (while also playing a varsity sport). I had no illusions of going professional in my sport, so I studied engineering at a technical institution. My time as a mascot afforded me an opportunity to continue my passion for performing post-graduation as I became a professional mascot for several minor league franchises in various sports (football, baseball, hockey, basketball), never realizing that being a mascot could be a full-time profession. In one of my early franchises, I was offered a full-time role as a mascot as long as I worked office hours (when not performing) on building a top-notched game environment.

After nearly a decade of moving up the ranks, both individually in my positions as well as level of leagues, I returned home to work for the University of Nebraska Athletics. From mascot to front office, I'm living a dream that I never realized could be a possibility. As a kid, I dreamed of playing four years for the Huskers. Now I have an opportunity to help kids with the same dream, only I don't lose my eligibility after just four years!

Andy Wenstrand, Market Dept., Univ of Nebraska

I was a senior at Princeton contemplating my career when, through a series of circumstances, I lucked into an interview with the CEO and Chief Creative Director at Young and Rubicam Advertising. The athletic director at Princeton who arranged the interviews told me to wear a suit. Well, the only suit I owned at the time was a white 'leisure suit' that I wore for my high school disco nights (it was the 70s). I was 6'3" tall and fully pumped from playing college football, and I had a full beard at the time. So I interviewed with the top execs at Y&R looking like a cross between Tony Manero and Grizzly Adams. The guard at the front door thought I was a messenger and tried to make me come in through the back entrance. BTW, I got the job.

Frank Vuono, President 16W Marketing

I was 15 years old when I was asked to be the starting pitcher in the Etobicoke Hardball League All-Star game. This was a big moment for my team, for my parents, and for me. It was a stellar game in many ways. Once the game and awards were over, a business executive from the Toronto Blue Jays approached me as he happened to be in the crowd watching. Impressed with my abilities, particularly the precision in my throwing, he encouraged me to apply for a position as outfield sideline warm-up catcher—not only did I not realize that jobs like this existed, but that I, at 15, could apply to work at the back-to-back World Series Champion Blue Jays!! After handwriting a letter and mailing it to my contact at my favorite MLB team, I soon got a letter back on Blue Jays letterhead. I anxiously opened it and skimmed through the words, and to my disappointment, I didn't get the job—the reason, I was not yet 16 years old. At that point, I realized three things; the notion of the possibility of working in sport, the importance of having connections to people in the industry who have insights that the average person is not exposed to (in this case, a summer job) and the importance to accept things that are out of your control, in this case, my age. I used this experience as the driving force that led to my eventual entry point into the sport world, working at Nike Canada in the middle of my university degree, which was found by uncovering an opportunity through a Queen's alumni. The early experience stuck with me and for that reason, I credit the Blue Jays for giving me my first learning experience in the industry that we are all addicted to.

Katrina Galas, Glideslope Marketing

My first day on the job after graduating from Syracuse University. I was an assistant media planner at Grey Advertising (now MediaCom). I was assigned to a media group which included Quaker State. On that very first day, my boss placed me in front of a TV with VCR and stopwatch. For the entire day he had me clock the amount of air time received by Ricky

Rudd's Quaker State car in the previous week's NASCAR race. I'm now an EVP at Shamrock Sports & Entertainment.

Dan Gracetta, VP Shamrock Sports and Entertainment

Technically my first job was being a graduate assistant at the University of Southern California. Two weeks after receiving my undergraduate degree from Southern Connecticut State University, I drove out to Los Angeles to pursue my master's and Ph.D. back to back, becoming a graduate assistant in the process. As a graduate assistant, part of my assignments was Head Volleyball Coach, Head Basketball Coach, and Director of Recreation and Intramurals. If that doesn't count, my first job was being an Assistant Professor of Physical Education at Brooklyn College, CUNY, where I was also Head Volleyball Coach ... and eventually became an Assistant Athletics Director.

Donna Lopiano, Women's Sports Pioneer and Hall of Famer

I was the mascot for the West Palm Beach Expos.

Ron Colangelo, Vice President, Public Relations, Detroit Tigers

Facts on File is a Manhattan-based news reference publisher, which before the era of internet was one of the most important go-to sources of information and news on a weekly basis. I was a writer/editor, covering Education, The United States Supreme Court and Sports. I always wanted to be a writer/journalist and this opportunity was a wonderful entry into this field. Not to mention that I had a crush on the Researcher/Librarian next to me. The day she quit, I asked her out in June 1972. We went to see *The Godfather* and then a week later, a Yankees-Orioles doubleheader. Lynn Rubenstein is now Lynn Abraham.

Seth Abraham, former head of HBO Sports and
MSG Entertainment, now independent consultant

My first job in sports was in the summers of HS and college when I worked as a recreation counselor at an HS and municipal park, respectively. Then my first job on the PR side was as student sportswriter for the school paper and then interning in the SID office with John Morris at Penn State.

Peter Kowalski, Manager of Public Relations,
United States Golf Association (USGA)

So I got out of Dartmouth in 1983, living with my parents in Westchester and was intent on getting in the sports business. I heard through a friend of a friend that Major League Baseball Productions might be hiring entry level "Viewers." The job entailed watching two monitors simultaneously of baseball broadcasts from the day before and charting every shot and every moment, from a big play to a fan dancing in the stands. I interviewed and, in addition to the traditional interview, I was given a baseball test—both past and current trivia. I passed with flying colors and got my first job out of college and my first job in sports. After 6 months of "viewing" I graduated to an associate producer and ultimately produced the official World Series film, official All-Star film and a weekly show for Sports Channel called the Pennant Chase. We had a really special group of young folks, this being the first job for many.

Mike Golub, President, Portland Timbers

I started as a ball boy at Tulane University back in ninth grade, which led to me attending school there and working as a student manager in football and basketball, and later working in the sports info director's office … the rest they say, is history.

Arthur Triche, Vice President of Public Relations, Atlanta Hawks

My first real professional sports experience came when I interned for the Boston Celtics in September and October of 1976, as an intern in the Celtics Publicity Office. However, the first professional sports experience I received that I received compensation for (assisting the Coordinator, preparing stories, writing features, assisting the media and the players, etc.) came when I worked for one week at the English Leather Men's Tennis Tournament in Stowe, Vermont.

Jeff Twiss, Vice President, Public Relations, Boston Celtics

I got an internship with the Cincinnati Reds and was the assistant to the traveling secretary during spring training. I did that for one season and I learned the way to get a job was by going through baseball winter meetings. So I stood in the lobby with a suit on and passed out résumés and talked to anyone who would talk to me. I got interviewed by Dr Bernie Mullin for the [Pittsburgh] Pirates and also by the Clinton Giants. Bernie hired me at the winter meetings, but before I started I got a call from the Clinton Giants asking me to be the assistant GM.

Mike Stanfield, Vice President, Ticket and Suite Sales,
New Orleans Saints

I worked as a student assistant at the University of South Florida during my sophomore year of college. I cut out newspaper clippings, was a statistician for the women's volleyball teams and was the Men's Tennis Contact.

Zack Bolno, Assistant Athletes Director, Media Relations,
University of Maryland

My first job in sports was working as director for sports publishing for Starwave, a Paul Allen start-up in 1993. Starwave was launched on Paul's rather simple and prescient notion that people were going to be using their computers differently than they were in the early 90s and that networked computers in particular would create opportunities for new types of products and businesses. My job was to figure out how that mission intersected with sports; we ended up launching a web site in 1994 that evolved into being espn.com.

Geoff Reiss, President, Pro Bowlers Tour

My first job in sports was Marketing Assistant at the Continental Basketball Association working for the VP of marketing, Bob King. It had only been a few months since the tragic plane crash in Sioux City where the Commissioner Jay Ramsdell had been killed and the Deputy Commissioner lived—Jerry Schemmel (now Radio for the Denver Nuggets). When I started the office was in a lot of transition because Jerry felt he couldn't continue there, so the CBA was in the process of interviewing for a new Commissioner and Deputy Commissioner. Because of all the change, I went very quickly from Marketing Assistant to having my hand in everything, to Director of Team operations (in 3 years). We were such a small office that I literally worked on everything—draft day, BOG conference calls, PR, all-star game, merchandising, etc. It was the greatest experience and career-changing job for me. It set me up for where I am today. I was able to see how all departments had to work together at the league level, but I also was able to work day-to-day with the teams, so I saw the league–team interaction as well.

Lara Price, president, business operations and marketing, Philadelphia 76ers

While attending Albion College, I worked as their student Sports Information Director (and was sports editor of the weekly school newspaper). Senior year I decided I wanted to pursue a career in sports information or in PR for a professional sports team. I sent letters and my resume to every professional team (NBA, NFL, MLB, and NHL) and to essentially every Division I university. Everyday I would get rejection letters (I still have them). I didn't get one lead from any of those letters. I did get some nice encouragement, and through my father (who worked for the *Detroit News*) I got an opportunity to meet with the Detroit Tigers PR Director. He told me to get more writing experience, to go to work for a newspaper, which is ultimately what I did and which led to me to eventually getting into sports information.

Craig Miller, vice president, public relations USA Basketball

For basics, I got started with junior year at La Salle in Philly. I interned at WIP for Eagles radio play-by-play man Merrill Reese for a year doing his stats and getting tape at Flyers, Sixers, and Phillies games for his morning sports reports. At the end of my internship, the Flyers PR assistant, some bum named Mark Piazza, asked me what I was doing senior year. Since Mark's boss did nothing but lock himself in his office, basically Piazza ran the department and I was his top guy. The 86–87 Flyers made it to Game 7 before losing in the Cup Final against Gretzky, Messier, and Edmonton, and I was there for it all. I wrote every article in the Finals program.

Chris Botta, writer, *Sports Business Journal*

Conclusion

In closing, this chapter should provide you with some guidelines on where and how to get started in sports publicity. The biggest thing that you need to have is practical experience. The academic side will hold valuable practical ability and is essential in understanding the concepts of writing, pitching, and note taking, which will all be discussed in the coming chapters. However, having a feel for the industry, especially on the event side, will give the new job-seeker the ability to ask the right questions and find the people who will be able to answer them and get them started.

Notes

1 Guber, Peter. *Tell to Win*. Crown Publishing, 2011.

3

READING, WRITING, AND SPEAKING—AND NOT JUST IN ENGLISH

Walking the walk and talking the talk

This chapter will take a look at the basics everyone will need not only in sports publicity, but in the general business world as well. Today's world has put us in a time crunch, so many times the writing that is generated is in short bursts; thoughts included in brief emails, on a blackberry, or in short notes. This chapter will look at the two essential skills, reading and writing, that can help set the great publicist apart from the good ones. It will also deal with the highly important area of public speaking, and how this critical tool will make the publicist more valuable in the workplace.

Reading

What to read and where and how to read it

When we first wrote this book, tablets were what Moses used for The Ten Commandments, and apps were those things you filled out to get a job or get into school or a driver's license. How times have changed. The volume of information has risen, all at the expense of the time we have to consume such info, so how does one make the most efficient use of time from a business perspective?

The good news is that the use of newsgroups, fan pages, and information aggregators has helped bring lots of pieces of news on a particular topic together in one place. The bad news is that by the time you are reading this, many of those sources on your mobile device or your tablet will probably have evolved into something else, or been replaced by a data scrub or clipping service that is even better than what is available as I write this in the spring of 2012.

That being said, the basic tools of business have not really changed since the first edition. Expanded and diversified yes, but not really changed that much.

There are new news sources that can be used for a resource, but many of the quality sites remain the same.

While it is true that some of this goes back to being able to sing and dance to get in the door, it also matters a great deal in helping you form opinions on matters of importance to your industry and organization. Being well read also gives you a greater understanding of literary style, will broaden your horizons, and give you more to talk about around the water cooler. One other thing about being well read is that it can help familiarize you with writers and editors that you may someday work with, pitch stories to, or even hire.

The more you understand and diversify your reading interests, the more valuable you become to an employer, a business partner, a company executive, or a university.

As we said earlier, students can receive discounts to a list of trade publications that will help them become more versed in the industry. That is step one.

Tip

Set alerts on your smart phone or other device, either through Google or another platform, to make sure that when news breaks or a relevant story hits, you are aware of what is new and noteworthy. Tailor and update your alerts weekly to make sure you are getting the right info from the right sources at the right time. No one in today's environment can work without a proper alert tool today. The same goes with RSS feeds from outlets, bloggers, and columnists. Setting and updating those feeds will save you time and effort and keep your reading timely.

List of key publications to read and subscribe to

- *Sports Business Daily*—Published every working day online, this is a great short synopsis of the world of sports. The small summaries make for easy references, and you have the ability to "click through" to the larger stories. The SBD is also available at a student rate and now has a more global version as well.
- *Sports Business Journal*—The weekly version of the "SBD," it provides more in-depth features on the world of sports business, with some of the most knowledgeable columnists in the industry. It is also available online, and will give you a good resource during "downtime" to catch up on ideas.
- *SportBusiness*—One of two key UK publications that are growing in scope and news and are a great source of a different perspective and voice.
- *SportPro*—Like *Sport Business*, the UK-based publication also takes a global, in-depth look at sport, featuring leaders in everything from netball to the NBA.

- *Team Marketing Report*—Published online and in print on a regular basis, it provides more of a look at quick trends and numbers in sports. Very good for research when doing larger projects.
- *USA Today*—Now that the publication has started to aggregate thousands of news sources, it has become more valuable than ever by combing a local and regional outlook. Sometimes criticized by academics for its simple writing style, *USA Today* has the readership and the columnists available to have a significant impact on any sports publicity effort. The search does not only include sports, it should include all sections to make the publicist as diverse in looking for ideas as possible. The online edition is also great for some quick trend-spotting.
- *Media Post*—Based in the US, *Media Post* has a series of "Best Of" offerings every day by category, from digital to marketing to women's topics to baby boomers, all summarized and presented via email.
- *Cynopsys*—An easy daily inbound email from various topics with the news of the day, their newsletter are very popular with senior sales folks around the world.
- *The Sunday New York Times*—Like all print papers, the *Times* continues to look for new and innovative ways to find its niche. It remains the "paper of record" in the US, and the Sunday paper and all its sections—along with the Sunday *Magazine*—will give the publicist not only a host of ideas for pitching but will provide some great fodder for discussions on every topic one could be involved with.
- *Inc., Fast Company, and Wired*—Both the print and digital versions have a plethora of trends, topics, and easy-to-apply profiles that go beyond sport but still apply to the business we work in.
- *GQ, Esquire, or Vanity Fair*—Some of the great feature writing is still housed in these publications, and the knowledge of what they write about in the front of the magazines is essential for having a well-rounded publicity plan.
- *The Rodale Publications*—These are grouped together because of their genre, which are largely health and fitness. Any combination of magazines like *Men's Health, Women's Health, Best Life, Prevention, Outdoor Life, Runner's World* and others should also be on the list. They give the publicist a good cross-section of both popular trends and fitness tips for various groups that can fit into any lifestyle pitch.

Anthologies

Anthologies are an excellent way to get a better feel of what good writing, especially sports writing, is. Everyone, every year should make sure their holiday list includes Glenn Stoudt's *Best American Sportswriting*. Not only is it an annual features collection that will help you learn about some diverse sports subjects, it will give you a clear idea as to who the best writers are and where they are coming from. Back issues will also be a great help, and tend to be readily available in libraries and online. It will help you become as well versed as you can be.

Other magazines

The other side of reading is what will keep you well versed in current events and pop culture, and in this day and age of sports and entertainment mixing as one, being well versed is very important. Always be able to glance at magazines like *GQ, Esquire, Men's Journal, Men's Health, Black Enterprise, Time,* even *People,* to get a feel for what topics may be able to meld sports into (think like Tess again).

Finally, and they are important today to the sports publicists as they have ever been, are the two mainstays in sports publishing today. *Sports Illustrated* and *ESPN Magazine* need to be included and read, or at least bookmarked, so that the features can be read at a later date.

Key to periodicals, websites, and blogs

- Keep the list diverse.
- Read the interviews.
- If you hear something being discussed by your colleagues then read it ASAP. Chances are, if it is water cooler talk it will be important for your career growth.

Newspapers

The ability for online reading and the lack of paywalls for many publications can make regularly pulling stories to read difficult. Try and keep a list of 10–20 columnists bookmarked, from both newspapers and online sites like Grantland, The Classical, Yahoo and The Big Lead, to download and digest when you are traveling or honing information. Aggregation sites will also be a big help, but it is always better to target and diversify your list over time and as your job needs vary.

Tip

Columnists still write regularly on the same day. Knowing the columnist cycle at a newspaper will make your time to search easier. Following those columnists on Twitter or other social media sites will also give you the chance at a glance to decide what and how to read.

A daily routine

There are some publicists who try and plan their reading schedule as follows. It is a good way to plan if you can.

Late night: After 11pm eastern time, make a quick check of key sites that post early for the next day. *New York Times, Washington Post,* espn.com have tomorrow's headlines and most features articles "today."

Between 6 and 7am on most days: Check bookmarked sites, minimum of 12–15 papers at 3–4 minutes per paper to see the news of the day.

7–9am: Read the *Morning Buzz* and related articles from the *Sports Business Daily,* go through various international aggregation sites on news from around the globe, and bookmark those of interest.

10–11am: Check relevant clips again, review your alerts.

Now, depending on where you live and what your time constraints are this may work—I know it works for me and gets me to keep those around me also informed. The other thing bookmarks do for you is to keep relevant information fresh, so that should you need archived information, you know where to find it. It is free and easy and will keep things relevant for you.

Also, always try and read your favorite writers daily. That will give you a solid, well-rounded base as you start to develop your writing style.

Tip

Create a printed "To Be Read" or "Have on Hand" folder for the off-hours, downtime, or trip reading. This can be articles literally clipped out of newspapers or magazines or printed from online that are semi-timeless and relevant to the business industry. They can also be articles that you can share with colleagues, business partners, or clients about the industry that they may need to know about and have not had time to read or find.

Writing

Now that we have gotten through step one and have looked at and studied what good reading should be, we can address how and what to write. In today's world of sports communications there are many more opportunities to write, and an even bigger opportunity for those who have a passion for using the written word to paint pictures and tell stories. We will look at a few basic forms here as the primer for what you will both need to get started, and what will help you advance.

The topics will include:

- the press release and advisory
- the feature story

- the blog/website entry
- media guides and game notes
- transcript writing.

The press release

Even in this day and age of the 24-hour news cycle, the basic premise of the press release remains the standard by which groups of all backgrounds and disciplines get out their mass news. The form, no matter how it is sent, remains pretty consistent. The style is reflective of what is being communicated. Hard news stories are usually very direct and to the point. Softer pitches can sometimes be more flowery and creative to set them apart. Regardless, all need to have strong grammar, quotes that communicate the basic information from the key spokesperson, and get to the point right away.

Attention spans are short and press releases are plentiful, so tell the reader what it is you are trying to tell him right away.

There are many reasons for generating press releases. The chief reason is very simple: the subject has news that is relevant to disseminate to a mass market. The crafting of the message to make it relevant, and to make it stand out above the flood of other information being generated, is critical. How to do that will be discussed shortly.

Another, and now more relevant, reason for generating press releases is to be "on record." By being "on record," both the publicist and the subject can show the time and date and volume of information that is being provided to the public and to the media. It is also a very simple way to build website content and create an archive for news. Also in today's electronic world, many "trade" websites (those dedicated to a particular industry) will take the electronic version of a release and post it as well. They do not have the time or staff for re-writes and are a great one-stop shop for the particular industry. The "on record" release fits them perfectly.

Distribution of the release is also another key element that needs to be factored in. Electronic distribution, and in some places still using a fax, remain the key methods, with each publicist tailoring their list for a specific subject or area of interest. For example, if a university is generating a release on a swimmer who has done well, the release will probably have a distribution list of email and/or fax addresses that will include:

- league/conference officials
- the hometown media of that student athlete
- trade publications that cover the sport
- internal university "officials" who have an interest in athletics
- booster club members
- local newspapers who cover the university.

This would be different from a Division One school that is putting out its men's basketball schedule, in which case the release would go to a much broader audience since the interest level would differ.

Tip

These lists are critical in delivering information and they have to always be updated and tailored. It is important to send, at least once a year, a message to everyone on the list making sure their information is correct and giving them the option to opt out if requested. It will save lots of time and even money.

There are a host of companies that will actually house lists for you if the money is available. These tailored distribution groups, who either sell the software or do the work, can make life a great deal easier. *Icontact* and *Constant Contact* are two of the best spam-free tools on the market. There are also a great number of quality news distribution services that, for a fee, will come up with a national distribution list for you. Companies like *PR Newswire* and *Businesswire* have been providing the service to publicity professionals for years, and many media organizations look to these services to filter out clutter and provide them with information they need.

Basic form

Despite many folks taking great creative license these days, the form of a press release should still be as follows:

1   *Main headline*. Bold type, 24–16 point—your only chance to make a first impression, right? Make sure you communicate who is doing what in the top headline; do not make the reader look for the basic information beyond the header.

Tip

Do Not Capitalize everything in a headline or, if emailing, do not put the subject in all caps. It will often times get caught in a spam filter.

---

2   *Paper size, spacing and margins*. Even if communicated just electronically, releases should always be done on 8 × 10in paper. Save the money on colored paper these days, as it will only annoy those printing with color copiers by wasting their ink. Leave wide margins if you can, two inches on

the top and an inch on the bottom. Spacing in releases these days should be single spaced in paragraphs. The old days of double spacing so that people could write in between lines are long gone.

3 *Stock header.* This will probably be provided to you by the company you are working with, but it is useful to keep logos and info on the top left hand corner of the front page, but not too big. Legible and small is important and useful.

4 *Whom to reach out to.* Whomever the contact person is on the information *always* goes on page one—either to the immediate right margin on the top (preferred) or at the end of the release on the left margin. Given the immediacy of information, it is strongly recommended to have two people (and where they are from), a phone, and an email address to respond to.

5 *The date.* This is one thing that has changed over the years, but is still important and extremely relevant. At the beginning of paragraph one, in **BOLD CAPS**, should be today's date and the location of where the release is coming from (**HEMPSTEAD, N.Y. MAY 16, 2012**). It gives folks a reference point for who and where the information is coming from when information has to be tracked. More and more people are also adding a time stamp, as information changes throughout the course of the day.

6 *The lead.* Here is the old journalism rule that still remains true, especially in the days of short attention spans and media overload. The lead should contain the five W's of journalism—who, what, when, where, and why. Think about how you can answer those as quickly and as easily as possible. The interesting facts should follow at the bottom of the paragraph—get the main news out first. You will be amazed at how that first line will be cut and pasted into stories.

7 *The paragraphs.* After the lead, which many times will encapsulate what is in the headline, try and have your best secondary fact or facts to close out paragraph one. From there paragraphs two and three (depending on spokespeople) should be a direct and to the point quote from whomever the person is making the announcement. The second quote in paragraph three should be a supporting quote if necessary, from the second most important person that the release is about. These should be short and to the point. Always keep in mind the first points you make will be the ones used—the further you go, the less chance you will have to get those facts out. Attention will be lost in the first 100 words, and go down exponentially after that. Following the quotes, relevant background information on the subject will go in, again be as concise as possible.

8 *The facts.* That's right, let's get the facts out. It is important to keep all the most relevant information possible on page one and to remember your audience for this. For example, if this is a strict news story—naming of a title sponsor, trading a player, signing a coach—the facts are straightforward and what you write will be used. If it is more esoteric—the results of a poll,

the announcing of a suspension, the explanation of a rule controversy—it may be essential to provide more background or detail than normal. Just remember, the easier the explanation, the better off you will be.

9   Use proper grammar and spelling. Many times in sports we tend to use colloquialisms or get very folksy and colorful in the way we speak. Although that may be helpful in a grabbing headline, it should be avoided when writing a release. The essence of the release is making a professional announcement of some kind. Therefore for the masses you must assume that they do not know what sports-specific abbreviations or phrases mean. So don't use them. If they are used in a quote that reflects the personality of the speaker then fine, but just be sure that you are explaining that phrase outside of the quote. For example, if you are writing about the New York Mets and have a quote from general manager Sandy Alderson about third baseman David Wright, it would be OK for Alderson to call him a "Third sacker" or a "stud hitter" in his quote—those are his words, not the omniscient ones of the release writer. Also spell-check, spell-check, spell-check—and then have *at least three* people proofread your work. We have become very reliant on using the great quality of spell-check; however when you spell-check "Knicks" it becomes "NICKS" and won't come up as a mistake. I know, I have done it.

10 *Length.* Most releases, if possible, should be kept to one page, especially ones that involve basic news and announcements. It is OK to be politically correct and go over to satisfy many masters—that will happen a great deal in the complex world we live in today. However, keep in mind that in the 24-hour news cycle only the first page of facts, and *especially* quotes, will be used in most cases.

11 *Bold and italic use.* If there are names, hometowns, and small important facts that need to be communicated in the body, then put them in bold and italic. They will jump to the forefront and be used more often and will be a great assist to the reader and media member. This is especially helpful for hometowns and universities and high schools for release subjects such as athletes and coaches. If this is geared to be picked up by out of town media, those points are essential and will drastically improve placement.

12 *Titles and nicknames.* If an athlete or school goes by a nickname, then use it. It is a sign of respect and accomplishment in most cases, and is preferred by the subject. For example, in New York Willis Reed will always be "The Captain." It is not his only name, but it identifies him and is important to the piece.

13 *The boilerplate.* It is very important that in closing the release, the proper boilerplate is used. This is usually given to you by the higher-ups and contains key factual information about the company, the organization, the university. It will never be used by the media, but it is very important for the record to have an understanding of who and what is putting this information out.

14 *The style guide*: Lastly, for all the little things—fonts, commas, use of titles, apostrophes, hyphens—use the *New York Times*' style guide as your base. In this day and age so many folks have developed their own style guide and companies spend millions of dollars developing a font and a "style" that the news can get lost in the glitz. Always go back to the basics, which are still held in high esteem by the paper of record—the *New York Times*. It is a great reference point and a great fallback.

The media advisory

Unlike press releases, the media advisory is really down and dirty, straight to the point information about an upcoming event. There is usually nothing left to the imagination. Just the facts. The style in an advisory is very simple. They literally advise the media as to an upcoming event and in this 24/7 world, can literally go out at a few hours notice.

The biggest difference between release and advisory is follow-up. The release is a re-statement of facts after they have or as they have gone out. The advisory is literally a call to action. Therefore it demands immediate action on your part. Every advisory needs to be followed up with calls to every media member to make sure they have been received and to ascertain interest in attending your event the advisory speaks to. The event can be a press conference or even a conference call. However, it is something which only makes sense if there is media interest. So you need that contact to get the folks on the call.

The other use of advisories is for the editorial and photo desks to make sure your event is on their "day" book. The day book literally is the basic listing of all media-worthy events going on in the geographic area for the day. The posting of your event by editors and decision makers is key to the success.

Basic form

1   Like the release, the form for an advisory is very straightforward. The header immediately tells folks what the event will be.

2   The body is a series of who, what, when, where, and why. The difference here could be in the inclusion or exclusion of facts. Since you do still want to break news with the release at the press event, it is important to confirm basic information but sometimes not all facts in the advisory. What is important is that there is enough information included to get media attention.

3   The contact information, which goes at the end, is the biggest key. At least two names, phone numbers (especially mobile ones), and email addresses should be included.

4   It should have each of the Ws in paragraph form, single spaced, with the contact information at the end.

5   There are no quotes and only basic facts included. The quotes come at the presser.
6   Last useful tip again would be emboldening information that will pique the interest of media members.

The feature story

In recent years, the worry was that the digital world and the use of social media might spell the end for the long form of writing, but in actuality the opposite seems to be true. The unencumbered digital world, and the thirst for content, has actually created a new opportunity for long form and features. Now, while many of these features may reside just in the digital space, the ability to share those features to a global audience has never been better. So, the feature story lives!

I am hoping that your love of publicity coupled with your love of writing will create some opportunities on your own. After all, chances are if you are on the team side of sports publicity, you will have the opportunity to write for an in-house publication or website. If you are in school you *should* be writing for your newspaper or website.

The feature story is a long length, in-depth piece that focuses on elements of the subject away from the game or the chief activity the subject is known for. It brings out the personality of the subject and is designed to help the reader understand aspects of the subject that they did not know about. It differs from the "event" story, which usually focuses on the aspects of what took place in the short term.

So with that in mind, I offer the following tips for feature writing, both on deadline and for long-lead publications.

1   *Tell a story that you think is interesting.* There are many opportunities to pick the low-hanging fruit and re-tell an old tale. Pick a topic that you think has publicity merit and make it yours. The great columnist Jimmy Breslin coined and created the "gravedigger journalism" genre, where he would go off and talk to the second in command about a key news story and get a perspective that the media pack didn't have. Always keep that in mind.
2   *Know your audience.* Always write to your audience. If you are talking about the passion of West Point football for a game program, then write in the fashion that your audience understands. Make it interesting but understandable. Make it something that you think people will want to read *and* save.
3   *Take great notes.* Use a voice recorder *and* write your own notes. Notetaking is a lost art and it is essential in capturing the essence of a story. Not only the facts, but how and why your subject answered a question. Make sure all quotes are accurate and honest. Don't paraphrase if you can avoid it.

4 *Ask good questions.* Questions with a yes or no answer are the worst ones. Engage your subject in conversation; see if you can get him or her to talk about topics that make them a *person*, not just a subject.

5 *Remember the time frame you are writing in.* If it is a long-lead publication, there is no need to ask about a game or an event from last night unless it will frame your story for the future. Conversely, if you are writing a game story, then do all you can to capture the essence of the event in words that fully tell the story, not just the box score.

6 *Remember to include all the facts.* Especially in game stories, sometimes folks forget things like team records, hometowns, and even scores. Be sure you have answered all the questions needed before submitting.

7 *Proofread, fact check, and proofread again.* Nothing worse than errors of grammar or fact.

8 *Avoid the cliché.* No need to sound like Grantland Rice or Ring Lardner. *Write* like them yes, but in your own words. Avoid the same phrases we hear all the time.

9 *Never bury the lead.* Just like in press release writing. Tell the folks the facts up front, give them the detail, and then tell them again in a nice tight package.

10 *You are a writer, not a columnist.* If you are writing a story to help promote an event or a person, write about them. There is no need for your opinion unless it enhances the story.

The blog

By definition, a blog is "a personal journal published on the World Wide Web consisting of discrete entries (posts) typically displayed in reverse chronological order so the most recent post appears first. Blogs are usually the work of a single individual, occasionally of a small group, and often are themed on a single subject."

The emergence and growth of blogs in the late 1990s (there are estimates of as many as 160 million blogs, although most are not active) began with the use of simple to use publishing tools that no longer required heavy data input to execute. Wordpress was born, and self-publishing began.

Blogs, the best of which are usually focused on one theme and have the ability to be interactive, can also be online diaries and, given the ease of multimedia today, can be highly graphic if the builder chooses to use those forms of media.

While in recent years the visibility of blogs has started to lessen, the written word as a way to merchandise and tell best practices is still very valuable, especially in a business like sports and entertainment, where there are always niche categories and the amount of content that can be posted is pretty rich. Unfortunately, sometimes in the quest for larger traffic, like in the earlier days of sports radio, loud, often uninformed opinions have gotten the most exposure.

So the question remains, what is the best use of a blog as an opinion piece to help you do your job better? Are you merchandising yourself and your opinion or the news and best practices of those you work with—also is the opinion being out forth biased or paid, or is it a legitimate third-party news source? The lines between editorial (free, unbiased opinion and news) and advertorial (an opinion or news from a paid source) can sometimes be blurred, and that balance has to be maintained to achieve a solid blog.

As a professional in the field, like in any form of social media, balance must be kept. Your opinion may be interesting, but in many cases the best content should not be about you and your rantings, it should be a good mix of news and information that will help make your blog a news source for those craving information they cannot find anywhere else. That may be insider's information, it may be fan access, it may be best practices of a team, a brand, an athlete, a skill set, but providing that information makes you and the blog a very valuable resource to those seeking it, and in some cases, those looking to put information out.

As with anything in the digital space, once information is posted it is available for anyone to see in perpetuity. So the same rule holds true for a blog post as it does for anything in cyberspace.

Remember your level of professionalism and *think before you hit send*.

Many of the same rules that apply for feature writing should apply to blogs. Know your audience, try to tell the interesting story that is worthy of promoting, keep the blog to the subject and not you. All are very important in maintaining credible, noteworthy information.

The best blogs also need to be consistent with content. In order to maintain a credible voice as a blogger, no matter what the topic, the content has to be consistent to maintain readership. It cannot be something that can be done one a month, or once every six weeks. The best blogs have a consistent voice and a regular post schedule, usually two to three times a week, sometimes daily depending on the news flow. The effective blogger is always thinking about an item that he/she can use as a hook, and then finds the time, usually in off-hours, to create and merchandise the post through his or her followers and other forms of social media. It is not a toy, it is an effective tool, and needs to be taken seriously about whatever topic is it is focused on.

Use the blog as the opportunity to champion the little guy in a very open and public forum. It may be your best opportunity for written publicity and for you to express yourself as a writer in this new era.

Examples of good blog work

Two professional sports owners who have used blogging to effectively tell their message are Mark Cuban, the owner of The Dallas Mavericks of the NBA, and Ted Leonsis, president and CEO of Monumental Sports, the owners of the Washington Wizards and Capitals and the Verizon Center.

Both men have varied interests and views on a multitude of topics from politics to entertainment to sports. Cuban's blog maverick.com is varied, with smart thinking on business, education, and finance in addition to sport. It is not a rambling about Dirk Nowitzki's hair or Jason Kidd's shoes—it is rarely about the Mavericks. It is about big picture issues with a tie to sports, and as a result is a great vehicle for Cuban to get out his opinion against the backdrop of being a successful NBA owner and businessman.

Leonsis, on his Ted's Take blog, gives regular information about his teams from an owners' perspective and is always looking for fan input. However, he will also mix in his other projects to expose them to a larger passionate audience of sports fans, such as his work in education and film. It is well positioned and well thought out and gives fans a good look into the inner workings of a very successful owner.

On the media side, David Schwab, Vice President of Octagon, one of the world's largest sports and entertainment marketing firms, has built a blog called First Call, which tracks the best practices of brands and properties in the sports and entertainment space. By looking not just at the thousands of personalities represented globally by Octagon, but at the entire marketplace in sports and entertainment, he has become an authority and a "go to" person for event buzz and value ranging from The Super Bowl to The Academy Awards.

One of the best sports-related best business practices blogs revolves around the business of minor league baseball, called "Ben's Blog," by Ben Hill at MLB.com. Hill is able to compile the best practices of hundreds of minor league baseball teams around North America, and provide information, video, and pictures of all those best practices on a daily basis to the baseball, and to the general sports community. It is a one of a kind compendium of baseball business that could be replicated in soccer, cricket, minor league hockey, or any other sport that has great information with innovative leadership spread over a wide geographic area.

Transcript writing

Transcript writing is a separate category for the reason that it is very important to be accurate, and often when starting out in sports PR, one may be asked to transcribe tapes or audio files from press conferences, speeches, and interviews from time to time.

There are transcribing companies that deal specifically with sports. One of the best is ASAP Sports based in New York, which does most of the world's major sporting events. The company was an offshoot of court reporting (the transcribing of all that goes on in a court of law) by a gentleman named Peter Balasteri. Peter learned through a friend that the legendary Virginia Slims Tennis Championships were looking for someone to transcribe their press conferences for their annual championship finals at Madison Square Garden.

Balasteri provided the service and has grown the business into a year-round international business that provides online and on-site word for word transcripts that are the standard for the industry.

Today there is also voice recognition technology, which will also pull and record audio back in a printed form, but it certainly does not catch the nuance or pronunciation as an actual transcription company would. In a multilingual world, technology is great, but the hands-on feel of a transcriber who can do the work almost in real time is still very important.

You may also try and do transcription on your own, playing back live audio feeds if it is not as time sensitive. If this is the case, always remember accuracy is important. Never forget that these transcripts can be used by journalists and company officials as actual spoken words and quotes, so you must be 100 percent accurate in transcribing. If a word is inaudible, then say it. If you have to review a tape ten times to get it perfect, then do it. If you need a name or company spelled, then get it spelled.

Especially in the 24/7 news cycle, once the transcript goes out, it is gospel and many times, unlike the release, it will be used in its entirety word for word.

It is very valuable to all, and can also be very dangerous.

Take the time to do it right.

Game notes and media guides

For those of you in team and individual sports communications, the media guide and the game notes will be perhaps your most valuable, consistent work that will give you the best opportunity to tell your story.

The media guide

The media guide is your bible and the ability to update news and information online and provide that e-book to thousands of media is invaluable. The media guide tells the overall picture of the piece of the sport that you hold, be it on the league or the team level. The media guide in many ways has taken several turns over the years. It started out as the basic stats book, providing names and numbers and some biographical information. The original form was just actually 4×9in and was devoid of most photos other than a head shot. The size was made to fit into a notebook or even the inside pocket of a journalist. They then evolved to the 8×10in size that is the industry standard on the professional level today, and basically the $8\frac{1}{2} \times 11$in size that most colleagues use for their revenue sports (men's and women's basketball and football) today. Revenue sports differentiate from Olympic sports in that they are seen as driving revenue for the university through television sales, advertising sales, and ticket sales. Olympic sports do not have this cache for the most part.

The guides actually took on their biggest changes in the 1980s, when in-house publishing programs became the norm, and many publicity groups were able to not rely on printers for design. Color photos, action photos, and longer biographies became the standard. On the collegiate level, the media guide also became a huge recruiting tool, to the point where several of the larger universities (the University of Louisville was the first) went to a hardcover version to set themselves apart. At that point, the cost spent on these books was spinning out of control, and the NCAA stepped in to regulate the color used in a book to make it more uniform for everyone.

Still, innovative design became the norm. Some of the best in those days were St. Joseph's University and Fairfield University, where the SIDs at these basketball-dominated schools (Larry Dougherty at St. Joe's, Jay Williams at Fairfield) each year would come up with very creative and unique themes for their books to set themselves apart from the others. Literally judging a book by its cover on the collegiate level has always been a great sense of pride and value. With the advent of desktop publishing, printing costs also decreased substantially, giving administrators the ability to become more creative with a new economy of scale. It also freed up the marketing side to be able to include advertising partnerships in books more easily and more affordably, leading to more creativity and holding costs steady.

On the professional side, the guides have largely stayed the same in size and form. Although most teams do use color in the book and it is used as a recruiting and sales tool in a few places, the need for media guides is to service the media. We will go through the basic information shortly. However, one of the biggest evolving areas in team publications also ties into the 24/7 world we live in today. The media guide, as it existed prior to the last few years, literally becomes somewhat dated the minute it is published and one game is played. The ability for downloadable, digital updates has again evolved the business for the better, both for the publicist and for the media.

There is a famous line from the TV show "The Odd Couple" that I always think of when people talk about dated publications. Felix and Oscar are trying to sell a car that they had gotten that is relatively new. Oscar contacts a woman named "Pushover Page" who buys used cars. Even though the car is literally brand new, Oscar is shocked to find out how quickly it has depreciated. Page's response was: "A car is like a new bride. Once it touches down outside the church, it's no longer new." The same thing holds true for media guides. Although they are a great source of history and records, much of the data becomes less than relevant on a day-to-day basis once play begins or players are traded or coaches changed.

So what to do? Change with the times. Sections are now updated on flash drive or CD and online on a daily basis so that media members have that information up to date and in the correct place. It also saves on reprinting, adding supplements, additional pages and the like, things which used to be standard when changes were made, and for the most part were wasted. That being said, journalists are still a tough lot to embrace change, and the concept of the hard copy is still something that will not go away in the near future. Media guides, at both the collegiate and professional level, still remain a great sense of pride and value.

So for those working on them, here is a look at what needs to be in.

Essentials for the media guide

The key for any successful guide is to have the *most* essential information at the fingertips of the journalist at a moment's notice. Therefore, some key elements which should be found in seconds should include:

- A schedule.
- Names, titles, phone numbers, and email addresses of key folks who interact with the media.
- A listing of the entire staff and player personnel and coaches.
- The previous years' final statistics and results.
- Player and coaching bios that should include not only statistics, but also personal information that would be relevant to the media wanting to know the athlete or coach more. (Rule of thumb is a page or less for rookies but no more than three pages for any one player—the media will usually only go so far in detail.)
- Bios of all staff that the media members may come in contact with *only*. (This is very important. The audience for this book is the media. Therefore if there are trainers, front office personnel etc. that work very hard behind the scenes but are not essential to media interaction, then it is our opinion that they should *not* be in the book.)
- Detailed historical info that is pertinent to the team.
- A significant effort on pages for community involvement or background on the university or city (again provides fodder for feature stories).
- Detail on the home arena or stadium.
- Key information on media that cover your team, with phone numbers and email addresses.
- Information with contact numbers of league or conference officials.
- Information opponent-by-opponent (again, this is something we believe has been done to the extreme in the past and should also be key to a minimum).

From there, it is your creative and budget license to round things out. Again **emboldening** vital information is a key factor. If you want it used, then make it stand out.

As the same with the press release, have no less than *three* sets of eyes go over every page. This is a very high-ticket item and once it goes, corrections can be both expensive and embarrassing.

As the business evolves in social media, the listing of Facebook pages, Twitter handles, and personal websites may also become standard information.

However, the bottom line is that the solid basic information, with an understanding of what the media members need, is still the most important aspect of a solid guide.

Game notes and fact sheets

Once again, another lost art is the compilation of quality and timely game notes for the media to use. Over the years, the advent of desktop publishing and social media has become both a blessing and a curse for the sports publicist. We are now able to make notes look like books—graphs, charts, big fonts, photos, even video clips, all have taken the place of what used to be simple typewritten pages of facts.

In all honesty, if your notes are innovative, accurate, and consistent, most media members would take them on a napkin and handwritten. This is a place where quality, not necessarily quantity, matters. It is also a place where the timeliness and accuracy of information is critical, since unlike reading a media guide, journalists will refer right to the game notes as fact in the middle of action and in their game stories with little or no time to check facts.

Key tips for good game notes

- Always use 8½ × 11in paper, single spaced, double sided. The old days of 8 × 14in notes are gone forever.
- Updated complete rosters with accurate numbers for you and your opponents should be first—any prominent injuries or recent roster changes should be here too.
- Series records and relevant facts (in bold) should always follow.
- After that, 10–12 updated key facts about your team and possibly the series should be next (this will become easier as the season evolves).
- Then always try and identify five or six small paragraphs of new and unique facts about your players and your team, listed with the most recent facts first.
- Try and keep most facts as relevant as possible. Most of the time, rule of thumb for notes or records set should only go back 30 days. After that they will no longer be relevant.
- Trends are very important to the media (Johnny has shot 52% over the last five games after shooting 27% in the previous five, for example). Always try and look at the cumulative short term stats (five to ten game stretches) as the benchmark. That is what most print and broadcast journalists will find helpful.
- Records "set or approaching" should be after the most current facts. These should include both team and individual milestones being approached.
- Following your most current notes, we feel it is very appropriate to have some recent miscellaneous non-game facts included—community events, attendance trends, mascot facts, holiday events—items that would be used

in a slow game or in a delay, or can possibly used in graphic form in broadcasts or in website information.
- The final section of your notes should be a play-by-player, more "macro," look at his or her season (for football it would probably be 10–15 key players). This would include larger trends—best stretches, best games, etc.

All told, notes should probably be no more than 8–10 pages on your best day, in addition to the regular statistical breakdowns. The numbers *have* to be accurate and updated each day, which is the greatest point of tedium but is also the most critical. Errors of fact (saying "last night" on a Wednesday when a game was on Monday for example) will occur, but should be avoided at all cost.

Also, know your audience. For lesser sports, smaller schools, we think it is still important to do a version of notes. Especially with online availability these days, chances are that there is a need to create and use relevant notes not just for media, but for league officials coaches, and yes, even parents and athletes.

And for those of you starting out in the business, it is the best way to practice and refine this lost and very valuable piece of work.

Other tips for great notes

- Read and take from other sources. Not just in your sport but in others.
- Collect and study other media guides.
- Ask media *what* they like and what they want in your notes that can be helpful. Many times this is not an exact science and what the radio play-by-play guy at the University of Central Florida will want in football, the TV play-by-play guy on Comcast Sports Net in Philadelphia may not want. Adjust to the needs of the market.
- Keep a file with the "best of" ideas over the years. Chances are you will find a place and time to use them throughout your career.
- Be innovative, but not cornball or insulting. Many times, it seems a good way to get through the drudgery that sometimes comes with notes is to be a wise guy or put something in that's off color. Don't do it. It may be funny once, but you need to be viewed as a professional, not a wise guy.
- Every time you make notes, think that someone is using them as a guide for the first time. What makes them fresh, interesting, and different?
- Even in the hardest times for the worst of teams, try to always find the glass half full. It is *very* easy to write negative notes for bad teams. However, think always that these coaches and athletes may look to you for some of the only positive thing going on in their season. It is up to you to find the positives. Now you cannot avoid facts or change them. What you can do, and it will be appreciated, is to look under every rock and behind every corner to keep things moving forward as positively as possible. Athletes and coaches who are not successful on the field do not need more pressure. You should be seen as the ally, not the wise guy.

Notes delivery. These days the quest for information to the fan makes the exportation of notes to fan groups and others very important as well. Whereas the audience used to be just media, now content is distributed through social media, fan groups, and website postings on a regular basis as well. While the audience may be different, the message is still the same—compelling information that an interested party would crave to have.

Now maybe the "public" information is much less detailed and delivered in one sheet, or posted on a website to be downloaded. Maybe there is a revenue stream that can be added in to get the information for fans. Regardless, serving many masters with the notes for a game or an event has become very important, and for teams of all levels is now a regular part of information dissemination.

Speaking—English and a second language

Now that we have spent time talking about good reading habits, and developing strong writing habits we want to close this out with good speaking presence.

As you have heard many times before, you hardly ever get a second chance to make a first impression, and in public relations, especially with the "pitch" ideas we will talk about soon, your opportunity to get to the appropriate media person, get him or her on the phone or in person, and clearly explain what you are trying to do, is critical.

Always remember that a media member has his or her agenda and deadlines (always be aware of that as we constantly say) and that trying to change that either in written form or in verbal form is sometimes difficult.

So how you speak, what you say, and when you say it are very important.

First: it's sometime not what you say, but how you say it

Always remember that when you are calling out or even when you are in the office or at an event, you should assume that you are the first contact this media member may have with an organization. You want that contact to be a positive one that will last. It is no different than sales. Believe in yourself and your product and know your audience.

Some basic tips:

1 Always know how to pronounce the person's name correctly and where they are from. Given them the respect they want and deserve. If an editor likes to be referred to as "Mr," then do so; if he or she has a doctorate, then honor that degree as "Dr" Make sure you know that "Michael" goes by "Michael" and not "Mike." Do your homework and it will pay off.
2 The firm handshake, and the first question should always be there. Put them at ease with your confidence.

3   Speak slowly and clearly at first. Make sure they understand right off who you are representing, how to pronounce your name, and how you want to be addressed: "Good morning, Bob, it is Tom Smith from XYZ Communications, how are you today?" *Then* go into why you are calling or reaching out to them. The more engaging you can be verbally the better off you will be.

4   Sports is a business, but it is a communication business. Properly communicate by being folksy but professional. It is not OK to get into off-color jokes, or use profanity off the bat—it is OK to talk about the weather briefly, to bring up a common topic (the more well read you are will pay off here), and work in your points.

5   Keep in mind deadlines when you are calling at all times. Make your initial point about *why* you are calling in the first two or three minutes and then follow-up with another salient point as soon as possible.

6   Always remember that this may be your first contact, but not your last with this media member or executive. Leave it on as positive a note as you can, regardless of how bad a day they may be having.

7   Finish with the understanding from your point of view, even if there is *no* interest on their part, that you will follow-up. No matter how bad it goes, there is always room for a followup note, email, or voice mail. You never know where that relationship will go or turn in your favor in the future.

8   If you are referred to someone else, be sure and understand clearly whom that person is and how to reach out to them—and still follow-up with the original person.

9   No matter how nervous you are on the call or with the meeting, be yourself and believe in yourself. If on the phone, have short notes with you to check off.

10 As soon as possible after the call or meeting, jot down notes about how it went and next steps for yourself. No matter what the outcome, you will then learn and build off of that call.

And finally, a note about speaking in tongues—no, not about being a religious zealot or having a miracle done for you—try and be able to converse, understand, and be respectful to folks in their native tongue, or at the very least, in a second tongue other than English.

Many of us have taken a second language along the way, in grammar school, high school, or college. If it was one of the romance languages (Spanish, French, or Italian) or one of the so-called "dead" languages (Greek or Latin), great. If it is Japanese, Chinese, or Russian, maybe even better. If you know a little Tagalog or German from your grandmother, that's fine too.

The point is, in this international field we are now involved in, understanding folks in their own language, even for a few seconds, *shows* that you have taken that extra step and will go a long way in helping you get them "on your side." Now that is not to say that you should disrespect folks by using slang or coming across as the "ugly American." Not at all. You need to show the respect for the language and the culture.

So hone up on that second skill. If you can write in it, even better. You will be ahead of 90 percent of the people in this industry. And more respected too.

4

HOW AND WHAT TO PITCH

No mediums should be rare when selling sizzle or steak

In this chapter we will focus on what, at the end of the day, is really the essence of what the publicity business is now and what it started out to be—getting ink for the client, no matter who or where he or she is. As you will see later on in the book, the industry has grown to the point where much of the focus is on the glitz and glamour, or the return on investment for a sponsor or an organization, or on maximizing company revenue. That is all very encouraging for an industry that continues to grow and expand.

However, the one fact remains that if you cannot essentially get coverage in media for whomever you are working for, the best business plans and multimedia presentations will all fall apart.

At the end of the day, the publicity industry remains very much a people industry. Just like selling a commodity, you are selling an image, or a story, or yes, even a product. Is there always a hard dollar attached to the sale? No. However, the idea of return on investment and building clip and video files is showing to be a larger example of success for companies than it has ever been before, especially in these days of cost-cutting on hard-dollar advertising.

Also, the great news is the 24/7 news cycle, the online world, the growth of niche and hyper-local publications, the explosion of the digital platform for sports television, and the competition for the disposable leisure dollar have all created more opportunities for the sports publicist. Whereas 5–10 years ago the value in placing a story in an online site was deemed as subservient to getting a story in a print publication, today correctly servicing that .com may be seen as your biggest success. The competition is always fierce for the larger, mainstream publications and media outlets. However, now building a stable of stories and contacts through smaller, niche publications that lead to the big hit is becoming more commonplace.

The reason for this is the value of the search engine. Nowadays when a major media company is deciding on covering an event, or doing a feature, they will go right to the web to find credible sources. One place they will look is the niche publications that have covered the sport, or the event, or the personality as they have emerged. If the positive clip file is found in their "family" of publications (the magazines, websites, and columnists devoted to the sport or company or event), chances are they will consider moving forward. If there is not a positive message out there, the chances that story will move ahead for consideration dims considerably. Those little placements now become the germ of the bigger story, like never before.

And that is how the pitch begins.

There are several basic rules that you will need to consider as you develop your pitch plans. We will list them here, and then get into the "type" of pitches that you can use in your publicity plan.

The pitching rules, or "How to deliver a strike":

- Know your subject.
- Cultivate the media.
- Set the strategy.
- Develop the pitch kit.
- Build the clip file.
- Follow-up and revisit.

Using these as the basis of your plan will help you to have a clearer, more focused sense of guidelines and timing as you begin.

There are also several forms of pitching that we will talk about. Each has a different approach to it, and although many times you can go to the same source for advice, or go back to the same person with many pitches, you have to be able to understand and make it clear to him or her that there are some differences. The pitches discussed will include:

- the long-lead pitch
- the quick pitch
- the notes pitch
- the feature/special event pitch.

So let's get started talking about the essentials.

Know your subject

The most important piece of a successful pitch is sometimes the one that is the most overlooked. By your "subject," I mean not just the person or entity you are working with, but the entire scope of the project. The most important thing before beginning is to ask questions, and then understand what areas of the pitch are the most important to the subject. That is how you will be judged on success.

Tip

Here is a simple rule of thumb when talking to a client and gathering information for the pitch. You have two ears and one mouth, so listen twice more than you speak. Everyone has an interesting story, letting the subject talk and then taking copious notes is very important, but the ability to *listen* to what the subject is saying is very, very important. There may be subtle messages or information which you as a professional may deem important but the subject may not realize is important when he/she is rambling at it. Listen to the content and then follow up.

Examples

The Olympic Community is very large, but the must-read every day is the online subscription service Around The Rings. While major stories about The Games break every day, ATR is still the most connected news source for goings-on that involve federations, athletes and countries every day. Based in Atlanta, GA, it may not be well known outside of the large Olympic circle, but it is essential within for all involved.

Tennis is a very large industry around the world, and the USTA is the world's largest national governing body for any sport. While I was there, we had several agencies as well as an internal team come up with a very successful series of pitches to promote the sport and the US Open specifically. However, much of the success or failure of the publicity pitches would revolve less around a feature in *USA Today* or a business story on MSNBC. They would revolve around what was written in a bi-monthly magazine called *Tennis Week*. The editor, the late Gene Scott, had a tremendous amount of influence amongst the insiders of the sport, and often would poke and probe at those insiders with a great amount of criticism. For a publicity pitch and plan to be successful, a strong relationship with *Tennis Week* was essential. For an outsider going in with a pitch plan that did not include *Tennis Week* would have been a major mistake.

Knowing what to pitch would include extensive research of areas like:

- *What media coverage has already taken place?* If it is a major sport, be aware of the beat writers and what has gone on in the last 30 days. If it is a niche sport, know the websites and what is covered. On the collegiate or league side, use a search engine to pull up stories not only about athletics, but as the entity as a whole. Have a solid set of clips going into the pitch.
- *What are others in the field saying/have said?* It is always important to know what the competition is doing, as this will make it easier to tailor your search. For "the other side" type of stories it will be good to go back to those media sources. However, it will also help to give you a list of media that will not be worth pitching because of coverage already done on a competitor or opponent. This will save you lots of time in tailoring your efforts.
- *What media are important to the subject?* It is very important in establishing the pitch to ask questions and know the priorities.

Example

I was involved in a startup called the International Fight League (IFL), a new version of mixed martial arts/ultimate fighting that involves a team concept. The founder was very interested in major media hits and pitches as the process evolved. However, his main priority at the start was to establish strong ties with the media that covered the sport. The reason? As one takes their pitch to the mainstream, one of the first places mainstream media will go for background on the effort is to the media that cover the sport with a passion. If you want credibility when making big pitches, it is important to have a solid relationship with those who are advocates of the sport first. This is a very example of establishing priorities and moving ahead. Without asking the question, we may have never had a starting point that made sense to the principal of the company.

- *What media are* not *important to the subject?* Once again, by asking questions you will save yourself a great deal of time and energy with your pitches. It could be that the principal you are dealing with already is well entrenched with their local media, so there is no need to go and pitch them on a story they would cover anyway. It could also be that the subject has no interest in business press at the time, a place where you may see a good pitch. Bottom line, if it doesn't matter to the subject, then it should not be important to your initial plan.

Example

There are many brands today that are totally consumed with activating against a very young demo. Therefore getting a business story placed in the *Wall Street Journal* may not have as much weight for them as cultivating relationships and getting personality pieces done with well-followed websites like a Bleacher Report or The Big Lead, which is where their core audience goes to get news. Getting that target list set and knowing what the "wins" are, can save a lot of time and effort in the process.

Startup companies or brands looking for funding may have more interest in a blog post with Darren Rovell on his ESPN blog than they would with a feature in a consumer magazine, because they know where their core audience is looking for news and where they want to be seen.

- *What problems or successes has the subject had with the media?* A search may be able to get you some initial answers as to how the subject has handled and is perceived by the media. However, that may not give you enough background to effectively tailor your pitch. Many subjects can be very media savvy, yet not have a great deal of comfort or trust in dealing with the media. Conversely, many people would like to be media darlings but say either too little or too much and create problems for themselves. Asking the personal questions and then marrying those answers to the media coverage will give you a better picture to include in your pitch plan.

Example

Hall of Fame quarterback Joe Montana was never viewed as having much of a problem with the media. Throughout his career at Notre Dame, then San Francisco and Kansas City, he was rarely if ever the source of a media controversy. He was rarely rude and seemed always to be accommodating to the media horde that would follow him. His outward "success" with the media was actually part of an inward strategy. His strategy was never to be quoted. He understood the media had a job to do and a success for him was not to be a part of the media process, and to give as bland or mild an answer as possible. It was a process that someone who did not know enough to ask him would never have discovered unless you combined what was written with what his perception was. It was not from a bad experience that he had had per se. It was more from his observations of the media and what he felt was best to handle those situations for himself as a personal choice.

- *What is the subject's timeline on measuring success?* One of the greatest issues in publicity is its sense of urgency. The 24/7 news cycle now makes that even more prevalent. However, that sense of urgency to succeed and start the pitch process may not be what the client wants to be done. Perhaps the company is trying to still quietly lure investors, or there are internal issues that do not lend themselves to coverage right at this moment. The chances are that you may be brought into a situation where media coverage is more immediate, especially if you are on the agency side.

Tip

Companies that are being bought or sold in the public markets, where stock is changing hands, will go through what is known as a "quiet period," in the United States, while Federal regulators are looking at all aspects of the transaction prior to sale. During that period, little to no public information of the company should be put forth, with the feeling that any information could influence a price of sale artificially. If you are working with a company during such a "quiet period," no information will be issued and very little news will be pitched or placed until after the period is over. It could be as little as a few weeks or as long as several months depending on the vetting process.

- *Does the entity have a set amount of goals for coverage?* Realistic goals for success are key. The only way to determine what those goals are is to ask. Perhaps it is a league which has had no success getting local coverage of its Olympic athletes in a major marketplace. Or perhaps it is a sports drink that has signed a series of major athletes with set endorsement media opportunities built into their contracts that no one knew about. The only way to know is to ask and see what the response is. Measuring those goals and determining what is realistic on a timeline will help give you a fair way to measure pitches, or to figure out how defined your pitches can be.
- *What additional forms of media can you bring to the table to help the subject be successful?* You are being brought in many cases as the expert on pitching and getting ink. Therefore it is your job to come up with that maximum plan for coverage. The subject probably has many other tasks at hand. Therefore, can you look at the broad scope of media and show the subject what alternative forms of media are out there to help define the pitch plan and satisfy the goals needed for coverage? Is it a series of blog posts or a podcast? Do Twitter posts by influential media help tell the story? Are there local news outlets or other small trade publications that can assist? All of which can bring "tonnage" to the table, and sometimes the casting of that wide net is what is best for the client, creating a steady string of news where the public cannot help but hear about the goings-on.

Example

Michael Yormark and Brett Yormark are twins who run successful businesses, the New Jersey Nets and the Florida Panthers. Individually they are great stories, but working together made for a family business story for *Entrepreneur Magazine*.

Example

Sporting Kansas City is a franchise built on innovation, especially with their arena Live Strong Park. The naming rights went to a cause, Lance Armstrong's charity, but the building was innovative in its use at the time of digital media for accessing fan engagement and activation. It's a nice soccer story, but it is also a great tech story. So the SKC team found a home for the story in *Inc Magazine*.

The Thom McAnn Theory

One key element of a successful knowledge of your subject is known as the "Thom McAnn Theory." Thom McAnn was a very successful shoe store chain in the 1960s and 1970s. Their base of success, along with a quality product, was to be a consensus builder for their clients. When someone came into a store, the customer was always right and it would be the salesperson's responsibility to take stock of that client, and try and know as much about them to help them make a good choice. It was important to make a sale that the customer felt good about and to listen and know what it is they would want by that dialogue. The other side of that would be to make sure that the customer was never the bad guy in the sales process. The issue in the wrong color shoe selection was never an argument with the customer. It would always fall on the salesperson to make sure the customer was happy with the choice and that the experience was positive. Like Thom McAnn selling shoes, knowing the subject in publicity is the key. He or she is never the bad guy. It is up to you to come up with the pitch that makes the most sense for their needs, and adjust accordingly.

Cultivate the media

With the ever-growing demands on the media it is important to have a fresh and updated database for when you are pitching stories. Staying ahead of trends today, and knowing who and what to pitch, is as much a 24/7 job as news coverage is.

The bottom line is that this remains very much a relationship business, and the innovation of all the technology today is both a help and a hindrance in media cultivation. Let's look at both sides and how we can use them both to our advantage to cultivate media for a pitch.

How technology is a help. The use of search engines, the availability of updated media files and listings online, the continued evolution of fan sites and niche websites, all make the names and addresses of media you can pitch much more available than ever before. You can now search stories by the minute and by the hour, and get an immediate response sometimes from an author. Facts are available to cultivate pitches on websites like never before. All that can help you define your pitch and connect with media in real time.

The use of new technology also helps you to deliver pitches directly to an interested member of the media, often including photographs and charts if needed. The days of going through editors or secretaries to find the right writer are basically gone. Being able to acquire an email address and direct a pitch has become much easier with today's technology.

Tip

Publications like *Bacon's*, the *National Directory of Collegiate Athletics, The Sports Fact Book*, the publications that many leagues put forward such as the NBA "blue" book (which lists all the media connections involved with NBA teams), the NFL "black" book (which lists media connections with NFL teams) are all tremendous sources of media information. Many of them also have an online database that is updated regularly. *Bacon's* also has books that will tailor media information to particular areas, like technology, multicultural publications, weekly and daily newspapers, and niche magazines.

Another important factor in media cultivation with today's technology is personalization. The mass blanketing with press releases and blind pitch letters is still part of the process for general announcements. However, being able to target media and personalize the pitch to their needs and interests is very, very important.

Example

Terry Lefton, senior editor for the trade publication, the *Sports Business Journal*, receives literally hundreds of press releases a week on all aspects of sports business, marketing, and publicity. Given his demands for time and the limited amount of space he gets both online and in the printed publication, he cannot look at everything that comes across his email and his desk. Being able to know what he like to write about, what stories are coming up in an issue, and what subjects interest him are critical in getting information in his column. The only way to do that is to develop the relationship, pitch according to his understood needs and not blanket him with needless pitches. The "mass blanketing" will actually have an adverse effect on having a successful pitch.

How technology is a hindrance—spam is neither something you want to eat or pitch. While the use of technology has greatly expanded our ability to pitch stories in a real-time basis, it has also made us in many ways *less* personal. As we have said before, this is a relationship business, and we have become even more dependent on email to make connections and get our jobs done. It certainly helps speed up the process. However, there is still something to be said about physically meeting a person and sitting down and discussing their needs and interests away from the workplace that is still a great part of this business.

We are able to "personalize" the business side of a pitch and make it effective. However, the social aspect of the business should not be hidden behind the wall of technology. Now this is not something that can be overcome sometimes on a national or even a regional scale. Especially large media outlets won't be able to take every call or every meeting to discuss a project. However a call, a handwritten note about a significant project that the media member is involved with that has nothing to do with your pitch (a good story, a new book, a website column) is a great way to overcome the impersonalization of today's society.

On a local level, it is critical that you have more than an email relationship with key editors, columnists, and TV people of influence.

Tip

Make a "hit list" of media, ranging from producers to editors and columnists, to have lunch with or coffee with face to face once a month. This process will help you learn more about what is going on in the industry and will help you easily refine your pitches. You will not be able to complete the list and will have to adjust to other's schedules. But making that effort and buying lunch or coffee will put you ahead of all those just on the email trail.

Another simple effort that needs to be made when cultivating the media is reading. The internet gives us all a chance to scan hundreds of newspapers and magazines and search by title and genre. As professionals, it is our job to be the experts for our clients (whether they are products or people) and have a strong working knowledge of trends and who is writing about them. By reading and maintaining a list of media you will need to call on, you will be more prepared for when you are getting ready to pitch.

Example of knowing what to pitch

Great idea, wrong day. A Friday in March was branded National Meatball Day, as fun a promo for brands that sell the product as there can be. Few people don't like meatballs and everyone knows what they are, whether you are fans of Swedish or traditional Italian. Only one problem, the promoters picked a Friday in Lent, when Catholics, and some other Christian faiths, abstain from eating meat. While some who don't observe may think it is nitpicky, it alienated a portion of those who could celebrate, which, if you are trying to drum up niche support, isn't smart. A move to another day next time with input from a forward thinking publicist who may have spoken to some media about the idea in advance, may make support may be even bigger at another time.

The other element that media cultivation gives you is another voice. The sports industry, despite all its growth, remains a very close-knit community. Many people follow trends and also are aware of those who do outreach and what kind of outreach they do. By working with the media as colleagues, you will be able to open doors more quickly when looking to pitch a story to a writer or a television reporter who you do not know that well.

"The up and down the ladder" effect. Another important aspect of media cultivation is what I will call the "up and down the ladder" effect. It's simple. As we go through our careers, we will run into many people in different jobs along the way. Cultivating media from an early stage and developing those long-standing relationships will help you in many ways, both as your career grows and as the journalist's career grows. You will meet the same people on the way up that you do on the way down. Here are some examples of that effect, and how I didn't know it at the time, but it helped me in my future pitches.

	Knew them when	They are now
Ian O'Connor	writer, *Poughkeepsie Journal*	columnist, ESPN New York
Mike Breen	reporter, WNBC radio	play-by-play ABC/ESPN
Michael Kay	broadcaster, WFUV radio	play-by-play YES
Steve Popper	student, Monmouth College	beat writer, *The Record*
Linda Cohen	reporter, News 12 Long Island	SportsCenter host
Stephen A. Smith	reporter Newsday	talk show host ESPN

Now, did I know any of these people would become such big personalities when I first met them? No. But they are good examples of cultivating personal and professional relationships for the long term.

For the print focus—columnists, editors and general reporters. In your media cultivation it is important to have a solid mix of:

- those who write news (reporters)
- those who write news and set their own topics (columnists)
- those who ultimately make the decisions on space and story (editors).

This is true for both the printed publications like newspapers (weekly or daily) and internet sites for the most part. Today we are seeing two separate groups emerge as well. It used to be that people worked on both, as well as managing social media and blogging. While that is true for beat writers, often times the growth of the digital side is placing larger amounts of staff dedicated just to that aspect. Now we are seeing more and more separate staffs assigned to the printed word and the internet word, both searching for unique content which you can pitch them.

It is very important to understand the chain of command at a publication and know how your pitch will be handled.

Reporters. Many times your cultivation will start at the reporter level and move on to the columnist if you are doing events they may attend or there is a cause or a unique story that you think they may have particular interest in. Most papers will also have reporters assigned to general "beats" (pro or college teams or high school and local sports) or to specific "sports" (NASCAR, golf, tennis, boxing, outdoors, baseball, etc., depending on what the readers and advertisers have asked for). There will also be a host of general assignment reporters who do much of the deskwork, and will cover the story that may be too big—or even too small—for the beat writer to cover (many times known as the sidebar). The beats are usually the most receptive and are out there trolling for good stories to raise their stature. They are usually a good sounding board for their bosses and what the paper is looking for. They are also important as they move up the chain of command. The cultivation of relationships with reporters is also important because they have the most regular presences in print publications and on websites, and they tend to write more about "news" than "topics," which is where columnists will usually reside. Reporters will also be more passionate about their beat, and when they move on to other beats will usually look to rely on their solid relationships from the past as well.

Example

Beth Marshall (now Vice President of Public Relations for the Atlanta Braves) was Vice President of Public Relations for the Pro Bowlers Tour (the PBA). She joined the PBA when bowling was in its doldrums, but new owners from Microsoft were looking to reinvigorate what was a very healthy sport in its 1970s heyday. In her quest for national exposure, Beth was able to identify that a writer at *USA Today* named Tom Clarke was an avid bowler. Clarke, who had handled many minor beats for the paper over the years, was very excited when approached about bowling's new outlook, and became a very strong PBA advocate for Marshall on a national level. He was able to bring strong pitches that may have been missed up the chain of command at *USA Today*. A result of identifying the right reporter? The PBA landed three *USA Today* cover stories in the span of three years. They were strong stories on the growth of bowling numbers, the flamboyance of bowlers like Pete Webber and the new investors in the sport, but without that connection and that advocate they might not have occurred. As a result, the PBA re-entered the mainstream because of the strong publicity efforts.

Columnists. The columnist is one of the most desired assignments for the print and internet. They will be general columnists or also "beat" columnists, although the beat columnists will usually take on larger areas of a sport or subject ("The University of Tennessee beat" as opposed to the "Lady Vols" reporter). General columnists usually have a set number of days during the week that they will write, and many times will write their opinion on the news of the day. The better columnists, such as the *Daily News* Mike Lupica, *Grantland*'s Bill Simmons, *Sports Illustrated*'s Jon Wertheim, the *Washington Post*'s Tony Kornheiser, ESPN's Rick Reilly or the *Detroit Free Press*' Mitch Albom, will often look for the off-news story of a major event, what was termed by legendary columnist Jimmy Breslin as "gravedigger journalism." (Gravedigger journalism came about in 1964, when Breslin chose to write about the man digging President John F. Kennedy's grave and what this great loss meant to him and his family, as opposed to the regular columns that were written about the tragedy. It means looking for an angle that no one else has thought of to tell a story.) They will use their own sources mixed with their opinion and solid writing stories to develop a column that forms and shapes a particular message to be sent to the public. Sometimes it is contrary to what the rest of the pack is writing on a major event like the Super Bowl or the NCAA Final Four or the Daytona 500. Sometimes it is more human interest.

Having columnists as part of your media cultivation is important, as they have the most dedicated space and can help shape opinions. They are also huge allies when you have stories that are "on the bubble" for coverage. Cultivating older columnists is sometimes difficult, as they tend to cover only major events and are rarely in the office. Using that "up and down ladder" idea for your pitch plan in the long term works best. However, knowing their interests and trends by reading their items religiously is the best way to grow relationships. The risk you run with a columnist is that his opinion will be what he writes. As long as that is understood going in, and realizing that his or her opinion will not always jibe with your agenda, the easier it is to make the connection with the columnist.

Tip

Many columnists also have the ability to write feature books on topics. They are always worth reading for background and for conversation. Also, many columnists will also have assembled anthologies of their works. These anthologies, ranging from Pulitzer Prize winners like Red Smith and W.C. Heinz to more recent writers like Reilly, John Steadman of the *Baltimore Sun*, Jim Murray of the *Los Angeles Times*, Gary Smith of *Sports Illustrated*, and Roger Angell of the *New Yorker*, will give you an excellent insight into a daily writing style of these gifted columnists. Also, magazines like *Sport*, *Sports Illustrated*, and even *Playboy* have compiled their best writing into anthologies. All, along with the "Best American Sportswriting" series, should be required for all assembling the pitch and cultivating the media.

Editors. The ultimate decision makers as to what goes in and what doesn't— website, magazine, or newspaper—is the editorial team. In this era, the team is usually segmented and decisions are made by a group as opposed to one central person. However, the Editor-in-Chief in most cases does set the tone for his staff. He or she is usually part of the "larger picture" of the publication or site, and has a say in other parts of the entity. The Editor-in-Chief these days is also in charge of finding ways to work with sales to drive revenue without compromising the integrity of the journalist. It is a fine line that he or she walks as the business of journalism is balanced.

Editors in this era rarely write, and rarely cover events. Long hours and new, sometimes earlier, deadlines keep them in the office overseeing the physical construction of the publication and all the elements that now go with that. Those include photo areas, video areas, audio areas, and additional online proprietary content. Some also have say in the content of the many "advertorials" that are now prevalent in many publications. The one common thread amongst editors is their rise through the ranks. They have an understanding of each of the jobs in their publications, and have the clearest vision of what the publication's audience is. Many times the best way to build that relationship is to visit the editor and then ask questions. Sometimes editors will also take meetings with prominent coaches and officials to have each side better understand the role in the media relationship. One thing is for sure, having a strong relationship with an editor may be the most difficult to achieve, but it is a relationship that can get your pitch to fruition the fastest.

For the multimedia side—reporters, producers and assignment editors. On the multimedia side, especially television and radio, the cultivation process also breaks down into three areas.

1   *Reporters.* Like the beat writers, they are the ones in the field surveying and delivering the news. Many times the immediacy of television or radio will dictate what the story of the day is. However, working relationships with reporters for the human interest or long lead pieces, or even making sure that the highlights of an athlete or a sport make the final cut, is important.
2   *Producers.* Many times producers can have a strong say in the editorial process as to what can go out and be shot. In this era of "delivered" video—raw footage, packaged pieces, and video news releases (we will explain each shortly)—the producer is the repository and can help get highlights into a broadcast. He or she is also a great sounding board for other areas of news that may be interested in covering non-game events or human interest stories, like morning shows or noon news broadcasts. Many times the producer will make more of these decisions that the on-air talent will. In these days of cost cutting, the producer may also act as his or her own camera man, and in some cases be the on-air talent his or herself.
3   *Assignment editors.* Like the publication editor, the assignment editor will have the final say with regard to the allocation of camera crews for the news broadcast. The producer and reporter will be able to make their case, but to have a relationship cultivated with this person, usually a newsperson not a sports person, is also important. The assignment editor normally has many tasks to juggle for the entire 30 or 60 minute show, of which sports

is a small segment. Therefore having a working relationship, and knowing how and when to use that relationship, is very important in many cases to get coverage of a feature or a non–game story.

Set the strategy

Now that you have addressed the agenda with your subject and have surveyed the media landscape with some solid contacts, it is now time to set the strategy for your pitches to begin.

It is always important to go into a pitch identifying the type of media that you would like to cover your pitch. Some things to consider.

What's the angle? The first and most important part of the pitch strategy is the simplest one. What's the angle? What sets your human interest story above everyone else's that will make it newsworthy. Again this goes back to knowing your subject and knowing the media you are pitching. It has to be simple and concise. Chances are if you can't explain the angle to "yourself" in two sentences, you may have to do a little more digging or refine your strategy.

A well-tailored pitch will fit well. The strategy has to make sense to the nature of the pitch. Carpet pitching, covering every outlet and hoping that something sticks, usually doesn't work. Knowing what the core media messages are for the pitch and what media will work comes from your media cultivation and using the correct source books, but it also comes from common sense. Pitching *Ad Age* on a new running shoe does not make sense if they just did a major feature on a new Nike or Adidas shoe the week before. If the pitch and the outfit don't make any sense, then don't pitch it there.

Is it time sensitive? Does the sense of urgency need to be factored into your pitch? Statistics, injury potential, etc. all need to be considered. Always be aware of media deadlines as well.

Exclusivity? Always remember that your pitch is most effective when it is proprietary. If it is exclusive to one reporter over another, always make sure that that media member will do the best job with the piece for you. Once you go that route, remember that you may be sacrificing coverage from all his/her competitors. There are ways to carve the exclusivity in some cases. Exclusive to a magazine or a business publication for example, as opposed to a sports story.

Have a backup. Even the best laid plans can not work out sometimes. If your media plan A falls through, figure out who you would go to for your next best pitch, and tailor it accordingly.

Biggest is not always best. Many times our subject has visions of the front page of the *New York Times* or the cover of *Sports Illustrated*. That may not always be the biggest impact. Sometimes telling your story to a secondary market paper or website can have the greatest appeal, and can create even more opportunity.

Example

The New York Mets, who, despite their home game heroics in 2011, were still playing second fiddle to the Yankees in terms of exposure. What do the Mets do … break a record. Not a baseball one, a crocheting one. Over 40 Mets fans at Citi Field, during the game against the Marlins in mid-July, crocheted at the same time to officially set a Guinness book of World Records mark. The event was led by crochet star, "Inside Edition" host, and Mets fan Deborah Norville, and got the team some worthwhile off-sports buzz for an event that really wasn't much of an event without the PR spin. It didn't get a magazine, but the photos and the stories got great grassroots coverage in blogs and notes columns, keeping the team relevant at a time when on field production was waning.

Don't forget the wires. Many times, especially in bigger markets, we downplay the significance of the Associated Press and Reuters, or the business wires like Bloomberg. Those outlets, especially on off-peak news times or days, can have a tremendous circulation across the country and around the world. In this era of immediate impact, the value of the newswire is sometimes forgotten.

A picture is worth at least a thousand words. We live in the visual era. The most control over editorial we have is through the visual. Sometimes providing a well-captioned photo or streaming video can get us the quickest and best coverage in lieu of the story. In an era where YouTube channels can be created and managed for any genre, or other video sharing services can bring key clips to millions, it is important to have both the still image and the video of an event ready to enhance coverage. It is always a good option to consider.

Example

One of the best examples of "sport" mixing virally is with the sneaker brand KSwiss and the fictional "Eastbound and Down" character Kenny Powers. KSwiss brought Kenny to life in a series of viral videos that lifted the profile of the show and the persona of Powers, by making Powers the character "spokesman" for their brand—even though he was fictional.

Example

Martina Hingis had just completed her first US Open championship and was the world's number one women's tennis player. She also had a few issues with some aspects of her English and being misquoted on a few occasions. Martina also had a deep love of horses, and the summer's other great sports story was the run of the thoroughbred Cigar to a near-miss triple crown. Cigar had come into New York following the Open for the Breeder's Cup as well. Given the fact that photographers had shot Hingis ad nauseum throughout the summer in a tennis background, the WTA media staff worked with the New York Racing Authority to have Hingis go to Belmont following her championship and meet this great horse. It was something Hingis was very enthusiastic about and created a great photo opportunity that was an easy pitch to worldwide media. The photo ended up running in tennis, horse, and mainstream publications, including both *Sports Illustrated* and *People Magazine*. It is not a pitch that would have worked with a writer, but the visual was incomparable.

Under-promise, over-deliver. You can only worry about what we can control. Therefore it is important in being realistic in delivering your pitch plan. You must be confident and be able to back up what ideas and items you think are deliverable. However, it is important that everyone understands that things do happen from when the plans are made and the events go on.

Example

David Robinson was just beginning his Hall-of-Fame NBA career with the San Antonio Spurs after a standout career at Navy. One of the big pitches his PR team had to arrange and deal with was to be on the cover of *GQ* in exchange for a men's fashion magazine exclusive interview. Robinson was very wary of how he would be portrayed, but went through the extensive project with the guarantee of a cover for the magazine. The photo and interview took place over several days, with input from the team, his agent, and his sneaker company. It was completed and as is the case with long-lead publications, the wait began to see when it would run. It was slated for their annual fall issue which focuses on the winter sports. The issue was ready to come out and then the bad news came. Robinson would have been the cover with one exception that was not addressed. He was bumped for Julia Roberts, who agreed only to talk to *GQ* with an exclusive cover guarantee. Although it makes for an understandable choice given the magazine demographic, it was not easy to explain to the client and puts the power of athletics vs. the power of entertainment in clear focus.

It is better to be lucky than good, but be ready for both. Every PR pitch plan should have at least one outrageous idea included in it. It is the call to the editor or the photo desk that is a long shot and may only be known to the publicist and the subject, but it is worth the shot. Those opportunities take a great deal of long-lead planning, but sometimes they will pay off. Knowing what else is going on in the area and including those events in your plans will also help those long shots sometimes work out. Sporting events, plays, musical performances, visits by dignitaries, all should be on the list.

Sometimes opportunity will fall in your lap, and it is up to you as the publicist to be able to maximize it.

Example 1

While public relations director of the Philadelphia 76ers, we were getting ready to honor Hall-of-Famer Maurice Cheeks by retiring his number "10." We came up with the promotion idea of having other "10s" join Maurice for his special night. We included many athletes who wore the number 10 during their career, and put out a call through a gossip item that we would like to invite the ultimate "10," actress Bo Derek, as well. (Derek for those of you who don't know starred in Blake Edwards comedy hit "10" with Dudley Moore in the 1970s.) We never thought anything of it, until we received a phone call the Friday before the event from Ms Derek herself. A friend had seen the item and she was indeed in the area (in Atlantic City for an event) but she could not attend. She was very pleased we had thought about her though, and Maurice was very pleased when he learned of the efforts we had made to make his night special. Once again it was a long shot, but the effort made almost turned into a great publicity opportunity. As it ended up, the fact that Ms Derek was aware and called still made it a highly publicizable event.

Example 2

The Cleveland Indians were able to turn a unique situation into a publicity pitch in with their then-budding superstar Jim Thome. In 1997, Thome was having an outstanding season while helping lead the resurgent Indians back to respectability in the new Jacobs Field. To celebrate his August birthday and mimic a tradition that only he had, on August 27 the entire team decided to wear their socks high in an "old style" tradition. The Indians went on from that point to post a 17–10 record and win the American League East title. The move also set a fashion trend amongst fans that the team capitalized on, and gave them a chance to tell the very unique story of Thome's socks to a national audience during the end of the season and the playoffs. Thome wore his socks high to honor his late grandfather, his role model and a lifelong baseball fan.

Stay focused on the goal. Particularly if you are working at an agency, or if you have numerous stories you may think are interesting to a reporter, it can be easy to get off track if you think that there may be the slightest bit of hesitancy on the part of the media member.

It is important to remember why you are making the pitch, and why this pitch is part of the strategy that you have set forth. Changing subjects or jumping to another idea will show you are indecisive with your subject in completing your strategy. Chances are if you make a strong pitch and it is even rejected, that you will have enough respect from that media member to come back a second time. If you switch in the middle of a pitch to another idea you may think is more "interesting," the person you are pitching to may see you as somewhat less than professional.

Can you plant a seed for another idea in closing? Or leave it that you will be back at them with another idea soon? Sure. But it is important to stick to the plan for the one subject before moving off and on to another.

Also, if the goal was to find three or four areas of placement and you felt it was realistic, then stick to that plan. As we said earlier, those little placements do add up and could lead to a larger one.

With these basic ideas in mind, it will be much easier to develop your strategy as you formulate the pitch plan.

Developing the pitch kit

With the plan, it is important to also have the right elements assembled. We will talk about the writing elements in a later chapter, but it is important to have the correct amount of elements assembled and ready to go as you make your pitch.

If you are still using traditional paper kits, as some still may, the elements of the basic kit should be as follows:

- A two-pocket, heavy-duty folder. The outside of the folder should have logo and website url if applicable, not much else.
- Inside on the right side up top should be your "news." Whatever the main one or two page element of the pitch is. Behind that should be proper clips on the person or event, no more than five pages if possible. Clips should be with the most recent or most informational on top and then go backward.

Tip

Assume the media may only read the top story as a rule. Color is probably not helpful for any images. If they cannot reproduce well in black and white then do not use them. You should assume that this information would be passed along and copied. Make sure the clips are legible after being copied. If they can't be read then they are useless. It is also much better to have nice articles printed off the web than fancy news clips from newspapers that cannot be read.

- Inside in the left pocket should be your background information. That should include a fact sheet about the event or person, and if possible on top, a personalized letter that briefly outlines what the essence of the pitch is. Any other information like historical backgrounders, timelines, or biographical information about the company or organization should go last.
- Any photos should be on a DVD or memory stick and placed in the pocket on the left side. The same with logos. The use of still images in a press kit and logo sheets is almost wasteful in this day.

It is also important that your contact information appear in at least two places. There should be a business card clipped to the inside left pocket, as well as the information in your pitch letter, once again assuming that these elements can be copies or passed on.

If you have the ability to do the kit digitally and the media member will use and accept it digitally, even better. The glory of emailing a press kit will save time and money.

The pitch letter

Once again, personal information and contact is key. It is not recommended to send blanket, blind pitch letters, and kits. The letters should be followed only after some initial contact is made. If the letter is not directed to the person with whom you have spoken with, it should be made very clear who it is you spoke with and why he/she recommended you send the kit.

The letter should be very concise. It should have three or four bullet points summarizing the pitch, your info, and the fact that you will follow up shortly to discuss potential next steps. The more personal, the less formal the better chance of getting something accomplished.

Building the clip file

Now that you have the strategy, the correct kit, and have worked the media well, the clips should come rolling in. Well maybe. However, the building of that clip file is important as you expand your pitches forward. There is one critical thing to remember with the clip file.

Quality and quantity do matter, depending on what that goal was that you set up with your subject. The quality placements are always the ones that most are judged on. However how you are able to merchandise those clips becomes important as well, especially in the smaller markets or the more obscured projects. Some things to keep in mind when doing the pitching.

Don't discard the hometowns and the small towns. Everyone has a hometown paper, and everyone in that hometown reads it. It doesn't matter if your "hometown" is Brooklyn, New York or Anchorage, Alaska. There is a weekly newspaper that has a small circulation that would love to be pitched. Chances are it will be receptive. Chances are you will get to tailor the copy and the photo. Chances are it will look good in the clip file.

Also, many of the small town papers are consolidated these days, and the story could run in multiple editions. Most also have websites that will take content as well. Nothing like being a big fish in a small sea.

Alma mater. We all get the quarterly magazines from whatever college, and many high schools. There are always many stories on some prominent alumni. Chances are that those stories have been pitched for inclusion. You are probably working with some prominent athletes or officials who have gone to school somewhere and would be well recognized by that community. No reason to go ahead and pitch 'em there.

The collegiate media. Again, college newspapers and websites have continued to grow as the communications industry has. More often than not, the chance about writing about a prominent alumnus exists, and if you can present it to the paper as an opportunity and a good story, chances are it will mount up for a good clip.

Ask for copies. Also important to building the clip file is to ask for clips to be sent or emailed. Many times the writers will take pride in sending on their work, especially if it is a freelancer looking for more work.

Niche magazines and websites. Another receptive area for pitching. Knowing your subject and his or her or its nuances will open up many doors, and will help make that subject more interesting to the mainstream.

Example 1

When he was with the LA Clippers, Baron Davis started to develop a great affinity for film production. That blossomed into a production company for rising artists. The team as able to take advantage of that interest and get a piece in *Variety* on Davis' passion, exposing the basketball star to a new audience for the next stage of his business career.

Example 2

Conchita Martinez was one of the top women's tennis players for over a decade, yet her popularity was lagging way behind the likes of fellow players like Hingis, the Williams sisters, Anna Kournikova, Lindsay Davenport, and others. However, the WTA Tour found that Martinez was a wine connoisseur. Where did it lead? To a pitch with Wine Spectator Magazine, which led to a prominent feature by very well-respected writer Bruce Schoenfeld. The piece exposed a part of Martinez's personality that the mainstream media were not aware of, and led to much more positive coverage of her as her career ended.

Once the clip file grows, and it will as you refine the pitch with a good angle, the more doors will be opened for large pieces. Quantity can lead to quality.

Follow up and revisit

Persistence, after you have done all the other work, remains key. We have talked here about the need to develop contacts, and trust those contacts. How you can tailor your pitch to the right media and then develop the kit and the clip files.

No matter what you do, you always must remember that the media need to work on their timetable, which usually is not yours. The amount of information that is pitched to them is astronomical. How you make your pitch stand out and get noticed will be helped by the tips provided already.

The persistence in attempting to deliver the pitch is also important. Keep in mind you are not just pitching for one story, per se. You are pitching to develop a relationship that will transcend this story into others, and a relationship that will grow as you as a publicist and the members of the media change jobs and grow in their business.

We have now laid out the foundation for how to pitch. However, there still is a fundamental difference in what to pitch and how to gear it to the right place. Let's now look at some examples of pitching types, and some formulas for success.

The long-lead pitch

The long-lead pitch usually falls under two categories:

- monthly magazines
- news shows.

Each of these categories requires a great deal of forethought on the pitch as well as a strong knowledge of the staffers involved. The magazines are always the most time consuming of the pitches. They always will be visually compelling and the pitch has to be able to stand the test of time. For the most part, monthly magazines will look two to three months ahead at minimum to secure editorial, therefore a pitch for a project usually can start as early as a year in advance. A strong knowledge of the magazine's editorial cycle is very important to make it both fit into your pitch plan and to have it accepted by the publication.

Example

Having the knowledge that *GQ* does its sports issue every October, and usually secured its participants by the late spring, is very important to know. Knowing that *The Sporting News* does its annual "Good Guys in Sports" issue in the early spring and will take recommendations two to three months in advance is also helpful.

Most editorial calendars for publications are readily available online these days. Taking the time to keep them on hand and knowing deadlines is key to successful advance planning. If you can't find a calendar online, call and ask an editor.

The long-lead feature piece away from the special sections is always a difficult one to secure because the magazine has to be able to catch the subject in a light that is unique to the publication. Therefore, it is critical that you have the right amount of information and access to the subject that will make the pitch a unique one. It is also important that everyone know the value and the amount of time such pieces take. Saying to a subject that a magazine piece will take an hour and an hour for the photo shoot is never realistic. However, making sure that both sides are upfront with the process and that the amount of time spent is worthwhile is also very important. It is also very important with long leads to make sure that they are upfront about the amount of follow-up time needed. Especially in sports, situations change in an instant and follow-up of that nature can rarely be avoided. However, to get a two-hour sit-down with a head coach or a star player and then ask for an additional two-hour period a month later can be excessive unless it is planned upfront.

It is also important for you to always remember who you are working for with the long-lead option. As publicists, it is natural to aim high and get excited about the opportunity of a major feature. However that feature and that writer will come and go. You as the publicist will be there day to day with the subject, and will need that subject for other requests again and again. Asking the right questions are essential. They include:

Focus of the piece. Especially if the topic is one that has been covered ad nauseum, the writer may literally not know his or her exact angle when he/she shows up. Therefore, you may have the ability to steer the writer to an uncovered part of the story, or at least give him/her some guidance as to what would make this story "fresh."

Length of time needed. This is a place where sometimes you have to think of the glass being half empty and figure out what the guidelines will be before the interview takes place. Now there is no reason if things go well and *everyone* agrees to give the writer extra time. However, it is important to set minimum time standards at best. It will always go long.

Use of stock photos and video vs. photo shoot. Another important part of time management. Most long-lead features will look for original photography to go with the piece. In the digital era, there may be a photographer who has shot a good amount of footage with or about the subject that has been rarely used. It is important to offer that up as a source and go from there. The photo editor may find something he/she likes, and it will help you grow your photo contacts. For a good photo shoot, no matter what is said, you need to allow at least 90 minutes, outside of setup time for the photographer. Also for the set shots, ask about lights, power, makeup, outfits, etc. Many times the professional photographer may not have been in the area where he/she is doing a shoot or may not be used to working with athletes. The more you ask the easier things can go.

Use of background clips. The writer and the magazine staff will probably be well versed in research on the subject in most cases. However, you providing a clip pack of articles that will be most helpful will give you the opportunity to make sure your side is covered. There is always the chance the researcher or author may miss a key fact in print because he/she was not reading that article. Always best to have the clips on hand. Also, it is always important to have other media members available for the writer to talk with who have covered the subject and both you and the subject know well. The more advocates you have the easier it will go.

Inclusion of third parties in the story. Since these long-lead pieces are usually very intensive, it is important to establish a "good" and "bad" list of folks who can be included prior to the writer coming. Many times a subject may not want family members involved. However, as the publicist you have to think about what will best shape the story from your angle, and proactively produce a list of folks who will be able to work with the writer to help tell the story correctly. He or she will have his or her own list to be sure. However, by coming up with a few "extras" that he or she may not know about—childhood friends, colleagues, business partners—it will show how important the piece is to you and the subject and possibly even steer the writer away from controversial figures. Of course, you should also speak with these third parties well in advance of the writer contacting them.

The ability to fact check and get an advance copy prior to printing. Given the 24/7 news cycle, the use of excerpts on websites, and the immediacy not to get "beat" on a story, the ability to fact check has started to wane. It used to be that prior to publication the publicist would get a call from a fact checker at the publication going over details. Many times now this process has been omitted and it falls upon you as the publicist to find out how facts can be checked. The advance copy is also something that should be requested, as far in advance as possible. Now, chances are that you will *not* be able to change anything, but it is OK to ask the question. Getting an advance copy gives you a few things that will help:

- It gives you the chance to review the piece and make sure there are no surprises when it comes out.
- If there are positive elements to the piece that you can promote to other media, it will help the magazine and the author.
- If there are "beat" media that are annoyed that you gave a long lead all the extra access, it may give them a chance to get some added information for their daily notes.
- It gives you the opportunity to do damage control if it is a negative piece. Being proactive in this instance is what is best for you and the subject.
- It also gives you the opportunity to know what did not make it into the piece that you can pitch other places.

> **Tip**
>
> Sometimes the unused excerpts can be beneficial to growing a website content area for either your group or for the magazine. If the writer is also a freelancer, you may also want to discuss with him or her pitching the extra material to a local newspaper or magazine. If there is a photo shoot involved, the same options should come into play. The added content for extra publicity is a very valuable tool, and often goes unused.

All these are important in the long-lead decision process. It is also important that you do your own research on the writer. Chances are this person is coming in and may not know a great deal about your media process or policies and how you can best work together to achieve the goals that everyone has laid out. Therefore knowing about the writer, his or her style, and having some examples both to show the subject and for you to talk about in that down time with the writer, is essential. Many times, taking that extra step to familiarize yourself with the writer will go a long way in winning confidence, gaining a little more credibility with the writer, and hopefully getting as much of your "story" in as possible.

The other item with long leads is that you will rarely be able to tell your whole story. Most mass market long-lead publications and shows need to balance stories, and it is my experience that most times they will do that if given the proper access and treated fairly. Will you win every point? No. Will you usually get the opportunity to turn a total negative around? No. But most times if you are professional, ask the right questions, and find ways to not say "no" but to find alternatives, you will have a strong chance of getting balance.

News shows

Most of the points listed above will hold true for the video medium as well. The "news shows" here are not the "Entertainment Tonight" type shows which will usually have short segments and short lead times because of the immediacy of the subject. The magazine format shows—national ones like 20/20 or "60 Minutes" or "Real Sports," or even the more frequent local magazine shows, morning news shows or "Sports Wrap" shows—can take a longer lead to provide more color and in-depth coverage.

The big difference in the print and the video side is simple. Compelling video, not usually words, make the video piece work. The time commitment for the video piece is usually much less than in the print piece as well. There are also so many more print options for the long lead, that the chances of having a video segment pitch accepted for a national show is much lower than the print side.

The one help that comes in the video pitch are the partnerships that your entity may have with national, regional, or local carriers. Chances are you may find a friendly rights holder who will be more apt to listen to the pitch, because it will help them as a partner to have added content on their air. However, the risk of a "neutral" piece making it to air is even higher than the print piece. The limitations of time, and the ability to edit the segment down and still keep it compelling, becomes probably the biggest issue with the video piece.

On the local side, the ability to bring the subject "in studio" as an enhancement to get the piece done is also an added plus. Many times limitations on crew and talent availability will hinder the ability to fully tell the story. However, being able to bring a subject in studio to save time and tell the story may be able to both complete a successful pitch and give the subject the ability to more clearly tell his or her story.

Also on video. Those who have rightholders for an event will also fall into the long-lead video pitch concept. The captive audience who is looking for extra content about their stars or their product is a natural pitch for when your product airs on your rightsholder. Many times this idea of pitching someone in the "family" is taken for granted.

The quick pitch

Many times the "quick pitch" idea comes out of the necessity of the moment—a moment of success or humanity that there is a short window to capitalize on for the subject with the media. Also many times the quick pitch results from an event that you as a publicist recognize as being interesting to the media and it opens the door for a story that you have been looking to tell for a while.

One of the biggest elements in the "quick pitch" is to again be prepared. Knowing your subject and all its positive qualities is the most important element of the quick pitch. In order to make it successful, you must be ready with the facts and figures, have a solid relationship with your subject, and have cultivated the appropriate media to make it impactful.

The best sources for the quick pitch are usually columnists or TV reporters looking for a story, and the opportunities will usually occur on an event day. Many times the "beat" press will not have the space or time to change subjects and give the larger coverage that a quick pitch will need. Therefore having information on hand will make it impactful.

SMTs, RMTs, Skype, and conference calls

Another quick pitch tool that can be used is the satellite media tour or the conference call. Following a successful event and to reach a large number of media, the publicist arranges, usually with the aide of a company that can handle many outlets, a 30 to 90 minute "tour," either by radio or TV or both, with each station getting five minutes of "personal" time. The subject is in one location, and has the schedule and message points with them, and will answer the questions asked by a reporter or producer in each market. It is a very effective way to get mass publicity in a short time, and satisfy many requests. In the case of video, an effective backdrop will also enhance the experience for a sponsor or an organization. Many times the SMT is also recorded for a news broadcast, so the time to make sure that a website, or certain stats, or a call-in number are included also exists. With the SMT, it is also important to remember that each network has a "news service" that should also be included (ESPN News, ABC Newsone, CONUS are some of the services). These will record a section of the tour and then rebroadcast it to affiliates that may not have been able to join in on the "tour" for time or space reasons.

Today it is also much more feasible to do pieces via Skype, giving the quality feel of video and the intimacy of the personal computer. Several companies, including the Cinesport brand as well as outlets like SB Nation and others, will have dedicated features done via Skype that can service hundreds of affiliates across the continent and, in many cases, around the world.

Tip

Always have large cards within sight distance for the subject with the station numbers and location, and another one with other info like a call-in number or a website address. The tedium of repeating certain answers or the excitement of the event can cause the subject to sometimes forget who they are speaking to or what they had or had not answered.

The other way is to do the media conference call. This is usually the case when media are scattered for an announcement and there is a need for the subject to take on a wide variety of questions. The best conference calls are done on broadcast quality lines (easily arranged by a provider) with muted sound. That means the only voices heard are the question and answer. The publicist is able to prioritize the calls as well to get maximum exposure. Many times the audio can also be used either in transcript form or as an audio file to further maximize exposure.

Here is an example of a successful "quick pitch":

Example

In the tennis world, a "media day" to get advance publicity for an upcoming tournament is becoming very common. The tournament brings a "name" player who will be participating into the local market for some media and sponsor events to help promote ticket sales. Usually the day is very much focused on getting the exposure with fans and media who will attend the event. One of the pioneers is doing a media day like this is the Pilot Pen, in New Haven, Connecticut. Every year the tournament would negotiate to bring a female player in the Tuesday or Wednesday following The Championships, Wimbledon to do local media. The Pilot Pen was late in the summer, and the flow of the tennis calendar usually produced an off week after Wimbledon while the players come back to the United States. It was a very successful strategy. One year the tournament director, Anne Worcester, worked with their PR reps, Alan Taylor Communications, to secure a rising American, Lindsay Davenport, for their media day. They confirmed the date in the spring with the hope that young Lindsay would have a strong showing along the way and garner some nice press. Turns out, the young American did so well she won Wimbledon, and Pilot Pen now had a major media opportunity less that 48 hours away. It was now a good problem to have. Their was a national media platform to promote, but there still had to be an effort to make sure the sponsor and the New Haven event got their local publicity too. The PR reps were able to use their contacts to secure a solid national media schedule, including the Today Show and David Letterman, as well as bringing Lindsay to New Haven to meet the local media. How did they do it? They were able to use their media cultivation skills to make sure that both Lindsay and the national media worked Pilot Pen into the questioning while satisfying all the national questions at the same time. They were also able to use local contacts to secure solid stringers in New Haven to service both the local and national print press, and use a satellite hookup to get some other media placements with a Pilot Pen backdrop. It was a quick pitch with some big hits.

The notes pitch

One of the more effective places these days to find room for inclusion in publications is the notes pitch. The immediacy of news and the chance to deliver some facts in a short, concise format has made this one of the more viable ways to deliver some key facts to a large audience. The notes pitch will often be a paragraph or less, usually with a lead to a tie-in phone number or websites for the public to access more information.

The one danger in a notes pitch is that this area is traditionally the first place editors will go when space is a problem. If the note can be more timeless, it is OK to submit the facts multiple times. Many times notes will make an online or early print edition, so it is important to find out each and every place the note did possibly "make it in."

Another growing medium for the notes pitch are websites and blogs, which are always looking for short, "noteworthy" content. Many daily papers which now have blogs by their reporters are always great targets for the notes pitch.

The notes pitch takes several forms:

Advancing an upcoming event. This is more along the long-lead idea, but it gives you the opportunity to alert the public to an upcoming event to watch or attend. The event notes pitch also works on the product side, alerting the public to a potential product release. The places to pitch such items include weekly newspapers, lifestyle publications, blogs, and daily papers. Rarely are there video opportunities available for the notes pitch, unless it is tied to an already existing story.

The follow-up announcement. This "after the event" announcement usually provides detailed information following an event or product launch. Items in the follow-up pitch will sometimes include items like website hits, TV ratings, amount of money raised at a charity event, event attendance, and product sales numbers. The follow-up can also be a retort or rebuttal by a subject to a story that ran previously. Pitching the follow-up usually will be in a "notes" or agate section in print publications, done by desk reporters or beat writers who cover the subject more frequently.

An effective notes pitch requires the publicist to have a good relationship with both the beat writer (if possible) and the desk where news comes in via email or phone.

Tip

Creating a series of notes in the form of a release, each bulleted, may also increase your chance of getting one or more points in a publication or on a site. The proximity to the date of an event is also a big help, as the closer the number can be released to the event (before or after) the better chance it stays top of mind. Also, releasing notes early in the day may be key to making an early edition, when space is sometimes more plentiful.

The special event pitch

This is where the promotional aspect of your "angle" will come into the most focus. It is working with the media or with the subject to create the time-less "special" event that media will look to cover and the public will always remember. This pitch will have you take in all that I have talked about to this point and will take the creativity to set your work apart from all others. Many times the "special event" pitch is the one angle that sets a basic story apart from all other at the time or in the category. It has to be visually compelling, tell a unique story, and strike a unique chord that the media will cover not just the subject, but the campaign as well.

Here are some good examples of the special event pitch

Where is Bernie? The Milwaukee Brewers held a state-wide scavenger hunt titled with Brewers fans searching for 1,400 Bernie Brewer yard ornaments (Bernie is the cheerful lederhosen-clad mascot who has been with the club since their return to Milwaukee) hidden throughout Milwaukee County parks and other parks across the state in Madison, Appleton, Kenosha, and Green Bay. Four hundred of the lawn ornaments had special prizes attached to them, including Brewers game tickets, and additional prizes including gift certificates for a night in a Miller Park suite, game-used memorabilia, Milwaukee County parks passes for golf, water parks, and the Mitchell Park Domes. In addition to the prizes, 100 of the lawn ornaments were also autographed by Brewers players and personnel. The team used all their social media platforms for hints and meetups for the little statues, which made for a fun and well-covered promotion for collectors, casual and ardent fans, and of course kids just getting ready to get out of school and hopefully follow the Brew Crew just a bit more. It is a great, low-cost, wide-ranging grassroots activation which can have a bigger upside in the future, tied to more media participation and maybe even a dash of local celebrity.

Quaker Oats cooks with the fire. The venerable Quaker Oats brand, a Division of PepsiCo, is never going to set the world on fire with cutting edge technology or over the top sponsorship explosions. They are who they are—a trusted, solid, essential, dedicated brand. However, as good brands do, they can be innovative in presentation. So how did Quaker Oats and the Chicago Fire of MLS team up to announce their partnership? The old fashioned way … with an innovative call to action *mailed* to media. The Fire sent out Quaker Oats custom designed oversized boxes packed with goodies, a release, and a customized Fire jersey (with the Quaker Oats brand across the front) to several hundred sports, soccer-specific, and trade media announcing their deal as official Breakfast Foods & Nutritious Snacks Partner of the Chicago Fire. The package was neat, effective, and easy to understand at a time when promotions are all about digital complexity. It had tremendous shelf life and showed that the Fire and Quaker Oats took the time to understand and think about each member. Big headlines for the announcement? No. Great brand statement that will foster future coverage? Absolutely. Money well spent by a team looking to cut through the clutter.

Put Thrash in jail. Although it did not keep the team in Atlanta, the NHL Thrashers (now the Winnipeg Jets) came up with a great promotion that went viral in 2010. Using their mascot "Thrash" as a foil, the team concocted a story about how Thrash stole the team's Zamboni and started to wreak havoc throughout greater Atlanta. As a result Thrash was arrested and put in jail, and supporters had to raise funds to get him out and back into the arena, where he was almost as popular with the fans as the team. The "bail" was a sale of 5,000 tickets for an upcoming game against their former star Ilya Kovalchuk and the New Jersey Devils. The fans loved the idea, rallied, bought the tickets (giving the team their biggest gate of the season), got Thrash back into the fold and created a ton of goodwill for the organization.

Dan vs. Dave. Perhaps one of the biggest special event pushes in sports history took place in the summers of 1990 and 1991 leading up to the 1992 Barcelona Olympics. Reebok, working with its PR agency Cohn and Wolfe, decided to identify to Americans who would be Olympic decathlon hopefuls and compete for the title of "World's Greatest Athlete" in 1992. The decathlon had become one of the Olympics' premier events, with folks like American Bruce Jenner and Britain's Daley Thompson capturing the public's imagination with their Gold Medals at previous Olympiads. The strategy was simple. Build tremendous public awareness in a two-year period leading up to the Olympics around Americans Dan O'Brien and Dave Smith as they competed against each other for spots on the US Olympic team and then as they went against each other for the gold. Both were good looking, telegenic and highly marketable and it would be a signature publicity campaign, supported with thousands of dollars in marketing and public relations efforts. The program called for year-round placement (even at the Big East basketball tournament in New York in March of 1990, where staffers snuck in and handed out Dan and Dave tee shirts to courtside fans). One athlete was designated as a "red" athlete and the other a "blue," to further accentuate the campaign efforts. National television was booked for both around the Olympic trials, with the assumption that whomever came out first would be a great story, and the challenger would continue along as well. There was one problem.

Dan O'Brien was disqualified during the Olympic trials because he "no heighted" in the high jump. That meant he could not gain enough points to even make the Olympic team. The entire campaign appeared to be lost.

However, the public group was able to reorganize and take advantage of the situation regardless of the on-field disaster. O'Brien, who was good natured about the campaign all along, continued to make appearances for Reebok (including a memorable one the night of his disqualification on the Aresenio Hall Show where he made a lighthearted joke of the issue). Smith did go on to make the Olympic team but the multi-year equity was not what had been hoped. The campaign then changed to show that anything could happen, and Reebok's investment in the brand, although not getting the initial end result, still reverberated with great name recognition to this day. Indeed, had O'Brien won the gold medal, the campaign may not have gotten as much recognition as it received with the critical blow.

USA Baseball cleans house. Sometimes a little clutter is the spark for innovation, and the folks at USA Baseball, the national governing body for the national pastime, came up with new incentive for those late on their spring cleaning. USAB remains an undervalued resource for many in the lexicon of baseball, many times placed between the quaintness of Little League and the success of the professional side. However nary a pro has made it to The Bigs without benefiting from the training or exposure that USA Baseball brings through its development programs, international and national tournaments. The growth of baseball as a global game would not be where it is, where it not for the work of USA Baseball working with its compatriots in other national federations or with MLB to help grow the game.

So it came as no surprise with all that work that a great number of valuable and unique mementos gather at the USAB headquarters in North Carolina from time to time. It should also come as no surprise, since USAB is all about young developing males who have taken to the digital world, that the governing body should look to the digital space to grow its footprint and exposure. So into the mix came a solid idea, hold a summer long series of promotions designed to get some unused "memorabilia" into the hands of fans, with the social media space as the catalyst. The result was a summer long promotion, "9 innings," which had fans join USAB's social media platforms in order to be involved in a giveaway for some fun items, ranging from signed Bryce Harper to Clayton Kershaw items. Each "inning" runs for ten business days, with an item going each day to a deserving fan. The result? Some good buzz and increased awareness for USA Baseball among casual fans, a jump of over 50 percent for the Federation's Twitter followers, and most importantly for those minding the storage space, closets which will now be a little more empty for the next round of items to come in from various elite events.

In a day and age where all entities are looking to grow following and move some distressed merchandise after a long season or series of years, USA Baseball came up with a fun and innovative one that helps everyone, especially those who love the game. A homer of a promotion with no downside and little effort, just ingenuity.

This promotion stinks. One promotion that I created in my college days involved a very talented wide receiver on a very bad football team. His name was Tom Garlick, and he went on to have a small career with the Philadelphia Eagles, but while he was at Fordham University he had a tremendous career that certainly garnered 1-AA All-America consideration despite the team's poor record and the fact that we were in a major market, with little media interest in college football. We devised a very simple way to cut through the clutter. We literally created a weekly flyer mailed to a few hundred media over a three-week period. It was entitled, "this Garlic stinks," and had pieces of chopped garlic taped to the flyer, followed by "this Garlick doesn't" which had Tom stats and his picture below. The piece cost less than 20 cents to make, but received national play and may have helped Tom make the honorable mention all-America.

"Is there a doctor in the house?" For a farewell salute to Julius Erving at their home game against Philadelphia on April 6, 1987, the New York Knicks chose the theme "Is There a Doctor in the House?" The game was the final farewell salute to Hall of Famer Julius Erving, and the Knicks needed to make this salute different and media-worthy apart from all the other gifts and testimonials Erving received in his final trip around the NBA. The Knicks decided to invite famous "doctors" to fete Erving, including Ruth Westheimer, Richard Chamberlain (Dr. Kildare), Vince Edwards (Dr. Ben Casey), Joyce Brothers, Dr. Seuss, Frank Field, Johnny Berardino (Dr. Steven Hardy of "General Hospital"), Bill Cosby (Dr. Clifford Huxtable), Dwight Gooden, Henry Kissinger, DeForest Kelley (Dr. McCoy of "Star Trek"), Ferdie Pacheco, Robert Young (Dr. Marcus Welby), and Bernard Meltzer. The event was a huge success, got national attention and set the bar higher for other promotional events in the future.

Best practices: Keeping sponsors coming back

Authors and researchers: Dr. Peter Titlebaum, Associate Professor at the University of Dayton and Research Director for ALSD, Todd C. Koesters, MSA, JD, Assistant Professor, University of South Carolina

---

Sport teams are more concerned than ever before about keeping sponsors coming back. A recent survey was completed by 38 sports teams from NBA, NFL, NHL, MLB, and MLS. The Top 10 responses provide direction on the best practices from the perspective of sport teams. While the industry is still dealing with economic change, it is a positive to see the ways teams are looking to keep sponsors happy. What they shared was a variety of tools they use to make effective renewal strategies part of their everyday business plan.

1   *Relationships should be based on knowing their business.* It's easy to fall into the trap that sport is the most important thing to them and they need us. Most of us hear or read about sports every day. However, successful partnerships are never one sided, and both parties need to feel valued. Knowing and understanding your client's business is vital to the value proposition for them. After all, a relationship is a two-way street with both parties delivering value.

2   *Maintaining objectives of the company.* While knowing your client's business is critical to developing the relationship, knowing their long-term goals and short-term objectives is crucial to delivering solutions. You must know why someone invested in sport in the first place. Additionally, do not assume that just because they made the purchase, they have a plan to implement strategies to meet their objectives.

3   *Results, top service, and experiences.* While a team will lose games, this should have little to no impact on the experience, as rarely does the marketing department impact on the field success. However, the marketing department can determine whether or not the event is a win or a loss for your clients. Premium pricing needs to deliver premium service. Little things like the quality of the food and service speaks volumes, and if you do the little things, they will feel like they and their clients have won, regardless of the scoreboard.

4   *Monitoring all aspects of the deal.* Life is in the details, and so is the contact. It might be easy to think that it's a three-year contract, so the team has plenty of time. Don't do it. Long-term deals are no longer the norm. All you have is your word, and they are expecting the team to fulfill its promise. It is not the sole the responsibility of the client to ensure they are utilizing contracted assets to the fullest extent. Properties need to monitor the contract throughout the relationship and assist clients in maximizing utilization of the assets.

5   *Over-deliver on the client's expectations.* While life is in the details of the contract, meeting contract expectations is sometimes not enough. As clients evaluate programs, they ask not just what is working, but what is delivering more than expected. Properties need to understand that just meeting contract expectations is not enough. They must over-deliver on the client's expectations. For example, the contract may stipulate that the client is to receive four escorted field passes during pre-game activities. Delivery and execution of the passes is what is expected. Having an assistant coach, player, retired player, or cheerleader say hello, sign autographs, and/or take a picture makes the experience much more valuable. The cost to the team is nominal while the value to the client is immeasurable.

6   *No surprises.* Sometimes things go wrong. It's how you handle these situations that can reveal whether or not a company will keep doing business with your organization. Be upfront and tell them what happened and what action is being done to rectify the issue as well as what you are doing to ensure it does not happen again.

7   *Referring business.* While sport teams have the power of a brand, it is easy to forget that teams are in the position to help their clients. Many teams have started B2B events and think that is as far as they need to go, but this may not be the case. Teams might have to play matchmaker and make the introduction.

8   *Create value by building and leveraging experiences.* Do not discount the value of everything you know as a professional. That experience needs to be shared with your clients who don't necessarily know how to maximize this investment, but if you assist them, then you and the property are more valuable.

9   *Premiums for early renewal.* Who does not like getting a gift? However, premiums are part of business today, and they take many different forms. They can be as simple as a discount, a creative payment plan, or a one-of-a-kind gift that is personalized for the recipient.

10 *Timely and on-going recaps.* Annual recaps have become the norm in sport today. However, the timing of recaps can be the difference between a renewal and a non-renewal. Recaps should be thought of as on-going progress reports and not just annual reviews. The team that continually reports progress is more likely to identify issues before it is too late. Additionally, keep in mind that the recap should be specific to the client's needs and objectives.

In summary, while these tools can be effective for making renewals possible, it is important to understand that it is a process. Renewals take effort and don't just happen. Also, you can follow all these techniques and still not renew the business. However, you will be farther ahead if you do.

Conclusion

In closing, this chapter will help you define what the goal of publicity is all about: getting ink in a professional and thoughtful way for your subject. It is important to use the creative skills you have to sell both the sizzle and the steak and make your pitches stand out as best you can. Most importantly, use the personal touch to develop those relationships that will help you throughout your career in every aspect of sports publicity.

5

WORKING IN THE COLLEGES

SID is not just the name of the accounting teacher

This chapter will discuss the nuances of working in the college sports information field as well as in a growing area of high school communications, and how it differs from other areas of the business. The college area in North America is one of the greatest for gaining both entry and experience in the field of sports publicity. It may be the most undervalued and most valuable position in the industry, because it seeds so many of the efforts of career professionals. This chapter will look at how the position has evolved greatly over the years, especially recently, and how the collegiate level of sports publicity can blend the academic background with the athletic exposure to form the base of the industry.

Unfortunately, the athletic communications position or positions at many schools has been viewed as a lower level, entry-level high-turnover position that is secondary to the development of the university. There are several reasons for this. One reason, ironically, is dedication. The people who get involved with collegiate athletics on the publicity side tend to start because of *just* their love for sports. They start as interns and work their way up into a full-time job. The thought of working on a collegiate campus is also very alluring. The changing of the seasons and the vitality and lifeblood of staying young stirs the interest in staying on the college campus forever.

Another item that attracts people to Sports Information Director (SID) work is the seasonal nature of sports, which remains constant at the collegiate level. One goes from football or soccer to basketball to baseball or softball without end. Spring football and recruiting periods are there, then the summer comes and although there is some downtime, it is time to prepare for the fall again. There is little time to look outside or appreciate the skills that one has to grow into other fields unless one plots a proper career path. It can be a very rewarding life in many ways, but can also lead one to get caught up in the same cycle with little room for growth.

There is also the personal growth to consider away from the professional side. The SID job in many ways is a young person's business. A great starting point, but a business where the best work is done by the young. Why? It is 24/7 work, and the ability to have the key components outside of work (family, children, financial security) are somewhat limited. The dedication that one needs to grow in the profession requires great commitment, and the ability to find a spouse willing to put up with that commitment and live the American Dream is somewhat limited. Is it a great starting point? Yes. Are there folks that are able to thrive in the position for a lifetime? Yes. However the combination of those two, unless there is growth into other areas of athletic administration, is limited.

There is, however, opportunity to grow on the collegiate level. Many schools offer the opportunity for employees to take classes, teach, or obtain a graduate degree. For those who show a penchant for athletic administration there is a chance to grow into collegiate sports marketing, work with a league, or develop other skills on the business side. But again one must have plans to enter into those fields. If someone doesn't take the time to think about the future it will be very easy to get caught in a very vicious cycle.

In recent years, as part of effort to earn more respect/appreciation, CoSIDA's (College Sports Information Directors of America) leadership has been pushing the athletics community to view this post as a "communications-based role" instead of an "information providing role." The thinking is that doing so will help others to see this role in a more global context.

The fact that these key roles reside at institutes of high learning should put these communications roles in positions of leadership or strength in the business of strategic communications in sport. There has never been a greater need for effectively managing the brand of a university, nor has there ever been a time where the visibility of athletic programs has been higher. So evolving the roles from "Information Director" to "Communicator" for these multimillion-dollar establishments is very, very important.

The evolution of social and digital media, especially amongst a younger demographic accustomed to 24/7 communication with various forms of media, puts the "SID" in a very valuable position for any university. He or she deals with the most visible people many times on a campus—college student athletes, marketers, coaches, and administrators as well as the media who cover sports—on a daily basis. So taking this evolving role of collegiate athletic communicators more seriously and in a much more valuable position going forward is extremely essential to the face of a university.

Every misstep by a coach, a poor text by an athlete, a slip by a booster, now has a very public place to reside in the digital space. So making sure that the school's daily public communicator and his or her staff are included, informed, and properly utilized can save a school literally millions in reactive crisis management and thousands of man hours in distractions when a problem does arise.

In that vein there is one thing to always consider when involved in college athletics. For those days when you are not sure what skills you have or what you can do with them. This was said to me by Harold Katz, who was then the owner of the Philadelphia 76ers. He was considering me for a job as Director of Public Relations, while I was still employed as Director of Media Relations at Fordham University. He had a simple thought which rang very true.

> If you can do publicity for all those athletes in 21 sports year round, you should be able to handle one sport with 12 players, shouldn't you?

Two weeks later I got the job.

So once again, why is the Sports Information Director sometimes the low person on the job totem pole? He or she is very loyal and very dedicated and is almost always a team player. In the collegiate setting there is always something to do, a sport or athlete to assist, a media guide or program to be worked on, a website to be updated, a blog post to be revised. However, many of these items cannot be quantified. It is the catch-22 situation that exists in publicity. There was a great phrase from the industrialist John Wanamaker when talking about advertising. He said, "I know that half of my advertising works, trouble is I never know which half."

That phrase also applies to publicity. On the college level these elements of the job are essential. However, since the SID usually did not have the ability to connect with how these elements can be monetized (because of lack of information or lack of time to grow outside the walls of a university as a professional), the traits can be taken for granted.

Learning how to do these things is essential for growth. Monetizing and networking will show you your worth in the "real" world, and can probably help you grow as a professional. You are a very valuable player.

Now let's take a look at what the typical SID does, whether he or she is at the University of Michigan or Ramapo College.

Primary responsibilities:

- publicity/promotions
- statistics compilation
- event management
- publications/new media
- sales and marketing assistance.

In many ways, the college sports information office may be the first touch point that members of the media have with that institution on a professional level. The SID is the central point for many folks in the university athletic department as well. He or she and the staff are, in many cases, closer to the athletes and the coaches than others in the university structure because of the day-to-day contact. Therefore, the value that the person has to be aware of rising issues or positive stories in the university system can often rest in the sports information office. Often times, the SID contact is the *only* person familiar with an athlete or a coach and how he or she is doing, and that sensitivity is invaluable to the growth of the university and its components.

The SID also has to serve many masters, many with the ability sometimes of monetizing how or what he or she does on a daily basis. Coaches point to won/loss records, athletic directors point to enrollment and graduation rates, marketing groups point to increased sponsor dollars, alumni directors point to increased funding. All of these work hand-in-hand with the SID to achieve their goals. The SID does have the ability to do the same.

First of all, when people talk about all the "free" publicity you get for the university, there is a cost associated with it. Good publicity, in terms of the man-hours put in and the investment in things like technology, even mailing and printing costs, does have a dollar amount associated with it. However, the *amount* of money generated by a good publicist will usually far outweigh the investment the university puts into the office. It is certainly cheaper than the advertising dollar invested to grow the university.

Example 1

"The Flutie Factor." It is commonly believed that Doug Flutie's November 23, 1984 touchdown pass to Gerald Phelan against Miami capping an thrilling 47–45 victory as time expired was responsible for boosting applications to Boston College in subsequent years. However, the greatest gain that Boston College received from that memorable moment was in the media perception that Boston College had arrived, and all the factors that the Boston College Sports Information office had to take into effect that year and in subsequent years to create and manage the publicity from that day.

In actuality, and perhaps this is also part of a good PR machine, especially at the collegiate level, enrollment only went up 16% in 1984 and 12% the next year (Cafehayek.com, May 2006). Where the university made its biggest gain was in publicity and exposure to the school by media who may not have normally wrote about the school or its athletes in years following that great day. The active pursuit of publicity kept the Boston College name alive, and has been a major contributor to the school enjoying increased revenue through their place now in the Atlantic Coast Conference.

Example 2

"The Patriots Pride." A second and more recent example of the value of publicity is George Mason University's run to the NCAA men's Final Four in 2006. The natural run of an underdog team with such exposure brings its own momentary exposure. Providing the story lines, the access and managing the media to fully capitalize on an event such as this for the university falls to the SID staff. The positive light painted by the coaching staff and players through the media was shaped by the SID staff, who as professionals were able to deal with the onslaught and maximize it for the best of the university as a whole.

Publicity

As discussed in previous chapters and throughout the book, pitching, acquiring, and merchandising publicity should be the biggest focus of the Sports Information Office. We are not "publicity coaches" on game days. We are professionals whose job it is to get maximum exposure and find stories that the general public and the university would like to hear about. On the collegiate level there are literally thousands of untold stories each year. Many of them go untold because we sometimes get caught up in the day-to-day duties and never have the time to look for the good story that is somewhat below the surface, or are aware of the forum in which to adequately tell the story.

The key to good publicity at the collegiate level is *communication*. We have said before that the SID office is the rallying point for so many aspects of the athletic department. Long hours and long road trips can lead to the unique camaraderie which will lead to unique opportunities coming to light. How those stories are portrayed is another thing. How you learn what is a promotable story and what is exploitive or uncomfortable only comes with experience. Hear are some simple tips to begin establishing the good story lines.

Questionnaires

They are simple—some will say old-school—but they provide the greatest amount of information in a simple forum for all your athletes, coaches, and business partners. They will answer the five Ws, but they will also give you insight into hobbies, movies, family background, etc. that you cannot get from anywhere else. American Express recently started their "My Card" project that is very popular. What is it? A simple questionnaire.

The other opportunity that these questionnaires give you is the chance to pool resources. Once you read them you may find out that you have a dozen athletes that love chocolate ice cream, or five athletes that crochet, or three athletes who are sets of twins, or you may have a marathon runner whose cousin is a pitcher for the Kansas City Royals. You would never know any of this unless you took the time to ask, communicated the information, and looked for the connection.

Example

The University of Nebraska is one of the most storied intercollegiate football schools in the United States. The level of success the school has enjoyed, especially in the 1970s under coach Tom Osborne, is legendary. Along with that success came some of the greatest student athletes and their own stories. It was the job of the sports information department to weed through those stories with a questionnaire, and see what stories could be promotable. In the late 1970s legendary Nebraska SID Don "Fox" Bryant noticed a young man named Isiah Hipp had listed his full name on his bio as "Isiah Moses Hipp." Fox noticed the unusual initials, went to the young man, and asked if he was OK with being referred to by his initials. It didn't hurt that young Hipp began his college career with several 100 yard rushing games. The name, as much as the on-field effort, caught the attention of *Sports Illustrated*, and the legend of all-America running back I.M. Hipp was born.

Managers, operations staff, and administrators

Once again, one of your most valuable assets sits right where you are if you take the time to ask. People who have the touch points with athletes—their coaches, the equipment room manager, the trainers—all know the fabric of athletes lives sometimes more than the athletes themselves sometimes. They are constantly engaged in casual conversation, and if they know what you are looking for in advance and can be advocates of the publicity process for you, the stories you never hear about will appear. Also, keep those staff members on your publicity list. They too can have some great untold stories on an event, an anniversary, or an athlete from past or present glory that is worth telling.

Know the media, and all the forms of it

We keep harping on about this point, but networking with media and getting to know them, whether in Los Angeles or Kalamazoo, is critical for when the moment strikes. Your questionnaire will have the local media contacts for athletes and staff which you will deal with constantly. However, it is up to you to create the casual relationships with the sports editors, the blog writers, the collegiate media, the online columnist, the alumnus in the media, so when the opportunity arises you are ready and are well connected. Is it easy to have the sports editor or columnist take a pitch and make it yours as the one he uses for that week? No. But do you stand a better chance because you have sent that outlet an item or two and complimented them on some other work that they have done prior to that pitch? You betcha. Invest the time to compile your own hit list in the summer, refine and update it yearly, and make sure you drop those notes and emails. The fact that the media members know you are watching them and reading them will make your job much easier when the story arises.

Create the unique opportunity

The Yiddish word is chach·ka or tchotch·ke (pronounced CHOCH KEE), and means "a cheap showy trinket." But that little trinket will go a long way in setting your collegiate pitch above the masses. Below are some unique pitches in the past that had great success in garnering some great publicity in non-traditional ways. Your pitch and your items must be able to stand out above the masses. They do not have to be big budget items; they simply have to be unique, and many times functional.

Example 1

Fordham University in the late 1980s had a struggling Division 1-AA football program, but had some great individual stories and great individual talent, one of which was a linebacker named Mark "Blaze" Blazejewski (pronounced Blah-ju-as-ki). On a limited budget, the university looked to create an item that would stand out and promote "Blaze" and his unique football talents. The result was an item that cost less than 50 cents to make—a matchbook. The University SID office had a thousand books printed that said "The fiercest BLAZE in America" on the front, and then "Fordham linebacker Mark 'Blaze' Blazejewski" on the back cover with all his stats. The result was national exposure in places ranging from ESPN to *USA Today*, all about the matchbook promotion, which in turn gained more exposure for his football skills and led to several 1–AA All-America votes.

Example 2

The Iona College Gaels had a long-standing tradition of regional collegiate basketball excellence in the 1970s and early 1980s, led by great coaches such as Jim Valvano and Pat Kennedy. However, the school had trouble establishing many of its blue-collar, hard-working players in the media limelight with a tough New York sports market. The result was to create an item they knew all media members needed to promote the All-America candidacy of guard Steve Burtt: a simple notepad with Burtt's image on the front and his statistics on the back. They were distributed to thousands of media members, and it soon became a tradition amongst the media to see how many "Stevie Burtt" notepads would show up at a press conference. The simple, useful gift was a tasteful and functional hit, and set Iona above all the other promotional campaigns out there for the year.

Keep it professional—remember the people and the university you represent

Sometimes in our thirst for publicity we can push too hard. However, always keep the lines of decorum firmly focused and make sure that you have buy in from above on your pitch. Remember *communication*.

Sell it internally before you sell it externally

Make sure that all who are involved, especially in a university setting, are on board with your pitch and are comfortable with at least the concept. Most importantly, make sure the principal person involved in the pitch understands your role, what you are looking for the idea to accomplish, and how you have their best interests and the interests of the university in mind.

Merchandise, merchandise

One of the biggest problems in SID work is that parts of academia have a bias against the big budget world of athletics. By once again *communicating* across the university and showing the results your office has produced, things will be much more accepted.

Tip

Do weekly or monthly clips to all department heads, either via email or hard copies. Make sure each department head gets copies of your team media guides as well. Inclusion is a key part of ensuring success and recognition.

In addition, make sure that the folks around the subject of a successful pitch—parents, high school coaches, team members, etc.—see your work. It will inspire more of a team approach to SID work, and will make the tougher pitches easier to sell the next time.

Some of the great collegiate publicity efforts to think about

Slippery Rock football in Ann Arbor

The uniqueness of Slippery Rock University's name has made it a college announcer's favorite for years. Dubbed "the Snoopy of college football," the university, according to its website, has the largest honorary alumni body of any school in the country, with the possible exception of Notre Dame. Sidewalk alumni fan clubs, official and semi-official, have been documented across the nation. There are fans who will call from all corners of the country to hear a final score, who will pull off the highway and spend $100 or more at the school's bookstore, who will stand and cheer when the public address announcer heralds another Slippery Rock *victory*.

That cult status came to a peak in 1979 and again in 1981, when the university played games at Michigan Stadium in Ann Arbor. Slippery Rock University drew more than 60,000 fans—to this day, the largest crowd to see an NCAA Division II football game—for their 1979 game against Pennsylvania State Athletic Conference Western Division rival Shippensburg and attracted more than 30,000 fans for its 1981 season-opening game against Wayne State (Michigan). The foundation for the trips to Ann Arbor were laid many years prior when Steve Filipiak, public address announcer at Michigan Stadium from 1959–1971, was one of the first people to report scores to big-time college football crowds. From those roots grew a trend. The media efforts to promote the idea both locally and nationally came from the SID office, and the exposure generated, and the managing of that demand, also fell to the SID staff.

Throwin' it back

One of those throwback campaigns was launched by Northwestern University in its desire to get proper attention on its stud quarterback Dan Persa and what could have been a Heisman-like season for their signal caller. Now the Wildcats have had their great years, and even some good ones since the days in the 1970s when they were a Homecoming trophy for everyone in the Big Ten. They reside in the number two media market in the country, and have a list of outstanding alumni in sports and entertainment media as good as anyone. However all that, and the fact that they are the smallest school in the Big Ten, does not make them media darlings. They don't have the blue field of Boise State, or the blue and maize of Michigan, but they do have a strong entrepreneurial following. So in the quest to break through the clutter, the Wildcats, led by marketing chief Mark Polisky and with at least some of the blessings of the coaching staff and Persa himself, got out of the gate first and fast with their push in 2011. The early campaign included billboards not just in Chicago but near ESPN's headquarters in Bristol, Connecticut, as well as a nice gift mailing to over 80 key writers of a Persa kit, replete with two seven-pound dumbells as a reminder of his number and stature. They also branded Persa "Chicago's Heisman candidate," another smart move to have a city rally around a student athlete at a school the city may not always fully embrace as their own.

Now, while some may say that a cool digital campaign is all that's needed, and gimmicks don't affect writers these days, they may be wrong. Saturday's *New York Post* had columnist Lenn Robbins devote a whole column to Persa and the campaign, along with a pledge from Robbins to carry the dumbell around with him every weekend this fall, and tweet about Persa regardless of what game he is covering. Others may say that the campaign is added pressure on an athlete who needs the support of everyone and doesn't need a bullseye or bulletin board fodder placed on him by opponents. However, these are the days of little secrets and lots of trash talk, so the campaign won't place any more pressure on Persa than his team will themselves. What if he fails or comes up injured? Not relevant to the branding campaign Northwestern has done. What was relevant was that the Wildcats have shown an interest in being different and one that supports a potential bigger than life star. They created a differentiator; one in a world of "what's next" should hopefully have other schools thinking about what fun promotions they can do to get recognition—not just for the Heisman but for athletes of all levels.

St. Joe's adopts Auburn football

The St. Joseph's University (Pennsylvania) Hawks have always been known for their tradition of basketball. "The Hawk Will Never Die" is the motto, and their mascot never stops flapping its wings during men's and women's basketball games. However in 1987, the school, which never had a football program, decided to adopt a school that did have one. Paul Laughlan, sports editor of the student newspaper, *The Hawk*, began a campaign supported by the SID office to adopt a Division I football program of their own. The voting was held amongst students, and Auburn had the majority of votes. The SID office then worked with the Auburn SID office to have St. Joe's student media become a regular part of the football beat, and even made sure Auburn coach Pat Dye was involved. Dye ended up inviting the students to Auburn's homecoming game. The whole publicity effort got St. Joe's national attention in a unique way at a time of year when the school normally did not receive much coverage.

American bending

Phil Bender Day at American University in Washington, D.C.—many of the students weren't quite sure exactly who Phil Bender was; he must have donated the money that paid for Bender Arena, several surmised.

The "Phil Bender" moniker was birthed by a group of pun-loving students in the early part of the first decade of 2000 in an effort to turn one game a year into an event. Their imaginary Phil came with an imagined caricature of a short, chubby, bald guy. The arena was actually funded by Howard and Sondra Bender and named after Howard's father. Who was called Jack.

That hasn't stopped Phil Bender from becoming American's Super Bowl, complete with celebrity appearances, corporate partners (free smoothies from Robeks and free quesadillas from Guapo's), extraneous rabble-rousers (activists handing out fliers in favor of Barack Obama and opposed to global warming), and a crowd nearly 100 percent larger than this season's previous high.

The event has even spread to other American teams at other venues. The field hockey and women's lacrosse teams play "Phil Jacobs" games at Jacobs Recreational Complex, and the men's and women's soccer teams play "Phil Reeves" games at Reeves Field.

Students sport "I Did Phil Bender" t-shirts and refer to the day as "State School Saturday," because of the one-weekend spike in a particular strain of face-painting, foot-stomping, profanity-chanting school spirit.

All because of a play on words and a great, opportunistic run at old-fashioned publicity.

The Gordie Lockbaum and Joe Dudek campaigns

The College of the Holy Cross has long been known for academic and athletic excellence. However, no one individual brought Holy Cross athletics more to the forefront that football player Gordie Lockbaum did in 1986 and 1987. The Crusaders' SID at the time, Gregg Burke, developed a long-standing campaign using all facets of media available, including Holy Cross' strong presence with national columnist Dave Anderson and television commentator Jack Whitaker, to bestow the virtues of throwback football player Lockbaum, who played both offense and defense throughout his career. By providing a series of strong arguments for the unique story, Burke and his staff continued to push the media for coverage on a national level that befitted Lockbaum's play, albeit on the 1-AA level. The campaign played out under the title "Back of All Trades—tailback, cornerback, and throwback," and it resulted in Lockbaum finishing third in Heisman Trophy voting in 1987, the highest finisher for a non 1-A player. This National Football Foundation and Hall of Fame scholar-athlete was also selected to play in the Senior Bowl, the

East-West Shrine Classic and the Blue-Gray game. He was a finalist for the Jim Thorpe Award as defensive back, and made the Kodak AFCA First Team All-America as a receiver.

A similar case occurred just one year before with another New England underdog. Joe Dudek was a running back for Plymouth State University in New Hampshire who was on his way to setting NCAA records for touchdowns at any level. The hard charging back had gained limited exposure throughout the first two years of his career, but the constant push by school SID John Garner finally caught the attention of *Sports Illustrated*, who elected to take a chance and put Dudek on the cover as he made his historic run. The battle to gain publicity for the small school had worked, and resulted in Dudek finishing ninth in the Hesiman balloting that year.

Expect a miracle

One of the more unlikely campaigns for national publicity took place at Oral Roberts University in Tulsa, Oklahoma during the 1970s. The new SID at the school was Brooklyn born Andy Furman, whose charge it was to use sports as a tool to promote the university. Furman was brought in by Athletic Director Bob Brooks to find unique ways to promote the school and its message. Always the consummate promoter, Furman took his charge very seriously, even though his religious affiliation was Jewish. The result was a series of unique promotions which gained great notoriety as the ORU team improved, including a run to the NIT in New York City. Along the way the team embraced Roberts' slogan "Expect a Miracle" as its calling card, despite some irreverent promotions which drew media attention and some new fans into the Tulsa arena. One of the best was when the school took on national power DePaul University. The irony of the Christian school playing a power with the nickname "Blue Demons" was not lost on Furman, who invited all of Oklahoma's occult worshipers to the game for free. He also created a Native American Night when the school faced nationally ranked St. John's, whose nickname at the time was the Redmen. Both promotions, which may not have worked in today's politically correct world, were a hit and got national publicity for the university and the team, as they rode the crest of several unexpected wins to unaccustomed recognition.

Wearin' the sweater

College hoops in New York had been dormant for too many years. In 2009–2010, not one local college even reached the NCAAs or the NIT, so all the good brand equity and loyal following that had been built over years of success for Rutgers, Seton Hall, St. John's, Manhattan, Hofstra, Fordham et al. has been lost.

For that casual fan to fill distressed seats, even on campus, can still be very elusive in this transitionary time. So what to do? Well, St. John's University came up with a great promotion for a pre-holiday Tuesday, holding "Ugly Sweater Night" on the Jamaica campus. Those showing up with the ugliest of sweaters get a discount on a ticket and a chance to win other prizes, including being part of a faux Guinness World record for the largest collection of ugly sweaters. The event paid homage to the Red Storm's legendary coach Lou Carnessecca, who was known for his garish collection of sweaters during his time on the St. John's bench. Does it get some buzz and create a fun visual at no cost? Yes. It also may move a few tickets at a tough time of year against an opponent, Bryant College, that no one would be lining up to see. On another level it sends a connection message to the current team and supporters of the glory days past, which is the team struggling may be troublesome, but in today's positive times, is a good message and connection. Now ugly sweater nights are not new, but to tie to a sometimes forgotten tradition it is a smart and easy promotion for the Johnnies.

Stats, stats, and more stats

For some reason, the image of the SID may always be tied to pocket protectors, calculators, and spreadsheets. Especially in this 24/7 world, the focus on statistics is even greater than ever before, and the job of making sure all that data is collected and compiled by the governing bodies falls to the SID office.

Is it sometimes tedious? Yes? Do people ever wonder why football stats have to be done with the same meticulous accuracy at Tuskeegee Institute as they are done at Notre Dame? Sometimes. However, the opportunity that records can be created and broken, that historical data can help be the lynchpin for publicity, is very, very important to the collegiate SID.

After all, if the SID office was not there to collect and disseminate the information, then a great deal of the efforts of these student athletes would never get even the slightest recognition. If you think of stats compilation in that vein—that you are compiling a historical platform and are using the process as way to add to the publicity pile—then the compilation takes on a broader perspective.

Also, look for innovation in numbers to include in your pitches. Creative numbers, fun numbers, unique comparisons will help add to the publicity push and set yourself apart again.

Example

Here is a rather humorous account of statistical keeping in an attempt to break a record. This was the winter of 1987, and Monmouth College was playing St. Peter's College at the Yanatelli Center in Jersey City, New Jersey. The Peacocks' starting-point guard was senior Kevin Boyle, and he needed just six assists to break the all-time St. Peter's record for career assists. The first half was slow but St. Peter's held a 22–17 lead. However, just before the half ended Boyle completed a pass that led to a basket for what was recorded as his sixth assist, the record-breaker. Keep in mind in 1986 statistics were still done by hand. There were no failsafe systems which made sure numbers balanced, like the programs that all schools use today. However, in the winter of 1986, one person would be keeping the scorebook while sometimes two or even three people would be keeping the other statistics. The announcement was made as the teams went to the locker room that Boyle had broken the assist record. However, when the scorer looked at the box score, there was a problem. St. Peter's had made seven field goals in the first half, two of which were by Boyle. That left a total of only five field goals for the rest of the team and created a little bit of an embarrassing situation for those involved. Luckily it was understood, the box score was rectified, and Boyle went on to break the record later in the game regardless. The story actually made some national notes columns which it would not have if it was a simple correct number. However, it does go to show the importance of accuracy and balance in doing the most tedious of numbers.

Event management

Another key area of SID work that often goes overlooked is event management. The setting of score clocks, hiring (or recruiting) of stats crews, credentialing, dealing with media, and basically making sure events are held in a timely fashion all fall to the SID department. Obviously the size of the event and the scale it takes place at any university will vary and dictate the amount of time spent, but event preparation and the ability to cover all the details is a key part of job development and is a skill that is coveted by the corporate world. The ability to juggle all those tasks and make the event run smoothly is key. The two biggest words again are *organization* and *communication*.

No matter what the event, organization and professionalism are key. It is important to establish a simple checklist to review with coaches and officials to make sure every aspect of the event is covered. It is your show, so treat it with the respect it deserves. Make sure that equipment and backup equipment is ready, rosters are approved by both teams, copies are available for even a few spectators, a timeline is planned out to begin the event, your cell phone is charged (especially for emergencies), and that you have a reporting list for all information post game. This list will obviously change for bigger events.

Publications and new media

A great deal of publications was covered in our writing chapter. On the collegiate level, there are many additional opportunities for publications that are handled out of the SID office. Things like schedule cards and calendars, photo selection, and recruiting pamphlets in addition to the media guides all fall under the SID office. As with publicity, one has the opportunity in the SID field to portray a positive image with some seemingly mundane tasks to a larger audience outside the walls of the gym. It is so important to pay attention to details, given the restraints of budget and the timeliness of putting materials together and getting them out. Some basic guidelines for the smaller projects are as follows.

Schedule cards and posters

- Make sure all events are listed by *day* and *date*.
- Make sure it is *clear* where events are being held. For the Olympic sports where a venue may shift or may be a little obscure, make sure folks are aware of where the event is being held.
- *Clearly* delineate between home and away events by using an @ sign.
- List the start time of each event.
- Make sure *all* spelling is correct and writing is legible. If you need a magnifying glass to read the information, then there is too much and the cards will get wasted.
- Make sure you have worked out a clear plan to distribute the cards and posters to the community. The worst thing that happens is a sponsor or team creates pieces and they sit in the closet and never get used. Review the plan with the coach and ask for help on distribution.
- If you are selecting athletes or coaches for photos, have a clear understanding as to who you are using and why. You will be asked by those who are not used.
- Use economies of scale if possible to further cross promote activities.
- Create a timeline to spot check and make sure the cards or calendars are getting pickup and use. Have a plan to replenish if necessary.
- Have a clear deadline of completion and distribution at minimum two weeks before the first event.
- Make sure that all information is also clearly communicated on the university website and is accurate with what is on the cards.
- If there is media covering the live event, even if it is online, be sure to list it. Those sponsoring the cards and those interested in the event will take pride in seeing the extra effort made for publicity.

Media guides/publications

Unlike your professional brethren, on the collegiate level a great amount of time you *can* judge a book by its cover. The collegiate "media guides," whether they are for football or for Olympic sports, will be used as a recruiting tool—sometimes the *only* recruiting tool to assist coaches. Therefore creativity, no matter what the budget, and accuracy are the most important things when designing and doing content for your sports.

Some simple rules for publication success

1   *Know your audience.* Communication with the coaches who will use these guides is just as important in many cases as what the media will need. Does the coach need a little extra text about the university? Is he or she less concerned with stats and more concerned with player interest? In basketball and football and other sports that may generate revenue, both are important with a larger budget. However, in many cases having a guide that is neat and informational and that looks professional is the most important thing.

2   *Maximize the exposure.* Once again, it is great to print 10,000 copies—it is awful to use 2,000 in an era where thumb drives and online tools can be just as effective. Kills a lot of trees. Make sure you have a defined distribution plan that achieves the purpose of the guide or publication. Who is it going to, when will it be used—make sure it is maximized internally as well as externally and don't forget your alumni athletes!

3   *Maximize the digital space.* Universities should be a source of great innovation, not just in the classroom but in the business of education as well. Websites, podcasts, effective streaming video, Skype, even text messaging are all essential tools to reach both a core audience and the broad interest world as well. The url to drive traffic to, and in many cases a twitter handle, are essential and should be front and center with every public-facing media element the office puts forth. It is not a sign of laziness to drive media to the website, it should be a source of pride, innovation, and effectiveness.

4   *Set yourself apart.* Especially in the yearly process, we sometimes don't have time or the drive to change fonts or alter contents or photos. If it is not a budgeting issue we would suggest keeping the publications as fresh as possible on a two-year cycle for historical material that can be rotated in.

5   *Be fresh and accurate.* Make sure that sections that do not have to do with your sport are always up to date (lists of alumni, building names, enrollment numbers, etc.) and make sure that all dates, times, and facts are always double-checked. Especially in the minutia of statistics on a yearly basis, an error of fact can quickly be accepted as wrote if never caught and corrected.

New media

Perhaps the biggest opportunity for growth that the SID has captured for the university is in the area of new media. Because of the lack of budget, the SID has always been at the forefront of new technology, be it stats programs, desktop publishing, or digital photography. The days of the fax and the ditto machine are well gone, but technology companies for years have looked to the collegiate world as their testing ground for sports opportunities. This began with companies like broadcast.com, Starwave and Statman going to small colleges to take their ideas and show larger entities how they can be brought to market. Out of those tests came "new" opportunites like goduke.com, the first "fan" site dedicated to sports, Marc Cuban's opportunities to show live Indiana University sports on the internet, and ultimately the birth of broad platforms like nba.com.

All started with SIDs who were looking to find new ways to grow their products in cost-effective ways. The same happened with desktop publishing. The days of typesetting were turning budgets out of control, so schools began finding ways to use efficient economies of scale to purchase desktop programs and learn the art and design business. In many instances, the quality and time turnaround for publications became more efficient, while costs dropped.

Following those points, the use of digital photography as a cost-cutting measure was next. This resulted in local publications and leagues receiving photos they were able to push to mass media in another cost and time efficient manner.

So where does this put the SID of today? In a position where he or she can learn to be the publisher, webmaster, and photo editor all at once—valuable and cost-effective tools for expanding one's stature at the university level.

It also puts the SID office today at the forefront of being able to mast whatever the next level of technology will be to capture as a cost-effective promotional tool. Web chats, blogs, and streaming radio are quickly becoming the norm for promotion. Will podcasts and streaming video be far behind as you promote your all-Americans? Probably and hopefully not. Will the SID be the first to come up with a strategy to used destinations like Facebook as ways to engineer sports publicity tactics at a cost-effective level? Hopefully.

As we all strive to find a way to create the next promotable technology opportunity, SIDs should and will be at the forefront.

Sales and marketing

No matter what size school you are at these days, the "return on investment" for monies spent is even more important today than it ever has been. Although we are well aware of the fact that justifying what we do in terms of dollars and cents is indeed difficult from time to time, working with the designated "marketing" person in the university or the athletic department is a growing component of the job. Again this goes back to thinking about key distribution points for publications, creating "buzz" or interest in local business partners and doing all those little things (thank you notes, PA announcements, etc.) to make sure those who are bringing in dollars are being rewarded on their return.

You again hold a key component in the process—you can make sure that coaches and student athletes are advocates of your business partners, and your "suggestion box" should always be open to finding ways to grow the business side, which will make you a more valuable player in the university setting.

What is CoSIDA? (reprinted with permission from CoSIDA.com)

CoSIDA was founded in 1957 and currently is a 2,700-plus member national organization comprised of the sports public relations, communications, and information professionals throughout all levels of collegiate athletics in the United States and Canada. The 2009–2010 academic year marked the 59th year of the organization, and a membership record was set in the early stages of the 2010–2011 academic year when the annual membership grew to 2,600 active participants for the first time.

The association is designed to help the athletic media relations and communications professionals at all levels. It is the desire of the members to have the profession take its rightful place on the decision-making levels of college athletics. Everything undertaken—the short- and long-term strategic planning and initiatives, year-long professional development opportunities, and the annual Convention/workshop—is geared to this objective.

Prior to the formation of CoSIDA, sports information directors as a group were a part of the American College Public Relations Association; yet, most SIDs at those ACPRA meetings felt that a separate organization was needed. There were 102 members at the original meetings.

CoSIDA's Board of Director leadership is comprised of nine elected officer positions (President, 1st Vice President, 2nd Vice President, 3rd Vice President, three Past Presidents removed, Treasurer, and Secretary-Digest Editor), along with 10 other Board appointees. These athletic PR professionals, along with an Executive Director, a Director of External Affairs and a Director of Internal Operations, compose the leadership group.

In addition, the association has been strengthened since the summer of 2008 with the creation of additional management teams: the University Division Management Advisory Committee (UDMAC) and the College Division Management Advisory Committee (CDMAC). The UDMAC and CDMAC were created as part of the Board's strategic initiatives in creating a more federated management structure within CoSIDA. The purpose and goal of these management teams is to encourage divisional leadership groups to take a more direct and personal responsibility approach in regards to division-specific CoSIDA matters.

CoSIDA's signature program is the Academic All-America® program, which honors the nation's highest-achieving student athletes for academic and athletic excellence across all divisions of play (NCAA Division I, II, III, NAIA, CIS, and NJCAA). CoSIDA members nominate and vote in selection of Academic All-America performers in 12 sports (men's at-large and women's at-large [multiple-sport category], baseball, men's basketball, women's basketball, football, men's soccer, women's soccer, softball, men's track and field/cross country, women's track and field/cross country and women's volleyball).

CoSIDA code of ethics—foreword

In order for members of College Sports Information Directors of America to enjoy professional status, it is imperative that a viable Code of Ethics be observed. This Code of Ethics must embrace and reflect the high ideals and moral fiber of the educational institution which the Sports Information Director serves.

It is essential that the Sports Information Director conduct and discharge his/her duties and responsibilities with dedication, integrity, sincerity, and respect of his/her constituency (peers) as a representative of an academic institution.

Members who do not wish to meet these basic responsibilities have no place in CoSIDA and such detractors should be referred to the Committee on Ethics for appropriate disciplinary action.

College Sports Information Directors of America code of ethics

The reputation of the membership and the organization as a whole depends upon the proper ethical conduct of all individuals related to the organization. We must set an example for each other, as well as other professionals, by our constant pursuit of the ethical standards of performance, professionalism and conduct.

The CoSIDA Board of Directors retains the right to bar members from functions, membership and events or expel individuals for actions in violation of this Code or CoSIDA by-laws.

Ethical practice should be everyone's utmost concern within the day-to-day activities for the members. This Code has been put in place in order to assist the membership with this pursuit. Members that do not wish to uphold this standard should not be part of CoSIDA. Membership in CoSIDA is a privilege, not a right.

CoSIDA presents these core values of the organization for its membership as an industry standard for professional practice in the field of sports information. These are fundamental beliefs that we find as a basic guide for our day-to-day decision-making process and are vital to the entire integrity of people in the areas of collegiate sports public relations/communications/media relations and information.

Advocacy

★ Those professionals in the areas of collegiate sports public relations and communications serve the interests of the various entities by acting in a professional manner.

Honesty

★ Collegiate sports public relations and communications professionals must adhere to the highest standard of accuracy and honesty in representing their interests to the public.

Expertise

★ Collegiate sports public relations and communications professionals must make themselves available to become acquainted with the latest technology.
★ Collegiate sports public relations and communications professionals must build expertise through understanding and creating relationships among a wide variety of constituents.

Independence

★ Collegiate sports public relations and communications professionals are to be held accountable for their actions and be ready to give counsel when needed.

Fairness

★ Collegiate sports public relations and communications professionals deal fairly with media, student athletes and the public, respecting all opinions and their right of free expression.

Conclusion

In closing, the uniqueness of the collegiate atmosphere makes the publicity effort at this level worthwhile and rewarding. The SID is able to use many of the skills that are essential to all publicists and, similar to agency work, apply those skills to many different subjects. Growing and understanding how the SID role fits into the bigger picture of sports publicity is the greatest challenge the SID has as the role becomes more important in the revenue growth areas of most universities.

6

WORKING WITH A PROFESSIONAL TEAM

The endless season

This chapter will look at the nuances of working with a professional team, and the differences that exist in the professional team environment that may not happen at the collegiate level, the league level, or the sponsor level. Some of the tips here can apply to the collegiate side, especially at the top levels of Division I sports in North America. However, the difference here is that at the end of the day professional sports is a job for the athlete. The amount of interest, even from the largest university, is different and because there are real dollars involved the perception, even though it has narrowed in the past 25 years, that these athletes are now "professional" as opposed to "amateur" collegians makes all the difference. Therefore the way some situations are handled, or event the time spent attending to detail, may be different.

Even at the largest collegiate institutions there are many opportunities to shift job focus depending on the time of year. The demands are year-round but they can become seasonal. On the professional team level, the demands for one sport in most locales have now become year-round. Between off-season programs, the draft, player trading periods, free agency, Olympic events, and the need to keep the product relevant to business partners and season subscribers as teams justify the bottom line, there is very little time for offseason work.

Like other roles in sports communications, the professional team publicist is evolving as well. The times of being the stats person, the media guy, the person dealing exclusively with the day-to-day has changed as teams look for more and more forms of publicity from the department.

As long as there is balance, the change is not necessarily a bad thing. The team communications staff now has to deal with many more masters and find ways to understand the business side of sports more fully than before, which will make them or her more valuable. It will also expose the person to more areas of publicity than before, ranging from entertainment press to business press and others. It makes the job more challenging, but ultimately more rewarding for those willing to take the challenge.

What you will find on the professional level is that many of the skills you have acquired in other places still apply, although you may have less time to use them. In many cases, desktop design and layout, website design; long feature writing, marketing and sales programs, and sometimes community relations fall into other professional areas of an organization. However, the fact that you have those skills and can relate to those departments will make you a better person in the team setting. They will help you break down barriers and get the job done quicker. The problem is that the level of importance of your media relations skills will probably give you less time to concentrate on areas outside of your chief function than before.

On the team level there are six principal roles:

- team spokesperson/public relations
- general media relations
- credentialing
- game operations
- publications/record keeping
- staff "coordinator"/budgeting/person about town.

In many instances, the importance of each role will vary by sport and marketplace. Examples of how bigger markets differ from smaller markets will be shown later in this chapter. However, the basic functions and the need to master each of them will not change in the general team environment. You work for a very recognizable brand in a sizeable market where everything your coaches and athletes do will get attention, for better or for worse. How you are able to maximize that exposure and help grow these very powerful brands will be the trick.

Team spokesperson/public relations

Unlike many college settings, the role of the team publicist in many instances is to be the daily face of the organization. Therefore he or she is dealing with various forms of media on a 24/7 basis. He or she also gets the brunt of the focus from a very hungry public looking for information, whether they are calling in with questions or complaints, season subscribers looking for information, or just the man on the street.

The position of the team PR person is a very visible one, no matter how he or she tries to be in the background. The need for media to get information on a timely basis makes the spokesperson the gatekeeper, and in many markets the gatekeeper can be the first and only contact with the public through mass media.

As the team's spokesperson there are many challenges that have to be carefully thought out. You are solely responsible in many cases of shaping the media story for the day, of putting out to little or too much information, of unknowingly creating news or knowingly withholding confidential information. You speak not for yourself and sometimes not for an individual. You speak on behalf of a brand, many times which is larger than many Fortune 500 companies. It is a very serious role, and one that has to always be taken as such.

Therefore, some basic rules to follow as a spokesperson are listed below.

1 *Think before you speak.* Many times the biggest issues arise because one is not prepared for a question, or one doesn't answer questions in the most direct way possible. Take a second and consider what it is you are saying before you say it.

Tip

The world of social media can often lull people into a false sense of security when using "private" or "personal" Twitter or Facebook accounts vs. one someone is using in an official capacity. Not true. Wherever you post, whatever you say, is reflective of your public position. If you think your words reflect poorly on your job or your team, then don't say it on any public-facing account.

---

2 *Know whom you are speaking with.* Especially in major markets, calls can come in from media or fans at any given time. Never answer questions or give out information without knowing whom you are talking to or corresponding with. It is the media's job to obtain information, sometimes at any cost. Always be aware of who is on the other end of the phone or the email or text.

3 *Make sure the information is accurate and approved.* You are speaking on behalf of the organization, so make sure that everyone is aware of what you are giving out and when you are giving it. It is much more important to be fair and accurate than timely. Acting too quickly can create a news cycle that is not needed.

4 *Off the record is usually never off the record.* In today's society the media need more and more information and need it quicker than ever before. Therefore the need to befriend media and go "off the record" becomes more and more of an "easy" opportunity. Always know that you are speaking, even if it is your opinion, on behalf of the organization. If you are not sure, then don't give out what it is you know.

Tip

Always think that your boss/coach/athlete is in the room with you when media ask to go "off the record"—is what you are saying what is in the best interests of the organization? If so, then take the opportunity—if not, then think twice.

---

5 *Going on background can be the way.* As opposed to going off the record, making sure that the media has the proper background from you, as spokesperson, is always helpful. It will help form the opinion and you will have made sure that the proper information is conveyed without giving your opinion. By background you are making sure that the media member fully understands the position of the organization as to what has already been made public record. You are making sure they have all the background, and do not assume that they are aware of details that they may not have taken into consideration that help establish your point.

6 *You are the spokesperson, not the story.* In today's world it is very easy for the spokesperson to become part of the story, either intentionally or unintentionally. The media's need for unnamed sources to fill out a story has become more and more important. Therefore it remains your role to disseminate information but not create news. In many cases it is even helpful to make sure your name is not a part of the new cycle. "Team spokesman" can be more than sufficient.

7 *Stay as Switzerland.* You are also the neutral party in many cases, and it is good to stay that way when disseminating information. Distributing the facts the organization wants out there in a calm, professional, calculated way is what should be done. Getting emotional or opinionated is not helpful to anyone.

8 *The customer is always right.* It is true in sales and it is true in public relations. The role of the spokesperson is to disseminate information to the media and the public, and sometimes that information is disappointing, controversial, or difficult to explain. It is your job to anticipate a negative response and make sure that you have your game plan to deal with the emotional or the disappointing. It is OK to placate hurt and emotional feelings so long as you are communicating the correct message for the organization. Your personal feelings here do not matter, you are speaking on behalf of a bigger entity and that must be conveyed.

9 *Always be organized and professional.* Rarely will a moment come up when you are interacting with a member of the public or the media when you will not have a chance to make sure you look and act professionally. Many times it is how you say as much as what you say that counts. Your

confidence is key. Believe in the message, have all the information, anticipate the basic questions—and always think before you speak.

10 *Remember the soundbite.* The media is very short tempered and short cycled these days. Make sure that the key message is short and to the point— make sure what you are conveying is the facts that the organization wants conveyed. Avoid going off on tangents. You are the messenger, not the message. It is always OK to say less than more.

The "public" relations aspect

Once again here there are many masters to serve. You as the spokesperson have to speak with the media, sometimes business partners, and sometimes fans. Never forget the audience and always remember the fans. These are the people who care about your product almost as much as we do, and sometimes even more. They are emotional, opinionated, passionate fanatics: they do not have to be rational. They don't even have to be sane. However, they are the consumer of your very expensive product and we have to treat them as the great customers that they are.

Many times this is the least interesting part of the position in a team professional sport. The fans are always coming up at the most inopportune times; they are sending the letters and the emails, leaving the messages most of the time they are upset about something. They are the end of the day, after the game calls. Many times they just want to vent. So let them. Also, many, many times they *do not* expect an answer. Take the time to listen and to read. If you feel there is a call to action needed, then occasionally surprise them and do that. The little acts of kindness will go a long way.

There is another, sometimes even more serious role to listening and reading. As I said before, sometimes fans act out of anger or frustration. There may be warning signs that come only to you of a more serious issue. Maybe they are considering a harmful action to themselves or to a team member or family member. If you don't take the time to listen and read, there may be a bigger tragedy afoot. In many instances a crank call or a hate letter can have serious implications and you as the public voice, the public face, have the ability to diffuse and protect. It is not your primary role as spokesperson, but it can be an important one.

General media relations

This is the essence of the team publicist. The biggest difference with the professional side is the daily interaction with media, the volume of daily media, and the ability to control media flow and access. In many professional leagues the media access time is mandated by the league and controlled by the publicity staff. The rules are easy to follow and are usually respected but usually not loved by members of the media. Once again here taking the time to prep, shape, and control messages is key. You may not be the person doing the speaking, but you have the ability to work with those of influence to make sure they are aware of who is asking questions, what is being said and where the daily flow of media will go.

Media training

More and more the idea of media training spokespeople is going from taboo to wrote. Keep in mind there is a *big* difference from what was originally thought of as media training, namely telling people what and when to say it, as opposed to what is being down with teams and organizations in sports and entertainment today. Today's focus of media training is much more about shaping what an athlete or team spokesperson is saying than what he or she actually says. In many cases, the goal is for the athlete to understand what his role is in a media setting and what control he or she has in setting the tone, controlling the message and making sure that he or she understands their responsibility in the process.

Why is this necessary? The media has a role to play, and especially in a professional team setting, the players and coaches have a responsibility to respect the media's job and deal with it in best they can. After all, the media provide the organization with its greatest amount of publicity, whether that is TV, radio, print, or new media. It is also important the athletes, coaches, and executives provide adequate and respectful answers to all topics, not necessarily just ones they want to answer. Properly executed media training will help everyone.

Another aspect of proper media training is that it helps make all those in the organization more responsible for their actions, and in many cases, the athletes themselves will help understand each other better and even police each other when media issues come up.

That being said, today's 24/7 news coverage dictates that media access be controlled and that those speaking fully understand the power that they have. That is where the publicist's role in training and shaping the message comes in. The publicist has to be responsible prior to media interaction to explain and help craft the appropriate message.

This takes several forms.

Formal media training sessions

These are done with all staff and players in the preseason. They explain the rules for interaction set by the club, some scenarios that have come up and how they can best be addressed, and a broad interaction and role-playing period in which media members or staff conduct mock interviews. Some teams will also go over whom the regular media members are, what their tendencies are, what has been done in the past, and how to be mindful of what could happen in the future. These sessions can last anywhere from 45 minutes to several hours. Sometimes there is video presented to show examples as well. A majority of teams now also use professional trainers, either former journalists or professional speakers, to address this group. Sometimes take-aways are also provided. In many cases on the professional side this is not the first time athletes or coaches have been taken through a media training program. Many colleges perform the service to a degree, as do sponsor companies that young athletes may be involved with. However, the training that is provided by the team is essential as the media scrutiny and expectations at the professional level is much different. The perception of an athlete as a professional is just that. He is no longer an amateur and this is a job, so the training needs to meet that standard.

Daily follow-up and prep

The daily follow-up is again a key component of media training. The publicist needs to constantly be aware of what issues his or her players and staff may face on a daily basis, and taking two to three minutes before the media interaction to remind the players and coaches of potential issues and answers is a big part of the job that is sometimes lost. The extra prep time can make the difference in avoiding controversy and gaining the trust of the athletes or having a scandal develop from nowhere. Again, the role is *not* to tell the person what to say. It is to merely remind him or her of the issues and the consequences and to make sure that they fully understand what surprises may be there. Is it foolproof? No. Will it be helpful? Absolutely.

The Q&A prep

For major press events and one-on-one interviews that are scheduled and substantial, it is best to do a full question and answer session with the principals involved. This prep on the part of the publicist could take upwards of a few hours and is the standard for most CEOs and spokespersons in the corporate world. It has not been the standard in sports until recently. The written Q&A gives the publicist the chance to think like the journalist for an extended period, and present the best and worst case scenarios to his/her athlete and coach. It will be wide ranging and extensive but is designed to make sure that every potential point is covered and that he or she is aware that anything can come up in an interview. The prep will also include the key messages that the subject needs to convey during the interview along with ways to make sure that he/she can always work in the key points. It is a very useful tool.

Who is your buddy?

One of the key things to remember in the course of media training is the buddy idea. Buddy is never an option with anyone involved in professional sports PR, although each person involved (with the exception of the athlete) will try and be someone's buddy along the way. The media member will try to buddy-up to the

PR guy, the coach, the player, the agent, as he tries to put himself into position for a story. It is also easy for the PR spot to become the buddy or protector of the player or coach or even do the media guy favors as a buddy. None of which will have a great long-term effect. The players and athletes should be aware of the buddy idea and realize two things: the relationship with the media should always be cordial but professional, and as soon as they do a favor to their media buddy, all other media become their problem. Consistency again is key, as is professionalism. The relationship with the player and coach can also be a transient one. It is the nature of the business. The PR staff is there to protect the best interests of the brand and of the players and coaches. That will sometimes mean telling them or getting them to do things they don't want to do for the good of the brand. That balance and professionalism again will lead the way to a good relationship.

Follow-up

Once any media interaction is completed, there is always time for review and follow-up. One of the biggest issues that can come up is that the publicist "checks the box" after the interview and moves on to whatever the next task is for the day. It is best to immediately review, take the temperature of the subject, get their opinion and always follow up with the media person on their thoughts. This is the best way that the publicist can tell if the training is paying off and also how one can anticipate issues.

Dealing with the demand

One of the great things about the professional side of sports publicity is the immediate media attention one gets. One of the worst sides of the professional side is the immediate media attention one gets. Therefore, the balance needs to be struck to make sure that you are best serving your constituents (the organization) while still feeding the demand that the media has. Prioritizing on the professional level is always the biggest challenge. Some tips for getting the job done follow.

Service long leads, but especially those who you see every day. The daily media—beat writers, TV, radio, and even internet—are your priority. These are the folks you will live with, your players will live with, and who are your best voice. It is important to always treat them fairly and evenly in good times and bad. This is a professional relationship and needs to be treated as so. They are *not* the enemy. They can be demanding but they have a job to do, as do you. You have to keep the best interests of the club at heart, and find ways to still service them. Going the extra mile for the little things—making sure you always call and keep them updated on facts, keeping their deadlines in mind when announcements are made, providing quotes and facts that they may not be thinking of, providing third-party quotes, making sure that technical information is explained in simple detail (on things like injuries for example)—are just some of the ways to keep your main media as focused as possible. Can you be their friend? It depends. You can be respectful and professional which is best. But being a caring person (knowing their family issues, wishing them happy holidays, making sure that they get the giveaways that go to the fans on game nights) comes with the job as well. In times of crisis, those little things can go a long way.

Be aware at all times the differences in the medium. In today's 24/7 world, there are becoming more and more issues between TV and digital media vs. print. The immediacy of news gathering and posting has made the competition that much stiffer. That being said, there are always instances where TV and radio reporters may have different needs and questions that the print writers who do not have to work in the soundbite. This has to always be taken into account on the professional level. Keep the needs for each in mind during media availability and figure out how to best service both groups. Will each be happy? Probably not. But if it takes splitting some media sessions into "TV first" to get their soundbites and then doing print, then so be it. The session may be a little repetitive but it will also be productive for all involved and both groups will appreciate the effort. Also, asking the media questions feedback from them as to how the sessions go in advance will also be helpful as you plan your strategy. Knowing their needs from their mouths will also avoid any problems if they do not get what they need.

Then there is the digital world, which is continuously evolving. The use of blogs, podcasts, and all forms of social media has created a need for more access, and sometimes less time, for those who need to be interviewed. In some cases, bloggers who regularly report about a team have no contact with the team. They may not be in the same city as that organization, and want to voice their opinion unfettered from the restrictions and interests that can be imposed on more traditional media.

In other cases the digital press may want to cover the team as traditional media do, but don't have the "name" or "coverage size" to warrant regular credentials. They may also be employed in other capacities which will limit their ability to attend events. That does not make them less credible or interesting or helpful to getting out a message.

Ignoring or trying to curtail that experience by digital journalists or bloggers is not smart. Instead, applying outreach to try and assist in coverage should be encouraged, whether it is a series of games that you can have dedicated space for, or practices where access can be given, or even access to conference calls. Now, if privileges are abused, that's a different story. If someone acts unprofessionally, that also has to be taken into consideration, just as it should with "traditional" journalists. However, by understanding and embracing the elusive digital medium will help to expand coverage and gain momentum, not just for small market or coverage challenged teams, but for all teams who can effectively work with the media to tell stories big and small. Yes, the digital coverage and its access is different, but is certainly should not be ignored or trifled with.

Example

While many Major League teams were leery of independent websites, the Los Angeles Dodgers embraced them and the concept of social media very early on in 2006. Beginning with their corporate blog, they extended into invitations for bloggers to come and spend a night at the ballpark covering the team and eventually extended the program to where they had a "blog spot" in the press box that received the same access as every other reporter. The result was significantly improved coverage (in volume and positivity) from independent websites and a much greater understanding of how the team operated from their perspective. It also helped usher in the Facebook and Twitter age and really understand the idea of direct communication with their fans.

Pitch and plan. Even with the great amount of media coverage on the professional level, there is still the need and the ability to pitch and plan for the quiet day. Make sure you know your players and staff, and what other things may be going on in their lives or careers that may be of interest to them in getting some publicity. Being able to cash in a favor or two to get those valuable notes in will go a long way. Also pitching some smaller but interesting stories also gives you the ability to assist the consistent writer or TV personality in their job growth. At the end of the day, the fans still want to know more about their athletes, and pitching stories, having a list of ideas, will help get those points out there.

Example

Perhaps no city was hit harder with the 2009 financial crisis than Detroit, and the sponsorships of the local teams suffered. However, the Detroit Tigers made a sound statement, one with positive long-term effects, by giving a sponsorship away for a year—to General Motors, Ford and Chrysler. The massive automaker was kept in its prime position, as were its competitors: Ford Motor Co. and Chrysler LLC. Tigers' owner Mike Ilitch gave the spot to each of the area's car companies this season at no cost instead of selling the space to other bidders. Some of Detroit-based GM's vehicles were displayed in past seasons at the fountain. As part of the plan, GM, Ford and Chrysler logos were erected on each side of the General Motors name. Underneath is a sign that reads: "The Detroit Tigers support our automakers."

Know the editors and the decision makers. It sounds silly, but even though you may *never* see an editor or a radio or TV executive at a game or an event, it is still in your best interests to have a relationship with those people. In times of crisis, or maybe even in pitching an idea or dealing with a minor issue, it is good to have an understanding of the bigger picture of the sports section of the newspaper or TV section, and being able to call that senior person from time to time will be a big asset. Don't hide behind email either. Still use the personal touches we talked about in the "pitch" section—the phone call and the note—if a sit-down does not allow.

Keep the front section in mind. Once again, the demand will come from the sports in most cases, but being aware of current and community events will also help deal with demand. If there is a crisis or an issue in a city that has nothing to do with sports, many times media outlets will look for the celebrity opinion. You can easily head this off by making sure that folks understand what they should or shouldn't comment on outside of their daily work, and the best way to do that is to make sure *you* know what the issues of the day away from sport are.

Know the columnists. Another issue we sometimes forget about is the influence of the columnists. They have the ability to shape opinion—sometimes just *their* opinion—even with more influence than the editor or the beat writer. It is very important to always know when the columnist will be around, who he or she is talking to, and how you can help them. It may be in casual conversation and sometimes may be very obvious, but many times columnists will show up not knowing what they want to write, and if you know their tendencies, you may be able to help shape an opinion. Given their stature at an entity as well, it may require a little more work on the day-to-day side, but the assistance and the "service with a smile" will pay off in the long run.

The little guys count too. One of the biggest issues in demand is dealing with the smaller outlets that will give you coverage: local cable networks, hometown papers, college radio stations, weekly papers, and niche websites. This coverage, welcomed in the minors and college, can sometimes be seen as a nuisance at the pro level. However, it is important to never underestimate the cumulative value of these outlets, as well as the fact that this is where many of your regular journalists got their start. Can they be given every courtesy and every point of access that the daily media gets? Probably not. However, setting aside quiet times for opportunities, acknowledging their work, asking them for copies of work they have done, and making sure that they are seen as members of the media is important in serving the greater public.

Example

The Golden State Warriors live and play in the heart of Silicon Valley. They have also always been challenged for media coverage, largely in part to the lack of on court success of the team. That has made their PR group, led by Raymond Ridder, one of the most proactive in sport. So in 2010, while many professional teams were trying to figure out how to work with digital media, the Warriors held a series of media days just for bloggers, giving them traditional access to players and staff. That extra outreach created tremendous good will for the team and lots of grass-roots support, that translated into more access and understanding of what the team was trying to achieve not just on the court, but across the board in community and business.

The long-lead management. Another big time management issue is the long-lead and lifestyle publications. These are high volume, non-traditional media opportunities that are essential in completing the professional publicity picture. They are also assets that can be pitched for great stories. However, there is a double-edged sword here as well. They will detract from media time your athletes and coaches spend with the regular coverage and because they can come in and out they are not as held accountable as regular sports media covering your team. Therefore, picking the spots, controlling the access, and making sure you understand their needs before agreeing to anything is very important. In many cases the dollars and man-hours they spend against a story is far greater than what your regular media would do. That has to be remembered and factored in. Also, always remember the risk you run is that the story can never appear if it is not meeting the agenda of the outlet. If there is not enough edge or freshness, the work will go to naught. Therefore make sure all involved from both sides understand that before making a determination.

Example

During one preseason, the New York Knicks worked with *Life Magazine* to do a behind the scenes photo shoot of what it is like to be at training camp. The magazine gave the team six digital cameras for players and staff to use over a one-month period, shooting behind the scenes photos that the magazine would then edit together. It was to be exclusive to *Life* and would run in early January. After taking literally hundreds of photos and passing up on two similar opportunities with other local outlets, *Life* determined that the photos were not edgy or creative enough, and the photo spread never ran.

National and visiting broadcasters. Usually this is more of a game day opportunity, but the ability to effectively use the national and visiting broadcasters as a PR asset is more and more valuable as teams grow their profiles to a more regional and national level. Given the turnover of players, the use of the internet to expose more fans to a brand and the use of more regional sponsors, making sure that the national broadcasters have up-to-date community and personality profiles on players, making sure visiting teams know what is going on with the franchise, should be a key part of the media demand. In recent years the focus was (and should still be) on the local broadcast as the way to communicate with the fan base. However, having messages and video delivered by visiting broadcasters and the national broadcasts is also a great benefit now as well.

Don't forget who pays the bills. At the end of the day, with all the media demands out there to prioritize, the rights holders, nationally and locally, should get the brunt of primary attention. Now, sometimes on the pro level this will cause great conflict. There will be times when a rights holder such as NBC Sports Net at the start of the Major League Soccer deal might not have the exposure or brand power as another potential partner (ESPN), but the dollars invested and the time spent in promotion make the decision a tough one with regard to access and coverage. At the end of the day, the rights holder "pressure" should make the decision clear, but in some cases the "weight" delivered by the dollar sign has to be considered strong. This is also a two-way street. You as the publicist should also be able to lean on the rights holder in a creative and tactful way to make sure that they are maximizing their time with you.

Book 'em. Another area of demand management will be in the booking of guests on shows. This will include everything from regular sports talk radio shows to national shows such as David Letterman or The Jay Leno Show. It is always important to ask some key questions before confirming the booking schedule. Questions should include:

- *Who are the other guests?* You want to make sure there are no conflicts of interest, or your person is not being set up for an uncomfortable situation.
- *Is it live?* You always need to know the difference between a show going on live or on tape. It can affect how a guest will feel about doing the show and how they come across.
- *What is the time commitment?* Many times shows may ask guests to arrive two hours prior to air. It is important to find out when their segment will be on the show.
- *Is there a preinterview?* The preinterview is actually very helpful. It will give both you and your guest an idea of what type of questions may be asked. It is usually done by a producer, sometimes as much as a day or two before the show.

- *Is it a sitdown or an activity?* Many times guests may not be asked, especially if they are athletes, just to sit and answer questions. If there is a skit of some sort involved, you have to be able to know and sure that the guest is comfortable with the interaction. Sometimes what seems funny to an audience or a host is not funny to a subject.
- *Have they done their prep?* Even if they say that all their background work is done, it is important that you send them whatever information you want included in the interview. Take nothing for granted.
- *Do they have photographers?* It's always good to make sure there are stills available for you to use in additional publicity opportunities.
- *Will portions that don't make it to air be posted online?* There are usually many ancillary pieces of a show that may not make it to air—behind-the-scenes encounters, interaction with an audience, green room talk prior to coming on air, etc. Asking when and what will be used and explaining the limitations of coverage will help avoid surprises for both sides.
- *Exclusive?* Many times shows will ask for an exclusive, namely that the guest does not appear in a similar show for a period of time before. When dealing with athletes on a media tour that is sometimes difficult to manage, and you may have to make some hard decisions to do or not do a show. The quantity over quality issue has to be addressed on a case-by-case basis. It is important to be upfront as much as possible with the show producer on this matter.

Those simple questions can help manage the booking process, and make sure that you are able to best deal with the interview process.

Dealing with the superstar in the team setting

One of the great experiences in team sports is to work with an athlete or athletes who are even beyond the gifted—the superstar. In this day and age, a sport as it becomes entertainment is even more susceptible to the "moment" for the individual in a team sport. The flamboyant and the unusual have become the media attention getter (see Dennis Rodman, Terrell Owens, and Manny Ramirez) as opposed to those who do their job (Steve Nash, Landon Donovan, R. A. Dickey) and become pillars of the community. Still with both groups, there is the amount of increased media exposure that (hopefully) sets them apart and makes the publicist's job more enriching and more interesting. When dealing with the superstar or the media star, there are always several rules of thumb to keep in mind, balance out, and make sure are communicated well.

Communicate effectively throughout the process. One of the biggest problems with the superstar is scheduling. Agents, sponsors, community groups, and team personnel will all pull at the superstar's time to satisfy their needs. It is very important for you as the publicist to unite the group and make sure that each minute is scheduled out, and not over scheduled. All sides should appreciate the effort.

Example

Longtime NBA player Marcus Camby is very focused on his community activity, and annually schedules a "March with Marcus" Day, when he goes to school, literally walking with kids through the streets as the kids begin the school year. He has done this in every city he has been in. Teams can work with him and use this as a time for access and publicity for other opportunities as well, such as making that day the first day individual or group tickets would go on sale. By combining that message with this great community event, you are able to get broader coverage for both the marketing and community sides, while helping the player promote what is important to him, his work with kids. Without communication, the groups would work in a vacuum and could do these events on different days, losing that combined media impact and even splitting media coverage.

Work to find consistent time for daily media. In some cases, team PR folks have worked to set up a special designated time each day after practice or before a game to make sure the larger group of media gets time with the athlete. As long as this is spelled out in advance and proper notification is given that this will be the media's only access time, it can work well when there is large demand. It is also important to coordinate this time with the home PR staff when on the road, so that all possible media are not overlooked.

Example

When he began his career in the NBA with the Golden State Warriors, there was a huge media demand in every city for Chris Webber. He was a member of the University of Michigan's "Fab Five," telegenic, highly drafted, and always a little controversial. Therefore, the Warriors established a time prior to the team arriving at the arena when media in that city could talk to Webber. It was usually at the team hotel, and made the process easier and fair for everyone. Some media objected about having to go the extra distance to talk to him, but overall it worked effectively for everyone.

Keep the athlete involved in the process. The media drain on an athlete on a daily basis can be significant as repetition sets in. It is very important to avoid surprises with the athlete and explain the reasons for the session. Quick updates on questions and answers are also important here. You are there to protect and maximize his or her time while still being professional. You will also know what his or her interests are better and be able to know when and how to push the right buttons to get stories done correctly.

Example

Serena Williams, in the late stages of a legendary tennis career, has become quite the entrepreneur. From clothing design to product endorsement, Williams spends the limited time she has away from tennis understanding and promoting various brands not just for the money, but because she believes in the products. In 2011, two of those brands were the SHEETS Energy strips and MISSION Athletecare, which pioneered a new technology in a fabric to keep athletes cool when performing. Williams' days to promote both products was limited, so the two came up with various national platforms, such as a workout on CNN, where she could go on and talk about both, giving the two growing brands the association with Williams in a way that did not cannibalize or seem contrived.

Example

Grant Hill has enjoyed tremendous notoriety as a role model both on and off the basketball court. However, especially given the health problems that he has experienced later in his career, his time with the media was very limited. One of Grant's other passions was collecting African American art. It was a side of Hill that not only showed off his off-court side, but also gave people a glimpse into what his post-career ambitions could be as a collector. It also gave Hill an opportunity to use his notoriety to expose some rising artists to a different world. The Orlando Magic worked with Grant's foundation and his agents to identify the opportunity and worked closely with him to create a tour of 46 pieces of his art in seven cities. He was thoroughly involved in identifying the cities selecting the artists and reviewing the media that could cover the exhibits. The result was a very big positive for all involved. It showed Grant's other interests, got him talking about basketball in other markets, and helped him grow one of his big passions, which made him a strong advocate of the efforts of all those who had helped him out as well.

Repeatedly review the requests. Keep constant lists of media requests and opportunities completed, and make sure that efforts are consistent to maximize exposure for all concerned. The one-on-one major hits may detract from some smaller more popular pieces, but over the long haul what is best for the brand is what's best for the process.

Use economies of scale whenever possible. If your star is doing a community appearance or a sponsor event, make sure that those media members who have not been able to get to him or her are aware and explain that this may be their best shot to attain the access. Many times they are surprised that the athlete is more accessible in that setting and can get them more time away from the usual media scrum.

Example

Peyton (Denver Broncos) and Eli Manning (New York Giants) may do a photo shoot on NFL apparel for Nike during the preseason. During the shoot there is usually a great deal of downtime, so both teams and Reebok worked together to find reporters, both on the business and the sports side, who had been trying to get the brothers together for a group interview. The result is a much more relaxed setting, and larger, broader stories than what could happen if they were talked to separately.

Make everyone the hero when media attend. By being the coordinator of events for the superstar, you are in a position to champion his/her causes or sponsors as well. Assist whenever you can (but avoid conflicts with team partners) and when the events do get media play, make sure the agent or business manager gets sets of clips/video as an FYI.

Use your rights holders as a benefit. Again, access is key. Giving the rights holder a little extra time as a "reward" for covering a community or business sponsor event is the right thing to do, and will score points with everyone. The rights holders are the local and national television and radio outlets who literally pay fees, usually in the hundreds to millions of dollars, to broadcast your team and/or your leagues games.

Don't become "his or her" guy or gal. Despite all the time and effort you may spend with the superstar assisting and prepping them, your primary duty remains to the team and the brand. Athletes will change places more than brands will, and it is important to make sure you pay proper attention to all of those on your team. Avoid the jealousy issue as much as you can, and find ways to include and work with everyone.

Be consistent and fair, don't be the apologist. In order to get and maintain the respect of the athlete, it is important to have him or her understand that you have everyone's best interests at heart at all times. There will be things that he or she may not want to do but will have to. There will be times when he or she does not want to speak to the media. These will happen. You will have to deal with them. Keeping a list of things turned down will help to show him or her at the appropriate time. Also having the agent or business manager as an ally is also important. If you treat them with respect, in most cases you will get the respect you need and deserve. Also, be true to your word. If you say an interview session is a half hour then try and keep it within that time frame. If a photo shoot will be all day then you also need to make sure they understand that and buy in with your help.

Include the coach. Sometimes in the rush to placate the athlete and his group we forget about the folks who are most directly affected by the demands of the media on the superstar—the coach and general manager. It is very important they too are included in the process from the beginning and that you get as much buy in as possible. A happy and healthy superstar will make the best story for everyone.

Credentialing the media

Another necessary evil in all sports, but especially on the professional side, is credentialing and media seating. Credentialing is the detailed assigning of media credentials to cover the team. Credentials are issued day by day or by the season, and each team is able to determine a pecking order depending on their requirements. The leagues will also issue season credentials to select national media, who are able to go from city to city. Usually these media will also be assigned a local credential through the home team. The process is similar but is usually less formal on the collegiate and event side, except at the highest levels of Division I sports. Credentials today may also include things like holograms, watermarks, and barcodes to make them easier to track. In some cases, teams have put barcodes on their season credentials, which media can then use as a debit card for media food and sometimes for access to and from certain areas. Traditionally most teams still use some kind of color differentiation system to distinguish both type of access (locker room only, pre-game, postgame, field access) and day when access is allowed (game day only, practice only, etc.). It has to usually be visually simple, so that security and staff can easily make a differentiation in a large crowd.

Post 9/11 and given the global nature of sport today, the need for more stringent crackdown on credentials has also become a key factor. Also the volume of outlets getting credentials and what are considered legitimate credentials as the professional level is different in most instances than the collegiate or minor league level, and will take up a good deal of initial time. The politics of credentialing numbers will also factor into the equation, along with figuring out seating arrangements on a game-by-game basis. In many instances, the final seating category can be relatively easy. However, the way credentials are administered is different in each city and for each team. While some teams may grant a good number of website credentials, others may not. International media, the largest growing amount of requests, is usually dictated by the league and then handed down to the teams for seating. Credentials also have to allow pre- and post-game access (both or neither), practice access, photo access, and space as well. The policing of credentials, and potential abuse by members of the media, is also another key component to the process. The language on all credentials is dictated by the leagues respectively, but the actual assigning is at the discretion of the team. The one thing always to remember is that the name and responsibility of the actions for all credentialed does rest with the team PR staff, and it must be taken seriously.

Example

A few years ago, there was a long-standing member of the New York media from a suburban small television service who was caught selling his season credentials from one team on eBay. He would use one credential for himself and then have a guest cameraman come into the locker room with him. That person would be whomever bought the credential. Although many times the cameraman looked legitimate, he was not. The abuse was caught and the person was both arrested and banned by all New York area teams.

Credential notes

1 Always have requests sent on letterhead from the editor or other assignor from the publication.
2 Photo IDs and wavers are a must.
3 No matter what level you are at, everyone is responsible for policing credentials.
4 Make sure whatever league or governing body you are involved with has final say on wording and sign-off.
5 Make sure you have adequate seating to rotate smaller publications, digital media, and groups into availability.
6 Never use the same credential less than three games apart. Never use the same credential look in consecutive seasons.

Game operations

On the professional level, the role of game operations usually does not fall to the public relations staff as it does in the collegiate level. For the most part there is a game operations group, usually overseen by the marketing group, that will handle many of the functions that the SID would handle. The PR staff is usually responsible for the essentials—clock and statistical keeping and the dissemination of information. However, the role of promotions usually goes to a separate group.

Volume of duties in the two roles is the reason for the difference. The amount of media coverage and the media needs take precedent over the regular duties at the professional level. You will be involved in the countdown and coordination of pre-game and in-game activities, but rarely will you be responsible for them. (In our minor league chapter this dynamic will be totally different). The duties of game operations falls to making sure all media are credentialed and seated, information is organized and disseminated, and all media availability is coordinated correctly.

During a game, the PR staff will mainly concentrate on media relations and trouble shooting for potential problems. The leagues also designate many of the on and off limits spots for camera positions, so the coordination of spots again is the principal role. It is extremely busy and demanding, but the great thing about professional leagues is that the duties are pretty clearly defined, and the support is provided to make sure you are able to handle the correct PR ability.

Publications and record keeping

Again, the good news here is that the volume of publications is greatly decreased from the college ranks. In many cases these days even the game programs have fallen away and are under the domain of the marketing staff. For the most part, even website management does not fall to public relations. What does fall is the media guide and the game notes, two very high volume pieces which are essential to team business. There is also a yearbook in many cases, which may also fall under team PR, but the chief function remains the other two.

The professional team media guide

Even though there is much more of a need for digital and e-books, the hard copy of the media guide, with all its information dated the minute the season starts, remains the backbone of team publicity publications. The color covers, color stock photos, and team historical data has changed little in over 25 years. It remains perhaps the biggest cost in the PR budget, albeit one that has decreased with the use of digital versions. The average across sports is roughly $75–100, and coupled with the mailing costs, easily takes up probably between 20–30 percent of most team PR budgets. The average page count in the 5 × 9in standard size is between 300–350 pages, with most teams determining the volume by size of market. For example, while the New York Knicks may order 10,000 copies of their guide for the season, the Sacramento Kings may order 4,000 copies.

The guide is rarely seen as a money maker. It is usually included in season subscriber benefits and is sold in-arena and in-stadium, but less than 10 percent of monies spent are usually made back. The guide is there to do one thing and that's to service the media. It is rarely used as a recruiting tool as it is in college, and its shelf life is limited because of the volume of games and length of a season in most team sports. Some teams with great brand value, like the New York Yankees, may also offer a limited run at bookstores as well.

What it is is a historical record keeper for teams. It houses all points of interest the media may need during the season, as well as player and staff data. It is referred to on a daily basis by media members. It is also distributed on a team-by-team basis to all media in their area. For example, the *Dallas Morning News* and the *Seattle Post Intelligencer* and ESPN all receive full sets of team guides—in many cases in boxes—at the beginning of each professional season. They are used daily by the staff. Beat writers receive their sets usually at home. So any mistakes are kept in those boxes and could be made useful at any time. Accuracy is key.

The value of the notes

Another aspect of team publicity that is grossly undervalued are the notes—game notes, quote sheets, daily updates all have great value to a media throng that continues to grow its thirst for information. The great thing about the professional team side is that the leagues all employ a stats service—the Elias Sports Bureau—to keep almost hourly updated statistical information that is done by the team and the league at the collegiate level. That lifts a great deal of time and effort off the team publicity staff. The effort then goes to discerning what information is needed and what is relevant for the media covering the team on a micro basis.

We have gone over the need for good and accurate notes earlier, but it is important to make sure that timing on the professional level is so key. There are a series of deadlines each league provides for when notes have to be provided for media access. The important thing is to make sure that the earnestness of posting notes does not lead to errors of fact. Again, the chief use for game notes may be at the game itself. However once notes live on the web, if they are inaccurate there is little chance to retrieve.

It is also very important to do your own checking with your media to make sure the information you are giving them is useful and timely, and make sure that what you are spending a great amount of time on makes sense to them. Collecting "best practices" from places also makes sense. Clean, concise and easy to read are key.

The same goes with postgame (and sometimes pre-game) quotes and facts. Keeping in mind the demands of media on deadline and what they need to complete their picture to your fans is key. Always be aware of career highs and lows, records broken, streaks broken and continued, and keep the notes and quotes short and to the point. The need for a transcription is rarely needed post-game—the need for relevant information about the games heroes and goats are most relevant. Also, remember that you are not the reporter in the postgame situation—you are the transcriber providing the service. Make sure that the tape has what he/she said exactly. It will greatly help avoiding controversy and the misquote by athletes and coaches.

Coordinating with others—balancing the business side and the "team sport" side

Although the balance of the team public relations function still resides with what goes on in and around the playing of games, there are still a number of elements regardless of what position you are on the staff that you need to always be aware of.

Cost justification and budget

If you are a department head, always be aware of what costs are. The biggest issue with public relations is usually it is very hard to track actual return on investment, which is becoming more and more of an issue as time moves along. Even with franchises that spend several million dollars in the business of PR, the actual number will be small considering the team operating budget. That being said, it is still very important to still look at needs vs. expenses on the little things that you may hit.

Here are some examples:

- Getting and making dubs vs. requesting from a service. In this day and age, most people have access to any number of recording devices for recording team publicity events. In many cases, the quality of those dubs are near to what you may get from a video monitoring service any way. *Always* ask for a dub or file from the TV entity you are working with regardless for your records.
- Don't order things such as still photos or high-end video stock for dubbing unless you really need it for a specific purpose. In many cases the volume you can buy at a Costco or Best Buy is just as good as what you can get from a distributor.
- A huge part of budget in many places comes from the overnight shipping industry. If you can use less expensive overnight costs, especially just going across town, then do it. Try and lower those numbers every year and make sure folks realize the effort made.
- Try and think like a finance department in advance. Always justify game night staff size, photo costs, and printing costs ahead of time. The last thing someone wants is that "this is the way it is always done." In this environment, that will not always work.
- If there is a high-end cost that is unbudgeted, don't hide it, explain and justify it.

- The budgeting process must be inclusive of the entire staff. The department head will be responsible, but like the PR project or game night event, everyone should be aware of costs before the fact. Buy-in is the key.
- Lastly, don't be cheap, but be professional. Spend wisely and review periodically. It will help you be a better-rounded person and get more respect from other members of the organization.

Understanding the business and marketing side

Because of the amount of time that is spend with team business, many times the PR group can suffer from a lack of awareness or aloofness with regard to the team business side. This was acceptable for a very long time, largely because of the time and distance that sometimes existed to get the job done. With the advent of cell phones and email, that distance is now shrunk, and the communication between the two sides sometimes falls to the PR group.

Especially in the offseason and in down time, taking the opportunity to meet and discuss other areas of team business, as well as giving input, will be a huge help in uniting these sometimes divergent groups. PR in many cases needs to be the advocate and the link to players and coaches from the front office—you have the opportunity to work both sides of the road without getting run over. It is a very rare opportunity but one that is to be taken as a challenge to improve the overall culture. Many times folks on the business side will feel isolated from daily team goings-on. Making sure that they are "in the loop" is a huge help.

Some small thoughts on unity:

- Use email as an ally to make sure that everyone in the front office is aware of team activity. If there are press releases, media events, special circumstances make sure that you are mentioning that everyone should be aware. The worst thing that a person in a team setting can feel is left out.
- Schedule time to talk to staff members not regularly around the team about team comings and goings and get their opinion on things—this is not to be a gossip or get "scoop" on players and coaches. It is to make sure that folks understand issues that you may be able to clear up.
- The easiest way to communicate clear information to everyone in the organization is through a monthly fact sheet. Simple data about the past, present, and future of the team provided by the PR staff can literally keep everyone "on the same page" and feel included.
- If things go wrong or there is a miscommunication that results in an issue with the players or a coach through another department, find ways to help fix the problem. It is very easy to pile on to a problem. It is harder to lift someone up when they are down.
- Conversely, when things go right with an event involving other parts of the staff, if you have the opportunity to mention something to a player

or coach about someone they may not know well, then do so. Make sure credit is given where it is due.

Conclusion

The team publicist at the professional level has to serve an ever-growing number of masters, perhaps more so than any area of sports publicity. He or she has to be able to make sure that the quality control of information released is fair, accurate, and consistent. He or she must make sure that the business side and the "sports" side are getting a fair return on their investment in his or her product. At the same time the publicist and staff must find new and unique ways to try and placate a 24/7 news cycle that is fair and still maintains the integrity of the organization at every turn.

All the while those goals must be achieved on a very tight budget and with limited staff. The cycle of work also has gone from "seasonal" to year-round, with very little downtime, making it ever more challenging as sports and entertainment grow into one.

7

WORKING WITH AN INDIVIDUAL SPORT AND ATHLETE

There's no "I" in team, but there is a "ME"

This chapter will take a look at what can be labeled a subset of the sports publicity field, but a very important and lucrative one. So far the team concept on both the professional and collegiate level in terms of publicity has been addressed. The next topic addressed will be dealing with the individual sport athlete, as well as looking at the individual sport circuits and the challenges and opportunities they each present for publicity.

The traditional individual sport disciplines—golf, tennis, auto racing, bowling, athletics, gymnastics, boxing (now mixed martial arts)—are still alive and well, both nationally and globally, and are thriving in most cases. However, the recent explosion of extreme sports, competitive gaming, Olympic sports, and even poker has made this area a potential growth area for sports publicists.

Whereas before there were usually opportunities for publicity only for a limited few, the opportunity to create publicity and deal with athletes in both major individual and in niche sports exists more than ever before. The faces that were identifiable to the general public in the past were the small group in individual sports. Tennis had John McEnroe, Jimmy Connors, Billie Jean King, Chris Evert, and Martina Navratilova. Golf always had its big names on top like a Nicklaus or a Palmer, and the other mainstream individual sports surfaced more in Olympic years. Now the growth of social and digital media, digital cable, and new lifestyle publications designed for niche sports, not to mention the video game boom, have developed a much broader area of exposure for athletes like Tony Hawk in skateboarding, Georges St-Pierre in mixed martial arts, Shaun White in the X Games, Usain Bolt in athletics, and Michael Phelps in swimming, just to name a few. They have their own websites and manage large-scale media opportunities, their own demographic that follows them, their own sponsors, and their own niche media. Local businesses are seeing these individuals as low cost, moderate to high impact to showcase their logos and products on a wider scale, and using publicity as the vehicle to do that with their investment.

Now there are some similarities. The involvement of agents in making media decisions, the team concept in sports like racing (where the individuals train together but there are clearly individual, as in auto racing and cycling), does play into the mix. For the large part these athletes are self-contained, almost individual contractors who are responsible for many of their own expenses, entry costs, and travel with the exception of the high elite ones. Many also fund their own coaches or are subsidized in some ways by national governing bodies, so the distractions and the duties are often more complex than a team sport participant.

The other difference in many ways is in their individual sport athlete's mental approach to things. Because in many cases the prize money and sponsor dollars are basically thrown out there for the best to get from week to week, many times they are more singularly focused than the team athlete. The nature of the individual sport is also more like the traveling circus. Because there is really no home, the tour or league moves from city to city around the world or the country recreating itself each time. Therefore, the opportunities for local fans to see, embrace, and identify with a number of individual sport athletes is very limited. Of course there will be breakthroughs: Michael Schumacher, Jeff Gordon, Roger Federer, Chuck Lidell, Venus Williams, or Tiger Woods. That is the beauty of the champion.

The advent of the internet, digital TV, webcasting, and satellite radio has greatly assisted in recent years in finding ways for the casual fan to connect to their individual favorite athlete more regularly. However, the ability to effectively promote the individual athlete on a consistent basis still represents its very unique challenges, and challenges which sometimes present the perception that the individual athlete is even less accessible than the team athlete. However, they are challenges which can be overcome with good planning, clear communication, and the ability to use and pool all PR assets to make a strong presentation. Some of the challenges are as follows.

Agents and sponsors usually rule the roost. Unlike team sports, where there is a general manager or league or union presence to control or assist in times of issue, the individual athlete is ruled by individuals. For most top-tier athletes—those who would compete on professional golf and tennis, bowling and track and field tours, those who race open wheel, NASCAR and the Formula 1 circuits—the be all and end all decision makers are twofold: the agent, who has the ability to negotiate fees, playing sports and sponsor dollars; and the chief sponsors themselves, who generate the interest and in many cases the prize money for the events. These two groups have to always be factored into the PR plan. It also has to be remembered that agents are not publicists. In most cases they do not want their behind-the-scenes work to be exposed in the public as it can hinder future negotiations. The most successful groups, such as IMG, and Octagon or William Morris, Wasserman Media, and Creative Artists (CAA) also deal in volume of clients. Their focus is on the sponsorship deals which bring in the money for their clients. Publicity is a secondary factor and for the most part these agencies do not assist their clients with publicity efforts.

The field of expertise for the agent is in the negotiation. Most are lawyers or accountants or both, and that makes the most sense since the biggest part of their job is negotiation. For the most part, that does not change with smaller firms that have individual sport athletes. Although many times the goal of these up-and-comers is to get publicity and build a name for themselves, they are not publicity professionals either. Building relationships with these groups and making them a part of the process while understanding what everyone's job is to do is tantamount to success.

Example

Octagon manages a great deal of individual sport athletes, many of whom are stars like snowboarder Ross Powers, as well as household names like Jimmie Johnson. Following Powers' gold medal in the 2002 Olympics, they brought him to New York to do media and get him exposure amongst sponsors. The snowboard federation, his personal publicist, and the Octagon publicity team was able to work with the New York Knicks, whose publicity team they had a long-standing relationship with, to bring Powers to a highly visible Knicks charity event and get him front row at a game, which generated a huge amount of publicity in the mainstream for him. This would not have happened if you did not have the agent buy-in and be able to build consensus or value as a publicity expert. The agent would have looked just for a sponsor dollar or a sponsor commitment with little value being seen in the building of publicity.

Travel time and practice time are high and fickle, media time is expendable. Because most individual sport athletes (with the exception of auto racing in the US) travel the way we do, commercially, they are beholden to the same weather and travel delays we are. They also have to deal with hotels, unpredictable transportation to events, and practice times that have to be fairly routine. Therefore the last consideration that sometimes goes into planning is media time during an event. Flexibility here is always key when dealing with an individual sport athlete.

Example

The media day for a certain professional golf event is usually scheduled for a Tuesday. However, two young up-and-comers playing in a tournament the following weekend are delayed a day because that tournament's weather pushed the final round until Monday. The young female golfer also did not fare that well, and her coach wanted her to try the new course on a Tuesday morning after an all-night flight. Since the golf promoters need the golfer to do well that weekend and make the cut to provide bigger attendance and television numbers, the events that are sacrificed or have to be rescheduled are the Tuesday media events.

When they are gone, they are usually gone. One of the biggest issues for the individual sport publicist is media just prior or during an event. Pull-outs and early exits are the bane of existence for the individual sport event publicist. Therefore, the more advance publicity one gets done (conference calls, phone interviews, satellite media tours, web chats) the better for the promoter and the less risk for the publicist.

Example

In 2005, American Express built all of its advertising and publicity campaigns for the US Open around American star Andy Roddick. Roddick's "mojo" was featured around the city and nationally in an advertising campaign. There were also numerous publicity opportunities built around an off day early in the two-week tournament. However, Roddick lost in an early round and with no doubles play to keep him in New York, he was free to leave. Hence, the long-term publicity and marketing opportunities were now gone. With team sports, an athlete is there for the rest of the game, the rest of the series the rest of the season. Once an individual loses or doesn't qualify or misses the cut or is injured, he or she is usually off to the next stop. A side note to this was that Roddick was able to make good on some of the opportunities and Amex did cut a funny commercial for use after he did lose, which helped save some of the opportunities. This is however the exception and not the rule to when athletes lose early.

Yes, they are gifted, but yes, that makes them different. The high-level individual athletes are the most gifted in any sport, just like a concert violinist is the most gifted at his trade or the Oscar-winning actor is the best at what he does. They are champions in an individual way. It is them against the world and the other athletes each and every week. This makes for a very focused, and sometimes lonely and tunnel vision approach to everything else around them. The camaraderie that is shared amongst team sport athletes is rarely there in individual sports. There is respect and downtime fun, but each week is survival of the fittest. Therefore, many times a publicist is left without the support or peer pressure to get things done with the media that comes with team sports. Being firm, direct, and professional will sometimes work, but without that backup it is not as strong as in team sports.

Example

Competitive eating may not be first on the sports fan's mind, but it is quite a promotable spectacle, especially when you have a unique individual like Takeru Kobayashi, arguably the world's most eclectic competitive eater. Philadelphia's annual Wing Bowl has grown into an entertainment event that rivals any niche promotion anywhere. In 2011, the event drew 20,000 followers and saw Kobayashi break the world record for wing eating in front of a crowd made up of radio promotional guests, competitive eating fans, and a porn star or two just for flavor. The event now garners international coverage with stars like Kobayashi, the king of competitive eating, and also has a great give-back element with food and dollars raised to feed the homeless of Philadelphia. A great tent pole event for Sports Radio WIP in Philly to kick off Super Bowl weekend. However for "Kobi" as he is known, it was a great opportunity to sit down with writers away from the competition to talk about healthy living, training, and his "taste" for the finer things in life. A different story, but a great way to position the athlete as a personality.

Things can get lost in translation. Many individual sports are also more global than team sports. Events that are taken for granted in the US in media and publicity situations are different in other parts of the world. This is especially true in women's sports, where in many cases chauvinistic attitudes still run rampant with the media that would not be tolerated in North America. Also there needs to be the respect of customs and language barriers, and even in some cases, the ability to adapt and understand the cultural clashes between officials and two athletes competing against each other (Israelis and Muslims in track and field, Serbs and Croats in tennis, for example). All these things have to be taken into account when dealing with publicity and the media by the publicist. Avoiding being the ugly American here is also key in international competition. The respect of a language barrier, and the planning of something like an interpreter, will go a long way.

Example

At the US Open a young Korean by the name of Lee Hyung-Taik unexpectedly made it to the fourth round to take on Pete Sampras. Because Lee was not expected to make it that far and because he was the only Korean in the field, little was known about him and he could not communicate well since he did not speak English. Things about his training regimen, his upbringing, his family were all stereotyped by the American press. It was not until the USTA staff was able to secure a translator from the neighboring Korean community that his full and accurate story was able to be conveyed. This differs from team sports, where in today's multicultural world if a team has a non-English speaking player, no matter where he is on the roster, there will be a translator readily available and all the background on the player will be firmly established.

Different places, different access rules. Also in the cultural realm that falls into the publicist and media issues can be the difference in media access space and time per event and per sport.

Example

The locker rooms at the US Open are open to the media. This is not the case at Wimbledon or the French Open, where media have to get timed passes to allow access to player areas. In golf, the clubhouse, TV, and fairway access for the PGA Championship is drastically different from the Masters. Each site has to be evaluated and the publicist knows the rules to make sure they are clearly explained to both media and athlete.

Every week is an education. Because of the traveling nature of individual sports, each week the publicist has to deal with new media, sponsors, and promoters who may not be accustomed or familiar with what went on last year or last week at an event. Therefore, refamiliarizing all the rules on a weekly basis is very important.

Examples

The Harlem Globetrotters may be seen as a "team," but they have unique stories that have to be constantly retold in every market every year. People won't really come to see competitive basketball; they will come to see the fun event and learn more about these unique showmen. Therefore it is essential to create buzz with local entertainment writers and media, as well as sport, each time the Globies hit the road. What's new and noteworthy with the team this year? In 2012 the troupe went big and small, bringing in 7' 8" "Tiny" Sturgess and 5' 2" Jante "Too Tall" Hall to round out their squad, and then exploited the matchup with a series of viral videos in advance of their tour. Repeated week after week, the media covered each market like new.

The PBA Tour will move from city to city every week. Since there is not the constant, consistent year-round media coverage in local markets, the local media have to be re-educated every stop on what player is a good story, what the trends are in the sport, and how the sport is being run this year. Advancing the tour—going into the city a few days early as the publicist to set things up—is one of the biggest roles the publicist has. This differs from the team situation, where consistent regular mainstream sports media coverage makes this not as necessary.

Remember who you work for. This can be a very good question, because in an individual sport you can be working for a sponsor, a league governing body, a local promoter, a media entity, or in some cases for the athlete him or herself. Like we have said in team sports, it is important to remember the asset that you are working with consistently, and figure out the best way to problem solve, act professionally, and find ways to get publicity for the person or group you represent.

Example

Using an athlete endorsement to leverage brand building when not a sponsor. Skechers launched a new running shoe "Go Run" during the fall of 2011 and had signed 2009 NYC Champion and Olympic Medalist Meb Keflezghi. The Leverage Agency worked with Skechers to maximize its presence producing a television show called "Go Meb Go Run Go NY." This documentary showed Meb's preparation leading up to the marathon and was broadcast the week of the marathon on SNY television and in taxi cab TVs as all the runners were driven around the City. Skechers also bought hundreds of bus stop "Go Meb Go Run" signs placed throughout the marathon route. In addition, they organized a press conference/ lunch directly after the NYC Marathon official press event for Meb and Skechers, and appeared on the Friday edition of Fox and Friends challenging the hosts to run past Meb and wear his new Go Run shoes.

Although Asics was the official shoe sponsor of the NYC Marathon, Skechers used its endorsement with Meb Keflezghi to steal some of the spotlight for its new "Go Run" shoe. The agency worked a great deal for their client around what the marathon could have done.

With those points as the base, you can now look to ways to create exposure points for individual sport athletes with the media that can be interesting, creative, and satisfy the needs of all involved. Here are some ways to do that.

Be a consensus builder. The individual sport has many cooks, as we have discussed. Your best bet to get publicity success is to pool resources, manage schedules, and over-communicate. You need to know the key people for the athlete, what that person is trying to accomplish with the athlete that week, and then develop the plan from that. Does the event sponsor want a charity photo taken? If so, how can you best use that photo to service a broad range of media? Does the agent have a special request from a sponsor for media that week? If so, then how can you use that for a note to get interest in off-sports publicity? Is his or her apparel company developing or unveiling a new outfit or piece of equipment? If so, find a way to work that in with the media. It is not easy or foolproof, but it will save you time and repetition, and help make you a hero with many of the people who have the athletes' touch points in their control.

This is different from the team publicity model because many times in team sports you have consistency from the league or even the team with regard to apparel company, charity affiliation, or sponsor that you may be working for. If you think of each athlete as his or her own team, in a tennis event you could potentially have 56 different groups to work with if the tournament has 56 players. Also, you may be working with a children's charity for the entire field one week, and the next week the charity of choice may be breast cancer. Building a framework of time and then plugging specifics into each event or each athlete is the best way to go. All of that will come by pooling the interests of each person involved.

Advance publicity and coordination is key. Many times we have to remember that these events that use individual athletes need almost as much publicity to drive attention, sponsor, and ticket sales in advance of the event as they need during the event itself. Therefore, creating a two to three month event calendar, knowing athlete schedules, windows, and ways to have events work together to garner publicity is another key element. It also gives the local fan a chance to understand and get close to athletes that they may not have the chance to during the event sequence.

Example

On the NASCAR circuit one of the most popular stops is Richmond, Virginia, the site of two Bush series (slightly lower level) and two NEXTEL Cup races (the top level of racing) each year. The place on the calendar makes this spot very desirable for sponsors and local media. Richmond is a hotbed of racing. However, each year the Richmond raceway PR team has to find strategic ways well in advance of the race to create media opportunities to drive interest in the drivers, the track, and the sponsors. One way they do that very effectively is to look to larger demographics like Washington, D.C. to create media events with drivers there. This is actually outside of their core market but it is a key area of development and media and sponsorship exposure for the sport. So the Richmond group will create media events a few months prior to the race in that area, hoping to broaden the focus of media and fans coming to the race. At the same time, there is a large track in Dover, Delaware, which also hosts races at different strategic times. The two tracks have to work together not to cannibalize media opportunities and let fans and sponsors know that the NASCAR brand is hot on several weeks. Therefore they will work together to find ways to promote the sport overall and their races specifically, without detracting from the other.

It is a traveling circus, so why not repeat the show? The bad thing about individual sports is that it is a traveling circus, packing up in one town and moving to the next almost weekly. The good thing is that it gives the publicist in many cases the ability to repeat effective media events and best practices in different towns that a "home" team's fans would find repetitive. It gives you the ability to effectively manage time and create a best practice that can not only be recreated weekly, but yearly upon return.

Example

The WTA Tour on the women's side of tennis and the ATP Tour on the men's side of tennis have created the FIRST Serve and ACES programs, respectively. These programs essentially work with tournaments to create programs that promote the tournaments, the athletes, and the sponsors from city to city, week to week, throughout the year. Many times the program is cookie-cutter and can virtually be repeated in every city since that media will view it as new. There is usually a charity component, a player human interest component, etc. It can even be the same player or story from city to city. The programs are great ways to centralize and promote tennis.

This is different from the team publicity model because it is virtually impossible to tell the same story with an athlete more than once in the same season. Usually team media will do a story, especially about an athlete, as a pack and then move on. Many times the notoriety of the sport on the team professional level will also have the story transfer from city to city as well. The daily coverage of team sports makes this type of repeat showing more difficult.

Know the media who cover the sport as well as the local media who help the event. This is also another juggling act, managing the time of the "circuit" media with athletes as opposed to the local media who are with the sport and the athlete for just a week or for a month. Each one has to be treated with respect and given fair and as equal treatment as possible, because they both have great value to the athlete and the constituencies involved. However, for the athlete this sometimes leads to a great about of naïveté amongst the local media, and a great deal of repetition of questions from event to event. This must always be clearly spelled out to the athletes before media interaction and is key in developing positive publicity. The local media will have long and lasting memories of their interaction with these athletes, which will affect media coverage for local events on a yearly basis. The "circuit" media will also be aware of the need for the locals, and will also look for extra time as they travel. Similar to the local beat writers in team situations, they should be given those little extras with your key athletes as time allows, or if they go to an event where media coverage is lighter.

Go to the video. Unlike in team sports where you have a home broadcaster, the amount of available weekly event footage can be limited or the quality may not be best. Therefore it is very important in your advance to make sure publicity events that are recorded can be kept as a rolling archive for use later on in the circuit. It will save you a great amount of time with both the athlete and with the media if you are able to provide advance video portraying the athlete in a positive light. It will also give you the ability to somewhat control an interview situation for the local media by providing them with more "canned" footage, freeing up their time to concentrate on the event at hand.

You must remember the sponsors and remind the athlete. Even more so than team sports, individual sports are carried by the lifeblood of sponsor dollars from week to week. The local sponsor can also vary from event to event, so it is key as a publicist to be cognicent of changes in both the athlete sponsor stable and the event sponsor stable and find ways to make sure that recognition is prioritized and communicated through the media. This can be in the form of making sure patches and hats are worn, names are worked into interviews, and backdrops are properly used.

Example

In sports like tennis and golf, the champion usually speaks right after the final match or round. The publicist will usually take the time to review a thank you list with the athlete usually seconds before he or she is to speak. The greatest sport in getting this process done is NASCAR. The prominent patch and apparel system, the elaborate backdrops, and the buy-in by drivers in acknowledging sponsors is the biggest reason for the growth of the sport in recent years.

This is different from the team publicity model because sponsor visibility and recognition is rarely seen in the US in team sports. The ability to keep uniforms clean of sponsor logos is much different than in other parts of the world on the team level, and with that clean look comes the cache that most team athletes do not use that acknowledgement. Logos will appear on backdrops for postgame interviews, and occasionally a logoed hat may show up as part of a sponsorship deal, but usually the sponsor recognition is missing in the team sports world.

Now this is steadily changing, as MLS and the WNBA introduce logos onto team uniforms, and all major sports except baseball allow some small signage on practice jerseys. However, the role of signage in team sports is still relatively pristine as we went through 2012.

Create the hometown hero. One of the great things about the individual sport athlete is that their success *just* to make it to the professional ranks will resonate very strongly in their place of origin. Ross Powers may not have had to have been an Olympic Gold Medalist to be important to his people from where he was from (Portland, Maine). The same would hold true for Georges St-Pierre in MMA, or Henry Cejudo in wrestling. What is in your favor as a publicist in this case is that they are professionals, people are interested in them in their region with their story to tell, and sometimes the lack of available regular news because of the traveling nature of individual sports creates an opening for you to get publicity through. The growth of internet opportunities, websites, blogs, and the interest in local business partners and sponsors to get involved and help use PR as a strong vehicle to help local athletes tell their story is a tool that has not existed in previous years, but can give you a leg up with individual athlete publicity opportunities.

A look at the difference in publicity on the individual sport "circuits"

We will now take a look at the individual sport professional governing bodies, and how they differ from team sports governing, especially in the US. Their structure from a publicity side can help create opportunities for the individual publicist, as well as needing publicity help for the governing body. This should help give you a better picture as to structure and opportunity with individual sports publicity.

The challenges with the circuit publicity

The challenges really revolve around an element touched on earlier for the individual sport publicist: consensus building. As a publicist for an individual sport circuit, you need to have your hand on every element of the sport from the grassroots efforts to the athletic results, and then be able to work with all those other elements that will make the sport itself successful. That will include things like television ratings, attendance from week to week, player rankings and success, player development, and even rule changes in the sport. It is close to what we will discuss about league publicity offices in coming chapters.

The difference between individual sport circuits and team sports leagues

It is the same challenge that you have working with individual athletes. It is not a set consortium of bodies all working as one. Circuits are made up of individual events and the athletes are basically independent contractors to those events. It is the circuit to try and pull everyone in the same direction and for the publicist to come up with common themes. It is much easier to do it on the team sport level because there is much more solid structure. All the teams play in the same league, and all the players are in the same union. The free agency side of the circuit makes it more unwieldy for the publicist.

Action sports

After years of fragmentation, many of the action sports genres have folded into the Dew Tour, both summer and winter, which showcase the phenomenal athletic prowess and personalities of everything from snowboarding to Motocross and BMX from city to city around the world.

The events have global sponsorship and activation programs and are usually tied to week-long festivals that include social media events, music, and other participatory projects that involve both fans and sponsors. The pinnacle of success for many action sports are the X Games and, in many categories, the Olympic games as well.

However, for week-by-week activation, the Dew Tour pulls in names and brands and fans like no other in the genre.

The biggest challenges remain mainstream consistent media coverage and the education of an older public in what the games are, what the levels of skill are, and who the stars are. A personality like Shaun White has achieved mainstream success well beyond competition, but many stars remain solidly popular with their followers but not outside their core group, although that core group can number in the millions. It is that core group which has to be engaged via a solid communications messaging platform, while at the same time educating the local media on the circuit with what is new and interesting for the casual follower.

Tennis

On the professional side, the sport is aligned in men's tennis (Association of Tennis Professionals/ATP) and women's tennis (WTA). Each is headquartered in Florida, with offices around the globe. For the most part the tournaments are operated as individual franchises on set levels designated by amount of prize money and tournament field. The top events, which include the four Grand Slam events (Australian, French and US Opens, plus Wimbledon), will draw the largest fields and have the biggest prize money, hence garnering the most publicity opportunities. That being said, each event, from Dubai to Memphis, will have its own press person in addition to the tour staff. On average, each of the two tours has a press staff of approximately 10 that work in conjunction with the event PR staff to coordinate opportunities for the players both in advance and during the tournament week (each tournament usually lasts seven days for the main draw, from Monday through Sunday. The four Grand Slams and two other US events, Indian Wells, California and Key Biscayne, Florida, are also multi-week events). The great thing about the two tennis tours is that each has created a program specifically designed to make sure publicity opportunities are done by all players in the main draw (the tournament playing field). The programs designate a minimum number of hours that each player must do leading up to and during the week in order to fulfill media and sponsor requirements. Those requirements are usually requested by the tournament officials and determined in order of significance by the PR staffs. There are also numerous opportunities by working with agents, sponsors, and federations to use "Economies of Scale" to produce effective results.

Also in tennis in the United States, the United States Tennis Association (USTA) is responsible for the growth of the recreational and in many ways, the professional side of the game. They have their own PR team, based in New York, which handles publicity for the US Open and other events, assists the American tournaments, runs the lower-level professional "circuit" in the United States (akin to minor league baseball), and handles the two team elements of tennis, Davis Cup for the men and Fed Cup for the women on an annual basis. The USTA's goal is to grow the sport in many ways, both on the recreational and professional side, and therefore it invests a great deal of time in effective publicity practices and opportunities. On the pro side that can mean assisting the two tours with player promotions, or creating events as publicity vehicles when there are events in the United States.

Most countries have similar federation assistance, and will help subsidize both grassroots and professional play. The Lawn Tennis Association in England, Tennis Canada, Tennis Australia, and the French Tennis Federation are the four largest outside the United States, and all have similar missions.

Golf

Like tennis, golf also maintains similar tours for men and women, the Professional Golfers Association (PGA) and the Ladies Professional Golfers Association (LPGA). Both are also headquartered in Florida. However, one of the biggest differences in the tours is that they are largely American based in terms of events and governance. They have offshoots that run worldwide events, but for the most part the sport of golf on the professional level (with all majors but the British Open held in the United States) is an American entity.

There are also other similarities on the pro level for publicity. The two tours work with local promoters, sponsors, and agents to garner local publicity, create national campaigns for athletes, and grow the game of golf. The difference is that the women's side of late has taken on a much stronger, more aggressive, and more non-traditional way of exposing their players' personalities than the men has had to. It is very similar to the tennis model: show your brand off in non-traditional places with aggressive lifestyle campaigns, designed to grow the image of the tour and its golfers while not sacrificing its athleticism. The results have been strong, with women's golf interest rising and name recognition of players in the mainstream media gaining ground.

The difference on the PGA side is the strength of the brand and the way many of the top golfers have a strong hold in name recognition amongst the American public. The Tiger Woods phenomenon speaks for itself in the way the world has taken to his telegenic personality, but the name recognition and the ability to promote other names as brands...from classics like Arnold Palmer and Jack Nicklaus to current stars like Phil Mickelson...is also very valuable.

Another big difference is with the national governing body of the sport, the USGA. Unlike the USTA, the USGA does not have any great investment in the professional game. As Director of Communications Pete Kowalski said in May 2007, "The USGA is what you see when you go to the golf course. We touch everything for the player, from the club regulations to the height of the grass. That is our principal focus." The USGA runs 13 events a year, 10 of which are amateur championships. Of the three that are not amateurs, the US men's and women's Opens, and the senior men's Open, that is where the only link with the pro game exists. The USGA staffs the publicity and marketing side of the US Open for the men, handling it in the same way the normal PGA publicity staff would. They run the press facility, deal with players and agents and their TV partner, NBC, to make sure the event is well exposed and that the access is granted. They also handle all credentialing for the event. Similarly for the women and the seniors, the USGA has a strong presence, but it does farm out some of the other aspects of running the event to event companies. The PGA Tour does have a small public relations presence at the US Open, but not to the extent they do at other PGA Tour events.

The other group that handles year-round publicity for golf on the men's side is the PGA of America. This is the group that handles everything for club professional golfers, not those on the pro tour. The PGA of America handles all the publicity efforts for the PGA Championships at Sawgrass each year, much in the same way the USGA runs the US Open. There is a presence of the PGA Tour at the event, but it is run by the publicity team for the PGA of America. Other than that one event, the PGA of America handles all aspects of publicity and information for those pro club golfers.

Also, like tennis, the PGA Tour handles publicity for it's up-and-comers through the Nationwide Tour, a series of events that gives young professionals the chance to qualify for the PGA Tour. There are similar local, grassroots publicity opportunities at these events, which also provide the publicist and the media with an opportunity to deal with rising stars, their agents, and new business partners at a very early level.

Auto racing

There are three big groups here with several layers for this fast paced, single person sport. Keep in mind the biggest difference for publicity in this individual sport as opposed to tennis, golf, or bowling is that the individuals are grouped by teams for ownership and sponsorship purposes. However, when racing the scoring and results are done by the individual. The team, per se, is the collector of data, sponsorship dollars, and technology for a set group of drivers and ultimately controls the biggest need for the publicist: access to the drivers calendar. The team, in most levels—NASCAR, open wheel, and Formula 1—has to balance the schedule for the driver amongst the various levels of sponsorship and media that he or she is needed for, usually depending more on sponsor dollar than on media opportunity. However, much of that is changing as racing again continues to emerge back into the forefront of the overall American psyche, much the way Indy Car racing was for a good part of the 1970s and early 1980s.

Like in tennis and golf however, there are differences in the way publicity is handled at each of the three major racing circuits: NASCAR, open wheel or Indy car, and Formula 1. Here is a look at each.

In NASCAR, which has become the fastest-growing sport in this country over the past ten years, the team controls the racers' time, especially with media. They will get input from various entities about opportunities. That includes the track needs during and prior to a race week, national NASCAR sponsors, the needs for television and also the interest in non-traditional media, and then plot out the schedule. Unlike in tennis or golf where the governing body has a decent amount of say in media opportunities, the ultimate decision here is left to the team, coordinating with the driver and his/her agent. In many cases, the pecking order goes from week to week, with the major driver sponsor getting the lion's share of the availability. If he or she is successful during a race week, especially a major race such as Daytona, then the governing body and the track will have a say in post-race media availability. Otherwise the publicists for various entities are left to work with the team to schedule out the time needed as the races approach, or if there is downtime. That's great thing about NASCAR. The key to its success on the publicity level is the understanding of the drivers and the teams to portray a very positive and accessible attitude to sponsors, fans, and the media. As the sport has grown, the opportunities for new publicity have increased exponentially. Therefore, managing that time is now the biggest challenge for the publicists involved.

In Indy car racing the stance is a little different. Because Indy car is still trying to grow back to where it once was on the national spotlight and there have been colossal financial failures with the sport in recent years, the governing body and the races will take a more hands-on and aggressive stance with media opportunities. Jeff Gordon or Tony Stewart are now prominent names not just in racing but in most American households, because of their exposure through NASCAR. Indy Car racing has struggled to achieve that cross-exposure PR in recent years. The basic formula is the same. Be as accessible as possible to fans, media, and sponsors and create opportunities to distinguish your drivers above other athletes available in the category. That has led in recent years to Indy car taking an approach to market the personalities of its drivers much more as a lifestyle brand. For Indy Car publicists there are growing opportunities using a hybrid of what golf and tennis has done well and incorporating the NASCAR element into it. The question is always timing and exposure and finding the right mix.

Formula 1 is arguably the most lucrative, yet unknown in the United States sports circuit in the world. Its drivers are some of the highest paid and most popular athletes around the world, in a circuit that runs in Europe, South

America, and the Far East. The chances at success in this country have been very limited and the interest in growing Formula 1 in this country has also been slow to take hold, much in the way America has not grasped the passion of soccer that the rest of the world has. For the publicist, the opportunities with Formula 1 drivers is perhaps the most stringent in sports. The drivers and their teams have all say on availability, with the Formula 1 governing body serving primarily as the licensee and rules governor for the sport. Herein lies a very simple, very strong, and sometimes, journalists feel, very un-American idea in granting access and media coverage literally paying for the time. Because of schedules, teams will literally carve out paid minutes during a race week for drivers to be accessible. This includes all sponsor time and media time away from the race. Therefore, any opportunities have to be fit in that agreed-to window and usually cannot go over it. It is perhaps the most business-like approach for publicity of all the racing disciplines, and has worked well to make drivers like Michael Schumaker into worldwide media and sports icons. However, the idea of such regimented access does not bode well for the publicist looking for growth opportunities. Formula 1, although lucrative and very solid in most of the world, is probably the most difficult medium for publicity for the rising publicity star.

Bowling

The PBA, the professional bowlers tour for men, was founded in 1958 and has taken many forms over the years as these individual athletes compete for prize money and points on a weekly basis. The tour became a single entity ownership in the early 1990s and is still trying to reachieve its glory days of the 1970s when ABC televised events each Saturday afternoon and made bowlers like Earl Anthony, Dick Webber, and Johnny Petraglia household names. Like other individual sports, the new appeal of bowling is its personalities. The tour recently also had the ability to take advantage of the other crossover sports and had a woman reach the qualifying level for its events, Kelly Kulick. This will once again enable a publicist to have even more opportunity for local and national opportunities, much in the way Michelle Wie has done for golf and Danica Patrick has for open wheel racing and now NASCAR.

The PBA events for publicity are structured similarly to tennis and golf events—the traveling circus mentality. Each local event has its sponsors and bowlers, while the PBA itself provides overall national and regional support for the PBA, the regional PBA qualifiers, and the Senior PBA Tour. Sponsor support is also similar to tennis and golf, as the tour has its umbrella title sponsor (Denny's) and its regional title sponsors in addition to all the local sponsorship dollars each bowler can bring in.

Cycling

Although mostly a European sport at this stage, the ability to garner publicity for cyclists on their American and Olympic qualifying runs in this country are out there for the right publicist. Like other individual sports, and in many ways similar to road racing, cyclists do work in teams for sponsorship and training opportunities. The most successful opportunities were obviously garnered by Lance Armstrong when he raced under the United States Postal Service team during most of his runs to Tour de France titles. However, for other lesser-known cyclists, the ability to get publicity through charitable ties and regional publications, as well as the hometown route, still exists.

Like in road racing, many of the opportunities for publicity will come through the team sponsor, since the team will control access around training times. However, the amount of time and the availability of time given the less than crowded media environment around cycling (with the exception of the Tour de France of course) gives publicists in this sport more leeway than in other individual sports run by a circuit or tour.

The Ultimate Fighting Championship

There is arguably no more global "circuit" that has grown more since 2000 than the Ultimate Fighting Championship (UFC). While some may still feel the sport is too bloody or unwieldy, its popularity as a brand cannot be questioned. Engineered by its leader, Dana White, with a cadre of athletic and diverse personalities, and appealing to a very strong male demo, the UFC is known from continent to continent and is well respected as a sports and entertainment event wherever it is staged. Its appeal as a circuit revolves around the globe trotting White and his marketing staff, who constantly travel to tell the story of these young men and their stories, from wine connoisseurs to military vets to Olympians. Using social media, digital television, and free cable to drive their pay per view and commercial broadcasts, the UFC re-tells their tale every week, many times to an audience that has not seen the story since the last time the event was in their geographic area.

The challenges of the UFC, unlike other circuits, are the limited availability of athletes to compete on a weekly basis. Rest, recovery, and medical limitations keep the best fighters at two or three events maximum a year, so the circuit is sold by the event and the excitement as much as on the actual fighters themselves. It becomes a happening when the UFC comes to town, no matter who competes, and when there is a big name star in town—from longtime names like Randy Couture and Chuck Liddell, to Rashard Evans or Georges St.-Pierre—the event gets an even bigger pop.

It should also be noted that there are other secondary mixed martial arts circuits, the biggest of which is now the Bellator Championships, which also follow the UFC spectacle model. However for global scope, media attention and marketability, nothing can come close to the UFC for a weekly amount of buzz wherever the show is that week.

Poker

While some may still not see games of chance as a sport, the draw of a poker tour for media coverage, technology, and personalities is also very strong. Poker became a big draw with the advent of digital media and the large push by casinos to grow beyond their walls, and as a result personalities rose from the championships staged not just in Las Vegas, but around the world. Casual gaming online gave the sport more of an interest, and as a result the World Series of Poker, the king of all card tours, gained a reputation as a media event with television partners like ESPN and a host of brands activating in the space where they could not usually gain access (brands like tobacco and hard liquor, which cannot crack through in traditional team sports, gained large followings again through poker). Now the sport and its tours have been slightly diminished because of problems in the United States with online gambling, but the personalities, from Annie Duke to Phil Hellmuth, remain large draws wherever they do play.

Educating the media town by town as to who is playing and what the stakes are remains a slight challenge, but the digital media space has made the process much easier than ever.

Other circuits

Athletics. Once a solid year-round highly sponsored professional circuit, the sport is now in a downtime. In the 1970s and 1980s this circuit was similar to golf and tennis in structure and publicity opportunities. The tour is still in existence outside of the United States and attempts to revitalize track and field with this structure are currently underway.

Boxing. Perhaps the greatest example of individual publicity opportunities in its heyday has fallen on hard times. Many of sports greatest publicists have worked in boxing, and the ones still involved in the sport continue to find great stories and get them out when boxing events occur. However, due to the lack of set structure in the sport, much of the uniformity in publicity has fallen away.

Figure skating. Once thought to be a solid professional year-round circuit, figure skating has become more of a sponsor- and television-driven exhibition sport. While still immensely popular and very lucrative, it does not have a formal tour for professionals in the sense that the other sports do.

Fishing. It is all digital, TV driven, and largely American, but fishing tours, including BASS Fishing, have gotten their share of media coverage and sponsorship in recent years. Like other traveling events, the personalities and the athletic challenge and strategy rule the day for coverage, so educating an entertainment and lifestyle media as to why the sport is relevant is challenging and full of opportunity every week.

Horse racing. The Sport of Kings enjoyed its heyday in the 1940s and 1950s, and remains regionally popular today, especially around the Triple Crown and on some years with the Breeder's Cup. There are efforts to have a more centralized publicity schedule and maximize the stories of the horses, jockeys, and others, but the efforts to date have not been what had been hoped.

Marathon/triathlon. The health and fitness craze, combined with a growing interest in extreme sports, has made marathon running and the triathlon business big in recent years. The marathon world has untied its internationals series for elite runners, and local races are starting to pull more dollars, combining sports marketing and philanthropy, so those who work with elite runners and tri-athletes have a story to tell market by market, much like golfers and tennis players. The story of the athletes can be re-told to a new set of media with every race usually regardless of result, and there are more opportunities for multi-event promotions as well not just for the athlete, but for groups promoting such races. The Competitor Group and IRONMAN have ramped up their work in recent years to put a more formal branding element to circuit competitions, making the efforts to market and promote much more cohesive than ever before.

Professional gaming. The professional gaming industry has had its fits and starts over the past decade, and with casual gaming and brand integration continuing to expand, the ability for professional gaming to find its footing on a consistent basis is still very high. However, the schedule is still a bit of a mish-mosh, with players drifting in and out of large-scale events. Attempts at creating a central mainstream professional gaming tour have been difficult because of the transient nature of gamers at the pro level, but those at the top of the industry still have great opportunity for media exposure, branding, and mainstream acceptance as digital and social media continue to be more ingrained in our everyday lives.

Some final thoughts on the individual athlete and publicity

Although there are sometimes more layers and complications that exist with publicity for the individual athlete, the relationships you build and the one-on-one contact outside of the team setting can be very rewarding, and can open doors to other publicity opportunities for you with sponsors, publicity agencies, and even national governing bodies. The amount of travel to different locations is also a plus, as is the international aspect which exists in most individual sports.

The other opportunities that exist for publicity with individual athletes also come from working for the athletes themselves. Many athletes form foundations to deal with their charitable work, or to manage projects they care about in their hometowns. They also sometimes have a great deal of outside business activity that their main agent may not get involved with, and the ever-growing field of publicity in that area is also a plus, and occurs much more with individual athletes than in a team concept.

The other good thing about publicity in the individual sport is that almost every week is a new opportunity or a new chance at victory or success. Yes, there are cumulative races such as the NEXTEL Cup, but every week the opportunity for individual success exists. That does not happen in team sports, where the end-game is obviously the team championship. Also without having a "home" team, fans, media, and business partners do look to recreate the same opportunities for weeks on end, which gives you as the publicist the opportunity to home your pitch skills on a regular basis, and in many cases recreate the same scenarios from week to week.

It is a traveling circus from time to time, but it can be very gratifying and a great way to learn a different aspect of sports publicity.

8

THE LEAGUE PUBLICITY OFFICE

Making the 300-pound gorilla warm and fuzzy

This chapter will address the function of a league publicity office and how it functions in relation to team publicity and individual athlete publicists. It will look at the role of the league publicity group, how it manages and administers certain functions, and how general media guidelines are set by the teams from the league level.

We have talked about how the publicist for the teams and the individuals should include those folks at the higher league level in the PR plan and use them as assets. However, there are great publicity opportunities at the governance level as well, and these involve various levels of skill and ability in order to be successful. There are also vast differences in how many of the major leagues handle publicity and how they are seen and used by the clubs that they are involved with. We will take a look at the differences and the opportunities that exist from a few leagues, as well as some ideas on how if you work at the league or National Governing Body level you can help maximize exposure for your sport, whether it is the Barclays Premier League or the NBA.

The role of the league publicist

Many times, the role of the publicists at a league level is determined by the league commissioner or president and his or her style. Depending on what the financial state of the league is and the way the league is structured as an organization, the publicists can be largely support services dictated by the clubs (such as the case in Major League Baseball) or they can be very diverse and proactive publicists working with the teams or clubs to aggressively identify media opportunities and set forth an agenda that is constructed in the overall vision of the league (the NBA). That being said, there are several similarities in the role publicists play at every league level. They include:

1   The dissemination of statistics records and rules.
2   League governance and policy setting.
3   Managing and implementation of national or international overall branding.
4   Overall national or international media management.
5   Running championships and special events.
6   Overseeing cumulative publications and internet activity.

Each of the league PR offices, at its core, will work with the club and serve as the liaison between teams, business and national TV partners, and other departments such as community relations, marketing, and operations to make sure all information is properly conveyed so that the sport runs smoothly and consistently. Examples of each are set out below.

Dissemination of statistics, record, and rules

It seems simple, but this is a basic and very essential function of the league office. The need for clear and correct record keeping, the settling of record disputes, the maintenance of all statistics (usually by an outside entity like the Elias Sports Bureau or STATS LLC) is one of the key functions of the league publicist. That includes staying on top of all the member teams to make sure information is sent in up-to-date and that when information needs to be changed, that it is sent out with *one voice*, clearly from the league level. Many times the league will work with the team to make sure that the media are notified simultaneously in a hometown about an accomplishment or an issue, but the ultimate say comes from the league office. One difference here is that the league will provide unbiased, clear reports of facts both on the positive or the negative. Sometimes teams will tend to avoid the negative reporting of facts, but since the lowlights are sometimes just as noteworthy as the highlights for the long-term establishment of records, the league will also make sure all information is included. You may not see the record for most errors by a second baseman in the Chicago White Sox media guide, but it will be in a league publication.

Also on the rules front is the clear settling of disputes by the league. This will always come consistently and clearly from the league office, since ultimately it is the league that is responsible for addressing the transgressions of its players. Many times, any type of this kind of media reporting will be coordinated with the club or clubs involved so that they have full background, but it is the league that will issue the information via press release.

The league will also be responsible for all awards balloting and information collecting, and then making sure that awards are adequately publicized with the input of the teams from a local level. This too is a big function of the league PR office: to make sure that balloting and awards reception is both fair and consistent to the teams and to the athletes. With the ever-growing tendency to *just* acknowledge stars and success for name value, it can sometimes become more of a popularity contest. The goal is for the league to provide an unbiased look and select those athletes most worthy for the time period considered.

Example

Each year it is up to the league office to publish a series of books for the media to use. The NBA will publish every year the official *NBA Guide*, which will list all facts and figures needed on a team-by-team basis for the year. That will include schedule, roster, team personnel, previous year's results, and a year-by-year breakdown of league standings, playoff results, and records. The *NBA Register* will list the year-by-year statistics for each current player or players in recent years. It will also have an all-time greats section and a breakdown of recent and current NBA head coaches. Many years these books are co-published with the *Sporting News*, and serve as mainstays for both teams and media reference tools for the year. The league will also annually publish all rules for the season for the media and teams.

League governance and policy setting

Since the publicists at the league level will work directly with the league president or commissioner and his immediate staff, the publicist will handle many of the issues with regard to how the league is run, what rule changes (on and off the playing field) will be made, and the tone and positioning of the sport as it relates to the overall sports landscape.

The league publicist will also be the repository for answering questions with regard to league rules. Many of the media questions handled by the league will involve rules interpretations that answer to the governance of the sport. The publicists will be the experts on such matters and the styles in which they will be handled.

In addition to general rules of the game, the league will also set policy as to how team publicists will be able to deal with issues such as credentialing, TV, statistics, and in many cases out of market media. The league PR staff is also responsible for making sure that media are treated fairly and respectfully from city to city and from team to team. Many times the league office will settle grievance disputes by media with regard to access time, credentialing, and other issues. The league PR staff will also set the overall guidelines for teams to follow with regard to overall media access and make sure that each team follows the same rules. In many cases the consistency of rules is almost as essential as the access itself, and it is up to the league office to make sure that all are on the same page despite differences in market size and media coverage.

The league is also responsible for monitoring the growth of new trends in media to make sure that all forms of access are given fairly. For example, policies on digital photographers and bloggers may be different from league to league, but it is up to the league to make sure its media rights holders are handled fairly and consistently by each of the teams.

Also along these lines, the league PR staff is responsible for overseeing the correspondence and availability of the top league staffers, including commissioners, presidents, and league governance staff. Shaping the message delivered to the media and the public by the league's top spokesperson is perhaps the most challenging part of the position, because his or her words, like those of any top executive, have to be carefully crafted and all divergent points have to be covered with the executive prior to speaking with the media.

Example

The league is responsible for communicating any suspensions and violations of league rules to the media, and then usually is the only party that will have official say on what a decision will be. If a player is suspended for a rules violation, for example, rarely will a team official criticize the league ruling publicly. Many times the criticism of a league decision will be followed by a fine if made publicly.

NFL exercises football message control

Proliferation of new media has helped fuel distrust and curtail access to information on players and coaches.

By Randy Covitz, The Kansas City Star, October 3, 2006

A few days before the season opener, two Arizona sportswriters noticed during the 30 minutes of practice open to the media that the Cardinals had shuffled some offensive-line starters.

The writers confirmed the position moves with the two players involved and reported it in the next morning's newspapers.

Coach Dennis Green wasn't happy.

"One of the things you guys (reporters) make a mistake is you see something and you write it as if it's true," Green chastised them. "The fans are counting on you telling the truth, and you don't know the truth."

Turned out the news was accurate as reported, despite Green's admonition.

Welcome to the sometimes contentious relationships between NFL clubs and the reporters who cover them.

The NFL is unquestionably the most successful and popular sports league in America, fueled by record attendance in 2005, off-the-chart television ratings and a TV contract worth nearly $25 billion over the next six years.

That kind of interest demands accurate, in-depth reporting by newspapers, radio and television stations and Internet sites, where fans historically have gotten most of their information on their favorite teams. It requires access to players, head coaches, assistant coaches, and practices.

But the proliferation of so much new media, including talk-radio and websites—not to mention the immense pressure on head coaches to win—has led to an uneasy coexistence and even a distrust between the teams and reporters.

Consequently, newspapers and other media wanting to provide fans with satisfactory coverage are running into roadblocks.

All but nine of the NFL's 32 teams close practices to reporters; some high-profile players don't speak with the local media; at least seven teams limit or deny access to assistant coaches; and on game day, only one local television affiliate per market is allowed an on-field camera. That affiliate must share its video with the other competing stations if they want to supplement already-seen network game footage in their sportscasts.

"My nightmare scenario is 10, 20 years from now, you will not be able to cover the NFL unless you pay a rights fee," said David Elfin of *The Washington Times* and president of the Pro Football Writers of America.

"As The NFL Network gets established and the teams' websites get established, and you have the whole ESPN machine, anybody who is either not working for the team or not paying a rights fee is not getting great access."

Indeed, the NFL itself has moved into the media business, having launched The NFL Network in addition to its own website and team sites that show the league and franchises in a mostly favorable light. In other words, you're not likely to find a story about steroids on nfl.com, or the news of Jared Allen's DUI on kcchiefs.com.

"We know the NFL wants to govern everything it does," said Andrew Lackey, director of the Donald W. Reynolds National Center for Business Journalism at Arizona State University. "Any business can try whatever it wants, but they have to realize they're part of a public trust and have a responsibility to the public.

"A lot of it is about control, but one place they haven't been able to control is the media. Because the media are all over the place, and their job is to find what's interesting, unusual or perhaps negative in some cases, what (the NFL) is doing is keeping these people from doing their jobs."

Greg Aiello, the NFL's vice president for public relations—who, incidentally, has a master's degree in journalism from Columbia—says that access to teams is better than ever. It's just difficult to spread the love to so many.

"There's more and more media covering a team," Aiello said. "It's more competitive than ever. If you watch television and read newspapers, it would be hard to conclude there is a lack of access to NFL players and coaches."

•••

The latest flap involves restrictions on what newspapers can put on their websites from game-day coverage. An increasing number of newspapers, including *The Kansas City Star,* are posting game stories and still photographs from games on their sites during and immediately after games.

However, the NFL will not allow newspapers (or any non-rights holders) to show their postgame coverage of news conferences or locker-room interviews on their websites. Even video from a newspaper's reporter asking questions of a coach or player at a podium or locker cannot be posted on the newspaper's site.

The NFL contends anything that happens on game day is proprietary to the league and its rights holders, NBC, CBS, FOX and ESPN.

"We understand the rights issues with (not allowing) game action," said Jim Jenks, executive sports editor of *The Philadelphia Inquirer* and the president of Associated Press Sports Editors. "But once you're in the locker room, in a media setting, at a postgame news conference where they bring in a coach and players, we don't understand why we can't use a talking-head video."

It's not just sportswriters and editors who are concerned about providing fans with better news. Any restrictions to newspapers' ability to provide information are unacceptable in the eyes of the Associated Press Managing Editors, said Otis Sanford of *The (Memphis) Commercial Appeal.* He is that organization's representative on dealing with NFL issues.

The Washington Post and *The Associated Press,* together with their attorneys, plan to ask new NFL commissioner Roger Goodell for permission to show postgame coverage online. Jenks will endorse the request on behalf of APSE, which counts more than 600 newspapers among its membership.

"Video from our stadiums on game day is one of our most valuable assets, including video of our people, players, coaches talking about the game," Aiello said. "The policy is designed to ensure that our rights holders, who have paid for access to that asset, receive the value they've paid for.

"At the same time, it ensures that news organizations have a fair, reasonable and equal opportunity to cover the news from NFL game sites. There's no limit to the amount of written NFL information that websites can carry."

Aiello emphasized that newspapers can post video interviews of players and coaches from weekday news conferences and open locker rooms on websites in addition to transcripts from game-day coverage.

"That sounds really nice, but the reality is the written transcript is very different from the audio or the video," said Bob Steele, a senior faculty member at the Poynter Institute, a training and research institute for journalists in St. Petersburg, Fla.

"Many of the users of Internet services will want to hear the coach talking or want to see the linebacker who bats down the pass at a key moment in the game. To say, 'Well, you can put written words on there, not the audio or video,' is creating a restriction that is going to limit the storytelling ability of the journalists. When you do that, it ends up as a disservice to the public."

To which Aiello responded: "Of course, they'd like to see the actual play. At some point we have to draw the line."

By prohibiting post-game video on the website, the NFL says it is following the Olympics model, in which the International Olympic Committee forbids any cameras at venues except for its current rights holder, NBC. However, the United States Olympic Committee brings athletes to the main press center, and nonrights holders are allowed to put video on their websites, though it cannot be live, said Bob Condron, USOC director of media services.

"The million-dollar question is whether this is a journalistic question for (the NFL), or is it just money?" said Emilio Garcia-Ruiz, sports editor of *The Washington Post*. "Are they going to take and sell the access they are denying everybody else? They'll go to a Yahoo or Google or AOL and maybe sell that for $50 million."

Aiello says no plans are in the works to sell the rights to postgame video. However, the league, like any billion-dollar business, is always searching for more revenue streams, and what happens if someone makes an offer too good to refuse?

"There is a smell here," said the Poynter Institute's Steele, "and it gives the impression that the NFL and the teams are more interested in their own financial protection than they are helping the public understand what goes on in the field with the players in the games.

"If that's the case, the audience, the public, is the loser."

•••

The NFL contends that there is more mandated access for the media than ever. After listening to concerns voiced by the Pro Football Writers Association and APSE, the NFL determined that locker rooms now must be open a minimum of four days a week instead of three; and for a minimum of 45 minutes, instead of 30.

On the surface, that sounds good. But on many occasions when reporters enter a locker room, key players are not around. They are in the weight room, training room, lunch room or meeting room until the 45-minute period ends. Some talk only on certain days. Others, like Chiefs center Casey Wiegmann and the Denver Broncos offensive linemen, do not speak to reporters.

When former Rams head coach Mike Martz returned to St. Louis on Sunday as offensive coordinator of the Detroit Lions, he was not made available to any media during the week of the game, even though he customarily has a Thursday news session. Nor was he available after Sunday's game.

Green Bay quarterback Brett Favre, the face of a publicly owned franchise who has been candid and cooperative throughout his 15-year career, is now talking to the media just twice a month.

"He has one bad year, and this is how he reacts," Elfin said. "What kind of message is he sending to the fans and younger players when things go bad? But they're letting him get away with it."

There are no repercussions from the league or clubs for players who refuse to speak to reporters. Other sports, such as the NBA and NHL, have guidelines that try to ensure cooperation with the media. In the wake of the NHL's labor stoppage, the league adopted a media policy that states, in part, "Cooperation with the Media, to the maximum extent, is obligatory."

To those on the outside, it wouldn't seem that the availability of assistant coaches is important. But on some teams, the head coach has very little to do with one side of the ball. And some assistant coaches are more eloquent than the head coaches and give the fan more insight.

However, the NFL is a copycat league. Once New England coach Bill Belichick, who like his mentor, Bill Parcells, denied access to his assistants and won three Super Bowls, other coaches followed. Historically, Chiefs' assistant coaches have been available to Kansas City media, but all requests to speak with staff members must now be cleared with coach Herm Edwards through the public-relations department.

Under former Chiefs coach Dick Vermeil, practices were open on Fridays, but now all practices are closed, except the first 20 minutes or so when reporters can take roll and see what players might not practice because of injury. Super Bowl participants Pittsburgh and Seattle are among the teams that open all their practices to local media during the regular season, along with San Francisco, Atlanta, Carolina, New Orleans, Houston, Indianapolis, and Tennessee. Philadelphia offers open practice on two days.

There's a tacit understanding between the media and franchises that reporters who watch practice do not write about strategy and trick plays, but depth-chart changes are fair game. Or are they?

Cincinnati coach Marvin Lewis threatened to eliminate the first 20 minutes of practice open to the media after a reporter asked who would start in case cornerback Deltha O'Neal was unable to play against the Chiefs.

Lewis announced it would be Johnathan Joseph, but when asked who would replace Joseph as the nickel back, he got testy.

"This is our business ... that's why the rules are the way they are," he said. "Otherwise, we'll shut it down."

Elfin, president of the Pro Football Writers, believes newspapers will gain a more sympathetic ear now that Goodell has replaced Paul Tagliabue as commissioner.

"Goodell is more hands on, more involved with us than Tagliabue ever was," Elfin said. "Roger grew up as an intern in the business sort of like Pete Rozelle was, while Tagliabue was a lawyer who didn't know anybody. Roger is a politician's son, he's a lot smoother, he does appreciate what we do and that we still are important to this league. That's a positive."

Managing and implementation of league branding

One of the other jobs of the league PR staff is to make sure that all the league brands, logos and nicknames and colors of teams, the league marks, and the marks of its business partners are being handled correctly by the teams and the media. The league PR office will usually put out a style guide once a year to get to teams and media partners to make sure that there is consistency and that any changes are implemented that are made in the offseason.

The league PR office will also make sure that if there are any special logo changes during a season—playoff patches, holiday or memorial insignias—that the message as to what and why is communicated to the teams and also to the media overall.

Another area that league publicists deal with is the overall creative look and use of footage within the media. Most leagues have their own creative arm, ranging from NFL Films to MLB Productions, to NBA Entertainment, which sets policy and creates vehicles for the teams to use for marketing, publicity, and general awareness. These high-tech, highly creative league arms have a whole range of publicity opportunities overseen by the league office, from technical and technological publicity to TV and personality opportunities. The league publicists also have the opportunity to deal with the business side of sports publicity, an area which fits into the branding concept that most teams do not usually get involved with. They will deal with business press on a national and regional level about the state of the game, the industry they are in, and the economic growth of their league from a television and sales perspective. All those type of numbers are collected and then distributed by the league office.

Examples

One of the greatest problems that have arisen is the placement of signage around a field of play and balancing that real estate with the needed area of media coverage for photographers to shoot the play on field or court. Now the use of remote cameras has helped ease some of the issue, but FIFA, the world governing body for the sport of football, came up with another idea. They decided for some major international competitions to dig a ditch around the soccer pitch, giving photographers a keen angle while not blocking the signage.

In 2006, the NBA implemented a special green uniform for select teams to be worn on St. Patrick's Day. The league publicity staff worked with each market and national business trade media to create a comprehensive rollout of the uniforms, which became some of the best-selling specialty team uniforms in recent years.

On the television side, each of the leagues will work very hard on a proactive basis to see if their team brands can be integrated into some of the most widely viewed television shows and movies.

Conversely, if there are shows being shot or movies made that may present the sport in an unfairly negative way, the league may choose not to grant permission to use team and league rights and marks. The critically acclaimed ESPN show *Playmakers*, about the behind-the-scenes lifestyles of fiction football players, or the 2011 film *Goon* did not present the NFL or the NHL in a positive light, so no assistance was granted in the creation of the projects. On the opposite side, Major League Baseball cooperated on projects like *Moneyball* and *The Rookie*, granting the producers the ability to use the rights and marks.

On the stage, the NFL lent its assistance to the play *Lombardi* in 2010, and the NBA did the same with *Magic/Bird* in 2012, giving those stage projects great credibility and marketing help as they went to Broadway, and then later on as licensed properties around North America to this day.

Overall media management

The league publicists should be the group that assists the clubs in finding opportunities for publicity, establishing best media practices, and making sure that the overall image of the sport as is projected to the fans through the media is being done consistently.

The maintaining of national lists for media contacts both in and out of the sport, the ability to maintain up-to-date data bases of newspaper editors by section and genre, the ability to maintain national lists of non-sports contacts, and the ability to make sure that all national media partners are treated fairly and are promoting the game, all of this falls to the league publicity office.

In many ways the league office will also serve as the sounding board for issues that the teams may not be able to deal with on a daily basis. The league publicist is able to be the consensus builder for trends in the media, and should be able to best present those opportunities to the teams in an efficient manner.

Conversely, the league publicist has the ability to also explain team trends and nuances to the media better than the individual clubs sometimes do. There may be very good reasons why certain things such as media availability, or the interviewing of a star player, is done differently in New York than it is in Sacramento, and it sometimes falls on the league publicist to make sure that there is a fair and logical explanation to such issues.

Another big area for league publicity management is on the community and grassroots side. The league, with its teams, is responsible for collating all the data and opportunities that its teams and players do to send a greater message through the media about community initiatives. In some cases, such as it is with the NFL, the league will also work in partnership with the players association (the classic example is the United Way campaign) to develop a national platform to tell these stories. The league marketing and community relations groups will also work with publicity to identify key grassroots iniatives for the teams to rally behind, and then find publicity opportunities on a market-by-market basis using the clubs as the driving force in bringing the message home.

The key here for league publicity is to make sure all efforts are being realized to their full potential. The coordination of community stories into the national eye, be it through league broadcasts, on the internet, or in national print publications, is usually done with the assistance and guidance of the league publicity office. Also, the league is able to bring clubs together to have athletes tell similar stories on a national or regional basis, or make sure that charitable endeavors are being recognized on a national level are worthy of such high praise. The NFL "Man of the Year" program is another example of how the league publicity arm is able to take a local story and make it into a much bigger deal on a national level.

There is also the growth of international and specialty media policing that exists now for the league office, and making sure that the right media members are being treated fairly and given, or in some cases not given, the access that they so desire. Because this remains a very new area for most of the teams, it is very hard for each market to judge what is a legitimate request from a non-American publication, as opposed to a person who just happens to be in town and wants to attend a game for free. The leagues for the most part also have extensive rights holders agreements outside of the United States that local teams may not be aware of. Therefore it falls to the league publicist to make sure that everyone is treated correctly. The influx of non-North American players into traditionally North American sports has also made this situation a bit more contentious. Now in addition to dealing with local media, team publicists have to deal with different relationships between athletes and the media from their own native lands, and things can literally get lost in translation. Therefore, having someone at the league level to be able to police these situations in advance, offer assistance and clearance in many cases, is a very positive service. The rise of social media has also created another dichotomy for the team publicist. Determining who or what is a legitimate request, and for some teams these requests can come in the hundreds throughout the course of the season now, can also become a full-time job. The immediacy of the reporting for many of these sites can also create issues both with accuracy and with rights holders as well, so once again having the league publicity office there to offer counsel and set policy is a huge plus for the teams.

The league should be the repository for all information on a macro basis about the sport as well TV ratings, social media, equipment sales, participant numbers, and should aggressively work with each of its clubs to make sure they have this overall information for when they are dealing with local media. Because many teams are streamlined in their PR opportunities, the league should also be have the ability to provide pitch stories from market to market to try and tell the best story possible.

Another key area that the league publicity staff will oversee is in regard to media seating. The leagues will review media seating and access areas in each arena and stadium and set minimum standards for the teams to follow. They will also regulate broadcast positions so that team broadcast rights holders all have consistent vantage points, and that both home and visiting broadcasters have an equal vantage point. This has become a bigger issue in recent years as teams look to increase revenue in prime seating areas, many of which used to be occupied by members of the media. In many cases, teams have shifted media seating away from prime areas to less desirable locations or decreased the amount of media seating. The setting of minimum standards and policing of these standards falls to the league PR group.

Example

The Major League Soccer publicity office will work with each of its clubs on a weekly basis to provide updated trends and league highlights for dissemination to the local media. The league office will also take in much of the information from the clubs about local activity and then find places to place those stories on a national level.

Running championships and special events

Unlike the day-to-day activities that go on with running a sport, the league office is ultimately responsible for the marquee events, championships, and all-star games especially. Here the league publicists take on a role which they do not normally have during the regular season or most play-offs. Since this is the crowning moment of the sport on the league level, the event with the most media coverage, where the message to a wider audience is usually the most accessible, it is the time where the availability of the sport and the governing body takes most precedence. At these events there are normally 50 percent more media than a team would normally deal with and knowing what each select group is looking for is impossible for the team publicist to handle. The credentialing for a largely national and international media contingent is also overwhelming for a team publicity group to handle, and dealing with each outlet needs well in advance, such as hotel, phone lines, wireless access, etc., is done much more efficiently by the league office.

The coordination of schedules and interview times is also handled by the league office for large-scale events, which frees up the team publicists to continue to deal with the day-to-day team needs during these busy times. It also goes back to the premise of "One Voice." With the league acting as the voice to the media for all procedural issues, there is much less chance for there to be confusion in the media as to what access is granted, what photo positions are available, what live shots can be done, and so on. The league publicists can handle those questions clearly and concisely, and most importantly, with uniformity.

Example

For events such as the Super Bowl or the NHL Finals, the league publicity office is able to work to determine media seating for the non-local press based on the amount of games the outlet attends, whether they are a rights holder (they pay considerable money for the right to exclusively show an event), or the size of the media outlet. Especially in international markets, this is usually not information that the local publicist would have. That media coordination also frees the team publicists to deal with their regular team issues, which usually grow exponentially by the time a championship comes around.

Normally most leagues will also bring in other team publicists to assist in major events. It would not be unusual to have the publicity heads of the Philadelphia Phillies or New York Mets, for example, be at a World Series game involving the Boston Red Sox or New York Yankees. These savvy pros are used by the league office to deal with every detail of the media horde that covers major events from around the globe.

Creating and running other special events has also become more and more of an overall league function, in conjunction sometimes with international governing bodies and the local teams, or sometimes even a third-party promoter. Two great examples of that type of league synergistic relationship are The World Baseball Classic and the NHL's Winter Classic.

The World Baseball Classic. Created as a non-Olympic year event to showcase the power of the sport of baseball on an international level, the World Baseball Classic takes players country by country, as determined by the rankings of the international governing body of the sport, the International Baseball Federation, and gives them the opportunity to show off some nationalistic pride on an international level. Usually every three years, the WBC takes place in the spring, now with qualifying events the previous fall, and has grown from a small undertaking to a multi-year 32-nation event, with many of the top stars in professional baseball from around the world playing to support their country. Major League Baseball works with the IBAF on all sales, media accreditation, broadcast and digital platforms to make sure that the event is run in a first class and professional manner that is reflective of the game of baseball.

As a result of MLB support, the WBC has been able to increase its amount of participating countries which in turn creates more publicity which creates more opportunities for younger people to enjoy baseball in emerging nations, as well as in those countries where the sport is popular.

The NHL Winter Classic. Although the first outdoor extravaganza was in Edmonton and Michigan, and Michigan State took the idea of an outdoor game to new heights in the 1990s, the joint project of NBC Sports and the NHL to make the Winter Classic, usually on or around New Year's Day, a league run staple has been tremendous. The league brings all the support with whoever is hosting the event in an outdoor venue each year, from Detroit to Chicago to Boston to Philadelphia to Buffalo and beyond, and makes the event a media priority for coverage and marketing. As a result the NHL now has a new tent-pole event to structure awareness and media coverage around at a time of year when hockey interest is just starting to crystallize each year. The result of the success of the Winter Classic has been similar events with the KHL in Red Square, as well as in minor league ballparks in places like Syracuse, NY and with college hockey in Canada as well. By managing the entire process, including on the communications side, the league has found a mega-event to grow around into the future.

Overseeing publications and developing digital and social media strategy

The other area where the league publicity office is heavily involved is with the regulation of publications, the inclusion of key information, and the policing of internet content. Being part of a league will bring with it a certain uniformity of information. There are many key national stories that need to be told with consistent content by the clubs. They range from overall community and branding ideas, to record keeping and information about league structure and rules. All are simple but very important messages that are needed as much by the hometown radio station as they are by the national broadcaster. It is the league publicity office's function to make sure that the language for these messages is included in all publications, and that any issues that arise are dealt with consistently and correctly.

The league is also in charge of the timing and accuracy of many publications, ranging from media information guides to rule books. Making sure that these vital publications are also in the appropriate hands, and most importantly, at the appropriate time, is also a key function. The league will also pre-produce interesting content for teams to include in their game programs and other consumer-friendly publications, giving each team a bit more of a national cache with regards to stories and fan access.

Example

The NBA requires each team to make sure there is a dedicated section to community events in each team's media guide, as well as making sure that each team has the directory for the NBA Developmental league. These are two categories which are important to the long-term health of the league, and categories which the media can sometimes bypass in the heat of the moment of covering the season. By having these pieces in each media guide, the league is able to make sure that the messaging is consistent and available to all members of the media across the markets, as well as giving the implied support of these programs by each team.

On the social media side, the leagues have taken on a more aggressive role in determining content, use, and frequency of all surrounding games in an official capacity. For example, as of 2012, Major League Baseball allows no mobile devices anywhere on the field of play once play starts. Coaches still use traditional phones to even call the bullpen, where pitchers may warm up coming into a game. The NFL has very strict rules on players using platforms like Twitter during games, with heavy fines levied for violators.

Conversely, a governing body like the UFC has been very aggressive in promoting the use of social media in its events and with its athletes, and actually at one point issued financial incentives for its fighters to engage in aggressive social media with fans.

On the college level

Although many of these policies may apply to the league publicist on the college level, especially at the Division I level, one of the biggest functions for the collegiate league publicist is to create the preseason and postseason media attention. The biggest ways to do that is through a media day.

Media days on the collegiate level

On the collegiate level, the media day usually occurs well ahead of the season, in July for football and late September for men's and women's basketball. It is the league publicists' job to strategically pick the site (usually a major market but sometimes will be a vacation destination with a media golf outing included), work with the schools to provide players and coaches as spokespeople, and then gather all the publications for distribution. The league publicist will also actively recruit media to come to the media day from all the participating schools, as well as all those media doing national previews. In most instances the league pre-season team will be revealed to create more news. Often times, especially on the football side, there will be 10–20 news crews set up at stations for coaches and players to go through. The league publicist will coordinate many of those details with the school SID. For the postseason, pre-tournament, or sometimes pre-Bowl season push, the league publicist will also coordinate details and media coverage for post-season awards, basketball tournament credentialing, and coach availability. Again this will all be in conjunction with the SIDs, but it remains a big responsibility for the league publicist at the most crucial times of the year for media coverage.

With the advent of new media, the governance, look, and content of websites has also begun to fall under league observance. The league publicity staff is usually the group that is the disseminator of key content to the public, and can be of huge assistance in helping teams find new avenues for internet publicity as well.

A look at cricket growth and governance

Six lessons from Twenty20 cricket by Jon Long, Head of Executive Programmes, International Cricket Council

In less than a decade, Twenty20 cricket has dramatically changed the landscape of one of the world's most traditional sports. Below are six simple lessons that the ICC has learned from this experience, but first here's a bit of background on the new format:

- It is the newest of cricket's three international formats with matches that last around three hour— the other formats are Test cricket (5 days) and One-day international cricket (7 hours).
- The first domestic Twenty20 match took place in England in 2003.
- Two years later the first international match took place between New Zealand and Australia.
- Two years after that, in 2007, the first global event—the ICC World Twenty20—took place. That event attracted live audiences of over 100 million and sell-out crowds in South Africa
- The following season the domestic Indian Premier League was launched. Cricket's first franchise-based league attracted bids of over USD 100 million from new team owners and the top players were paid over USD one million for the six-week league.
- A year later, 2009, the ICC World Twenty20 became a joint men's and women's event, breaking broadcasting records for women's cricket and achieving 96% attendance rates at the host venues. 2009 also witnessed cricket's first Champions League competition, bringing together the top club sides from six leading countries for an event valued at USD 900 million over 10 years.
- In 2010, the USA hosted its first top-level Twenty20 matches and China's first international cricket venue made its Twenty20 bow at the Asian Games.

Against that backdrop, here are the lessons we've learned so far …

1   Know your audience, know your sport.

Twenty20 cricket is a product of market research but, and this is a big but, it is also a format that reflects and complements the sport of cricket and its values and spirit.

Let me explain. Twenty20 has its roots in a piece of market research by the England and Wales Cricket Board that was commissioned to find out why attendances at domestic cricket were so low.

It turned out that while people were interested in the sport, they didn't have the time to invest in following long matches.

The proposed solution was not complicated. Twenty20 is based on a format that has existed in schools and communities since time immemorial. To put it simply, its core innovation is shorter matches.

And this is where the 'sport' is important. Unlike some of the other shorter formats of cricket that have been tried in the past, Twenty20 closely mirrors the other formats of the sport. It uses the same field size, same number of players, same equipment, very similar playing conditions and requires little adaptation for participants.

2   Don't be afraid to lead.

The timeline presented at the start is a seamless upward curve but it's very easy to write history with the benefit of hindsight.

Twenty20 cricket's success has been based on foresight, belligerence, and good fortune—pretty much in equal measure.

The original decision to proceed with a domestic competition in England was approved by a slender 11–7 majority and that skepticism was mirrored at international level.

Cricket's biggest national federation, India, wanted nothing to do with the format in 2006 and the first global event was pitched as an "invitational" due to concerns some of the leading countries might not take part.

In the end everyone showed up. And although several of India's most experienced (and marketable) players asked not to be considered for selection, a youthful India side—that had only played one international Twenty20 match before the event— beat Pakistan in a fairytale final.

This gripping match was the biggest television event of the year in South Asia and the rest, as they say, is history.

3   Think big, think global.

That first ICC World Twenty20 helped consolidate the sport's power base, not just in India but in other established cricket markets too by attracting new demographic groups to the sport, particularly females and families.

After the demographic growth, we are targeting new geographic markets.

Cricket is a long way from being a major league sport in the USA but the combined Caribbean and South Asian expatriate populations provide an audience of up to 10 million potential cricket fans and there are tens of thousands of active social cricket players.

This is why we decided to break with tradition and give the USA a wildcard at the qualifying event for the ICC World Twenty20 in 2010. It ruffled a few feathers but inspired an uplift in the performances of their national team and brought American cricket to CNN for the first time. From 2012 the ICC World Twenty20 will be broadcast live by ESPN.

That same event saw another great success story, Afghanistan, complete a remarkable journey to the top level of the game.

We hope this might be the start of a new cricket rivalry that has already been noted by the US Secretary of State, Hilary Clinton who said: "If we are searching for a model of how to meet tough international challenges with skill, dedication and teamwork, we need only look to the Afghan national cricket team."

The global growth will continue in 2014 when the global qualifying system for the World Twenty20 will embrace 100 countries ahead of a finals event which has been expanded to 16 teams.

4   Think different.

The first World Twenty20 was just a men's event. The next time we ran it we included the top women's teams too.

And we tried something different. The men's and women's semifinals were staged in the same venue on the same day as part of the same ticket package. Our broadcasters supported the venture by televising both matches and the unprecedented exposure has given women's cricket an immense boost, helping stimulate rapid growth in both profile and participation.

Twenty20's initial success was fuelled not only by the content but the packaging too. It came wrapped in cheerleaders, loud music, and dunk tanks but our research tells us that fans are following the game first and foremost for its cricket content. The focus of our 'packaging' is subtly evolving, therefore, to the things that matter most to spectators in the ground and at home.

We worry a lot about simple things like the comfort and shade of spectators and their access to food and drink. High-quality big-screen presentation and PA announcers are essential and the music follows the action rather than the other way round. When we took the event to the Caribbean in 2010, our marketing campaign was simply "Bring It", in direct reference to the perceived over-corporatization of the previous major event we hosted in the region.

We are using social networking to bring fans closer to their heroes. One of my personal favorite innovations is the inclusion of good luck messages and photos chosen by fans in the players' dressing rooms.

5   Understand the economics, know your limits.

Twenty20 cricket has been so successful in such a short timeframe that it has stimulated a rise in both supply and demand. Unfortunately the two are not necessarily growing in harmony. On the supply side, the success of events that sit within the IF/NF pyramid has encouraged private entities to enter the market.

Some of these have already faded into history but others remain live and real threats—in both established and emerging markets.

We have had to completely overhaul our regulatory framework to address these threats, introducing both non-objection certificates for overseas players and new regulations and penalties governing official and unofficial cricket.

Also on the supply side we have opted to strategically restrict the volume of international Twenty20 matches, leaving breathing space for the other formats and, we hope, successful domestic leagues.

We know that we can't grow the game on our own and that global events might not be the best means of expanding our foothold in North America. A domestic professional league might be a more effective option or, in the same way as the NFL has staged regular season games in London, some of the domestic cricket leagues could decide to stage matches in New York or Toronto.

On the demand side, some consumers are screaming for more Twenty20 but—interestingly—not at the expense of other formats.

In almost all of our major markets our research suggests that consumers are satisfied with the current volumes of Test match and one-day cricket. Over 30% of consumers would like to see the ICC World Twenty20 take place every year but after being forced into that schedule in 2009–2010 we are planning to run it in a two year cycle in 2012 and 2014 and may even lengthen the cycle when we next take our rights to market.

6   Don't neglect your heritage and core audience.

My final point relates to the heritage of a game that was first played internationally over 130 years ago. Since the explosion of Twenty20 cricket, we have spent more time and energy researching, restructuring and promoting the other formats of the game than worrying about Twenty20.

We are confident at present that all three formats retain strong public appeal and there is excellent cross-over interest. Each of the formats claims over 600 million of the 700 million passionate fans around the world.

Our focus now is two-fold:

- better-differentiating the three formats in the minds of the consumer; and
- introducing greater context to the calendar and events in the other two formats.

We think context is as important as content.

We are going to introduce a World Test Championship for the leading teams in the most traditional format. This event will not replace the historic series like the Ashes between England and Australia. Rather, it will complement these iconic series and enhance the context of series that don't benefit from the same levels of brand recognition and public interest.

So in summary, those are six lessons that we've learned from our new format.

We have many more to learn. And some big questions still to answer.

Twenty20 might be the format to take cricket back into the Olympic Games.

Some think there may be another format out there—perhaps sixes cricket, beach cricket or the indoor game—that will take our sport into smaller stadia and/or multi-sport games.

We have our hands full at present balancing the three formats we are fortunate to have and, for the coming years, balancing and promoting these will be our focus.

A look at media access policies set by the league

Each league sets its own media policies with regard to player and coach access. These are usually set as minimum standards and teams need to adapt to them so that all media get fair and equal access on a regular basis. Non-compliance with league media policies by the team can result in fines to the team. The regular media covering the teams usually serve as watchdogs with regard to access, and the league publicity heads will usually rule on access controversies.

NBA

On gamedays, coaches and players must be available following their morning shootaround (the gameday morning practice which usually lasts an hour). Locker rooms are open between the 90-minute mark and the 45-minute mark prior to the game. Locker rooms are then open to the media following a 10 minute cooling off period after a game. Players and coaches are made available to the media following each non-game day practice as well. Most teams practices are closed to the media. Any additional time is not regulated and is set up by the team publicity department.

NHL

On gamedays, players and coach are made available following the morning skate for 30 minutes or so. The lockerrooms are closed prior to the game and then open again following a cooling off period after the game. Hockey will also make a player or coach available to the TV broadcaster following each period if needed. On practice days, most media are allowed to watch practice and the lockerrooms are opened after practice.

MLB

Because of the amount of games, the major league baseball clubhouse is probably opened the most to the media. Clubhouse access is from 3:30pm until 45 minutes prior to first pitch (if at 7:05pm, then it's 6:20pm). It is then open again following a cooling off period after a game. There are rarely any practices during a season.

MLS

Major League Soccer requires clubhouses to be open to media up to one hour before the start of games, and clubhouses to be open to media no more than 15 minutes following a completed match. Most clubs allow at least 15 minutes of media access to practices during the season as well.

NFL

The opposite of baseball because there is only one game a week, the NFL media policies are probably the most structured. Rules stipulate that the locker room has to be open four days a week, 45 minutes per day and it is up to the individual teams to structure the week as best suits the team and the media. Locker rooms are closed pre-game and then open following a cooling-off period post-game. One difference is that media have access to the field post-game and many times may get a player before he goes into the locker room as he exits the field.

Other sports

Tennis

The ATP and WTA both make players available after their matches if requested by the media. They also have access to players by request at other points during the week. Both tours also legislate a comprehensive non-match publicity effort designed to grow the game, ACES for the ATP and FIRST SERVE for the women. The players in the field are obliged to do different levels of activity away from the court: media, sponsor, community, as part of giving back to the sport.

Golf

Both the PGA and LPGA will make players available after matches. Depending on the course, access to the clubhouses is limited. Most times media will also find players on the practice areas for time.

Colleges

For major colleges, there is usually one day a week where the conference coaches are mandated to do a general media conference call, especially with major conference football. Traditionally, either regional areas will do a once a week luncheon or call for notes writers, where many of the college coaches gather to report on their teams, or major colleges will do a once-weekly luncheon to make the head coach and sometimes a player available. This is also similar in some markets with basketball. In big markets there may be a weekly luncheon which many college coaches attend depending on schedule, or in smaller markets the league or the school may do a weekly call for the media. Other than the preseason media days and the weekly football call, rarely do college leagues have any say in media availability for coaches and players.

NASCAR

The media availability for a NASCAR race week usually begins on Thursday. There will be some availability earlier in the week, but Friday is the major availability day, after qualifying is completed. Once race weekend begins, time is limited for drivers.

Conclusion

In closing, the league publicist has to be the consensus builder and the rule keeper. However, there is great opportunity to be entrepreneurial as well, as you are able to combine teams and information to tell big picture stories to national media and shape the position of your sport more than most teams will be able to do. When there are big-time events, the league PR team generally the biggest influence.

9

THE SOCIAL GAME

This chapter was researched and written largely by the work of Columbia University graduate student Rikki Massand. We are very appreciative of Rikki's work in helping explain the latest opportunities in the area of social media and sport.

When this book was first published, the dawn of social media had just begun. Facebook was in its infancy, there was nothing to tweet about just yet, many people were still going through the discovery of MySpace, and YouTube was still in the distance. For as much as we conceived sport and news being 24/7, that experience was largely passive. We could watch and react, usually not in real time unless we were using the voice or text messaging, but it was not anywhere near immediate as what we have today.

Now we are all about positive and proactive engagement in a 24/7 world where you can communicate peer to peer or to millions at once. The information we send out from various devices is essentially non-retractable, so discretion and understanding of the medium we use is essential.

The chapter going forward will look back on how we got here and give some best practices in the effective use of social media for communication, from the college ranks to the highest levels of professional sport.

While it's been well documented that the rises of the Internet and social media have redefined the rationale of consumer-based marketing, the explanation of sports' growing involvement in the virtual landscape is often overlooked. Today, each sport reaches its fans in more ways than one can count, a stark departure from standards held in the late nineteenth and twentieth centuries—first in person only, then print, then radio, and later television. From the early 1960s until the late 1990s, the only major changes in the media spectrum involved the number of outlets in each medium that covered sports as well as substantial growth in deals for broadcasting rights. Talk radio and TV shows within the genre of sports talk were the only real outlet for fan integration until the Internet arrived. Now media is social; anyone can write or create podcasts or YouTube videos and upload sports-related content for the masses. Professional and collegiate sports have had to keep up and explore the many ways to tap the online and hand-held market, and several examples are presented within this chapter.

Sports, like most other industries, must now be heavily involved in social media in order to do twenty-first-century business. Teams and universities have studied how many of their ticket sales come from people who use different social media sites, taking that data into consideration of how to promote their brand and market future news and events. There is no faster and more concentrated effort underway in the professional sports landscape than building and selling a team's presence through the various outlets the Internet has provided. But how and when social media and sports publicity interact is a constantly evolving dynamic, one that is now a key in constituting the business plans of the most dominant sports entities, including the NFL and every other American professional league.

From 2010 to 2012, the Super Bowl kept topping its own television viewership mark for honors as the most watched TV program in US history—up to 111.3 million viewers in 2012—and it undoubtedly looked primed to do so again for years to come. But it is the "two-screen" consumer that networks have coveted the most; those who consume sports and other programming on TV as well as through a smartphone, tablet, or computer—simultaneously. For sports, this audience extends to those at a game or match while using one of these devices. According to data released by sports medicine company KT Tape (kinesiology tape), 83 percent of sports fans check sports on social media while watching a game on TV, and over 63 percent did so while they were at a game.

Baseball at its core is a conversation-based sport, and in recent years one niche that its online presence has attempted to fill is that of fan interaction—a.k.a. virtual customer service. The Oakland Athletics were the first MLB team to feature a quick reference "Twitter roster" on their website. Instead of the traditional scorecard in-hand to track the game, a fan can keep track of each tweet that a player sends out, also in-hand, as mobile devices allow for a revolutionary method of information gathering. Want to know what the players were saying after their teammate was hit by a pitch? No need to wait for the 10 o'clock news to spell it out for you. In fact, an injured player can receive well wishes from fans as he or she visits with their doctor, and provide the public with up-to-the-minute updates.

As of May 2012 Brazilian soccer star Kaka had accumulated over 10 million followers on Twitter. The next most-followed athlete was another soccer star, Cristiano Ronaldo, who had 8.5 million. Future NBA hall-of-famer Shaquille O'Neal had just under 5.5 million, while LeBron James had over 4.2 million to round out the top four most-followed athletes. The phenomena of Tim

Tebow during his college career and the Broncos 2012 season owes much to social media as "Tebowing" took over social networks. On January 7, 2012, just after Tebow threw to receiver Demaryius Thomas for a game-winning touchdown against the Pittsburgh Steelers, his name set a Twitter record of 9,420 Tebow-related tweets per second.

Marketability, anyone? Certainly this kind of effect and the legions of fans Tebow drew helped the New York Jets make the decision to trade for him two months later when Peyton Manning took over in Denver.

As technology's future unfolds daily, if not weekly, sports publicity will continue facing a myriad of questions. Do certain sports have a higher percentage of tech-savvy fans than others? Do people at work or school log onto sports websites or engage in sports debates via social networks? Is a sports story topping Yahoo!'s "most popular" list each day because Americans are in need of their sports fix online? The answer to each of these questions is yes, but knowing isn't enough. As a product of creativity, digital space leads its users to come up with innovative ideas and ways to get noticed. People who work in sports marketing, new media, and communications have all contributed ways of enhancing their brands and capitalizing on a newfound way of attracting customers. Sports is certainly inherently social, so will platforms that combine the two—a company like PlayUp which was launched in 2010 and used the free mobile model to give fans not just a common ground to chat but a place to also pull in live statistics, video, and other data in a real time environment—be a key area of publicity and effective communication on a global level? Will using multiple screens to disseminate information be the best way to go to communicate? All need to be factored into the social discussion.

In this chapter you will learn about certain successes and attempts that future sports publicity professionals should consider.

Although the Internet and social networking websites are inherently unpredictable, sports franchises and individuals have found their fair share of success through exceptional social media strategies and concentrated efforts in SEO—search engine optimization. Those strategies will be examined in this chapter with specific advice to boot.

Developing a strategy

The United States Olympic Committee (USOC) has a varied take on the integration of social media into its mass marketing. In April 2008, at the USOC's Media Summit held in Chicago (a marketing technique itself, as there was real hope for a bid to bring the 2016 Olympics to Chicago at the time), social media was absent from the largest gathering of 150 Team USA athletes and over 400 journalists. Most attendees got their first taste of that incarnation of Team USA by meeting the athletes in person, save for some of the obvious NBA and professional sports names. In 2008 the main online component for information on US Olympic athletes was a standard webpage with basic bio facts on each athlete—TeamUSA.org.

After the Beijing Games in 2008, social media became a focal point in the USOC's marketing efforts, and a clear strategy was developed. Website content, Facebook, and SEO components would go under the direction of USOC's Department of New Media. Scott Cronk, Manager of New Media for the USOC, explained the marked difference between sites launched in early 2008 for the Beijing Games compared with the 2012 version, launched on April 5—just 10 days before the USOC Media Summit was held.

"The 2012 version was significantly more dynamic, mover visually appealing and contained much more social integration with Facebook, Twitter, YouTube, Google+, and it contained more technology integration with android, tablet, and mobile apps available for download," Cronk said.

For summer 2012, with the games set to take center stage, USOC planned for a new data app to be available on the android and Apple market.

Cronk said that in 2012 each individual Olympic sports division developed web content for their team, and the team sites integrated Facebook pages for each athlete. A function called "follow your sport" was developed for USOC's main Facebook page to steer fans and casual web browsers to whichever sport might have interested them the most.

Cronk referenced Samsung's launch of the US Olympic Genome project in 2012—an app that "personalized the 2012 Olympic experience for viewers"— as a breakthrough way for fans to stay connected with Team USA athletes. Upon its release, Samsung and the USOC stated that through Facebook, fans could "reach out to people they may have not been able to otherwise." At the same time the application allowed US Olympic athletes to share information about themselves and the behind-the-scenes experience in London.

While from 2009 through 2012, Facebook and other avenues fell under the USOC's new media strategy, Twitter was seen as a strategic communications tool for fan and consumer engagement. Cronk said that his digital media department of three individuals focused on Facebook, the USOC website, and framing Team USA's online presence "through what is tangible."

Rather than a user experience, Twitter was seen as more of a word-spreading technique, akin to the traditional press release—albeit with a personal touch in this case. Leading up to the Vancouver 2010 Winter Games and the 2012 London Olympics, USOC's tweets were handled mainly by Patrick Sandusky, director of communications for USOC. The communications department made the decision to personalize its Twitter communications through Sandusky, who often tweeted messages on a variety of subjects such as travel, US news, and general sports topics—even if there was no relation to USOC or Olympic athlete activities.

Throughout the first half of 2012, the USOC had its eye on its SEO success by working with outside consulting companies "to make sure we were doing the right things to try to get our pages and technologies recognized," Cronk said.

"We had to make sure our SEO was done the right way and that we weren't URL-ing ourselves into oblivion—in other words, making God-awful URLs that are not optimized, not searchable, and not findable," he explained.

Cronk said more than sport-specific terms, keywords that would pull TeamUSA.org or its affiliate sites to the top of SEO ranking would include "US and Olympic" or "team USA" as well as its campaigns—"donate" and "Olympics" were one example. He added that the names of some of the up-and-coming Olympic athletes would be an asset for SEO rankings, whereas NBA superstars' names such as LeBron James would probably direct traffic elsewhere than Team USA.

While Kronk said there had not been a specific plan in place to direct computer or mobile app users from viewing one sport of their choosing to another sport, he admitted that the conversation had come up in the new media plan for London 2012.

"How do we cross-populate our fan base? It's a difficult thing to assess. If you're a fan of the Olympics you are already cross-populated. But a fan who is dedicated only to Olympic hockey, for example, maybe not come on the site unless their sport is in the news," Cronk said.

Another example: The Australian Open

Serving up social media. While Americans are mostly asleep during the hours the Australian Open is played, the Internet offered ways for social media to come to the forefront of a continent's most recognized sporting event. The Australian Open has engaged fans in a multitude of ways in recent years, all while tapping the market potential of the home country. Engaging fans interested in the Australian Open was a concerted effort, started as early as 2006 with the rise of social media.

Statistics helped push social media creativity in the Australian Open's marketing efforts. The number of Australians on Facebook hovered around six million for two years, 2008 and 2009. In 2010, it was reported that there were 7.9 million Australians on Facebook, 6.9 million of which were over 18 years old. By 2011 Facebook claimed to have over 11 million Australian users. The largest age group of Facebook users in Australia is 25–34 year olds, followed by 18–24 year olds. Per log-in, the average Australian spent an average of 26 minutes on Facebook.

Encouraging the growing number of social media users to be part of the tennis conversation as it took center stage was the strategy. When tennis fans tweeted about a player or 'liked' them on Facebook, they increase their social ranking and helped raise them up on the Fan Centre social leaderboard. AustralianOpen.com prompted fans to participate with the tagline "Every mention and like counts! Get behind your favorite player and help them reach the top." Naturally the well-known stars like Rafael Nadal and Maria Sharapova lead the way, but journalist Cork Gaines of *Business Insider* wrote, "while those players are familiar to the casual sports fan, the rest of the social leaderboard is great way to learn which players we should be paying attention to."

In 2012 the Fan Centre included interactive contests such as "Caption It," where users had a chance to add their own captions to photographs from each day of the tournament. "Fan of the Day," sponsored by Kia Motors, was another promotion and there was even an initiative to have fans create short films online called "Changing Ends." For a more comical take on the goings-on at the Open and some on-the-court items that fans might have seen, such as comments or odd snapshots, there was "Popcorn Tennis." At the end of the tournament, Popcorn Tennis featured a comical version of best performance awards, with categories including "The Marat Safin Award for Racquet Origami," "The M★A★S★H Award for Longevity," and "The Curse Toast."

The Australian Open Fan Centre also had interactive tools with "AO Trivia" and "Pick 'Em" in which fans selected their picks for each day's high profile matches (such as the 2012 Men's Semifinal with Novak Djokovic taking on Roger Federer) to see how they compared with friends and others. Online users could also invite their friends to join in on the action, and Fan Centre posted a leaderboard to show who got the most picks correct. The top-ranked fan on the 2012 leaderboard had 259 picks correct. Many users gave feedback to the Australian Open web team, directed at "AO," that they wished the other Grand Slam tournaments provided the same type of interactive games and features.

SEO techniques

Glenn Gabe is the president of G-squared Interactive, a firm that provides SEO, social media marketing, and web analytics to clients. Gabe, also a columnist for *Search Engine Journal*, was previously the lead search strategist for the US Army, Exxon Mobil, Bertolli, and Lunesta.

Gabe presents some unique perspectives on SEO, website-building, web marketing, and social media. One of the more intriguing ideas behind SEO he has spoken about is the ineffectiveness of story or clip headlines, offering insight for those in charge of drafting press releases or articles for online. From Gabe's *Search Engine Journal* article on July 29, 2009:

> Creative and clever headlines aren't great for long-term sustained traffic from natural search. Most SEOs recommend creating descriptive titles based on keyword research. The reason SEOs recommend descriptive titles based on keyword research is because many have analyzed traffic across numerous sites and know how important optimized title tags are, which are often pulled from the title of the article or blog post. I said

"often" and not "always" and I'll explain more about that later. When natural search can sometimes be a majority of a site's traffic, it's hard to ignore optimizing content to attract longer-term, sustained traffic from organic search.

Another web content element that Gabe speaks on is the visual side of websites. With the expanding capabilities of visual elements reaching users on smartphones and tablets, many web designers look to create the most eye-catching sites possible. But that can actually hurt a site's visibility on the web. Replacing HTML content with full Flash pages or a significant amount of Flash can cause problems with a site's SEO. Gabe suggests that web developers with their mind set on adding more flash content to your site and utilizing SWFObject 2.0 should provide search engine friendly alternative HTML content.

SEO and viral videos

Nearing the conclusion of a very tumultuous season in 2011–2012, the Orlando Magic prepared a video previewing the NBA playoffs and adopted a late-season slogan—"We All We Got"—as the team veered toward an under-dog role as a number 6 seed. The video and slogan drew significant attention on the web, said former Lexis Nexis developer Brian Austad, who advised Dan Savage of OrlandoMagic.com about SEO and social media. Savage is also the resident twitter-person for the Magic, sending out messages about the team and its upcoming events.

This campaign may have been one of the only ways of even attempting to turn the page after a season in which the team saw its star player, center Dwight Howard, and head coach, Stan Van Gundy, spar in the media while attempting to soothe things over in person, all of which came to a head during and after All-Star Weekend which was held in Orlando. After Howard was ruled out for the remainder of the season in early April, the team made a show of unity very publicly with its slogan, breaking its in-game huddles with the saying. Van Gundy adopted saying the phrase and even asked players including forward Glen "Big Baby" Davis to have t-shirts printed with the slogan.

Working hand-in-hand, a video the franchise hoped to would go viral and a new message helped distract Orlando's fan base from the poor public relations saga that Howard, Van Gundy, and the front office went through during the season.

Gabe offers similar advice to clients on the importance of having online video go hand-in-hand with other marketing components. A quick video alone won't cut it.

"Don't create a 30 second spot … please. Sure, you might get some views on YouTube, but I firmly believe you need to have people interact with your campaign I think it's a great idea to have video as part of the campaign, but not part of a one way viewing experience. There are so many ways to have people take part in your campaign, especially with web-based campaigns," Gabe said.

Gabe adds that branding an online campaign of any form gives people an easy way to communicate it to their friends—"helping with natural search, tying easily with your concept and creative, and obviously making it memorable." A friend had told Gabe about MLB's Actober campaign in the fall of 2007, and Gabe remarked that without the name branding people would simply search for Major League Baseball. He suggests to clients that each campaign be accessible instantly, and to add a directory matching the title of the campaign. For example, a proper destination to send people would be: www. yourwebsitename.com/yourcampaignname.

The other benefit of this format is building on an established web presence. Gabe says that registering an entirely new URL is not an effective strategy because it will be a brand new domain that needs to build its own search power versus inheriting the trust from your core domain. With the use of subdirectories, such as yourdomain.com/campaigntitle, your campaign will leverage your trusted domain, rank faster, and help build links for your trusted domain. Gabe says that is a win–win.

Keywords are key. The SEO your video receives will most likely depend on this subtle information about it. Remember to not skip the area where you can add a description of your video. This will really help your video's SEO, so fill it with many keywords.

Keep in legal. Gabe also cautions clients that before a campaign hits the Internet and social media, have your legal counsel review everything.

"Legal is a necessary element to successful marketing campaigns. Make changes based on a lawyer's feedback and get final approval before moving forward. I'm fanatical about this stage of a campaign—listen to your lawyers," he said.

MLB and social media

Major League Baseball: On April 5, 2012—Opening Day—Sam Laird wrote an article for *Mashable* reviewing the latest in Major League Baseball's social media efforts. For the 2012 season, this included assigning "social media-savvy real-time correspondents for all 30 of its ballparks to provide on-the-ground updates and content," Baird wrote. Correspondents are paid by the game and provide short updates and photos of players' pre-game routines, lineup cards, and other behind-the-scenes features. MLB also launched Tumblr and Pinterest accounts for every club at the start of the 2012 season.

Baird's article quoted Arturo Pardavila, MLB.com's director of social media content, to explain the move.

Once the game starts it's not sitting in the press box, it's getting out with fans in the crowd, talking to who caught foul balls and home runs, and making the ballpark a social and mobile experience for fans.[1]

Twitter was also used as a marketing strategy to kick off the 2012 season. On Wednesday, April 4, the @MLB twitter account was used to post trivia questions with attractive prizes such as iPads, XBox 360s, Roku devices, and PlayStation 3s. The promotion was to have thousands of fans re-tweet the hashtag for MLB.TV's new streaming service, MLBTVme. The twitter plan was a success as the hashtag was mentioned over 57,000 times on the eve of the baseball season.

Individual team marketing and promotions campaigns helped pave the way for MLB's social media integration. In 2010 the Cleveland Indians implemented the first-ever social media-only section in professional sports at Progressive Field: the Tribe Social Deck.

Invitations to the Indians Social Suite are distributed to fans on a game-by-game basis after they fill out an online application from the Indians' website. Fans who were selected to attend gave rave reviews of the experience, saying there was no pressure to be a live game reporter through their social media updates. In fact, the organization took an extra step to create a laid-back environment for its customers through an email sent to those in attendance at the Tribe Social Deck.

There are no expectations around in-game tweeting or live updates for this event. We, as an organization, wanted to reach out to the social media community in recognition of their efforts and provide a new-age variation of the press box for those who attend.

In an official statement Indians' President Mark Shapiro acknowledged the value of the new wave in brand strategy.

"Social media's popularity—600 million Facebook users overall worldwide and 300,000 new Twitter users per day—represents a fundamental shift in the way people interact and acquire information. We are incredibly cognizant of social media's growth and have developed a comprehensive social media strategy to address it," Shapiro said.

In 2011 the Social Deck was replaced by the Indians Social Suite, an entire group suite at Progressive Field catering to social media users. Also in 2011 the Indians launched also a social media ticket offer, available only via Facebook and Twitter. Fans were given the opportunity to share the ticket special via social media to receive an even deeper discounts on game tickets.

Example

In hockey the Devils found their "mission"

In addition to the great work in baseball, other teams have been using social media for better engagement, and one of the best has been the New Jersey Devils of the NHL. In 2010, Devils launched "Mission Control" on the third floor of the Prudential Center in Newark, New Jersey. The Devils, once at the bottom of professional sports in the fan engagement category, have become one of the leaders in a league (the NHL) which probably does the digital space as well as any other sports property.

The goal was to have a central location where fan leaders, part of their "Army" can monitor, engage and join in the real time conversation on any social platform possible. Thoughts from fans can be pushed out instantaneously, problems in the arena can be fixed right away, promotions can be created and activated with sponsors at a moment's notice, media can chime in with what is going on, information on injuries and other topics can be relayed very quickly to all those in the space who are engaged, all from one central hub. It is a bold and costly step for a team which has a strong online following but still limits the access to players and coaches during the season, a long-held stance that the team continues to stick to. Still, this type of broad-based and centralized engagement can lead to maybe bringing injured or inactive players or team officials into the conversation during games as well.

Between period, interviews and analysis can be uploaded via Skype or stored in podcasts, and broadcasters and bloggers can also chime in with their perspective with additional shared content.

It was the latest step in digital fan engagement for the team, who earlier in the year started renting iPads during the games to fans to provided an added experience on top of what was being done on video boards and with traditional in arena contests. It also helped show that the team is committed to finding ways to engage their fans and stay involved despite all the talk about the franchise being for sale, at least by part of their ownership group. In many ways the launch of "Mission Control" became an even bigger enhancement for owner Jeff Vanderbeek should he need to go find new partners in the ownership group. The team was also able to bring in sponsor engagement for "Mission Control" and help set a standard for in-game social media opts that others have replicated going forward.

How the web can help sports programs

Often colleges have looked to the negative aspects of social media. Many high-profile athletic departments have viewed social media as an undesirable avenue for their players to slip information out or simply make comments that will come back to haunt the program in some fashion. In 2010 the University of Miami ordered players to shut down their Twitter accounts after a tough loss because it served as a distraction. Texas Tech University did the same after one of its players tweeted an inflammatory remark about the head coach. But for one college in northeastern Pennsylvania, the interaction of athletics and Twitter has only helped their brand, mostly due to strong management planning.

Julie Oltman, Assistant Athletic Director for Technology at Lehigh University in Bethlehem, Pennsylvania, approached social media integration from an athletic perspective as she spent her career as a soccer and lacrosse coach at the University of New Hampshire, The Ohio State University, and Lehigh. From 1998 to 2009, she also served as a regional coach for the US soccer Olympic development program.

> If you're a coach and you're not fully aware of social media and at the least engaged to a level where you understand the culture, then I think you really are missing some tremendous opportunities in terms of creating relationships with prospective recruits, trying to promote your program in the light you want it to be perceived as, and also reaching kids you might not have reached before.[2]

Oltman was a key player in developing Lehigh's social media presence.

> We made our first footprint into social media back in 2008 and 2009, and that was really led by the sports information department as they opened our first Twitter account and got Facebook going because they saw that there was a need for that—people were asking for that. There really wasn't much of a strategy at that point other than reporting scores and getting news out—really an extension of what traditional sports information department material.[3]

Oltman explained that as social media became more important to everybody, Lehigh recognized the need to balance its social media process and come up with a strategy. In the past sports information directors had spoken to teams and individuals about "how to be smart about speaking with the press," according to Oltman. These days that conversation has shifted to the use of social media.

Around 2010 Oltman formed a "social media strategy team" at Lehigh with the university's multimedia/special projects manager and a person from the university's business office who had private sector experience utilizing social media. The group's first order of business was developing a social media policy for student athletes and personnel at the university who might draw attention. Oltman said the goals were to help Lehigh's athletic programs get on Twitter and Facebook, provide a set of guidelines to each sport's leadership and players, and help each party utilize these new media tools throughout their season and the calendar year. Lehigh developed a model social media guidelines and policy to serve those needs.

"A big part of this was teaching the understanding of what these tools were designed for and what the space was about, but also we wanted people to be aware of their statements from a PR perspective," Oltman said.[4]

That year, 2010, saw the first of two opportunities for national exposure for Lehigh athletics. The men's basketball team drew Kansas, the 2008 NCAA champion and a number 1 seed, in the first round of the NCAA tournament. Oltman said that on the day of the game Lehigh's website traffic jumped to 25,000 hits, up from an average of about 4,000 per day. But she notes that in 2010, social media was not as big as in 2012.

"We didn't really have a way or position of leveraging our website traffic in 2010," she said.[5] A lopsided loss to Kansas also deflated the temporary momentum that Lehigh saw that year.

However, in 2012 Oltman and Lehigh officials were left to consider the capitalization of an SEO sensation. When Lehigh's men's basketball team, a number 15 seed, beat number 2 Duke in the opening round of the 2012 NCAA tournament, 75–70, Lehigh gained much exposure for a 24- to 48-hour news cycle. The Mountain Hawks were quite unknown to most of America as a New York Times article mistakenly referred to the team as the Mountain Lions.

On Google on Saturday, March 17 (St. Patrick's Day of 2012), "Lehigh" was the number one search term, a notch ahead of "corned beef and cabbage" and nine notches above "Duke." The high-profile opponent certainly helped, but the fan frenzy surrounding the NCAA tournament played the biggest role. According to Nielsen Media Research, more people tuned in to the tournament on Friday, March 16, 2012, than on any first Friday of March Madness. Oltman expected some of the web drama.

> We knew there would be a spike in the web traffic, just like against Kansas, but there were some factors that we knew of but couldn't quantify. We knew people would be connecting via mobile devices, which grew substantially over 2010, and people tweeting throughout the game, which generated conversations that we had not had before.[6]

While watching that Duke game, she followed the conversation on Twitter, saying that once it seemed apparent that Lehigh could pull off the upset they started trending on Twitter. Oltman was also following live data from Google Analytics, which led her to an excited reaction that the traffic could possibly crash Lehigh's website as there were over 44,000 site visits during the game. Oltman attributed that to the exponential growth of people who use mobile devices which connect to the Internet between 2010 and 2012.

"Now with smartphones and tablets you are much more likely to be sitting and watching a game with that in your hand or on your lap—you don't have to get up and go to a computer, you can be at a bar and check our site," she said.[7]

Twitter did make much of an impact for Lehigh that night as music superstar Justin Bieber gave the university a much unexpected boost. Oltman said that Bieber was the second-most followed person on Twitter behind singer Lady Gaga, and during the Duke game Bieber tweeted "That guy on Lehigh was for real."

Bieber was referencing the Mountain Hawks' C.J. McCollum, the 2012 Patriot League Player of the Year, who scored 30 points as Lehigh slipped past Duke. Scores of retweets ensued. Overnight from March 16 to March 17, 2012, 1,500 people started following McCollum on Twitter, according to Justin Lafleur, Lehigh's assistant sports information director.

From Lehigh's view, school policy did help in this instance as Oltman said C.J. McCollum was "pitch-perfect" with his tweets throughout the 2012 NCAA Tournament as he represented himself and the Lehigh athletic program in the best light. She says that McCollum is just one example of a dedicated effort, starting in each player's freshman year, for Lehigh to promote what its teams and programs are about, instilling certain messages in players over time.

> It has to be a reoccurring theme—this is our culture, this is what we're about, and these are skills for how to leverage social media and talking to the press that are going to be helpful when you leave here too. Athletes want to come out of a university working like a professional who has every career path ahead of them that they want to have.[8]

Now with that strategy laid out, here are some additional thoughts on the use of social media platforms for integration into communications.

First, it's not for everyone. Just like parties or driving fast cars, social media is not a practice for everyone. Coaches, athletes, even some brands may be risk averse or simply not have that much to say. Therefore participating in a social media campaign of any kind is not something that everyone must do. Understanding and following what is going on from a distance makes sense, so being on Twitter or Facebook from a monitoring standpoint is a great thing to do. If you have nothing to say, or add, then don't say or add anything.

However understanding what is going on is important. Silence can be the best form of intelligence.

Second, size doesn't always matter. When social media exploded there was a burst to get to large number of followers. However, social media is about peer-to-peer engagement of thoughts and ideas. Making sure you, your client, your business partner have the right followers, whether they are 20 or 20,000, is just as important as having a million in many cases.

Third, know who is in your posse. Many people sign on to Twitter, Facebook, or Google Plus or engage in LinkedIn or any other social platforms and never bother to see who is following them or why they are following them. Ask from time to time; check your lists for spammers or unusual content; block those who are offensive to you. Just like people at a party in your house, responsibly managing your lists is an important piece of business maintenance. Then, knowing who and what is being said amongst your user groups will make your social media engagement just as valuable and effective as anything else you do in communications.

Four, ask questions. Make sure you ask people why they are following you if you don't know. Drop a question from time to time to some followers. It is important to be involved in the social space if you choose to be, so engage when you can.

Five, speak when you have something to say. Many people fall into the trap of speaking just for the sake of saying something. Don't. If you have an idea, a link, a story to communicate then do so, and make sure it is reflective of your overall social strategy. Don't just post something because you haven't said anything in a while and feel a need to do so.

Six, remember who you represent. Sometimes people think that they can separate their personal thoughts from their professional by using a "this is my thought not my company" disclaimer. That can be a big mistake. We are all intertwined for better or worse, and the alter ego idea in the digital space does not work. You speak for all those you represent at all times, so always have those around you in mind.

Seven, watch the chains that bind you. It is very easy to comment on a photo or a public chain in social media. Once you are on it you can lose control of those ties and they can spin very easily into a questionable area of comment, whether you are still commenting or intended to be part of a conversation that grew or not. Cut the ties after you comment, it will save you a lot of headaches.

Eight, watch the inference. We lose all nuance with the printed word, despite the addition of emotions and small catch phrases. If something gets lost in the printed word, pick up the phone and call the person. A little voice contact can take much of the sting out of a misguided email, post, or tweet.

Nine, think before you post. The biggest mistakes made in social media come from those who react emotionally. Be professional, pause and then say what you have to say. Once a thought is out, the amount of time taken to retract or clarify will cut away from all the productive time you have.

Ten, be genuine and creative. Don't use social platforms to create white noise or endless useless chapter about a subject you are working with or promoting. Make your platform as much editorial as advertorial and as diverse as you can. It is social, so be social while balancing the work effort. Social media provides lots of opportunities for us to connect with people from around the world that we would not normally be able to.

Network away, but watch what you say.

Conclusion

In closing, the social space still remains vastly uncharted. In the time we started this revision at least five new platforms have propped up, and others have disappeared. What platforms we will be using in the future may be different from what is being used in 2012, but all will be manageable, personal, and effective with the right level of usage and engagement.

Notes

1 *Mashable*, May 2012.
2 http://articles.mcall.com/2012-03-17/sports/mc-lehigh-buzz-ncaa-tournament---20120317_1_mountain-hawk-lehigh-alumni-lehigh-coach-brett-reed.
3 Ibid.
4 Ibid.
5 Ibid.
6 Ibid.
7 Ibid.
8 Ibid.

10

THE PRESS CONFERENCE

If it ain't catered it ain't journalism

In this chapter, we will take a look at one of the key ways to get your message out, creating, implementing, and following up on the press event itself. We will look at what or what not to include in an effective press conference, how to use creativity in creating an event, how to speak with one voice.

We will look at the PR process for two types of announcements in this chapter:

- the long-lead announcement
- the spontaneous announcement.

The biggest element a publicist has with event publicity is timing. Ample lead time for an event is always a bonus but even when events are impromptu, such as in a crisis or a sudden news story, it is always important to think and plan. One of the biggest problems in public relations in this era is reacting too quickly and not effectively thinking through a strategy. Even if you have five minutes to get your story out, it is *very* important to take the time, step back, and *think* about what it is you are about to do or say, or make someone available to say. Spontaneous reactions are the ones which will always get us into trouble.

The long-lead or planned event

As publicists, we are always looking for time: time of day to make an announcement, time to plan and prep, time of the week to be impactful, time to hire the right people, time …

Budgeting time with the long-lead announcement is critical to success. Time gives you the ability to think strategically, to effectively prepare and provide messages to the speaker, and most importantly to review your steps to make sure that you have thought of everything, including the unexpected, as you plan for an announcement.

Also, to clarify what is meant by *long lead*. It is very simple; having a longer time than usual from when an event is being discussed to when the event will actually happen. Sometimes these events can be almost timeless—the announcement of a logo, for example. Or the events can be around the same time every year, such as when a schedule is announced, or when a league draft or college signing day is. They are events which the publicity team knows will happen, but the immediacy of the announcement is not actually at hand.

Like the good news story, it is important to follow some simple reasons for having a press event.

- Why
- Where
- When
- What
- Who

Let's take a look at each.

Why call a press conference?

The structure, cost, and formality of calling a "press conference" leads to many other questions that publicists need to be prepared to answer. In this day and age, when conference calls, video conferencing, transcription services, online chats, and phoners are the norm, calling a formal event can at times lead to more cost, and sometimes embarrassing timing, more so than anything else. There is that time issue again by the way. Given all that is going on in our world today, the immediacy of an announcement will also have a great deal to do with your decision.

So why have a formal press event?

Breaking major news. The news we have to tell the press is immediate, and usually there is more than one party involved who will be a voice. It is the opportunity to control the message and be both proactive and decisive. Examples would be:

- Changes in organizational structure—a new coach, player, or organization head will be introduced to the media and fans.
- The announcement of major business news such as new business partners, new arena, rules of the game, or logo change.
- The announcement of an award bestowed to player, coach, or organization.
- A major community initiative.
- Crisis management.

The need to address many members of the media in one setting. It is much easier to have all the media come to one central place, be able to address them through statements and Q&A, and actually see them, then try and take hours of one-off sessions or miss people with conference call formats.

Example

It is not every day that a backup quarterback in the NFL draws a crowd, but that was not the case in the spring of 2011 when the New York Jets signed Tim Tebow. A quiet Monday morning turned into a media circus with over 250 media showing up at the Jets practice facility. Rather than cramming people in, the team set up an availability on the practice field and gave the media ample time to have at Tebow. The result was a positive for all involved, and a great win for their Toyota sponsor, whose name was on the backdrop and was seen in news feeds around the world. It made for a much better setting than to try and do things piecemeal, especially with the large turnout.

The need to publicly show unity. Especially in a crisis situation or when a trade or organizational change is made, it is important to physically see that all involved are united on a decision.

Example

The Philadelphia Eagles suspend controversial wide receiver Terrell Owens. It can easily be said that losing such a talent will hurt coach Andy Reid's offensive set, or that Donovan McNabb and management may not be on the same page with the decision. However having Reid, McNabb and owner Jeffrey Lurie available in the same setting shows the world that the team is speaking with one voice.

The need for the photo opportunity. One of the most basic needs is for video and still pictures of an event. In this ever-increasing visual world, the short soundbite and accompanying pictures have become essential to showing the impact of an announcement.

The need to show our partners the "impact" of this announcement. Giving the principals their due is another motivating force for having a formal press event. It also shows that the organization is taking this announcement very seriously and it needs the attention of the top of the organization.

The need to take a minor announcement and make it "important." Many times it sounds silly, but this is the motivating factor to have a press event. It is important to keep an entity or an ideal "topical" in the minds of the media and constituents, and by having regular announcements that the media can attend, one can create news. It also sends a message to our competitors that we are active and making news.

With that as the basis as to the "why", here are some thoughts on "why not."

Bad timing. You cannot have the proper speakers there to answer questions, or the folks you can provide are not newsworthy enough. Here is the example of when it is a good time to have a conference call to address issues in a short turnaround from wherever the principals are at the time. Having an under-served event makes the organization look disorganized or disinterested.

No news. Try never to "cry wolf." If you are asking the media to attend an event, then you should have something substantial to get them there. If there is no real news being announced, the more times you do this the less chance you have of either making an impact or getting media to show up when you have an announcement of significance.

Minor news. Especially in niche sports or for minor announcements, in this day and age you are better off doing the press release and the follow-up calls as opposed to trying to make something big out of something small. You can invest a great deal of time, money, and energy into an event and have a negative effect.

Example

The Westchester Golden Apples of the defunct United States Basketball League wanted to have a press conference to announce their new coach Jim Bostic. However, the timing of the announcement, on a summer Friday, was bad, even though that is when the owner wanted to have it. The result was that no local media showed up, embarrassing the owner and the coach. The easier thing would have been to do the announcement in a time or place where it could have been impactful, or to put out a release and get the coach on the phone with a local media rep.

The news is already out. In the 24/7 news cycle, this is becoming a bigger issue. When you are dealing with multiple media and multiple sources, the story gets out with all its details and you are left to have a press conference to basically repeat or confirm what is already out. The more extra information you can give the media when they show up, the better off you will be. Once everyone has spoken, it is hard to create the buzz again. Now, this is a bit difference with personnel changes in team sports. If a coach is changing or a player is traded, the news cycle can usually last a few stages and a few days, especially if folks are coming from various places. However, if there is one main focus and news gets out and is accurate, the follow-up presser can lose steam quickly.

Example

Although not a sports specific example, this one fits the profile. TWA was ready to make an announcement with new flights coming into Chicago O'Hare airport, which would bring millions of dollars into the local economy. The problem was that in order to get media a little more interested, the Director of Public Affairs gave the background of the story to the *Chicago Tribune*, which ran the information in the morning paper. With the news now out in one outlet, the other local newspapers chose to pass on the press conference, and the video angle was lost when forty minutes prior to the event there was a major fire in downtown Chicago. By giving the information to just one paper, the news cycle ended before the formal event could take place.

The jury is still out, or the news is limited. It is much worse to call an event and not be able to speak than to not have an event and go with a press release. If you are trying to control the amount of information that can be put out, the last thing one wants to do is create a situation with dead air, where the principals may say more than they should. It also gives the air that the organization is looking to create news.

Conflict in the marketplace. All publicists will deal with situations beyond their control when it comes to press events. Weather and disaster are two common ones. These will affect attendance. However, many times we are so focused on our task that we forget to look around in the general landscape to make sure there are no conflicts already scheduled that could affect attendance. Is there another game or event going on in town that media always attend? Is there a political event going on that will always draw TV? Are we doing an event at a time when TVs have to be back putting together a news show, or when reporters are on deadline? All those have to be factored in when we have the long-lead planning.

Injuries or serious accidents. Due to the changes in the Health Insurance Portability and Accountability Act (HIP-AA) in the United States in recent years, the amount of information that can be given out about accident or injury to an athlete is limited to whatever is agreed to by the athlete involved. There have been many cases where doctors or officials, with the best intentions in mind, have spoken too much on an injury or been misquoted by a media that is clamoring for information and is not savvy to medical terms and the results are long-lasting and very damaging to all involved. The amount of technical terms used to explain nuances for specific player injuries can get very dicey as well. Therefore, many leagues have mandated that little basic information be provided for injuries, so that everything is consistent. When dealing with million-dollar athletes or the careers of student athletes and the investments made in them, simple fact is much better, and this can usually be done in a press release form.

The best recent example of this involved former Cincinnati Bengals quarterback Carson Palmer. The following is the AP story the following day.

Doctor calls Palmer's injury "devastating"

NFL.com wire reports, June 12, 2006

CINCINNATI (Jan. 12, 2006)—Carson Palmer's knee injury was "devastating and potentially career-ending," involving numerous ligament tears, a shredded ligament, damaged cartilage and a dislocated kneecap, his surgeon said.

The Cincinnati Bengals quarterback tore ligaments in his left knee when he was hit by Pittsburgh's Kimo von Oelhoffen on his first pass during the Steelers' 31–17 playoff victory.

The team announced that he had torn the anterior cruciate and medial collateral ligaments. The damage was much more extensive and severe, but Dr. Lonnie Paulos said surgery went well and Palmer could be back for the start of the season.

Palmer had surgery Jan. 10 in Houston. Doctors used grafts from other parts of his body and donated tissue to fix the damage during an operation that lasted more than two hours. Palmer headed back to California on Jan. 12 to do his rehabilitation.

"It's not just like it was a torn ACL," Paulos said in a phone interview from Houston. "It's a magnitude more difficult to recover from and repair. It can and has ended careers, without a doubt."

"However, I feel very comfortable with Carson as an athlete and the heart that he's got. In the end, that's the bottom line. I can see the look in his eye already. He's ready to get going."

Paulos, an orthopedic surgeon who has worked with the US Ski Team since 1983, replaced the anterior cruciate ligament, which runs through the middle of the knee and provides stability. He said the medial collateral ligament, which runs along the side of the knee, was damaged "real bad."

"On a scale of 1 to 3, it was a 4," he said. "It was off the chart. It was pretty badly damaged—shredded is the better term."

The kneecap dislocated when Palmer was hit, damaging tissue around it. There also was some cartilage damage, he said.

Paulos was able to repair the knee without removing pieces of cartilage or soft tissue, a good sign.

"The things that were torn could be repaired," he said. "They were not torn beyond repair. So he's got all his parts in there, which is good. We're optimistic, actually."

If rehabilitation goes well, Palmer could be running in a couple of months and might be able to play in the first regular season game, Paulos said. The 2006 schedule hasn't been set.

Palmer has worn a protective brace on the left knee since he sprained it near the end of the 2004 season. The knee bowed inward on von Oelhoffen's hit even though Palmer was wearing the brace,

"The brace didn't function well in this environment and should have done better than it did, frankly," Paulos said.

The plan is for Palmer to wear more substantial braces on both knees when he returns.

"No brace is perfect," Paulos said. "No brace can prevent every injury, but they do help."

Paulos saw the replay of the injury and wasn't surprised at the extent of the damage it caused. Palmer has absolved von Oelhoffen, saying he didn't think the lineman was trying to hurt him. The lineman said he was trying to sack Palmer, not injure him. He wasn't penalized for the hit.

Palmer made the Pro Bowl in only his second season as a starter, throwing an NFL-leading 32 touchdown passes. The club extended his contract through the 2014 season.

The issue here is that the doctor, although speaking from facts, used words like "devastating" without Palmer's knowledge, and turned what was already a bad situation into a worse one.

Where to call a press conference

Once again the logistical planning for a press conference is almost as important as to what is being said. Some background follows.

Make it in a controlled space. There are many times where we think that having a press conference in an open stadium, or with a beautiful scenic background, will make for a great photo opportunity. Photo ops are for afterward and can be moved to another location. Quiet, indoor spaces with great lighting and clear sightlines are the best, no matter where you are. If one can't be heard or seen by the media, or if he/she can't see the media assembled, it will be very uncomfortable. This also avoids having folks wander in or having distractions arise to disrupt the flow.

Make it easily accessible. The simpler place, the better. An easily identifiable restaurant, room, or office works best. The last thing you want is for media, or the principals involved, to get lost getting to the event, or media who can't get equipment up and down stairs to leave or not attend. Also always remember the *closer* you go to *where* the media are, the better off you will be. If there is any question of attendance for important media, it is almost as important to move the principals than to move the media.

Have another space ready for prep. Again, the more prepared you can be the better, so have a side room or hallway ready for your principals to relax and be ready to go when called for. The less intermingling the better off you will be and the more focused you can keep those involved. A little air of mystery for even the most mundane announcements helps the event go smoother.

Know the area where it is being held. Even in the simplest announcements, always know the space yourself and walk it many times before getting ready to go. Where is the power being supplied from? Do the windows open? Does the room get too hot or to cold and where is the thermostat? How far are the phone lines or the media work space? All these will make you be secure when everyone arrives and you are ready to go.

Be aware of the time restraints. Even the most perfect and accessible space can become disastrous if there are others using the space either too long before or too soon after. Delays can always occur, and you always want the space ready to go before, and make sure it is yours afterward, so your efforts can be maximized.

Try and make the space significant and positive. Even with controlling the space, it is great to have historical or geographic significance that ties into your story line. Announcing the new men's basketball coach at St. Francis of Pennsylvania's "Mo" Stokes Center (Maurice Stokes was one of college basketball's legends from the 1950s) makes much more sense than having the presser in the cafeteria, for example. Conversely, try to avoid any discomfort as well. Having an event in a locker room space where a player injury occurred may not be the best way to avoid negative past feelings being dragged into a positive announcement.

Record and stream. Making sure that whatever area has the proper Wifi connections so that a group can stream and live tweet and blog from the event as it happens is key. Many times older venues still do not have this capability and that limits the effectiveness of the event.

When to have a presser

This sounds simple and logical, but depending on what your goals are there may be differences here in the normal, traditional rule of thumb. The traditional rule of thumb said you always had a presser:

* as close to midday as possible
* in the middle of the week
* away from holidays or other significant events.

While that may hold true in many instances, when trying to carve your niche, many people will look to optimum times when the 24/7 news cycle is actually slow to get their story out. If you are looking to drive maximum exposure, then those principles hold true. However, if you are looking for a slow news cycle to make an event noteworthy, you may look to those areas to help fill a void.

From a non-sports perspective, a great example is New York Senator Charles Schumer. Senator Schumer has a great understanding of the news cycle, and holds a press event every Sunday during the afternoon in various locations to address a particular issue he is involved with. Because he is a popular public figure and it is a slow news day, the television coverage he gets on Sunday night news is always significant, and in many ways is welcomed by the media to help fill their shows.

On the sports side, legendary sports publicist Joey Goldstein would always work on holidays, especially Christmas and New Year, pitching and planning stories to get into the papers. His theory is that he is one of the few people working to get his clients "ink" on those days no matter what the story is, and many times he was successful. Now is the circulation of papers down on those holidays? Yes it is. However in today's news cycle the amount of times CNN, or a website, or an all-news station will run a story on a slow news day can increase exponentially in comparison to a busy day when there are many events going on.

One thing is for sure. You need to have your event when you are able to get the key folks there and when the news is ready to be made. If you choose the quiet times to have events then your clients must also realize that you may not have the column of attendees, but the long-standing coverage may increase. It is a gamble, but for some stories may be a gamble worth taking and should be considered.

Time of day and day of the week are two other factors that seem to be changing as the way news is covered evolves. For example, if your goal is for live TV, then maybe doing an event in the noon hour or in the five o'clock hour will get you local news coverage. Those pre-six o'clock eastern times can also get you ESPN news, various websites with streaming video and other live shots that were not available in previous years, along with live pickup from websites and audio services. The immediacy of news on the web has also led to greater competition between websites and print media. The later in the day one now goes with an event in the day, the better chances that websites will rush to post while newspapers file for their online sites to get the jump. One thing the publicist should always be aware of with time of day is the deadline for early editions for print. This will not only affect news coverage but could also affect photo coverage for early editions and get some extra placement both there and on the websites of publications. In the time factor there is now a global issue as well. If your news is worldwide and you are on the east coast of the United States for example, early morning may work best. In the financial world, the gearing of announcements around the 9:30am eastern time opening of the Nasdaq or NYSE has always been popular, and for more sports and entertainment related businesses using that as a worldwide launching spot have found to be optimal. The bottom line is you have to weigh in what the norm and what the end-all goal for coverage is, and make sure that your constituents are happy with timing.

Day of the week, as mentioned in the two examples above, is also evolving. The traditional, high impact areas in mid-week are also the most crowded and tend to have the biggest risk as far as mass coverage. In cities in the fall where football is king, early week coach press events can drown out any other coverage. So effective planning is the most important thing, especially in the 24/7 cycle. That being said, there do remain natural breaks in the calendar which every year are slow news days and are not holidays.

Tip

The two biggest breaks occur:

- The day after the Major League Baseball All-Star game (usually a Wednesday) in July. The day has become ESPY and WNBA All-Star day now because of the lack of traditional sports programming There is no NFL yet, basketball and hockey are over, NASCAR is just past midseason, there are no majors in golf going on and tennis is between Wimbledon and the rise of the US Open. For long-term announcement planning it is usually a very smart day market-by-market.
- The day after the NBA all-star game (usually a Monday) in mid-February. Again after the Super Bowl and NHL All-Star games, college hoops is not into tournament mode, baseball is in a lull, Daytona is done, tennis and golf are quiet. This used to be ESPY day before the NBA lockout in the late 1990s, and remains the second quietest day on the calendar for planning.

Again these are all great planning options, but your success will be determined by timing and impact. One great thing is the publicist of today does have more options than he or she had in the past with regard to day, time, and date.

What should go into a press conference set-up?

Now that we have looked at why, where, and when, let's examine the "what" that goes into a successful event. We will deal with who the speakers and their prep, etc. next, but first let's look at the press conference and its basic elements for success.

Like the Boy Scout motto says, "Be prepared"

When setting up your event, make sure that every possible detail is on your checklist (end of the section) from the first planning stages through the end. Let's start with the advance planning.

1 *The advisory*. Make sure the finalized advisory includes all the facts, as well as the basic information that will pique the media interest without giving away the store.

2 *The invite list*. Make sure that all contact info on your media invite list is fax, phone, and email correct, and that you have reached both the decision makers and the writers. It should be organized by level of importance for the event and the participants and everyone involved with media outreach should be working off the same copy. Duplicating invitational calls is OK. It is better to call the same outlet or writer more than once than not to call at all.

3 *Doing the inviting*. Split it up, and make sure all are called with an invite and track responses. Bring the list of confirmed attendees to the event and have the greeter check off as they arrive. It is not acceptable to have someone blind fax or email without follow-up. Also make sure that everyone gets the correct invite, from the wires and papers to TVs, radios, and the weekly newspapers. Never assume someone knows.

4 *Know the audience*. Make sure that you are thinking about the media needs for the event, and have your mult box (the mult box is the box usually set up by sound technicians in the back of a press room so "multiple" media can plug in and get clear sound. It avoids having the rash of microphones on the dais and gives everyone clear, consistent sound) set up for sound, there is ample power, seating is appropriate for the size of media expected, photographers have room to shoot, and cameras have a strong unblocked position to the podium. Key media also deserve special attention, so a call from you after initial contact goes an extra mile.

5 *Know who pays the bills*. In this video-driven age, the importance of messaging on your backdrop is almost as important as what the speaker is saying. Make sure that the information on your repeat banner (the banner in the background which is visible to the media. It literally repeats the logo of the sponsor or the organization many times so that each one is visible to the attendees, especially the photographers and video cameras) whether it is a logo, a ticket sales number, a sponsor or a website (or a combination of all) is clear, correct, and in the media eye. The lack of legibility cannot only be an embarrassment for those speaking, but could also be a critical violation of a sponsor agreement.

Another low impact but thoughtful touch is the mic flag on the podium. In today's age, the use of a mult box as a central resource for sound is more efficient than ever before. Therefore having just your mic flag on the podium will get your logo, sponsor, or website more exposure in still and video image. You now have the chance to brand both behind and in front of the principals better than before.

> **Tip**
>
> Asking photographers or camera crews to "site" the image for you with lights on to check for glare and clarity is an important factor as well.

6   *It's your party, treat everyone like guests.* Even though the media are not getting elaborate hand-engraved invitations, they are your guests and your messengers to the world for your news. Treat them as guests no matter what the news is. Make sure that they have all the things they need to do their job—power, lighting, phone lines, or wireless and internet access (if applicable), etc. You never get a second chance to make a first impression, so make sure that whoever is at the door is courteous, respectful, and aware of the needs of the media coming in. He or she may not know the key columnist from the weekly blogger, but if he/she treats everyone with equal parts respect, there will not be an issue.

   Also remember that this is your house, and would you let anyone in without offering them something to eat or drink? These folks will get there early and leave late, and although budgets may not allow for a full spread of food and drink, making the gesture of having water or soft drinks and some snacks available is usually very welcome. It may also be a way to find some creative sponsorship through a local restaurant or on-campus caterer or beverage provider in exchange for some in room signage.

> **Tip**
>
> Have a bag of extra batteries, pens, an extension cord, audio recorder and paper around for those media members who arrive late or unprepared. If you have logoed pens and pads even better, as they become a grateful takeaway from the event.

7   Make the press kit crisp and impactful. Like a game program for a sporting event, the press kit from an event can have a life of its own. Many times extra copies return to press rooms and offices and are used for follow-up time and again. There is an opportunity to get information, both the primary announcement and all the background, out to a larger audience. Once again, think here what your message through the media is to be. The basic press kit for an event should include:

- press release
- bios (one page each) of each of the principals speaking
- background material on the event (testimonials, career stats, timeline, etc.)
- your business card or the appropriate person or persons for follow-up.

In this digital age doing items on a CD or memory stick is nice but may have limited use. However, they are much more useful (correct logos, photos) on disk or stick than to put photos in a press kit. The days of using stock prints are almost totally gone.

For the television side, having b-roll (background footage to fill in the story) available for local television stations to use, or streaming video for websites to download, is also a big help in saving those media time, and also controlling what footage gets used. We are not talking about footage from the event here. I am talking about action footage or stock shots that support the event, images that media may have to search for or pay for without your help.

Keep in mind that anything more than three to five pages per folder pocket will be useless for the media in most cases.

Tip

I have always found it useful to prepare a sheet of third-party testimonials for media to use as background. For example, if it is a hiring or a trade or signing of a player, or for a milestone, having a one pager of third-party quotes available. This serves three strong purposes:

1 It saves the media time from making the calls themselves.
2 It gives you the opportunity to control and give credit to some key people.
3 It saves those influential third parties time talking to many media.

---

8 *Visuals are nice, but keep them impactful and to a minimum.* If there are trophies, statues, awards, artists renditionings, models, etc. it is great to have them in the room as photo ops. Blow-ups of great photography are also very interesting for down time and posed photos. However, they are part of the day, not the real focus. Press events are usually about people, and the people should dictate the event. Keeping visuals in play is important, but it shouldn't detract from the focus.

> **Tip**
>
> If your principals in the press event have been featured in a newspaper (in a positive way), you may want to have a blow-up or two of the photo to include in a photo op. It will get you a nice website or paper shot in that publication.

9   *Got gifts?* It sounds silly, but the far-reaching effects of hats, t-shirts, pens, and notepads as take-aways can get you more exposure and keep you top of mind with the media sometimes longer than what your actual news was. Free stuff. Most people will wear it and use it and sometimes pass it on to friends and colleagues. Therefore it is always nice to be able to have some low-cost but useful items available as part of the press kit or as an exit gift for media. The media will remember when and who they received gifts from, and it may be a key way to influence them to come back for other events.

10   *Set the dais, view the room.* The way your dais is set and the way your room is structured will set the tone for the press event.

- Make sure that the room, no matter how large or small, has balance. Equal seats and space on both sides. The podium or dais or both should be the center focus of everyone in the room.
- Leave space in the front row for unexpected guests such as families, VIP officials, sponsors, etc.
- Determine what your post-event photos will be and where you will do them beforehand. Make sure your photographers know what the photo op will be, and maybe ask them for an opinion on where and who should be included so that they are maximizing their shots.
- The same thing goes for your one-on-one area, if there will be one. Make sure the area is clearly marked, even if it is another room. Make sure your video folks know where it will be and whom they will get and if possible make sure that the area also has the appropriate back-drop (this may sometimes be too cost prohibitive).
- Like the room set-up, make sure the dais is balanced. Try and keep an equal number of speakers on both sides of the microphone position.
- Table tents should be used no matter how famous the speakers. The use of table tents give each speaker the knowledge of where you think they should sit and will help you balance the room. Also never take for granted that media will know who every speaker is. It will avoid having them guess at whom to shoot, who is speaking, and who to direct

the questions to. Table tents also give you another chance to display a logo for photo and video, as well as make sure that everyone's names and titles are correct in photo and video use. If Twitter handles for the participants are relative to the announcement, put them on the table tent. If there is a hashtag to drive interest, list that as well. Whatever is relevant should be included for the press to use in referencing and reporting the event.

- Find a place to make sure that there is bottled water available for the speakers, and that the speakers know where it is. If it is a sponsor on the cups or bottles, even better. *However,* if it is a competitor make sure to remove the logos from view.
- If there are props to be used in a post-event photo, have them hidden and in the photo area. They should be readily available once the photo ops begin. The same is true for other VIPs who will be in photos. They should be aware that they will be included at the right time and they should be in the area (front row preferred) when the event starts.
- Check that all microphones work, and then check again. Know where the on switch is and who the sound guy is if you are using a sound-board. Feedback is a killer.
- For post-announcement Q&A sessions, try and determine who will ask the first question and where that person is in advance. Like the photography issue, ask a writer if he or she will ask the first question. It will save you time and keep your event running along very smoothly. Many times you may want it to be a beat writer, or a wire service person, or someone who you are familiar with. It will avoid surprises in most cases.

11 *Go to the audio and video record.* For every event it is critical that the PR staff have at least one digital recorder and the ability to get at least one raw footage video dub. The audio file is very important, especially if it is possible to convert it into a file to email out to media unable to attend or to post on a website.

It would also be very helpful in many cases to have a word-by-word transcription, or at worst a Q&A, of the press event as well. Transcriptions become very important when participants are misquoted, and are useful for pulling out sound bites for promotional pieces. The sound bites are essentially a best selection of the quotes from an event that can be used in additional press releases, on websites, and in stories in the future. The transcription lists exactly what was said in the order it was said and is the living record of the event for future reference.

The video file is important for similar reasons. It provides a solid record of the event, and gives you the ability to dub raw footage copies to get out to outlets that could not attend, as well as posting streaming video online. Video also gives you the ability to reconvene with the principals at the appropriate time to review how they answered questions, and will give you the opportunity to actually see what the event looked like and how it flowed so you can adjust accordingly in the future.

12 *Do the run of show.* Like a game, you as the publicist need to have a run of show, listing what should be happening on press conference day minute by minute. The list should include every breakdown from when the kits are assembled, to when the food is brought in, to when the doors open, and when the event starts. It will also include ample time to meet with participants, review speaking order and potential Q&A, and all post-event activity, ranging from photo opportunities to one-on-one interviews.

When you review the run of show with staff the morning of the event it will give you pause to think of what you could have missed and will give you time to think through everything that is needed and planned out.

The other key in doing a run of the show is that it gives you the opportunity to effectively communicate with the principals what their role is and what the timing is. This way any questions they may have are out of the way well in advance of the event.

Another key in doing a run of show is that as the emcee of the event, you can effectively orally communicate to the media both when they arrive and when the event begins exactly who is speaking, in what order, when Q&A will occur, and what the photo opportunities will be. This will avoid a great deal of confusion by late arriving media, and will show to everyone in the room that you are firmly in charge of the situation.

Who should be involved in the press conference

We have now gone through the essentials for the event, and thought through potential trouble spots. Now the main question that remains is who is speaking, what are they speaking about, and when are they saying it.

There are several rules of thumb with the process. The dais, which as stated earlier should be the focus of your room, should be confined if at all possible to those with whom the announcement is for, those who will take questions from the media, and the person who is running the event. In some cases, usually for moral support, one of the subjects chooses to have a key family member or members on the dais with him or her. It is my opinion that this should be discouraged for several reasons.

- It puts someone directly in the focus of the media (such as a child or a spouse) who probably should not be there.
- If it is another official, it creates an uncomfortable situation to have someone up there who is not speaking. (In most cases when given the choice, that person will opt out of being a silent head on the platform.)

- It creates distractions (especially when they are family members) for the people who are speaking.
- It creates confusion for the media as to what everyone's role is in the press event.

These additional family members and officials, who are in a non-speaking or ceremonial role, should be treated with warmth and respect. They should be in the front row, acknowledged by you as the emcee when the proceedings begin, and be given every courtesy that they deserve for photo opportunities and possibly one-on-ones after the press event is over. This way it gives everyone the chance to focus on the task at hand and lets the event run smoothly.

The amount of speakers in a press event should if at all possible not exceed four, in addition to the emcee, and they should speak in order of importance. Usually the highest ranking official speaks first to welcome everyone, then the second-highest ranking official until we get to the principal person making the announcement or is the subject of the press event.

Remarks should be short, no more than two or three minutes each, unless the principal person is clarifying a negative situation and needs to speak more. It is also important that someone on the dais acknowledge all of the family members and other VIPs in the room at that point. It is usually left to the second in command, but it is the emcee's job to police and make sure all bases are covered.

Tip

When planning the seating, it is easiest to have the speakers come from outside in. The final speaker should be right next to the podium so that he has the shortest distance to go when he or she speaks, and can pose for a brief photo after his or her remarks. If any presentation is being made to the speaker, it is easiest to do so briefly at this time, with bigger group photo ops. after the Q&A.

Following all the remarks, it is the emcee's job to police the Q&A. The easiest way to do Q&A in a press conference setting is for the principals to remain seated and take questions one at a time from the audience. If mics have to be passed around or parties have to get up and answer questions, valuable time can be lost. It is the job of the emcee to keep questions balanced across the room, keep the questions to one per person, and never let the Q&A run long. This is the most dangerous time of the press conference, and where people tend to let their guard down. Therefore, keeping the mass Q&A to 5–10 minutes at maximum is critical.

It is also important to try and lead at least one question to each person at the dais if at all possible.

One important note to always keep in mind: if the news is of a negative fashion, or if only a statement is going to be read by participants, it is *critical* that is understood by the media. Furthermore, it is *not* suggested to make an antagonistic situation with the media if there are subjects that the principals do not want to or cannot address. Two steps need to be taken here:

1   The emcee makes it clear prior to the Q&A that the participants will take questions only about what has been discussed here. Do not make it any more specific than that, because there may be members of the media who do not know about an issue and this could raise it.
2   The participants must be aware that despite your best efforts, in all likelihood one member of the media will ask a question on the topic simply to get a "no comment." That is fine, and the participants can issue the "no comment" once or twice if need be. If the questions persist, it is the emcee's job to police and end the Q&A early.

To assume that the media will not ask the question is a mistake.

After the formality is over

Now the formal press conference is done, the less formal break-up sessions then take place, and should go in the following order:

1   Group and individual photos in the predetermined location with all principals and other VIPs involved. The group photos should last no more than 5–10 minutes.
2   One-on-one interviews, coordinated in a list in advance. Normally the rule of thumb is to do television first, followed by radio, and then print, given the deadlines that most organizations are under. Of course, given different deadlines, this may change. Usually one-on-ones are also determined by market share and circulation, or impact of a columnist. It should be noted that each participant be aware that these one-on-ones are essential to the process, and usually take longer to do than the initial formal press event. The order should be determined ultimately by the publicist, and should be coordinated for each of the principals so that he/she knows exactly where he/she is going at that time.

Also at this time it is important to note where other VIPs and family members are hanging around, perhaps taking them to a quiet room with drinks and snacks to wait, or giving them the option of leaving. The more coordinated the effort and the more streamlined the media requests are, the less confusion occurs.

Once all media is over, it is important to review with staff who attended and who did not, compile a quick "hit list" of those who were there to follow up with, and then review your checklist again to make sure the event was as impactful as possible.

The post-event process should include:

- Servicing photos to outlets.
- Email of transcript and press release to a larger audience.
- Full use of all social media platforms to transmit messages, photos, and video.
- Distributing event b-roll to media outlets not able to attend.
- Making sure all information is up to date on the website of the organization you are with.
- Monitoring websites and social media for immediate reaction.
- Collecting clips for distribution the following day.
- Following up with long-lead publications.
- Getting feedback from all involved on the event.
- Sending out thank you notes or emails to all involved in the event.

When the final box is checked, you will be able to see if you had a successful, well-planned event regardless of the news. You can only control what you can control!

The spontaneous announcement

Now we will describe the surprise press event, the impromptu or reactionary press event. Usually these come on event days or as a result of some unusual activity. They usually cannot be scripted and the environment can be chaotic. It is the publicist's job to calm the seas, make sure the information coming out is accurate and work as the singular voice for the organization. In short, don't panic!

There are usually four key areas when the spontaneous presser occurs. They are:

- injuries
- bad news/bad game/bad performance
- record breakers
- reaction to news outside the market (scandals, accidents, etc.).

What will always happen is that the media in their quest for a voice on a subject will always go to the person they know best, or the authority figure, or the loudest voice in the room. He or she becomes the authority on everything. He or she is also the person with whom the publicist should have the strongest rapport with for just these situations. That person should be the first one that the publicist is looking out for when these news cycles begin.

In many ways the impromptu presser *is* actually controllable. Since it does require more than a few members of the media to make it an event, it needs to be during a regular media access period where the press is assembled. That gives the publicist the element of time that he/she usually needs, even if it is just a few minutes.

The overall goal here is the same as the planned presser but bears repeating. The difference here is usually situational. The impromptu presser usually happens in a hallway, a locker room or on the field, where the external circumstances can create sound problems, loss of focus, and often large and uncontrollable crowds.

The common word used for this mass of mass media is *the scrum*.

The biggest problem with the scrum is that the questions often come rapid fire and from all sides. They can come from anyone, with every person there trying to get his or her soundbite. The jostling for position, the position of mics and cameras, all create large tension problems and sometimes do not give the speaker the ability to think before he/she speaks or get out of the situation as cleanly or as quickly as he/she possibly can.

The tension arising from a scrum situation can be palpable, and can sometime adversely affect the relationship between the media and the athlete or coach for a great amount of time. Some of the classic examples of a scrum that got out of control have occurred in the larger media markets. In New York, a long-time *New York Post* columnist was once challenged by former New York Jets quarterback Richard Todd for comments he made that Todd thought were antagonistic following a practice. Todd promptly deposited the columnist in a trash can.

In Los Angeles, former Dodger manager Tommy Lasorda, one of baseball's media darlings, once went on a five-minute profanity-laced tirade after receiving what he perceived to be a silly question following a loss.

Another situation I witnessed first hand came on the tragic night when Loyola Marymount star Hank Gathers passed away in 1992. I was the Director of Media Relations at Fordham University in New York, and we were playing LaSalle University of Philadelphia in the Metro Atlantic Athletic Conference Championship game in Albany, New York. Gathers was from Philadelphia, as were many of the LaSalle stars, including future NBA players Lionel Simmons and Randy Woods. Fordham's star small forward was Sanford Jenkins, also a Philly product. All of the group were long-time friends. Shortly before the start of the game, a reporter mentioned to Jenkins that Gathers had passed away, and Jenkins got word to the other LaSalle players who had not heard. The media rush to get immediate comments and reaction from the players on this shocking event, especially to Simmons, was swift and immediate, and he was not given space to react on his own and didn't think the questions were appropriate given his response. He also became angry at Jenkins for what he perceived to be insensitivity to tell him at that time. There again, a seemingly innocent comment between friends was able to spiral into what could have become an ugly situation.

All three situations occurred in the uncontrollable scrum environment, and in all cases the participant was not warned beforehand of potential trouble before media came in, and the subsequent interaction became the stuff of legend.

With those scenarios in mind, let's take a look at what can be done to control the impromptu as best we can.

Injuries

As we mentioned earlier, the HIP-AA laws today prevent much if anything from being said about injuries unless all parties agree. Still, the third-party view of an injury and its severity, or what an athlete said, becomes the bigger issue. Also with injuries, athletes who have suffered a similar fate are always asked to elaborate as well. An example here is with the rash of micro fracture knee injuries in the NBA in recent years, to stars ranging from Antonio McDyess and Allan Houston to Kenyon Martin and Amar'e Stoudamire. Each injury is different, yet each was asked to comment on the other.

The easiest way to address this is for the publicist to take the time *before* media are let into the locker room to remind the coach and players about caring for the privacy of their teammate first and never to get into speculation. That one minute prep can avoid a great deal of the speculation that follows injuries.

Bad news/bad game/bad performance

This of course is the classic impromptu scrum: the reaction to poor athletic performance. Once again, the key is to address this before the locker room opens and remind the athletes and coaches about calm reaction vs. the emotional ones. The phrase "no comment" here can usually go away to diffuse the scrum.

One of the best at this was Hall of Fame quarterback Joe Montana. Montana's career goal was never to be quoted in the papers. Therefore he would answer questions simply and benignly and always took the high road. Another person who has done this very well is the Yankees Derek Jeter. Jeter will rarely get caught up in controversy with the New York media because he has taken the time to breathe, think, and then answer, and it is usually with the same expression.

Record breakers

This is usually a positive for the impromptu, because it reflects positive on-field or on-court performance. The key here for the publicist comes in those brief moments before media access. Remind the athlete to be thankful to those on his/her team or his/her coaches early as possible, and then have them talk about the performance and its feeling. The emotional aspect of the accomplishment should be the memory that reaches the public, almost more than the words themselves.

The other side of the record is to assist he/she whose record has fallen, or who was beaten in the record-breaking performance. One of sports classic moments occurred in 1951, when the Giants Bobby Thomson hit his classic "shot heard round the world" home run off the Brooklyn Dodgers Ralph Branca to win the National League pennant. Branca's spoken words of "leave me alone," and "how do you think I feel" were the lasting memory to many a sports fan. This is perhaps the most difficult situation to deal with and one which obviously must be handled carefully. However, the relationship the publicist has with an athlete will go farthest here. If one can remind the athlete what is to be gained by being respectful as opposed to being surly and disappointed in public, it will go a long way.

Reaction to news outside the market (scandals, accidents, etc.)

Although we mentioned the incident with the Philadelphia-area players above, a situation like that is usually pretty rare. What is more common is for athletes to be viewed as authority figures and quoted about topics that are well beyond their realm as spokespeople. The topics can range from the BALCO scandal to world current events, and many times the athlete becomes a voice in a controversy that he/she was not even aware they would have been involved with.

One example involved the New York Rangers and their all-time great goaltender Mike Richter. Richter was always known for his social consciousness and philanthrophy in addition to his great athletic skills, and would often have discussions with members of the media about current events to pass the time. Following the US invasion of Iraq in 2002, Richter made some comments which he thought were just "in passing" to a writer, and it ended up as major news in the front of the paper. Here was a socially conscious athlete with his own personal views that became the focus of everything he did through several news cycles because a reporter viewed him as an authority.

The importance of the publicist again here is to be the screener and the protector. You have the ability to think outside the game situation, know what is occurring out there, and make those key figures aware of what they should or should not say.

Now once again, you are just suggesting. In this instance there may be a voice that the athlete would like to have. For example, following the tragedies of September 11 the NFL had a great debate over whether or not to play football the following Sunday. In 1963, there was a landmark decision by then NFL Commissioner Bert Bell to play football following the assassination of President Kennedy, and the decision haunted Bell, and his then-assistant Pete Rozelle, for the rest of their lives. While the teams were deciding what to do, the Jets Vinny Testaverde, himself a native New Yorker, came out on his own and said he would not play on the Sunday and would have his teammates not play even if the league decided to play. He also implored other team spokespeople to do the same. It is not known if that was the deciding factor, but the NFL did postpone play for the week.

With those scenarios as the base, it is important to use the same principles that were outlined for the conventional press conference and apply them as best as possible to the impromptu event. Namely the publicist should want to:

• Make sure the facts are presented clearly by the principal speaking.
• Make sure the subject understands he/she only has to answer questions that he/she can answer. If there is a question that the subject cannot or does not want to answer it is OK to say *no comment*.
• In the case of a tragedy, make sure the emotional aspect of the reaction is factored in.
• Have him/her think before they speak.
• Try at all costs to transcribe quotes or record the session to have an accurate account of what is said and to avoid the misquote

Overcommunication can overcome difficulty

One big difference with the impromptu presser is the fact that key decision makers may not know what has been said by whom. After all, this was probably not planned, so owners/business partners/university officials, even coaches, may not be aware what has occurred and could be blindsided by media asking for their comments. Therefore it is *very* important that the publicist pay careful attention to comments and then overcommunicate to those higher-ups with all the facts so that they are not caught unprepared. Sometimes this may be as simple as a phone call or a note, or one may have to run across a field to find a coach, but whatever the physical exertion, the better everyone is aware.

Also in many cases the impromptu presser is both an opinion and a reaction, neither of which can usually be scripted. Therefore, as Einstein said, "For every action there is an equal and opposite reaction," or at least one sought out by the media. In order to stop the chain of events, or the chain reaction, overcommunicating is key.

As we look back, there are the same principles that apply to both of the press conference settings. The importance of the control that the publicist has and the trust he or she has with the newsmakers is critical. And as we said at the beginning, you always have the *time* to make an impact, regardless of whether that time is two months or two minutes. Use it wisely, and both types of events can be successful.

11

CRISIS MANAGEMENT

*A little foresight and planning can go
a long way*

In this chapter we will look at the sometimes overlooked, sometimes trivial but nonetheless important area of crisis management. This chapter addresses what types of issues the sports communicator may have to deal with, how they can be dealt with, and what can be learned from each situation.

One thing the communicator should always consider and always keep in mind when an issue arises is that in many cases the crisis is sometimes only as big as those involved. In many cases, an internal issue only becomes a public one because someone chooses to make it so. We are all aware that in this business none of us are solving hunger or curing cancer. We are working in a services industry, a very fast growing and exciting industry that does involve billions of dollars. That being said, there are some very serious issues that this industry can get involved with that need extreme care, thought, and caution. The 24/7 nature of news and media today also may seem to bring both more immediacy to an issue and may bring more attention to a potential crisis with the media, but even though more people will hear about something short term, unless it is a sustained story, the "crisis" usually passes quickly to the outside world.

It is also important to maintain the chain of command in the crisis, and make it clear who will speak on issue and who are the decision makers. Many times the publicist is directly involved but not at the top of that chain. It is important to keep the chain clear and equally as important is the necessity to surround the decision maker with the right information so that the choice made is clear.

While some may see social media as a creator of crisis—when individuals tweet or post thoughts without thinking about what they are saying or who they are speaking on behalf of—social media can also be a great resource in a crisis in getting out clear and useful information. Although the use is growing, only 25 percent of companies encourage their employees to use social media channels to share messages about the company, but in a crisis that shared accurate information can be critical. Twitter's paid sponsored followers for example, can be one of the best crisis resources, as it will help very quickly identify thousands of followers who can help amplify the information spread with Twitter's targeted follower acquisition strategy. Of course that type of social use is also evolving for the positive, using best-case scenarios of everything from natural disasters to man-made threats.

There are several kinds of crisis situations we will look at:

- The physical plant crisis—escape plans, security, blackouts, bomb threats, etc.
- The on-field crisis—game injury; fan injury; and unruly behavior
- The public tragedy—untimely loss of life; crimes; family issues for athletes, coaches, and executives; suicide
- The corporate/internal crisis—financial shortfalls; teams or entities being sold; sponsor leaving; hirings and firings; changes in reporting structure, etc.
- The player personnel crisis—trading the hometown star; dealing with the fallout.

Most issues we will deal with will fall under one of these five categories. Before we get to them, let's set up some general guidelines to consider and apply to almost every situation.

Prepare for the rainy day

In this post-9/11 era, most human resources departments have assembled what is known as a disaster plan: if such and such action happens, here is where we assemble, where we go, what we do. It is important for the publicist to be aware and have a copy of the disaster plan should something critical arise. The publicist should also know the history and background of issues that have previously arisen at his or her place of business, and how they were handled. It will give you good insight into how things could be handled and how key people may react when something does come up in the future.

It is also important to be cognizant of issues in the media that have been viewed as a crisis and how *other* organizations have handled them. How did Major League baseball deal with steroids or the Tour de France with alleged blood doping? How did USA Basketball deal with Bob Knight after he threw a chair at an official in Puerto Rico? How did the local little league deal with disorderly parents? All of those are different degrees of a crisis but can have an impact on what or how your organization would do when faced with a similar situation. In many cases in a crisis, no matter how large or small, you as the spokesperson will probably be looked upon for input, and having a rainy day file will be a big help.

Speak with one voice

No matter what the issue is, it is important for the publicist to guide the organization away from controversy and differing public, or sometimes internal, opinion. Gossip in a crisis is a killer, and you will spend a huge amount of time dealing with the trivial while the important escapes out a window. Gather the facts, determine the plan with the decision makers, have everyone communicating and working off the same page.

It is also very important to determine who that voice will be. In many cases it may not be the person involved in the controversy. It may be the publicist; it may be the athletic director or league or team head. It should always be the person who can be recognized as an authority figure, can speak clearly, commands respect, and can stay calm and on-message.

Listen to opposing sides

It is amazing in a crisis situation how people forget the simple process of listening. Telling people "thank you for the information," or "you are right," even when they may not be, will have a calming influence and will help you get more of the basic facts out in a faster period of time. Many times we will find the truth is somewhere in the middle, and it is important to not just hear what everyone is saying but to listen to them as well. This holds true with the chain of command as well. The leadership from the top and the ability to clearly explain to the higher-ups the need to listen and then evaluate will be key to good decision making.

Ask questions

Many times when a crisis arises, the gossip and the panic is the first instinct. It is important to have in your rainy day file a simple list of questions and to literally check the box to make sure they are answered. They are very simple:

- Who or what was involved in the situation?
- Who knows about the crisis?
- Where are all involved?
- What is our timeframe to speak publicly about this, if at all?
- What are our next steps?

These are questions not only to ask others, but also to ask and answer yourself. You will be amazed that by physically looking at the questions it will slow you down and give you pause to think and act a little more clearly.

Be as consistent as possible

Especially in the current news cycle, if media are aware of a crisis, even if it is just the campus radio station or the weekly newspaper or website, there will be a need to constantly ask or give updates. It is your job as a publicist to hold the line and give updates *only* if there is new and relevant news. Setting a timetable for updates is always a dangerous thing. It is much better to be consistent and let the media know that new information will be furnished when it comes available. The same is true for internal communication. One great way to avoid gossip is to gather and inform staff, and let them know that they will be informed when situations change.

If you are consistent in any crisis situation, the process will run smoother. Also, by being consistent, many times when a different situation arises those around you will have an idea as to what the process will be.

Do not operate in a vacuum

If it is a big deal to you and your organization, then seek help from those who have been there before. Chances are there are folks in the industry who you know (and maybe through your crisis file) that you can call upon and get counsel. The more you keep things to yourself, the more you may second guess or slow down actions. Now this is not to say that you call 20 people and try and build consensus, because that may slow down the process even more. However, having two or three people on call for a situation, especially those with a different experience who may be able to provide an unbiased eye and a calming influence, can be a big help. In many cases when you are in a team situation, those people can be the league officials, who have dealt with a myriad of situations over the years. Confidentiality here is also key.

If the media does not know, then probably don't tell them until you have to

Many times we as publicists feel compelled to "come clean" with a story because we think it will become public knowledge. Because those around us are so close to a particular issue we think it will be the end of the world if it does get out without our spin. Here is a very important thing to think about, especially in this era of accessibility. Sometimes if you don't tell the media, it never becomes a story. There are so many issues that are going on in the sports and entertainment world, what is seen internally as a "big deal" may be viewed as trivial to the media. Also, one should never assume that the media, even in today's world, is all knowing. Yes there are many sources and information streams. However, those streams do not give the media the opportunity to concentrate on every detail, so some things you "assume" people know they may actually not be aware of.

This is *not* to say that you are hiding things. You can be fully prepared when media members do find out about the situation with a plan or a statement. However, to do their jobs for them in this situation may either create a situation that didn't need to become public or make a situation worse.

Now that those basic steps have been established for most crisis situations, let's look at some scenarios and examples.

The physical plant crisis

In a post-9/11 world, the need for a physical disaster plan has taken on even more of a priority than it had before. Whereas before 9/11 the plan was often an insurance formality and was done by building operations and internal security people, it is now an intricate detail that involves police, security, building people, public address announcers, ushers, organization heads, and the publicity staff. For the most part the physical plant crisis comes from an element that is totally unpredictable while an event or a workday is going on—natural disasters or man-made problems, ranging from electrical problems to bleacher seats collapsing.

The publicist's role in these plans is to be another voice, another pair of eyes that can look at some of the other logistical issues that the day-to-day folks have not thought of. Issues on things like player and staff family relocation, where the media attending the event will go and where they can't go, accounting for players, coaches, and game night staff should all be on his or her plate. He or she should have copies of all working documents of the physical plant so that if questions do arise from the media as to an evacuation plan and issues need to be communicated to the media then he or she will have that information.

Since the physical plant crisis will usually be immediate and may happen very quickly, the publicist needs to stay calm and communicate information to the media that can be readily made available to the public. The knowledge of a key area both where team officials are assembled, and a separate area where the media, both those attending the event and those who will be on the police "beat" (the news media who would respond with the police when an incident occurs), should be in the advance plan. Both should be separate areas where a plan of action can be determined and then separately communicated to the media.

Also in terms of communication, especially given large areas where officials could be spread out, such as tennis or golf events or large stadium events, two other key elements have been installed and help a great deal in alerting folks that there is a potential serious issue without initially alerting the public. The first is a key phrase that is communicated through the PA system throughout the complex, one which only those on the "crisis" team are aware of.

Example

At The Championships, Wimbledon in the late 1980s and early 1990s there was a coded call to action phrase that alerted key officials to a bomb scare. Most times the scare was just that and the public rarely needed to be aware that the system was functioning and in place.

The second system in place where public address and sometimes phones need to be placed on silent is through the use of all mobile devices. Each member of the crisis team has his or her device set to receive a key message sent out to all, alerting them to a potential issue and where he/she needs to report to.

Both systems work very well and give those in the know a jump on the public for even a few minutes to ascertain the situation and implement a plan if necessary.

If there is a need for evacuation at the event, the key is to remove everyone safely, assemble at the desired locations, and then formulate, with the right officials, what needs to be presented to the media. Many times, security concerns will limit the amount of information that can be made available, and once again it is very important to be consistent, speak with one voice, and *not* provide updates on demand. As those in charge determine the information that needs to be communicated, then that can be passed on to the public. The important thing is to first remove those who could be in danger from the danger area, and then communicate effectively to the media.

If there are injuries as a result of the action, it is always important to follow the lead of a larger municipal group such as the police or the Red Cross, to determine protocol for distributing information.

Tip

It is very important to remember that when you are dealing with any type of crisis situation that many members of the media sent to cover the event are not in their normal environment. It is also safe to say that you may not know many of these media as well as you will know your regular media. Therefore, *do not* take anything for granted, including such simple things as where they can find electricity, how names are spelled, any other media policies which you take as rote. The more answers to simple questions you can think about and provide upon their arrival, the easier things can go. They can also use this naiveté to help exploit some confusion and gain access to information or areas, which would not be appropriate, as they try to get a better story. Make sure you are aware of who the media are, where they are from, and try and be both respectful and develop a rapport. In the long run it will help the organization.

The other part of the physical plant crisis involves incidents that happen away from game days, or in the office during a normal workday. This again should fall under an institutional plan, but you need to be apart of it. The following is part of the experience that the New Orleans Saints went through during their relocation caused by Hurricane Katrina.

The New Orleans Saints were in the midst of training camp preparing for the 2006 season when Hurricane Katrina hit New Orleans. The devastation to their home field, the Superdome, which was used for a preseason game just the week before, has been well documented. The relocation of the team, including offices, equipment, and personnel, from New Orleans to a temporary home in San Antonio was massive. Although the team practice facility was not terribly damaged, much of the team essentials were not immediately brought to San Antonio. As a result, their makeshift homes and offices at the Alamodome in San Antonio consisted of borrowing from other folks in the area. The staff of the San Antonio Spurs of the NBA pitched in to help, as did several former professional sport publicity professionals in the area. Luckily, communication via the website remained one clear link. The fact that the team and many of their family were able to move en masse was also a plus. However, without immediate knowledge of the extent of the damage the team had to find make-shift ways to get regular work done, as the NFL season was to begin shortly. They also needed to establish solid communications with their fan base with regard to an uncertain return to New Orleans. There were also the efforts on behalf of the team to continue to be a solid and positive voice for all the displaced citizens of the city. All of that crisis management took place with the Saints PR group delivering messages and information, handling a huge amount of media requests and still being able to manage the day-to-day tasks of running a football operation. It also had to be factored in that the staff and their families were still part of the great hardship of the millions of displaced people in New Orleans. They had to maintain a clear and positive public attitude while wondering about homes, savings, belongings, and friends left behind. In the end the PR staff performed tremendously. The displaced team functions took place with few hitches, and the team remained focused and on message while delivering a great amount of hope and humanity to their fans through the media. The biggest issue as the weeks went along was a return to New Orleans. The team played most games either in Baton Rouge or San Antonio while still maintaining a return to New Orleans, which took place in 2007.

The longer lasting physical plant crisis, such as what developed with the Saints, will be ever evolving and can rarely be predicted. For example, the blackout of the east coast in 2004 forced an immediate postponement of a WNBA game at Madison Square Garden. However, a game the next night between Team USA and Team Puerto Rico was not canceled right away, or at least until other officials such as Mayor Michael Bloomberg's office closed down the city well in advance.

A smaller but still impactful crisis regarding weather also involves the playing of games in bad weather. For example, an NBA rule stipulates that a game be played so long as the two teams and the referees are able to make it to the arena. Yet several times fans not willing to lose money on tickets will brave the weather to attend games while many other events are canceled.

The plan on how to deal with season subscribers, communicate weather issues, answer questions about letting or not letting fans move into unoccupied seats all fall into the physical plant issue.

The on-field crisis

This area of crisis management deals with events and occurrences that go on before, during, and after the game. They can involve things like the impromptu presser we talked about in Chapter 10, but for the most part they again involve outside influences which are many times unexpected. How to appropriately handle these crises is a crucial function of the publicist.

Just the facts, ma'am. In terms of an injury to a player during the course of action, we have mentioned this before but it does bear repeating. In the United States, HIP-AA laws dictate that if a player does not consent to releasing information, then the team can do little legally to put information out. It is very important to be in constant communication with the trainer and the doctor first, to make sure that whatever medical information is agreed to is communicated exactly the way it is supposed to be. The difference between sprain and strain may seem subtle but can also be critical. The same thing with what was injured. Many times ankles and knees, as well as even left or right, can be confused in the heat of a crisis. Speak with one voice, and double check the facts.

Also during a game or event, if there is live television and or radio, they may have the highest level of importance to communicate the information correctly to the masses. The most direct line can also include the various social media outlets that the team has employed as well. Keep in mind if the injury is serious or looks serious, the athlete's family and friends are probably watching or listening and will have a great deal of angst. Although it is recommended that the athlete's family have the ability to deal with him or her and the doctors first (by phone or in person) prior to going out to the media, the TV or radio may be the next best thing.

The print media in attendance should also be given the same information in writing at the same time, via press statement. Many times in the hurry to speak to everyone and not put information out in writing, there can be confusion on spelling or terminology. Putting the information out in writing eliminates that. This can also be effectively communicated through social media platforms, leaving little doubt for accuracy.

The third group to be addressed are literally the witnesses—those fans and officials, and even teammates, in attendance at the event. A posting on a scoreboard or message board, on social media outlets, a PA announcement (although unusual), or even the passing out of a statement will help address that group as well.

At one point website posts were not seen as a first line of dissemination. However, in this age now the first line of accurate information media and others may turn to is the Facebook page, Google Plus page, or Twitter feed. If that is your first place to go, make sure it is in lock step with reaching other media. The calling of local outlets, from TV and radio to websites who are following the game and are not in attendance is a solid follow-up, but posting information on a website gives the team or the event a chance to accurately control the facts.

Following the initial information, it is standard procedure to remember to use the standard press conference and update guidelines in other chapters as to how to handle the next steps on injuries. Keeping everyone informed and on the same page is the most important factor.

The fans. With regard to fan injury, many of the same rules apply. The big difference here is the factor of personal injury and all the legalities that go with it and the fact that so much of the video and still photos by those in the crowd can make it to the media well before the team or the event has the ability to accurately ascertain what has occurred. If there is a fight in the stands and security are involved, it may be different than if a child is injured by an object coming off the field. In many cases this will immediately become a matter for the authorities and information will be directed to the local authorities or to police or security. It is still the publicist's job to make sure the information communicated is accurate, and to have on hand all the security measures that are taken in stadiums to keep fans safe. The alcohol policies displayed and announced throughout most professional stadiums and in arenas in this country, and the penalties that go with abuse, should be always on hand. Also keep in mind that you will be looked upon as the expert by the media and by authorities for dealing with the media, and you should confidently assume that role.

If it is a case of a fan injured by an onfield activity such as a hit with a puck, a ball, a stick, or a bat there are "own risk" standards that are well known throughout sports in this country and others, although how those standards hold up in a court of law is for another subject.

Example

However there are exceptions, such as the incident that happened in Columbus, Ohio in March 2002. A 13-year-old girl named Brittanie Cecil was killed after an errant shot by Espen Knutsen struck her in the head while she was in the stands watching the Blue Jackets play the Calgary Flames in Nationwide Arena. As a result of her death, nylon mesh nets have now been installed in all NHL arenas above the area behind the goals to shield spectators from flying pucks.

The reaction of all those involved was appropriate and professional. Information was given out through the team to the media and then hospital officials took over with the process. The team and its players expressed the appropriate remorse and were well versed and sincere in their response. The NHL's PR team also got involved with the greater issue, also assisting the club in their words and actions.

The Blue Jackets wore "BC" initials on their helmets in her memory and have since created the Brittanie Cecil Memorial Fund, which to this day collects donations at every Blue Jackets home game. The event was viewed as a far-reaching tragedy that affected venues around the country.

Brittanie's parents received $1.2 million in a settlement with the NHL and other groups, according to a statement released April 14, 2004.

The other aspect of crisis with the fans is the recent "fans gone wild" episodes in sports. Streakers, assaults on coaches, and attempted flag burnings have all fallen under the lore of crazy fan action in recent years, as folks do stupid things to make themselves part of the action. The proximity that fans now have to the field or court also has created issues as well, and the age of decorum and respect that fans have shown in the past toward athletes has significantly decreased. There have been many documented cases of fans going on the field and athletes going into the stands in recent years. The Houston Rockets Vernon Maxwell charging into the stands in Portland, the Boston Bruins Terry O'Reilly jumping over the glass and into the stands at Madison Square Garden and the ugly incident between the Detroit Pistons and Indiana Pacers at the Palace of Auburn Hills are offset by acts of fan unruly behavior.

On April 25, 1976, the Chicago Cubs outfielder Rick Monday entered sports lore by snatching a flag from a father and son who had run onto the field, doused the flag with lighter fluid, and attempted to set it on fire. Then in September of 2002, Kansas City Royals first base coach Tom Gamboa was assaulted by another father–son duo who ran on the field and attacked him while he stood in the first base coaches box at Chicago's US Cellular Field.

In each case, the team reacted swiftly with police to make sure that the facts were made clear and that the key spokespeople were presented in an appropriate time frame to the media. The teams and the leagues involved also made sure that the law was understood by the media and that the penalties for such actions were communicated clearly and correctly. Usually the public role in such actions is not to create or organize the news, but to make sure that all of his or her constituents get the information correctly and get it in their respective stories.

Tip

Many times in the case of fan unruly behavior, it is important to work with the media to make sure that the incidents, no matter how innocent they seem, are not played out by the media as to encourage more unsocial behavior. Incidents such as fans running on the field, streakers, etc. are now avoided by the broadcast media (with strong encouragement by the publicists) with the theory being that if the fan does not get media attention, less copycats incidents will take place. However, that cannot stop the viral nature of such incidents getting publicity. Publicizing the names of the guilty as a form of embarrassment and public record is one thing, working with the media to explain the incident and then not glorify the action is another. You can only minimize damage and exposure these days due to the proliference of mobile devices, so controlling what you can control is the best course of action.

The public tragedy

This is yet another area which has gotten more and more play in recent years due to the accessibility of information, athletes, the growing news cycle, and the advanced state of technology that has made things like cell phone cameras and voice mail "weapons of publicity" for the general public.

We have also had to deal with a larger rash of untimely deaths and a series of mass tragedies, from the two plane crashes in recent years that took members of the Oklahoma State athletic department to the larger disaster in Russia in 2011, which took the lives of all the members of the KHL Lokomotiv Yaroslavl. That is in addition to the very public suicides of players like former Baltimore Orioles pitcher Mike Flanagan and NFL great Junior Seau.

Many times the family crisis is usually one that does not directly involve an athlete, coach, or administrator during the normal course of work events. It is the after-hours or offseason story, usually when an athlete is on his or her own time, that these instances occur. They are the front-page headlines, the gossip column stories, the police blotter, all the instances in which the celebrity status of today's sports figures have to deal with as the dark side of fame. They will usually start with a late night call from a media member and then go from there. The worst part of these stories is unlike many of the other crisis, the attention to the story will probably come from someone outside alerting the publicist as the team official. Those calls will come from members of the media, the police, or a security person. Rarely will they come first from the athlete him or herself. That means that the story is already out and that in many cases the athlete is now in a strange environment he or she cannot control with little to no of the support system he or she is used to.

We will go through several instances shortly. First we would like to put forth a set of basic ground rules to follow when these stories arrive. Some rules for the family crisis are:

1   *Check the validity.* As we all know, rumors can wildly circulate, especially when prominent members of the media are called. It is important to get confirmation on the incident from a credible source such as another team official like a coach, a teammate, or even if it involves police, a police source or security person themselves. Many times a member of the media will chase a wild lead in the hope that you are able to confirm a story or give them information that they did not have. Like most crisis situations, it is most important to think before you speak.
2   *Get the information to the right people.* Once you know, it is most important to find out who else of influence in the organization knows what has occurred. Write down what facts you know meticulously—location, type of incident, who else is involved—and make a quick list of who needs to know immediately. It is okay to place a few calls too many. It is better

than having a coach, school president, athletic director, team president, or team owner find out from watching TV, getting a text via social media, or hearing it from another source.

If he or she is a professional athlete and is represented by an agent, that person should also be in the loop. Many times he or she will have the most information and will have spoken to his or her client before a team official does.

3   *Build consensus and then identify a speaker.* Again, the only sense of urgency to speak comes from a very rabid media corps looking for quotes. It is the communicator's job to collect the facts, review the chain of command, and work with the officials to speak on behalf of the organization. Even if another person such as a police official, a lawyer, a family member, or an agent has already spoken, it is your job to think and represent the organization and what is best for the long term. A quick reaction can have very long-lasting effects.

4   *Remember that he or she also needs support.* In the US, everyone is innocent until proven guilty. This person or persons represents your school, your team, your sport. Therefore he or she needs to know that there is a friendly face in the area. Getting to where he or she is and helping fend off the media that may already be there will help everyone, regardless of what the issue is. Also, you as a calm, professional official may be able to find out more about the actual situation than those who are emotionally involved.

5   *There are two sides to every story.* No matter what is said or how egregious an act has been committed against another person, there are two sides to every story. Be patient enough to list and if possible ask questions so that you can assist in any way possible.

6   *Remember this can be strange territory.* If you are lucky, situations like this will be very rare. However, when they do occur it is very important to remember that more often than not, the media you will be dealing with will not be the members who you are accustomed to dealing with, and if it is a serious issue, the numbers may be much larger than what you normally experience. Extra caution is always needed here.

7   *Make sure someone tells the team.* It is also important that someone informs the team before the media can get to them about what may or may not have happened. In the instances that his or her family is not aware of anything yet, it is also important that their first news come from a familiar face or voice, not a policeman or member of the media, if at all possible.

8   *It is a larger than sports issue.* Like the media who cover this event, the event itself now becomes more a social issue than an athletic issue. When that occurs you may be put into a secondary or advisory role, rather than the primary one. The chief spokesperson may be an agent, a law enforcement official, or a high university official. Egos should not exist at this point. Actually your job may actually become more valuable to those involved as you work behind the scenes as opposed to being out front.

9 *Your world has changed.* Lastly, remember that, depending on the magnitude
   of the issue, this will dominate your world as a publicist for as long as it
   goes on. Make sure that you are not forgetting about your core job functions in the interim, and that you have folks who can cover off on the day
   to day. Many times issues like these can define an organization, a sport, or
   a university for a long time.

With those points in mind, let's look at the publicist's role in a few of the
largest family issues of the past 25 years.

The Kontinental Hockey League Lokomotiv Yaroslavl air disaster

The Kontinental Hockey League (KHL) had undergone tremendous growth
and a gain in global popularity heading into the 2011–12 season in September
of 2011. A number of NHL stars who were raised in Russia and other countries outside of North America had come back to the KHL to either finish
or extend their careers, and the profile of the league as being a safe, fun, and
engaging alternative to the NHL was on the rise. New arenas were being built,
fans were turning out in larger numbers, media attention was increasing, and
the leadership of President Alexander Medvedev was bringing the KHL to new
business heights it had never seen before.

A good deal of the goodwill and positive imagery took a temporary and
devastating hit on the afternoon of September 7, when the plane carrying the
Lokomotiv Yaroslavl team to its opening game of the season in Minsk, Belarus,
crashed near the Russian city of Yaroslavl. Of the 45 on board, 43 died at the
scene; one of the two rescued from the wreck, Alexander Galimov, died five
days later in hospital, and only the flight engineer Alexander Sizov survived.

While the news of the tragedy started to get out, the KHL and its communications advisors at global PR firm Ketchum were faced with numerous
challenges. First, most of the KHL leadership was scattered around the country at other opening night events, and Ilya Kochervin, the Vice President of
Commerce and Communication, was on another flight and could not be
reached. Because of communication issues and the location of the crash, initial
information coming out was misleading and inaccurate. The team also had a
number of players from outside of Russia, so getting information in a time-
sensitive manner to those families was also critical, as was getting word to the
families of Russian players who may have been from smaller remote villages.

The league also lacked a disaster plan at the time on how to deal with such a
mass tragedy (the NHL did and does have one). Literally those league officials
who could be reached had one main source of information in a country where
social media was still growing—and that source was CNN.

The fact that the incident would also involve multiple layers of government, aviation officials, and multiple jurisdictions of law enforcement made the

process quite daunting in the chaos surrounding the first few hours. However, as mentioned, the KHL did have the benefit of crisis communicators on call, and despite the fact that several were either Europe or US based, they were able to begin the task of fact gathering and messaging while officials went about the grim task of dealing with the initial parts of the tragedy.

A war room was constructed and all senior KHL officials were brought on board to make sure that any and all messages from the league to the public were carefully plotted out. The messages had to address the gravity of the situation and the remorse of a grieving nation while not pointing blame or causing issues with the larger government investigation that was rapidly beginning. The KHL worked with their players association to make sure that all families of the players, coaches, and staff were contacted regularly as the grim tasks of identification were going on. They worked closely with the highest levels of Russian government to make sure that all the facts came out in a clear and orderly fashion, and were not reactionary to rumors and guesses that would make the process worse.

KHL President Medvedev suspended all play and travel for league teams for an unspecified period at first, making sure that all league members had time to adequately grieve and understand the magnitude of what had occurred. The memorial services were carefully planned to be inclusive and respectful of the fans and the team, and more importantly the league began a period of working directly with international officials to make sure that all aspects of the tragedy, regardless of ultimate blame, were being dealt with.

Perhaps most importantly in the crisis, the KHL took a stance of complete transparency in its investigation and in its process of dealing with the tragedy. They immediately assembled international media to talk about the crash and all the issues, answered questions clearly and succinctly, and never placed blame. The message was clear—right now is a time to grieve and assist those affected, from the fans to the players to the families of the deceased. There was no room for finger pointing or cover up, and any issue as to what caused the plane crash would be found out and corrected to avoid an incident ever again.

Over the period of days, the league dealt with the harsh questions regarding the safety of the charter airplanes teams flew, and the government dealt with the larger overall safety of Russian commercial travel. The league consulted with players and other international officials and resumed play the following Monday, following a massive outpouring of global support for the families and all those involved.

In the weeks and months that followed, the KHL dealt with the scathing criticism of the issues with charter flights that were substandard and addressed every issue on the tragedy straight up and with a solid, positive voice. There was no hiding of issues, and zero tolerance for rumors that were unfounded. The legal issues kept some questions from immediately being answered, and at the time of this writing many longer term problems are still being addressed.

However, what came out of the tragedy for the KHL was a positive process led by league officials and their advisors at Ketchum. The messages were clear and consistent, the issues were dealt with head on, there was little room for speculation, and the lessons learned from the tragedy hopefully will lead to a safer, more thoughtful professional organization going forward.

What could have been amazingly chaotic and a death knell to a rising league turned into a tragic learning experience for executives and communications professionals, one which hopefully can be studied and not repeated anytime soon. However, if it is needed, the precedent for an effective process has been spelled out by the KHL and its crisis team.

Len Bias

Len Bias was one of the most gifted and popular athletes ever to come not just out of the University of Maryland, but also out of the Atlantic Coast Conference. The Maryland native had a storied career at the University of Maryland and was the second pick of the 1986 draft, selected by the Boston Celtics to be the next great NBA star, joining the ranks of a second year player for the Chicago Bulls named Michael Jordan. The draft took place in New York on June 17. Less than 48 hours later, Bias collapsed and died in a University of Maryland dormitory. He suffered a fatal cardiac arrhythmia that resulted from a cocaine overdose. Few people even knew Bias had used cocaine, and his death came as a shock to everyone who knew him, especially those at Maryland and the team that had selected him, the Celtics.

Because of the timing of his passing, the Celtics really had no initial role in the media circus that followed. They had not yet signed him, and he was still home in Maryland with family. Therefore much of the initial dealing fell to those who were in the area, his agent Lee Fentress and a young publicist at the firm that had signed him (Advantage International) named Meredith Krugman. The early morning initial call that something had happened to Bias came from Bias' legendary coach at Maryland, Charles "Lefty" Drisell to Krugman, who had just started working with Bias on a number of post-draft promotional and media ideas. Prior to the call, the media had already been alerted through both the police department and the hospital where he was taken after he collapsed. Meredith's role was initially to get to his parents' house and help the family deal with the media who were now descending in droves into the area. Hundreds of media showed up by the time she arrived, literally camping out on the Bias' front lawn. She, along with an Advantage colleague, were able to dodge media and get into the home. By now the news had been confirmed that Bias had died, but not the official cause. Again working without the help of a huge support system, Krugman worked with the family to speak to the media and provide updates on a half-hourly basis. Usually there was no new news and the family was not prepared to speak, so the media descended on anyone who arrived in the area to fill their vigil. Eventually as the day wore on, Krugman worked with Bias' uncle to come up with a statement on behalf of the family. She alerted the media in attendance (there was obviously no need to contact additional media), worked with the family and all his friends and representatives as to what was going to be said, and then assisted the relative in delivering the statement with no questions, and the respect for privacy for the family.

Keep in mind that this was over 21 years ago, and the devices we have mentioned earlier to communicate in crisis situations, Blackberrys, laptop computers, internet access, pagers, cell phones did not exist at the level they do now. It all had to be done with conventional phones and paper and ink, and the statement had to be strong as to give the message of respect to the media but adequately express the feelings of the family, without addressing many of the now rampant rumors that were circulating.

The message delivered, all parties brought on board, and the media satisfied temporarily, Krugman was then assigned to coordinate the media for the extensive memorial service that would then be held two days later at Cole Field House. More like the conventional news conference, hours went into the planning and messaging of speakers, the messages that had to come forth (it was now confirmed that cocaine had been in his system) while still supporting the family and the community.

The long-lasting effects of the way Krugman was able to coordinate the initial reaction of the news to the media and serve as both the sounding board and spokesperson for the family was key in the way the Len Bias tragedy was portrayed by the media. She recognized the media had a job to do but that the family needed time and respect, and was able to juggle both in this family crisis situation to make everyone satisfied with the result.

Ray Lewis

Baltimore Ravens linebacker Ray Lewis is arguably one of the greatest ever to play the position. He is one of a handful of players to win the NFL Defensive Player of the Year more than once, and his role as defensive anchor was key in helping lead the Ravens to the Super Bowl title in 2000. However, his image was publicly tarnished following a Super Bowl party on January 31, 2000. He was arrested along with two other friends for the murders of Jacinth Baker and Richard Lollar. Baker and Lollar were stabbed to death outside a nightclub during a fight in the Buckhead district of Atlanta. The media circus that followed for months afterward was legendary, with one of the most respected publicists in the business, Ravens Vice President of Media Relations Kevin Byrne, front and center.

Byrne was able to work with Lewis, his representatives, and the Ravens officials on all their public statements as Lewis maintained his innocence to the charges and all the bizarre circumstances that followed in the months afterward. He was able to assist wherever possible in dealing with the media, and was able to stay clear and keep the Ravens, their longtime owner Art Modell, and head coach Brian Billick's best interests balanced throughout the process.

With all the legal ramifications, the impact of the franchise, the city, and the NFL at stake, there were certainly many sides to be heard from and many positions to be used. The bottom line was that silence and clear thinking had to be the key to Byrne's consistent role as the process took its twists and turns. Rarely if ever was there a knee jerk reaction to a rumor by the official Ravens spokespeople, and team officials were always buttoned up and well prepared for the latest news of the day. The team business on the publicity side also continued to move along, as Byrne balanced out the tasks at hand while still dealing with the regular non-sports media that showed up during the weeks and months that followed. He also worked with Lewis on what his lawyers needed him to say and what the team was doing, while still balancing the tasks of the rest of his job.

However, one of the key moments in the publicist relationship in this "family" crisis came to bear the day that the trial ended in June. Lewis was able to maintain his innocence and charges were dropped. As the verdict came down, the media which had shown a strong bias towards Lewis throughout the trial, painting him as guilty without much proof, now wanted to hear him speak. Many of Lewis' family and friends, as well as Lewis' own lawyer, advised him not to speak to the media, rather to let his lawyer speak on his behalf as he left the courthouse through a back entrance. The emotionality of the trial, along with what many felt was an unfair portrayal in the media, had left those close to him very bitter. However, Byrne, who did not have the emotional attachment to the issue, viewed things differently.

He was there in the courthouse with Lewis and his family and observed the emotional reaction that Lewis was receiving from those closest to him. However, Byrne saw the bigger picture, the opportunity to have Ray Lewis as a man and as an athlete speak for himself in his own words. He was able to get in front of Lewis, pull him aside, and carefully explain the pluses and minuses of his actions and how it could be viewed in the media. He explained to Lewis that he now had a one-time opportunity to take this very personal and very public crisis situation and turn it into a positive result. By speaking to the media, with several carefully worded talking points, and no questions, he would show the world on live TV that he was an innocent man and was now getting ready to start the rest of his life again. It would be a proactive, one-time chance to thank those who supported him, and begin a very public resurrection.

In this case Byrne had tried to be the consensus builder, he watched the "back" of a very public figure who was now vindicated, and he had the best interests of his club and the sport at hand. He was able to use all those things as a positive to show a very public athlete how he could control this crisis situation and make it as positive as possible.

Lewis listened, delivered the points in front of a horde of media as his lawyer stood by, and began his return to the higher ranks of professional football. As a result of that Kevin Byrne intervention, Lewis' turnaround has seen him be the cover of *Sports Illustrated* following the Ravens Super Bowl win the following season, and on the cover of the popular Madden 2005 NFL video game, both only given to NFL players held in high public regard.

Dealing with suicide

The 24/7 nature of the news today means that sometimes stories of great tragedy are able to make it to the news media or on to social media before officials can track the accuracy of a story. This happens more often when a person is on his or her own time or out of the spotlight. Unfortunately one of those instances can involve the suicide of an athlete or prominent official. Recently we have seen this tragedy with athletes like German soccer star Robert Enke, former NFL stars Junior Seau and Dave Deurson, NHL players Wade Belak and Rick Rypien, and golfer Erica Blasberg. We also dealt with the crisis first hand with the death of popular Mixed Martial Arts athlete Jeremy Williams. Williams' death provided us with access to suicide counselors and prevention specialists who gave us insight into how to deal specifically with the aspects of a suicide with high profile and popular personalities.

Some guidelines:

1   Confirm all the facts in stages. Unless there is a first-hand account of actions, and many times there are not, defer to the law enforcement officials for help. Sometimes what looks like a self-inflicted injury could have been an accident, and rushing to conclusion stigmatizes and confuses the situation.

2   As in all tragedies please think of the survivors and their families. Many times those actions occur when family members are away, so helping to control all official statements until family members are notified will help alleviate some of the immediate grief.

3   Identify through the organization's medical team an appropriate spokesperson who can speak in general terms about the issue of suicide. This is a very, very complex issue, and working through the media to make sure messages are communicated properly to prevent copy-cat instances by ardent fans in a time of intense grief is very important.

4   Support the family but be guarded in glorifying the tragedy. Many times the rush to throw platitudes toward the victim can have an adverse effect on fans in the grieving process. Therefore speaking carefully and accurately about the deceased is much better than over-speaking about the person's virtues.

5   Have suicide prevention and counseling phone numbers accompany all media messages about the tragedy. This is a very important fact provided to us by those who deal with the aftermath of suicide, especially with an athlete or personality with a loyal following. There is an immediate chance to assist those who may also be having such thoughts, and by providing proper messaging in lock step with news announcements about the tragedy can actually help to save lives.

6   Be there to support those around the victim. The devastating effects of suicide often linger for a very long time, so watching those on a team, a league, or with a personal relationship with the deceased is very, very important to make sure the loss is not compounded by the loss of another in a similar way.

The corporate crisis

This type of event has really become a bigger part of the sports publicist world as the business of sports grows. Even on the collegiate side, the justification for spending dollars, all have made "sports" into "business."

This is not necessarily a negative in many ways. On the collegiate level it gets the publicist out of the SID world a bit and shows us more about sponsorship, marketing, and ticket sales. It teaches us how to run budgets and account for dollars. In the old days the business was very cyclical and could become rote as the years went along. Now, especially since Title IX, many colleges and universities look to the athletic department for spending and revenue the same way it looks towards its development office as a way to grow the university base. That in many ways for those who have been in the business for years can be unsettling, especially in the push to drive publicity. However, it has to be looked at as an opportunity to grow a career, and with that comes the challenges.

The same in many respects can be said on the professional level. The publicity and marketing arms of professional sports teams, leagues, and National Governing Bodies are tied more and more together. Public and media relations now deal more with the sponsor side and the business side, as opposed to being holed up with just the sports side. The offices of the PR group, sometimes sequestered away with coaches, are now literally closer to the business side in many cases. More and more also on the professional side, sole or family ownership of sports teams have given rise to boards, corporate ownership, and companies looking to leverage the sports avenue to grow other areas of their business and vice versa. The branding of sports teams today is most directly tied to business growth as it is to wins and losses.

For the publicist, this can be seen as an opportunity to expand one's horizons and flourish, or it can be seen as a chance to move on to another area of the business. The days of just doing stats and pitching stories just to the "back of the paper" are over.

With the benefits of becoming part of a more formal business structure also come the challenges. On the collegiate level, that may require more reporting into a marketing group or a university relations staff as just opposed to an athletic director. On the pro level it may mean more meetings with a business affairs department or a team president to grow the business side. It also means more of a watch on the financial side, and if it is a public company, thinking about how things may affect the stock.

Now all of this is not entirely new. Teams have been under corporate ownership for years. The Yankees were owned by CBS in the 1960s, Madison Square Garden and its teams, the Knicks and Rangers, have been owned by companies ranging from Gulf and Western to Paramount to Cablevision. The Green Bay Packers have always been a public company with the fans owning stock. Still, the days of family ownership of sports team has really dwindled. The Maras (Giants), the Hunts (Chiefs), the late Al Davis (Raiders), and the Rooneys (Pittsburgh), along with the Buss family (the Lakers) and the late George Steinbrenner (the Yankees) are a few of the franchise that remain more privately controlled than public.

Here is a look at some of the issues that can fall under the corporate crisis mode, and some tips to be able to deal with them.

Issues that will arise include:

- team layoffs and downsizing
- public reporting and coverage of financial matters
- the dealing with immediate tragedy
- the buying and selling of teams, the changing of the guard at the top.

Now most of these are everyday issues in the non-sports and entertainment world. Unless layoffs are massive at most public companies, the loss of jobs rarely becomes news. The reporting of financial issues for most companies is a regular occurrence, and usually affects or comes of interest to stockholders and those involved in running the company. Companies are bought, sold, and merged every day. Most companies review their long-term strategy and make changes accordingly away from most of the public eye.

However, sports franchises, and those companies involved in sports and entertainment, make these adjustments under great scrutiny. While major corporations will have writers from media outlets following them on their financial "beat" from media outlets, most do not have the daily public face that sports entities do. Therefore the amount of news that needs to be generated, and the amount of scrutiny every change has, grows exponentially because of the nature of sports. Yes, most papers do have business sections. However the visibility of the business of sports is much higher and appeals to a much larger audience than the daily workings of most businesses.

Corporate policies may have to be adjusted and business plans adhered to in order to make the sports venture a successful one. The most successful companies in this area are the ones that are able to devote the resources and personnel to make the business of sports successful. The ones that traditionally struggle, and sometimes fail (such as the Fox purchase of the Los Angeles Dodgers, or Disney's venture with the Anaheim Mighty Ducks) are the ones that do not make the adjustment to the business of sports securely. All of those new responsibilities fall to the publicists to sometimes adjust, work with new staff, and morph into the job that grows beyond the traditional sports publicist.

Some basic principles that apply to the corporate crisis as a publicist should include:

1 *Avoid the gossip.* Especially when the worlds of sports and business are thrown together, the gossip will begin. This is a natural thing when change occurs in the business world, but it is the publicist's job to try and stay above the fray, maintain the best interests of the company and maintain a level of professionalism at all times. Of all the crisis situations, this one may actually be the most personal to you and those with whom you have worked with for months or years. The more you can stay away from the water cooler talk and be respectful and professional, the better off you will be.

2 *Balance the good old days with the new reality.* As the person who usually will have to deal with both the traditional sports staff and the new corporate environment, it is important to have a solid understanding of both. Indeed, people from both sides may approach you for counsel as to why things are being done a certain way now or why they were done a certain way in the past. As Billy Joel says "The past never was good enough, tomorrow ain't as bad as it seems." It is the publicist's job to try and maintain the traditions that make sports such a special place, and marry those traditions with the new business reality.

3 *Change is inevitable.* It is important to be able to study what other similar organizations have gone through and how they have adjusted and reacted publicly. Tradition is important but reticence to change is very problematic. One thing that folks will not want to hear is "that's the way we have always done it." Without a show as to why, problems will arise.

Also, keep in mind that the change could very well involve you or your staff. Whereas in previous years, the public or media relations staff remained one of the constants in the business world, these days new administrations may already have people in mind to fill jobs. If you are affected in this way, it is important to maximize your opportunities and always look forward instead of looking back.

4 *Try and find the positive.* Especially when it comes to sales or financial change, the new owners or new executives are not making decisions in a vacuum. Many times changes have been discussed for months, and every aspect of the organization has been examined. Perhaps they have yet to meet the people, but they have a good understanding of how the system works or doesn't work. Even if the publicist has not been involved in the process, he or she will have to be involved in the first public announcement. Coming across as positive, informational, and an asset to those coming in can make you very valuable in ways the new faces may never have thought of before. An open mind will open a great deal of doors.

5 *Do not speculate on speculation.* This is one of my former bosses' (Isiah Thomas) favorite sayings. As the winds of change blow publicly, instant

speculation will begin from the media machine. As in the family crisis, many of these requests may come from media that you are not familiar with. It is very important not to get into debates about information, or get caught up in the media flow, on or off the record. Report what you hear to the higher ups, and show your ability to be a team player both to those in place now and then those who are coming afterward.

With those five principles in mind, let's look at the business crisis situations and how the publicist deals with them.

Layoffs, downsizing, and corporate restructuring

This has long been an art of the North American corporate culture, and now with the dollars spent in sports and entertainment on all levels it has become inevitability in the sports world.

One of the differences here, as opposed to many other crisis situations, is that many times the people affected by these changes are not in the public eye. They are usually administrators, sales people, or regular staff. Many times they are the "worker bees" of the organization. Therefore the need for public acknowledgement of these people by the media is sometimes minimized. Also, because most sports entities are not made up of very large staffs, these moves are usually contained to a few people. I cannot recall an announcement that the "Philadelphia Philllies today laid off 300 people." Indeed, their 2006 media guide listed only 196 employees (not including players). This is not General Motors. It is a very concentrated, albeit very public business. Most teams that are part of corporations these days will undergo layoffs as part of a larger company plan. Also, always remember that in the case of public companies, rarely do team on-field results affect the price of a stock.

Now, there will be instances where the media will seek out these employees to try and build a story of corporate change vs. the folksy nature of the way sports used to be. This is especially true when longtime employees or those who have been friendly with the media are let go. However, the goal is probably to keep these people's names out of the paper, many times out of respect for their families. People we know are laid off all the time. Only in sports can the cycle dictate that the name of a secretary or clubhouse attendant becomes newsworthy enough to appear in a paper.

There are two key elements for the publicist to work on in these cases. First is the external element. Be aware of the changes, be aware that the changes and the names may be circulated by a third party to the media, and be ready to explain the changes should media inquire. This way it becomes one line or a note, and it does not take on the "coverup" atmosphere that the media may be seeking. There is no need for a press release or even a comment from a top team official in most cases. Even in public corporations, most of these moves do not need public comment.

The second element is internal. It is very important to make sure that the higher ups communicate the reasons and the issues down to the remaining staff, and many times it is left to the publicist to push that information through. Most of the time these changes are both unpopular and unpleasant. But to stem the internal tide of negativity, there needs to be adequate communication, whether in oral or written form. This in many ways will humanize the move even more, and it will fall to the publicist to work with the decision makers to have that transition go smoothly.

Public reporting and coverage of financial matters

Again with the growth of sports media and sports business media, this area has become more and more a focus. Reporting the earnings of corporations have long been the standard, however, the reporting of team and athletic department financials were never given a great deal of thought.

Given the great amount of money spent on collegiate athletics, the recent labor actions taken against players by teams (the hockey, basketball, baseball, and football lockouts), and the advent of the salary cap has made team financials a new aspect of public business. It is not just important to understand the financial matters that teams or entities must deal with, but it is important to be able to explain them to the media if needed during a crisis.

Many times the sports media will know what the term salary cap is, but not understand exactly how it works, and their interpretation of the rules to the public becomes a self-fulfilling prophecy. Having some simple facts on hand to explain financial matters to the media will go a long way in avoiding the financial crisis stories. Like in all crisis matters, it is important to fully understand the issue, and to speak with one voice.

It is also very important to understand, with both not-for-profit agencies like National Governing Bodies as well as with public companies, what numbers are available in the public domain. The enterprising reporter may be able to gain sales numbers that you may not have, or that were thought to be confidential. He or she may also be able to obtain salary figures through what is reported to the IRS. Making sure that they have accurate information without giving those more than they have is critical when this comes up.

It is also important for the publicist to know and understand when these figures are reported and for what time frame they are being filed for. If it is a university reporting football and basketball revenue, the SID should be aware of when that posting is done.

Once again there is no need for the sports publicist to go out and offer up this information. Even in positive times this is not something that most companies want to offer up there. Financial windfalls in an era of seat licenses, high ticket prices, and huge salaries can actually have a negative impact of the fan base, especially if a team or entity is underachieving on the field.

Having the information on hand and being reactionary and confident in the figures is much more important.

Now will there be cases where entities want to show the public a great turnaround story? A team that was floundering is now doing well? A university that was struggling is now close to turning a profit? A racetrack that was close to bankruptcy has now gotten things back on track for the community? Yes, there will and those stories have to be very carefully plotted out as to how they are handled. Here is a great example of one.

The New Jersey turned Brooklyn Nets

Long the brunt of jokes, despite their on-court success, the Nets and their new owner, Russian billionaire Mikhail Prokhorov, chose to take an aggressive approach to building brand identity for the team and changing its financial fortunes. Previous owner Bruce Ratner had hired former NASCAR Chief Marketer Brett Yormark to recreate his business model and build equity in the team and that process continued as the team moved from the IZOD Center to the Prudential Center in Newark, New Jersey to the Barclays Center in Brooklyn in the fall of 2012. Whereas many teams were reluctant to talk about new financial gain, Yormark and his publicist, Barry Baum, were very bullish. They openly talked about bringing in new sponsors, creating aggressive financial ticket incentives for staff, and showing the dollar value that increased with team growth. The result was a huge increase in business press coverage and renewed interest in a franchise that many thought was dead, especially with it abandoning its New Jersey location for a future one in Brooklyn, New York (in an arena and area that Ratner controlled through his Forest City Ratner Development Company). As a result of this aggressive approach, problems that arose that may have been seen as major setbacks in the past, such as the financial reporting of losses, or the slowdown of the building of the arena, were minimized. The team still struggled financially in some ways. However, the perception to the sports fan was that the team was now vibrant and aggressive in its business model outweighed the negative stories.

One more area where the publicist is affected by the potential financial crisis is in the naming rights area. One of the largest areas of profit for teams, and universities is in the naming of stadiums and facilities. It has become a billion dollar a year business, as everyone looks for a solid stream of revenue and maximizing a return on its investment. However, with those new names, and they do change when deals expire and companies are sold, comes great pressure on the publicist to make sure that the new name is applied and the old one removed. Billions of dollars are at stake to make sure all the changes go smoothly. It is not an easy process to rebrand either.

- *Look at Philadelphia*: The CoreStates Spectrum › CoreStates Center › First Union Center › Wachovia Center › Wells Fargo Center.
- *In San Francisco*: Candlestick Park › 3com Park › back to Candlestick Park.
- *In Miami*: Joe Robbie Stadium › Pro Player Park › Pro Player Stadium › Dolphins Stadium › DOLPHIN Stadium › Land Shark Stadium › Sun Life Stadium.
- *In Houston*: Enron Field › Astros Field › Minute Maid Park.
- *In Phoenix*: America West Arena › US Airways Arena.

All new arenas? No. Same arena, different name. Many of the changes have even occurred in mid-season. I was actually in America West Arena on a Tuesday and US Airways Arena on a Thursday. Changing the mindset of what the public thinks and also what the media *reports* can be a huge issue and can create the kind of financial issue that needs to be corrected.

The publicist in each case must make sure that all publications, website, and stationery are properly changed at the appropriate time. That even includes things like area signage, business cards, and sometimes website names. He or she must make sure that all media services are monitored for the changes and that television and radio broadcasts, from fonts to announcements, are being done correctly. Especially in the mass media, the smallest backslide can be a big issue.

Some changes occur because of the expiration of a contract. However, the bigger ones that create crisis are when public companies holding naming writes for millions of dollars go belly up. This was the case in Miami, when Pro Player, an apparel company, went out of business, and even bigger when financial giant Enron collapsed in Houston. With Enron, it was not just the issue of not having the financial gain, it was the everyday stigma of having the team, the city, and the stadium associated with the biggest financial collapse in the history of American business.

On the collegiate level, a big challenge came at Villanova University, where their basketball arena was christened with a grant from the duPont family as the duPont Pavilion in 1986. In future years, one of the principal benefactors was involved in a highly publicized crime in the Philadelphia area, and the university made a decision to remove the duPont name, rather than risk the name association, from the facility and not seek any additional corporate funding for the building, now known just as the Pavilion.

In all cases it is the role of the publicist to make sure that these changes are adhered to and that the current sponsor gets the proper bang for his or her buck.

The buying and selling of teams, the changing of the guard at the top

The business-like nature of sports and the high price tag that goes with it also puts the publicist in a unique position when change comes at the top. The buying and selling of teams, the rumors that go with it, and the change in corporate philosophy can directly affect the publicist, the way he or she does business, and the way that the media work with an organization.

Many times the acquisition of a team can become a very public and drawn out function, especially when the sale is between two public entities. The amount of man-hours that goes into the process can be staggering. In the meantime the uncertainty, loyalty, and angst amongst employees is very public. It is not different than the regular business world of today, but it can be more public.

Many times, the fan loyalty or disharmony is tied to an ownership group. The Steelers will be forever linked to Pittsburgh through the Rooney family. The love that Chicagoans feel for the Veeck family when they were involved with the Cubs and later the White Sox is legendary. Conversely, the mention of Art Modell in Cleveland (where a set of events forced him to move the Browns to Baltimore) or the Irsay family in Baltimore (where they were seen moving the Colts' offices in trucks during a winter's night to new offices in Indianapolis) will bring great resentment. Unlike businesses, the emotional ties to sports franchises are a huge factor.

Therefore it is the publicist's position when these situations arise to again be the sounding board, perhaps for both the incoming and the outgoing group. The messaging to the fans through the media to create a positive situation for both groups is essential. So therefore using the rainy day file again to study the positives and negatives of previous changeovers also becomes a big part of the publicist's job. Being open minded, working away with both groups, and keeping everyone as informed on the process as need be is critical.

Here again internal communication also is very important. Making sure that current employees have a feel for the new regime and that the outgoing group also feels appreciated by the staff and vice versa will also be important. Having the publicist as the sounding board here remains a big factor.

With the ownership change also comes change at the top in many cases. The change may not come immediately, but it will come eventually. It is a fact that most people like to have their people with them—the ones who they can rely on and make a smooth transition. Therefore, making sure that the publicist knows everything about the incoming group without forgetting the needs and egos of the outgoing group is also important.

Some key items for the publicist with both executives and ownership groups may include:

- a listing of all the key media in the market, with a brief description of each
- a forum with local editors and newsmakers as an introduction
- an explanation of existing team policies with regard to media and how things have been handled in the past
- a file with team best practices with media and the community.
- a description of media training opportunities, including what has or has not been done in the past
- the suggestion of meeting other folks of influence (coaches, alumni, etc.) in the community through your contacts.

The Penn State crisis

There is perhaps no greater crisis of personnel that may change the face of an institution than the alleged crimes committed by former assistant football coach Jerry Sandusky at Penn State University, alleged crimes which came to light fully during the winter of 2011–2012. The scandal brought down the leaders not just of the athletic department in Athletic Director Tim Curley and legendary head football coach Joe Paterno, but they also brought down the President of the University, Graham Spanier, and numerous others in the administration who may or may not have been aware of the long-time issues going on with regard to alleged child sexual abuse by Sandusky.

The crisis split loyalties at the university, brought into question to power of individuals in athletics, the accountability of administrators, and the core values for anyone ever associated with the famed school in State College, Pennsylvania.

There were a couple of key realizations that the administration, from athletics to the top of the university, became aware of early on. The magnitude of this scandal, especially with both the administrative leader (the President) and the athletic head (the athletic director) compromised made this much bigger than the university could handle. They also realized that any crisis plan they had developed did not account for a roadmap for such widespread issues, so they began to look outside the parameters of the university to find advisors who could be of counsel and were agnostic to the goings on of a school that took a large amount of its funding from a tax paying public.

In so many complex issues such as this where the public is screaming for their perceived version of justice, there is a need to make sure that justice indeed is carried through. There is also the need to make sure that any legal issues are not affected, even while millions on TV see the rioting going on with students on campus and the reaction of the media and others to hold Sandusky and others accountable regardless of letting the justice system play through. The system as we know is not one which will occur over minutes, days, hours, weeks, or months, and the situation at Penn State following the arrest and the uncovering of news is changing by the minute.

Still the board of trustees, with an obligation not just to those personally affected by the allegations but to those who live, work, and attend Penn State, as well as taxpayers, alumni, and many other groups, held their ground. They issued statements as warranted and worked with the athletic department not to stonewall information but to control the flow, much to the chagrin of the public and the media wanting more information, and probably more controversy, by the hour.

In the first few days a number of independent consultants were brought in to try and assist every constituent with message control and in some cases damage control as well. The Board brought in the crisis team from Ketchum Public Relations, who immediately began their task of ascertaining damage, monitoring the news, and helping prep the board and new University President Rodney Erickson with the correct messaging not just for the short term, but for the long-term benefit of the university. They were able to align the groups who may be approached for media comment, keep all aware of the latest developments, work with the appointed officials looking into the matter, media train select spokespeople, and most importantly, prep for what seemed like a foregone conclusion, the dismissal of legendary coach Joe Paterno, who was not directly implicated but would be one of the leaders who would have to step down because of the allegations and the things that allegedly happened with a direct subordinate.

The advisors were deeply immersed in the first few days in the culture of Penn State, which gave them a better understanding of the unique nature of this type of crisis. They were able to talk to get a perspective not just from students, workers, and alumni, but from senior officials who had such a passion for the school and its leadership that they too were having health and personal issues as a result of the scandal. This was not a one-off tragedy where the healing could begin immediately, like in an accident. This was on-going and had been for years, and as a result even the innocent were suffering from great guilt and were admittedly not thinking clearly.

The Board also had to deal with larger issues of governance outside of the day-to-day, minute-to-minute developments in the case. There was an Attorney General and other politicians closely watching the goings-on, not to mention thousands of both pro and con intercollegiate athletics who would look to use this case on a national basis to trumpet their own agendas.

The one thing that needs to be made clear through the chaotic time was that those advising on all communications issues were doing just that—advising the decisionmakers. That is a clear distinction and a key point that has been made in this chapter, and played out very well in the early stages at Penn State. The advisors were able to assess and provide counsel but ultimately it was up to the board and the President to act on that counsel. Although many discussions were kept confidential (and still are), the public saw some moves, such as taking the board's story to highly visible forums in various cities, as a bit controversial, but prior to that move counsel was provided as to the pros and cons. Also during the process there were numerous other advisors brought in, most notably former Clinton advisor Lanny Davis, to provide another look at what steps should be taken. Regardless of the number of cooks, the Board and the President stayed unified in the quest for clarity in decision and unity in their resolve.

With the idea of clarity, President Erickson worked to develop a five-point promise that became the rallying point for his administration, and ultimately for the university itself. It includes:

- a promise to reinforce to the Penn State Community the moral imperative of doing the right thing the first time every time
- leading by example and expecting others to do no less
- a commitment to transparency
- respect and sensitivity to all victims
- a promise by the administration to provide the resources and information to the task force so that they can do their jobs.

The university also made a landmark decision, with the aid of crisis counsel, to take the money earned from qualifying for the TicketCity Bowl and start to fund a victims' crisis center on campus for the first time: a loud message that the healing was underway and was being taken seriously by all, especially those in athletics.

At the end, while some may say the university did not react swift enough and was forthcoming enough at first with information, the crisis counsel provided built a foundation that PSU and other places were similar crises will arise that can withstand a battle internally and externally. At the time of this writing the case is still ongoing, but it is worth noting from a business standpoint that both donations and applications rose following the first few months of crisis work with the Sandusky case, something that many experts will attribute to both the passion of those who are part of the university and the work that the Board and their advisors did in consistently assessing the damage and taking the steps to fix what was viewed as a systemic problem. It was not easy, it was very challenging and very fluid, but the biggest wave of crisis, one that was brewing but not totally foreseen, was handled well by the team involved.

The Women's Tennis Association

One example of a crisis in change at the top occurred in 1996 while I was vice president of communications and special projects at the Corel WTA Tour. The outgoing CEO, Anne Worcester, was ready to pass the reins on to the new CEO, Ric Larson, who was then vice president of marketing for the PGA Tour. The search to replace Worcester, who had led the world's most popular sport for women back from the brink of crisis, was an arduous one, and the committee had interviewed people from various areas of expertise from all over the globe. The choice of Ric had taken a while, as he and his family were based in Florida and the move to the head office in Stamford, Connecticut had been a stumbling block. Still, the decision was made and the announcement set for early January 1998, prior to the start of the season in Australia. There was enough time over the holidays to effectively plan the announcement and even insert his bio into the Tour media guide, which was now at the printer and ready for shipping to events around the globe. His hiring was also seen as a positive for tour sponsor Corel, which was in the final year of its title sponsorship, was having some financial problems of its own, and was questioning its future in women's tennis. Bringing in someone from outside, especially from the successful world of the PGA Tour, was seen as a huge step forward for the sport.

We had prepared all the facts for Ric as he readied himself to take the position at the top. The release was scheduled to go out right after the New Year, with a conference call with media to follow and then formal introduction later in the month in Australia. The release went out on a Tuesday afternoon, with the presser to follow via phone to worldwide media the following morning.

As we arrived in the office for the day of the conference call, with all the prep done and approved and the announcement out, we received a call that Clarson had backed out. The ramifications in the tennis world could have been extreme, both on the sponsor side and with the media, who had always been cynical about the professionalism of the way the sport was run.

We were able to pull together a group of executives and continued with the conference call to announce very carefully, Clarson's change of heart, our respect for his decision, and the re-establishment of a search committee to re-visit candidates. The call was done by Worcester and the chair of the committee Bart McGuire, a lawyer for the Tour, and their professional attitude and spin, all the while sticking to their bullet points, allowed the media to take this potentially embarrassing situation and diffuse it. The spin involved talking about the positive direction that the Tour had taken and the facts that the players and the game were strong, and that is what the public should be concerned. The solid footing the game was on would take precedence over a shift at the top, and everyone on the committee recognized this as a mistake, and was relieved at the early timing of the change rather than months later when new agendas could have been well entrenched.

The committee then re-convened and within 48 hours had installed McGuire as the defacto CEO, with Worcester staying on for a transition period. It showed decisiveness, familiarity with the organization, and gave a quick end to what was a difficult and potentially disastrous situation. The communication, consensus building, and timing were critical both with the announcements and with the news. Everyone worked from the same page, consulted players, sponsors, and business partners, and was able to reach a decision that was the next best, and probably ended up being the best decision for the sport under the circumstances.

The one other issue that remained and needed to be addressed was one of publicity. The media guide, printed on a limited budget and ready for literally worldwide distribution for the entire year, now had to have this embarrassing situation literally cut out. We were able to repossess thousands of copies, and took exacto knives as a staff to remove the errant pages which contained the former CEO's biographical information. Hence, the crisis was literally cut out within a 48-hour period, and the Tour with Bart McGuire at the helm continued to flourish.

All of these can help make the transition smooth, and give the publicist a good opportunity to avert crisis and build consensus with new owners and executives.

The player personnel crisis

Now we come to one of the most common crisis issues, perhaps biggest in the sports field. I have chosen to put this one last because in all actuality, it may seem like the most immediate at the time but many times can be the most fleeting in sports. Given the changing rosters of teams today, it is also the one that may come and go the fastest. However, at the time it is the most immediate, the most pressing and the most stressful.

This is the trading of the star or popular player.

We are all aware of the star value in sports. The stars create our memories, captivate our attention, help us buy products, make us watch and spend countless dollars supporting our teams. It is a great emotional bond that exists in very few places.

With that bond comes a price, sometimes financial, sometimes emotional, sometimes both. It is also inevitable that those bonds eventually leave as the star moves on either through trade or retirement. Usually the parting is not pretty, as that is the nature of sports. The publicist does not have a say as to when these events occur, but they can contribute as to the how, and make sure that the blow is as short as possible and that the replacements are received in a positive light.

Because of the marketing dollars spent on teams these days, the use of player image in campaigns has to be clearly defined and thought through. Players today rarely spend their entire career in one city. Therefore the use of their likeness in campaigns needs to be addressed. The popularity of those players as we know is a prime source of fan interest and revenue as well. Therefore equity built in can be a dangerous thing when the trade is made or the decision not to resign goes through.

Some key points when addressing the departing player crisis:

1   *Always take the high road.* Even if the split is very public and very acrimonious, make sure that the messaging for everyone speaking when the move is announced is positive, and is looking forward to the future. There is no need to look back and readdress issues. Acknowledge his or her's success with the organization and move on.

2   *Accept the negative.* Do not think or prep with rose-colored glasses. Spinning an unpopular move is very difficult to do. Rather than trying to change opinion of the leaving player, look to the traits of the incoming player or potential players as the positive.

3   *Live through the news cycle.* Again, the trade news cycles are relatively short in this day and age, and then the media move on to a new story or the new players or coaches. Be willing to make sure everyone involved knows and is realistic about the news cycle and is ready to move forward in advance of when it ends. The faster you are able to get the media looking forward, the better the messaging will be.

4   *Be ready for the return.* In many cases the return of the athlete is sometimes an even bigger news story than the trade itself. It is important that the organization decide how that return is handled sooner than later. Some organizations take the time to welcome home the conquering hero with his new team, while others choose to treat the day as any other. It is up to you as the publicist to make sure that whichever approach is taken, that it all happens smoothly.

5   *Welcome the new faces.* Even with strong ties to the outgoing athlete, it is important to make the incoming athlete feel at home and welcome in his or her new surroundings. He or she may have a tough transition and be the subject of trivia questions for years on end. However, he or she now represents your future, and the better off you will be making him or her feel that way.

6   *Make sure all tracks are covered.* As with any player move, it is important to make sure that the surprise factor to key participants is minimized. Your rainy day file should have a list of who should be contacted—players, family, agents, other staff members—so that there are as few surprises as possible when the news breaks.

7   *Out of sight, out of mind.* It is also important to work with those who have used images—arena folks, marketing campaigns, host broadcasters,

publications folks, webmasters—to make sure that all information goes through a quick and thorough change. One of the greatest embarrassments is to have a player image still on a billboard a month after he or she is gone. Also, sometimes the inevitable happens and a player is featured in an upcoming promotion or in a local campaign that can't be changed. It is important not to ignore the situation. In this day and age most will understand the cycle and planning that goes into such things and reacts accordingly. However, everyone in the office should be aware of the cynical media response if the campaign or promotion cannot be changed.

What you will find most times is that if you can use these as a guideline, the sting of the move will pass quickly, especially if it is in season. You cannot control the on-court performance, but the shaping of the image of the players and the organization as first class and respectful will be the long-standing memory to fans, officials, and business partners.

Conclusion

In this chapter, we have spent extensive time looking at all the potential crisis touch points big and small. It is an interesting reflection of where sports are today that this may be the most wide-ranging chapter in the book, and the one that may not be thought of most often, but when these situations do arise they can be the most defining moment of a publicist's career.

I hope that it is kept as a guide and rarely used.

12

PROMOTING SPORTS IN A GLOBAL ENVIRONMENT

The Meat is not proportional to the amount of the Cheese

In this chapter we will take a look at the differences in publicity in sports around the world. We will look at the different perceptions that the global sports community has in promoting sports, the value of regionalization, the ways to approach pitching in different places, and how to deal with media that American publicists may not be familiar with.

Again, some of the principles here are the basic ones, but since the global spectrum of sports is ever-growing and opportunities from online to digital television and global branding are quickly advancing, the ways to apply these principles to specific global trends and have the publicist be successful are really essential to explain in this format.

The global landscape in all the business world has changed and sports is no different. The advent of the internet, digital TV, and the growth of sports worldwide, the opportunities to carve a niche, and work with worldwide media to identify and publicize sports, from poker to basketball, are very exciting.

With that in mind, the important thing when looking at these opportunities is to not think like the ugly American. Yes, many opportunities for growth do exist around the world for fans to want to "Be like Mike," as the popular slogan for Michael Jordan used to say. However, there are many nuances that are important for you to learn in order to get off on the right foot and grow your publicity opportunities on a global basis.

Now there are several sports that have long been established as worldwide entities, and their participation numbers reflect that. Tennis, soccer (known everywhere else as football), basketball, and figure skating are probably the most promotable on a global basis. There are also the Olympics and the other global events that we will look at in this chapter. Those too have their challenges as you go from global region to global region, and it is important to understand not only the culture of those who play, but those who watch, and those who cover the game as you grow your business plan.

We also have to always keep in mind as publicists that sports are also ever growing as a unifying social phenomenon. Whereas this used to apply to just Olympic competition, it now applies across the board because of the ability for athletes and fans to communicate in a real time, 24/7 universe. Sports are both a social glue and provide an opportunity for transmitting basic values that every society holds dear—elements like justice, team work, sacrifice, and honor. They have contributed to racial and social integration, and even to the development of slang, as sports terms and expressions slide into everyday usage. This is true around the world, where the passion for local soccer and cricket clubs, and the rituals that goes with that understanding of passion, binds itself to other groups globally.

As publicists, it is our job now to incorporate all those elements into a careful global landscape.

So let's again set some basic rules of thumb when looking for PR opportunities on a large geographic scale.

1   Gain respect before you expect to get it.
2   Learn the nuances needed in each situation for a proper pitch.
3   Understand the social importance of the sport or event where you are pitching it.
4   Learn the local media and how they work.
5   If dealing with non-American media in this country covering a non-American athlete, understand the protocol and traditions and how they adapt to the States.

Each step will give you a better opportunity to succeed as you refine your pitch and navigate the deep waters abroad.

Gain respect before you expect to get it

One of the common misconceptions when working in sports and entertainment is that everyone wants to be and think like the American business model. As we said above, I do believe that most *fans* of sport, and even many athletes and businesses, do want to "Be Like Mike," at first glance. However that being said, there are many, many traditions and styles that are well bred in sport around the world, and many journalists, athletes, and sport officials *do not* want to easily adapt American ideals and principles to the way they conduct the business of sport.

There is a resistance to the way American sport runs itself in many ways, including the way athletes are treated in the world of sports publicity and marketing. Therefore in order to succeed, it is very important to gain the respect of the media, the national governing bodies, the event organizers and the athletes themselves to be successful.

Here are some ways to move in that direction:

- *Do your homework.* If you are going to work in the UK in June on an event, it would be important to understand that, for example, on the middle Sunday of Wimbledon there is no tennis, or that the Royal family is almost more important to some Brits than the Prime Minister. Learn how the public transportation systems work, make a stab at learning some basic language as opposed to assuming everyone speaks English. If in Asia, know the customs of respect when exchanging business cards or leaving a room. The more time you take to understand the basic customs of a land, the easier most people will accept you into the workplace.
- *Understand the value of local heroes of sport and the rules.* If you have the opportunity to work in the Caribbean, for example, knowing that Hiram Bithorn is the father of Puerto Rican baseball, or the great standing the Springboks rugby team has in South Africa, or event some of the rules of Aussie Rules Football and when it is played, will also give you the casual knowledge needed to get ahead. We as Americans assume when people come to this country that they want to understand how sport works here and what our rules and regulations are. Yet when we go abroad sometimes the assumption is that these folks again adapt to us. The more you can know and be able to carry on an informed conversation with the colleagues and media you will be working with, the better off you will be.

Learn the nuances needed for the proper pitch

Again it sounds basic, but in order to work with the media outside the United States you have to be aware of their needs, styles, and customs. It is important to talk to those who have worked in the area you are going beforehand to learn what is important to go into the proper pitch. Are there local sports daily newspapers in the area? Do the media in the area have a longstanding appreciation or a longstanding bias toward a team or product that you are working with? Has there been an issue with the national federation that would prevent the state newspaper from covering an event or an athlete? Do all the newspapers in the area file only feature stories? Does anyone in the area speak or write in English? Do you need a translator or a transcript? All these differences are essential to know before you go in.

Understand the social importance of the sport or event

The meaning of fan is derived from the word fanatic. Here in the United States, the allegiance to a team, athlete, or sport is very passionate and it becomes a part of our social experience. However, for only the most loyal or die-hard fans does their life revolve around the actions of their local club or favorite athlete. American society simply offers too many other opportunities for other forms of entertainment. As Americans, we are also not raised in that type of local devotion these days. There was a time when that devotion did exist. The stories of the Brooklyn Dodgers and their passionate fan base are the stuff of legend. However, even in that instance, sport as a business took over and the team was moved to their present home in Los Angeles because of the lure of larger profits in a new market by their owners, led by Walter O'Malley.

For most of the rest of the world however, the devotion to a local club, or the following of a legendary athlete or a sport, goes well beyond the casual social significance. In the Barclays Premier League in soccer, for example, devout followers of Arsenal or Manchester United build their lives around the club. The clubs have a vested stake in the community and the loyalty to the club surpasses player transfers and won/loss records. Loyalty to clubs is passed down from generation to generation. The same holds true for cricket clubs in India and Pakistan, baseball in Japan, Australian Rules Football, and Gaelic Football and Hurling in Ireland. The devotion to the club is seen as a social contract more than a following of a team.

That fervor also increases when national teams are formed for international play. Other than the 1980 US Olympic hockey team, the 1999 US Women's soccer team, the Ryder Cup team, and maybe the USA Basketball "Dream Team" that competed in the Barcelona Olympics, Americans rarely put all their focus on international competitions, especially on the team level. Even in most of the cases where national teams do captivate the American landscape, the fervor is driven because of the individuals on the teams rather than a sense of nationalism. Our cosmopolitan society does not really dictate that type of fervor. Even in Olympic years we have seen plummeting ratings and broadcasts more as "shows" on tape delay, as opposed to live full scale event broadcasts.

Conversely, the rest of the world usually stops when their country is competing in international events. I happened to be in England during the 1992 World Cup, and streets normally choked with traffic leading into London from the suburb of Wimbledon were literally deserted, as were most restaurants. Even during the World Series in a city where a team is participating, there is rarely the total stoppage of life to revolve around a sporting event. Some may say the Super Bowl is like that in this country, but even there it is more toward the event—and the commercials and the gambling—than it is the game and who is playing.

Example

The fervor in a home country follows below, with author John Genzale in Umbria, Italy for the 2006 World Cup, won by Italy over France in penalty kicks.

Italy wins the World Cup … from John Genzale in Umbria Italy …

What a night! Italians dancing in our streets all night. Thousands and thousands. They came streaming out of their homes to join the crowd who watched on the big screen in the main piazza. Delirium. Euphoria.

Mothers and grandmothers dancing with their daughters. Frenzied fathers with flags and fireworks … sons on their shoulders. All singing patriotic songs.

All over Italy.

It's like nothing you've ever seen. There was no rough edge. No fighting. No loss of temper. No one throwing up on your shoes. (That's New Orleans, not Italy.) No ugliness, just joy.

(Italians, as a rule are neither drunkards nor overly patriotic.) Cops cleared the way for an endless parade of cars overloaded with revelers and way too many airhorns. My wife, Jenny, got a kick out of some guys dancing among hundreds of waving flags to a disco version of the Italian National Anthem without their pants. Tidy-whities. "Until you stand in the middle of the chanting, screaming, hugging, dancing, you can't even imagine the passion that Italians have for their game," she said.[1]

Keep in mind that this support and passion was also on the heels of the potential of a very large scale gambling scandal just being investigated in the Italian "Serie A," the top level of Italian professional club soccer. Despite the undercurrent of scandal, the country unified behind its patriotism and the joy for its national team unlike anything that happens in the States.

So when gearing up your pitch and coordinating activities, it is very important to know your audience, their passions and their following. The media will follow accordingly.

The following is a great example of social acceptance that, although it takes place in suburban Chicago, shows how a publicist can adapt a story with non-traditional American understanding and embrace it to do his or her work. It also is a prime example of how understanding social or religious differences benefits the publicist in doing his or her work.

Hunger on hold

By Tony Baranek, Chicago Daily Southtown, December 2003

Coaches and teammates in two suburban communities near Chicago take measures to ensure that Muslim athletes are able to observe Ramadan.

Over the past two seasons, the football team at Stagg High School, in Palos Hills, Illinois, has received many an ovation from its appreciative fans. That results naturally from qualifying for the state championships twice in a row and coming tantalizingly close to making it to the final rounds.

But third-year coach Tim McAlpin says he was genuinely moved by one particular cheer. This one, though, came from the players. It occurred near the end of the regular season in 2002, when the coaching staff gathered the team together to explain why things were going to be just a little bit different at practice and before ballgames that November.

Members of the Chargers who were Muslims were beginning their annual month-long fast of Ramadan, a holiday during which those who practice Islam celebrate the good fortune in their lives by fasting during daylight hours. It's a particularly challenging time for Muslims who are high (secondary) school athletes, a group becoming significantly larger in the United States.

The most critical games and matches of the fall sports season take place during November in football, girls volleyball, girls swimming, and cross-country. Yet for the Muslim athletes, there is no lunchtime or after-school snack. Showing up for practice means doing so without having had nourishment of any kind for nearly 10 hours.

McAlpin told his team's players that they would need to sacrifice a few minutes of practice time at sunset to allow their Muslim teammates to sustain themselves.

"One of the assistant coaches pointed out how awesome it was that [the Muslim players] were doing this," McAlpin said. "He said that that was their religion and we will respect them for believing in that and doing what they needed to do."

A family atmosphere

How did the other athletes react to this?

"The whole team gave them a standing ovation," McAlpin said. "But that's kind of like the family atmosphere we have here at Stagg. We have a whole lot of different cultures here, all being together and working together."

In the 2002 state playoffs, Stagg advanced to the semifinal round. Throughout the playoff campaign, not once did starting defensive lineman Ahmad Abdel-Jalil eat or drink during daylight hours. "But he just kept going and going," McAlpin marveled. "He hung in there and played well."

Mahmood Ghouleh, a senior at Reavis High School in nearby Burbank, Illinois, is a wide receiver and strong safety on that school's football team. He says that celebrating Ramadan simply is all part of being Muslim.

"It's tough, but you get used to it," said Ghouleh. "It's how we show that we're thankful for what we have, instead of taking everything for granted."

In 2003, Ramadan began on October 27 and continued until the last week of November. As always, it was intended to be a period of reflection as Muslims commemorate the time when the Koran, the Muslim holy book, was revealed to the Prophet Muhammad in the seventh century. During Ramadan, devout Muslims pray and abstain from food and drink between sunrise and sunset.

Ghouleh says the 10 Muslim members on Reavis's football team were remaining firm to their convictions and would continue their fast no matter how far the Rams advanced in the state playoffs. This conviction doesn't surprise Kareem Irfan, chairman of the Council of Islamic Organizations of Greater Chicagoland.

One of the five pillars

"This is a very fundamental obligation for a Muslim," Irfan said. "Fasting is one of the five pillars, and you really cannot call yourself a Muslim if you're not fasting. The youths know that. They realize that in order to do justice to the name they carry as a Muslim, they have to do this with conviction."

"For athletes, it helps to have good role models, too," Irfan continued. "In the past we've had professional athletes like [basketball player] Kareem Abdul-Jabbar. Akeem Olajuwon [another basketball star] was an outstanding role model. He played his [league] games without giving up on the fasting."

"Role models like these are an inspiration. I know my daughter [a high school basketball player] is inspired ... to see somebody like [that], at that high level of professionalism, still adhere to the fundamentals of Islam, to fast, and be able to keep up that level."

Ghouleh is a 6-foot-1-inch, 161-pound senior strong safety and wide receiver who sees plenty of playing time each week in the Reavis High games. "Mo is doing very well [physically]," his coach, Jim McDonough, said. "Actually, all of our [Muslim] kids seem to be doing pretty well. They're pretty tough kids. Plus, at this point [when the weather cools], practices aren't as physically demanding as they are earlier in the year."

Yet there can be still be complications from fasting for such an extended period of time, for athletes as well as non-athletes. The most serious is a natural shrinking of the stomach. "You don't really get that hungry after a while," Ghouleh said. "You'll feel like you're real hungry, but once you start eating you get full right away. Even after we're done fasting, it takes about a month to get over it."

A support network

Nonetheless, says Irfan, the average Muslim teenager is well equipped to handle the rigors of fasting. At around the age of eight, Muslim children begin fasting in small increments, gradually building up their resistance before taking part fully in Ramadan when they reach puberty.

Ghouleh tries to minimize the effect of dawn-to-dusk fasting by having a good breakfast. "I tell my mom to wake me up before sunrise," he said. "She wakes me up at around four in the morning. I'll eat a bowl of cereal or pancakes and then just go back to bed until it's time to get up for school."

Soad Halim, a senior at Stagg and a member of the girls' volleyball team, also subscribes to the very-early-to-rise meal along with her younger sister, Sanabel. "We do that, too," she said. "It's just a regular breakfast my mom makes. We just eat and go back to sleep. That helps us throughout the day."

Football coaches like McAlpin at Stagg and McDonough at Reavis do their part to respect the Muslim players' beliefs by making adjustments in their practice and pre-game routines.

"They have to say prayers at certain times," McAlpin said. "What we'd do was come out for practice and they'd go off to the side and do their prayers for about six minutes. We'd wait until they were done and then start our practice. Then, when the sun would go down, I'd tell them, 'Whenever you have to stop and eat or pray, you stop. Go off, and eat your lunch or pray. It's not a big deal. We'll move on, and when you get back, you'll go back where you were.' And they were real good about doing it on their own."

Ghouleh brings a small amount of food—an apple or a sandwich—with him to practice. The players begin their workouts at 3:15 p.m., and practice until shortly after sunset, when McDonough blows his whistle and takes the players off the field for about 15 minutes. "We give the whole team a break. There aren't any problems at all," the coach noted. "I think it's an excellent experience for all the kids to see some of the other things that go on in life."

Stagg girls' volleyball coach Colleen Hyland also calls a timeout at her team practices so that the Halim sisters can grab some food around five in the afternoon. "Sometimes my teammates bring me things, give me pretzels or peanut butter and jelly sandwiches," Soad Halim said. "They're very supportive. Most of them have been friends of mine since kindergarten, so they know everything about Ramadan. There was this one girl, though, a non-Muslim, who tried it and said it was pretty hard. She lasted two days!"

Summoned for a feast

In mid-fall 2003, Reavis's football squad competed in its first state playoff contest since 1995. If the game had begun in the early afternoon,

Gouleh and his Muslim teammates would have had to play without having eaten for more than seven hours. As it was, they had been without food or drink for nearly 11 hours when they began warming up at four-thirty p.m. Shortly after the sun set about a half-hour later, coach McDonough stopped the drill, and the school athletic director, Tim Smith, summoned the Muslim players for a feast.

"All the [Muslim] players went inside and ate. Then, after a few minutes to digest, we went back out and continued [our] pre-game [warm-ups]. I didn't really overeat. We knew we had a game to play. I ate half of a sub [sandwich], and saved the other half for after the game."

Surely, he savored the second half of the sandwich—but not nearly as much as he savored the victory that moved his team to the next rung of the championships.

Learn the local media and how they work

This is perhaps one of the biggest challenges when one leaves the United States. Understanding what the media wants, how they work, who is important, and who is influential. It is not as cut and dried as it is here in America. Also unlike the United States, the printed word still holds great standing in most countries. The internet and television do not have the power that they have here, especially in countries where television and radio are pretty much state run.

The daily sports-only newspaper in most European and Far Eastern countries is also a huge source of coverage that reaches the avid sports fan. It is not a section; it is the entire paper dedicated to dissecting the most intricate details of every match or game. Papers like *Il Gazetto dello Sport* in Italy, *L'Equipe* in France, and *Sports Nippon* in Japan are dedicated just to the coverage of sport in the country. In addition the amount of tabloid newspapers per country is much larger than here in the United States.

Tip

Did you know that there actually was a daily newspaper devoted just to sports in the United States? Unfortunately it was ahead of its time, just before the rise of sports radio and ESPN. *The National Sports Daily*, or *The National*, debuted January 31, 1990 and folded after only 18 months. The newspaper was published daily (Sundays through Fridays) and had a tabloid format. Its editor-in-chief was sports journalist Frank Deford and its writers included columnists like Mike Lupica and Ian O'Connor. There were attempts to regionalize it as well (this was also before the growth of the web), but it folded after mounting substantial financial losses.

Example

A typical newsstand in London can have as many as 12 daily newspapers for sale, compared to just three or four in New York. Here's a look.

London:

- *Daily Telegraph/The Sunday Telegraph*
- *Financial Times*
- *Sunday Times*
- *The Guardian/The Observer*
- *The Independent/Independent on Sunday*
- *The Times*
- *Daily Express/Sunday Express*
- *Daily Mail/Mail on Sunday*
- *Daily Star/Daily Star Sunday*
- *The People*
- *The Daily Mirror/Sunday Mirror*
- *The Daily Sport/The Sunday Sport*
- *The Sun/Sunday Sun*

New York:

- *New York Times*
- *New York Post*
- *New York Daily News*
- *Wall Street Journal*

In addition to the amount of coverage, the style in which stories are written, and also pitched, is much different than it is in the United States for the most part. Sports journalists will still tend to write in flowery and flowing terms about each detail of an athlete, and rely much less on the quote from the athlete. Developing their own style—many in the States would refer to it as old school writing—is almost as important as the result itself. A big reason this is done is because of the lack of available television for sports in many parts of the world. Like in the United States before 1960, televised sporting events are still limited to major events, although with digital television that has begun to change.

Because of this, access to athletes and the stories that writers will use is different than what most American sports publicists are used to. The sports daily writers will be more inclined to write about description and results than background. Another difference in the country-by-country coverage is the fact that most of the dailies have covered the star athlete since they were playing on younger club teams or junior competitions. The turnover on these beats is very low, so the familiarity the athlete has with a corps of writers is very high.

Example

Swiss tennis is not neutral. It is not out of the realm of possibility to have Swiss tennis champion Roger Federer, for example, have dinner with the Swiss tennis writers or have them come to his room in a hotel for an interview. Conversely, the politics with this corps of writers can also be quite tough to navigate for the publicist as well. Swiss champion Martina Hingis for several years would only speak with certain Swiss writers because her mother's boyfriend and her representative, Mario Widmer, was also a former sports editor and played favorites with newspapers. This caused the WTA sports staff some problems as she developed into a world number one, and impacted some of the negative coverage she received in Switzerland and throughout Europe.

Another issue with the coverage of sport outside the United States is that it still tends to be very sexist in nature. The acceptance of women's athletes for their athletic ability is still very slow to come. Part of this is the way stories are written, which we mentioned above. The grace of an athlete, and his/her form, takes dominance. Therefore it would not be unusual for a journalist to ask a female player about her weight, or the size of her thighs for example (I have witnessed this with Lindsay Davenport in the Wimbledon press room and Venus Williams at the French Open, by the way) and the journalist not think there was anything wrong with it. Therefore once again for the publicist, the ability to pitch stories for female athletes also has to be structured differently.

Example

Sports Nippon is the tabloid that enjoys the highest circulation in Japan. It is a part of the Mainichi Shinbun group, which is one of Japan's three major newspapers.

Sports coverage fills much of the paper and consists mainly of stories related to baseball, horse racing, golf, soccer, sumo, track bicycle racing, motorboat racing, boxing, and fishing. The paper is geared towards a male Japanese audience, mixing in equal parts of sex and scandal, along with suggestive ads and cartoons, amongst the reporting. Stories about female athletes, especially tennis players like Anna Kournikova or Maria Sharapova, will get solid play but will talk more about looks and body movement than actual match results.

Another big difference between the American press corps and the non-American counterpart is the use of incentives in exchange for coverage.

The American angle

In the United States, for example, the separation of church and state has become even greater that journalists cannot accept any gifts—tickets, freebies given out at games, Christmas gifts—that could possibly "influence" coverage. Most large newspapers, such as the *New York Times* and *Los Angeles Times*, require reporters to submit receipts in exchange for any kind of tickets for events. On the television front, the use of "pre-edited" footage, commonly known as the video new release, now can only be used by stations with a disclaimer on the bottom saying that the footage was given to them from an organization. The only exception most news gathering organizations will make is if it an actual hard news story that they were not able to cover.

The non-American angle

The non-American angle still will show a bias for coverage, and if there are incentives offered for journalists—tickets, airfare to an event, meals—they are welcomed as a way to improve the amount of coverage that a sport, an athlete, or an event gets. The negotiations that go on for the size of complimentary incentives have sometimes gotten into thousands in recent years. Surveys at the USTA carried out amongst journalists have shown that even at events like the US Open, the more free rides and food served, the better incentive it is for journalists to cover this event, one of the world's largest sporting events. The subtitle of this chapter for example, is a direct quote from a very respected journalist ("The Meat is not proportional to the size of the Cheese") when he was asked about how the coverage of the US Open could be made better by the media staff.

Now there are real financial reasons for the incentives. The growth of information on the web has created a real hardship for a large amount of newspapers, not just abroad but in the United States as well, along with the 24/7 news cycle. However, whereas American newspapers for the most part have opted out of the incentive for coverage ideal, many non-American media will take the incentive. Whether or not it influences coverage is the subject of much debate.

Another learning curve comes in the TV and radio area. We are all familiar with the amount of television coverage that sports gets in this country. In many parts of the world, although the quantity may not be able to reach the great masses it does here on a regular basis (hence the need for adept print coverage), there are parallels. The ESPN networks on the TV side, especially in Latin and South America, continue to grow and expand the depth of their coverage, while ESPN and its European competitor, Paris-based Eurosport, continue to make substantial moves across the continent. One of the biggest differences with pan-European events is actually location and language. The need to broadcast in many languages creates a huge cost issue in Europe, which leads to Eurosport doing many of its single language broadcasts from their massive studio complex in Paris. In one room you may hear as many as 10 languages broadcasting the same real-time feed to their respective countries. In Bristol, Connecticut, ESPN's multi-lingual teams could be doing the same thing. This, as a publicist, presents several issues. First, all the time and prep work that goes into making sure a broadcast delivers notes and messages can literally get lost in the translation or not used at all. There may be literally 15–20 broadcasters who you would not be able to meet and give ideas to while you are at an event. How to be able to work with the in-studio producers to be able to leverage your message to each country, and then track that message, is one of the biggest challenges.

Tip

The other challenge with "host" broadcasters for events is that many of them also tend to be journalists covering the event as well. In order to save money, outlets will split the cost for coverage (in addition to whatever the sponsor or event will kick in). Therefore the journalist/broadcaster may choose to withhold information that could go into the broadcast for his or her newspaper story the next day. He or she may also be able to gain an "exclusive" with an athlete by using TV as the hook. Therefore seeing however you can negotiate the biggest bang for your pitch with selected journalists is an added challenge. This rarely happens these days in the United States. Although many journalists will also do television, stories tend to break in one or the other. The more a print journalist breaks a story on TV, the less he will probably write for his outlet.

Similar to TV, radio also presents a big challenge. In many parts of the world, the conventional radio story and its satellite partner are still the principal way folks will receive news and information. In this country, the growth of satellite radio—Sirius/XM—presents great opportunities. The advent of sports radio on a market-by-market basis also has some great opportunities, but many times the opportunity for a guest and coverage is limited to national news and profile, and the local event. The mid-market event suffers. Outside this country, however, the opportunities for radio exposure are much larger. Entities such as the BBC, the world's largest radio service, provide the publicist with the opportunity to reach millions of people in areas where conventional television and radio broadcasts do not work. Knowing how the BBC and other large outfits work, how to pitch the right shows, and how to acquire and track the right coverage is a challenge, but one that is an essential part of your media plan outside the States.

Finally, having the conversation with the locals—athletes, federation, event staff—to know the media of influence and importantance is also very important from a micro standpoint. It is no different than in the United States in establishing the priority. However, in a strange land, the differing priorities will help gauge success, and the only way to really know that is to use this as a guide and do the homework beforehand.

Use the non-American press in the United States as a tool to grow your media base

As sports becomes more of a global entity, the amount of non-American athletes displaying their wares in this country continues to increase. We have seen it in basketball, baseball, hockey, and even football. There is more and more interest in soccer. Cricket has even tried to make some inroads. That is in addition to the other traditionally global games like golf, tennis, track and field, and boxing.

Athletes like the New York Yankees' Icihiro Suzuki and the former Houston Rockets star Yao Ming brought throngs of journalists from Asia to the United States to cover their every move in their own unique style. Colleges have increased their recruiting bases in sports like tennis and soccer to include more non-American athletes. It has also seen a large increase in the amount of ethnic newspapers and magazines in this country, along with the amount of non-English radio and television broadcasters and websites, who now cover sports as a whole. Yet we as publicists in this country tend to look at these non-American outlets as a nuisance sometimes, or an oddity as they follow these athletes from place to place. Instead of viewing them as an anomaly, we should be able to embrace them, speak to them, and learn how they cover the sport, the athlete, the team both for the multi cultural community here and for the people in their native land.

Another opportunity to gain perspective and build alliances in this country is to work with the non-American athlete as he or she learns how to deal with the American sporting press. This too can be an issue. Like most Americans, the press corps can tend to view athletes as somewhat of an anomaly, especially those who do not speak English. Now the stereotypes have changed from the 1950s and 1960s, when athletes like the Pittsburgh Pirates Roberto Clemente were viewed as "hot dogs" because of the way they played baseball and the fact that they spoke with an accent. Still understanding these athletes and how they are treated by their media in their home country and having them have positive experiences here with the American media can also be challenging.

One of the first things is to not create or perpetuate the same stereotypes that exist in many ways when we think of non-American media and athletes, or even ethnic media and athletes that are based here. Here are four good examples of situations gone awry.

- *Ferrari spins its Chinese wheels.* In the spring of 2012, Ferrari celebrated the 20th anniversary of its entry into China by laying rubber on top of an ancient Chinese wall using a dragon-adorned Ferrari 458 Italia. The PR ploy quickly turned into a PR disaster. The event was cancelled and Ferrari had to extend an official apology to China. The wheel-spinning stunt left tire marks on top of the 600-year-old Nanjing wall, possibly causing permanent damage to the Ming Dynasty-era monument. The bottom line is that a lot of people were embarrassed about what was essentially a high dollar version of a high school parking lot antic. Chinese officials shut down Ferrari's event, and it caused a great amount of cultural problems for a brand that has always prided itself on quality of service to its partners.

- *Linsensitive?* The meteoric rise of Jeremy Lin from afterthought to sensation for the New York Knicks in the winter of 2011 brought with it a series of changes and challenges. One of the most documented was the use of the phrase "Chink In The Armor" when the Asian American Lin faltered in a game after a long winning streak. It was rightfully seen as a play on words with a derogatory slant, and ESPN apologized on air and disciplined the editor who posted the phrase. Lin, whose family is from Taiwan, or Chinese Taipei, also had to walk the fine line with the media who referred to him as "Asian" or "Chinese" or even "Korean" on several occasions. Understanding the nuances became more critical as Lin's star power rose.

- *Maybe you should ask?* Two seasons in a row, Jewish Heritage Day has belonged to first baseman Mike Jacobs. On August 21, 2005, the California native electrified the hometown New York Mets fans when he was called up from the minors as a pinch hitter in the fifth inning of a game against the Washington Nationals and hit a three-run home run on his first swing in the Major Leagues. That day happened to be Shea Stadium's Jewish Heritage Day, and the heavily Jewish crowd of 42,000 erupted.

  Then, in June of 2006, Jacobs's new team, the Florida Marlins, celebrated its own Jewish Heritage Day at Dolphin Stadium and handed out free T-shirts featuring his name and jersey number. Only one problem— no one asked Jacobs if he was Jewish ... which he isn't.

  The Marlins did say the promotion was just a coincidence. However, they did take out a full-page ad in a local Jewish newspaper.

- *Respect the flag and the anthem.* Knowing which anthem is which country, especially in the war-torn Balkans, is very important. The subtle differences between knowing which anthem your competitor from the former Yugoslavia is theirs is pretty critical. Just ask the USTA. The US Davis Cup team faced Croatia in a Davis Cup second round tie at the Forum in

Los Angeles in March of 2000. The team, led by captain John McEnroe, had defeated Zimbabwe in the first round, and came home to play for the second round. These events are usually filled with patriotism and good will amongst competitors and this was the same. The only difference was when the teams lined up for the exchange of National Anthems; the US played the Serbian National Anthem. It was called to the attention of the US immediately after it happened—the two anthems were on the same cassette tape, and the team officially apologized. However it is little things like that which makes the US athletes sometime seem disrespectful towards foreign opponents, and could have created a public relations nightmare.

Not only will it increase the scope of what you do here, but it will give you an advance understanding of the area outside of the United States when you expand your pitch scope.

With those five rules in place, we will take a look at the following sports and how they differ both in the United States and abroad.

The Ryder Cup

The ultimate team event in the sport of golf is staged in the US against the world format every four years. All the media for the event is handled by the PGA of America, which is the professional organization of America's teaching golf professionals. PGA of America also handles the publicity for the PGA Championships every year (the USGA handles the US Open). Credentials for the Ryder Cup are accepted a year in advance of the event. Media is done in a team format following each round, and prior to the first day of competition. No other media other than the rights holders are allowed to film on the course, and filming is limited to designated areas only. All media interviews are conducted in the media tent only. There is no interaction with the media other than the designated media times, and times assigned by the PGA of America.

The Olympics

The summer and winter Olympics are handled now in two-year alternating spans. Credentialing for the Olympic are done in a variety of ways, with the National Governing Body of each country (the USOC) having final approval. There is a set criteria for the number of pre-Olympic events media and staff must cover in order to be able to get credentialed for the Olympics. The host committee public relations staff and the International Olympic Committee oversee final credentialing and interaction between athletes and the media during the Olympic events. Other than post-event and pre-event opportunities, media are allowed to enter the "mixed zone" areas where they are able to find athletes who are not competing for that specific event at the time. The National Governing Bodies are able to also work with media to assist in media interviews, although those opportunities are severely limited.

Tennis Grand Slam events (Australian Open, French Open, US Open, The Championships and Wimbledon)

Credentialing for each of the Grand Slams goes through the host tennis association (Tennis Australia, The French Tennis Federation, the Lawn Tennis Association, and The US Tennis Association). Credentialing is done on a year-by-year basis and is reviewed with a number of criteria, including the amount of other tennis-specific events the media outlet covers during the year. Preference is also given to media from the host country and to television rights holders. Interviews are conducted post-match, with early rounds on a need-only basis. The ATP and WTA Tours assist with arranging all media interviews during three of the four Grand Slams. The one exception is Wimbledon, where the staff are on site but the interviews post-match are timed and are done by members of the All-England Club. With the exception of the US Open, locker rooms are closed to the media. Individual interviews are scheduled on non-match days for players through the ATP and WTA. Non-rights holders are allowed on site with the exception of Wimbledon, where only rights holders may have a camera on the premises.

How the NBA expanded globally—a report by former head of international communications for the NBA, Terry Lyons

Since its founding in 1946, the NBA has become a global phenomenon that transcends national boundaries. With 30 teams in the United States and Canada, NBA games and related programming are broadcast to 215 countries and territories in 43 languages. The NBA is one of the largest suppliers of sports television and Internet programming in the world. Through NBA Entertainment, the league's award-winning production and programming division, the league produces NBA TV, a 24-hour television network, weekly television shows, and exclusive content for each of the NBA's team websites, and the league's official sites, NBA.com, WNBA.com, and NBADLeague.com.

International media coverage

The NBA services media members from thousands of newspapers, internet sites, magazines, and television and radio stations from around the world.

During an NBA season, over 3,000 media credentials were issued to international reporters from a minimum of 50 countries and territories.

Television around the world

NBA regular season games and programming are seen in over 230 countries around the world with broadcasts in more than 45 different languages via 164 different television partners.

- NBA Games: Fans overseas can catch the best basketball action during the NBA regular season, NBA All-Star Weekend, the NBA Playoffs, and NBA Finals.
- NBA Action/NBA Jam/Specials/Greatest Games: NBA Entertainment produces TV shows for sports and basketball fans around the globe with highlights of the best plays each week, along with all the latest in news, quotes, and statistics from around the NBA. From the news of the past week to the most memorable action from the league's archives.
- NBA TV: The league's 24-hr television network features a live NBA game every night, classic NBA programming, behind-the-scenes specials, and feature programs such as NBA Action. NBA TV is broadcast in 41 countries worldwide.
- NBA TV Daily/NBA Live: Provides game highlights, statistics and league updates from the previous night's action direct from NBA Entertainment and allows telecasters from around the globe to keep their viewers posted on NBA news.
- Multimedia: NBA Entertainment provides real-time statistics, scores, photos, highlight video recaps for media outlets and international websites.

Technology/NBA wireless

The NBA was the first North American sports league to provide video on phones in China through its new relationship in the region with Nokia.

NBA.com

The NBA is one of the most popular US-based sports internationally and the first professional sports league in the US to offer international web destinations for fans. Among English-language sports league websites, NBA.com draws the greatest number of users from outside the United States with 53 percent of all traffic to the site.

Basketball without Borders

Basketball without Borders, a global basketball development and community outreach program, visits four continents. The program, a basketball instructional camp for young people that also promotes friendship, healthy living and education with an emphasis on HIV/AIDS awareness and prevention, features current and former NBA players and team personnel as camp coaches. Since the inaugural camp in 2001, Basketball without Borders has featured more than 200 NBA players, coaches, and team personnel from all teams as camp coaches for the more thousands of young athletes from over 100 different countries and territories. The NBA family and the campers have traveled more than 100 million miles and logged more than 1 million hours of community service participating in Basketball without Borders.

NBA international player milestones, events, and attractions

The NBA stages a variety of events and attractions including goodwill trips, basketball clinics for players and coaches, preseason games, player appearances and grassroots basketball activities to cultivate interest in the sport. Activities include:

- NBA Jam Session: Features non-stop basketball entertainment, interactive events and exhibits, as well as on-court activities in various cities around the world.
- NBA Madness: An interactive touring event featuring NBA lifestyle attractions and tests of fundamental basketball skills.
- Basketball tournaments such as: NBA Basketball Challenge and Sprite NBA Basketball Challenge
- NBA 3 × 3: A grassroots traveling event for fans of all ages and skill levels.

Global business

More than 200 licensees make NBA products that are promoted worldwide and sold in more than 120,000 stores in over 100 countries on six continents.

- Over 25 percent of merchandise sales are generated from outside the US
- NBA merchandise is sold at more than 20,000 retail locations in China.

Global promotions

As the NBA has grown in popularity in recent years, global partners have taken a more in-depth and sophisticated approach to their international promotional activities with multi-faceted platforms featuring:

- NBA-themed advertising in 215 countries on six continents
- NBA-partner-themed promotions and events in 50 countries throughout the course of the season
- NBA player tours
- grassroots events
- special packaging.

Conclusion

In closing, it is important to take this chapter and the examples provided as a base for how you employ the education of the American publicity machine and include it in an ever-shrinking global sports publicity field. The examples provided should be able to give the publicist ideas to think about and a basis for learning as he or she takes many of the other examples included in this book and factors them into what is not a traditional publicist work environment. It is certainly a growing environment, but it is one that will take adapting traditional work standards and practices and adjusting them to the climate and the principles of those directly involved with the project.

Notes

1 Genzale, John. "What Passion They Have." *Street and Smith's Sport Business Journal.* July 10, 2006.

13

AGENCIES, MEDIA, AND BROADCAST PUBLICITY

Growing up you wanna be Joe Namath ...
when you are older you wanna own
Joe Namath

In this chapter we will take a look at sports communications from a different angle—from the agency perspective as well as from the perspective of a media company, be that television, print or digital.

Now the agency side has many different aspects to it. First of all, a description of what the agency actually is. This is perhaps the place where the beginnings of all publicity work stemmed from. The very first publicists were press agents. Namely, they went out and were responsible for image creation, damage control, and positively representing their clients, who paid them a fee, to the public. Sports and entertainment have always been key components of this field, as we have discussed. The agency today is comprised of publicity and image experts. They are structured from the most senior staffers; many times they are partners in the business, just as they would be in a law or accounting firm. The partners run the business, oversee client relationships, and cultivate new business. Below the partner level, depending on the firm, can be account executives, vice presidents, managers, group directors etc., all with the task of working on teams for clients to create publicity, handle crisis management, manage marketing partnerships, etc. The clients then pay fees to the firm, and they can be on a weekly, monthly, or annual basis, or be on retainer to the firm. Many times firms will keep billable hours for a client's work (this is especially true in a firm that is part of a public company) and in turn the amount of time is divided by client. For the most part, folks in an agency will rarely be working just on one client, and in many agencies a publicist will work alone. The time needed to effectively handle the full needs of a client is usually best served by the team, each with their own area of expertise. In today's world, the rule of thumb for most managers and above levels of publicists is to divide their time evenly amongst maintaining the client base, overseeing accounts, and also developing new business. Therefore, the social aspects of agency work—attending conferences, reading trade publications, developing relationships—is much more extensive than it would be on the client side. The biggest different between agent and client is very simple. The agency has the expertise that can show a client return on investment that the client does not have in house. For that, there is a fee schedule.

Here are some basic categories that will be examined:

- Large public relations and marketing agencies which deal with a myriad of sports and non-sports properties and find ways to marry them together.
- The sports-specific agencies that concentrate more on the public relations side and touch on the other aspects of agency business.
- Small groups or individual consultants who will work chiefly in one sport or in one aspect of the sports and entertainment world, like the sports television business.
- Agencies or groups that represent a specific athlete and all of his/her business interests.
- The entertainment representation agencies which have now started to grow into the sports area.

The role of the agency covers many categories. Some agencies have chosen to specialize in a particular area of expertise or partner with consultants on a case-by-case basis to make themselves as all encompassing as possible when developing a pitch. In recent years, large companies have also been able to segment their work off more and more, dividing activities between large strategic agencies and boutique agencies that have a certain area of either geographic or demographic expertise. For example, company x may have a large agency, like a Matter-Edelman, on retainer for crisis management across the board, but if they are looking for event-specific work to launch or run a tennis tournament in Los Angeles they may hire someone like Brener-Zwikel Associates, a well-respected Los Angeles based firm that specializes in sports events, especially in the Los Angeles area.

Also, in recent years, companies and sports-related businesses have started to view this area of their business like they view other areas of revenue. Whereas 15 years ago, there was not a long-term vision for a sports practice or project, now there is. The goal is a well-planned, well-executed strategic opportunity, just like consumer product marketing to any other core group would be. On the company side, the marketer looking for PR help can also fall into three groups as they plan their strategy.

- They know the sport but are not sure of execution.
- They have a strong brand and are trying to reach consumer x, which is a core sports audience.

- They just acquired a sports-related property and are unsure of both how to execute it through PR or exactly what the market should be.

Their request to find an agency will vary depending upon where their needs fall.

The acquisition of some of the larger agencies in recent years by holding companies like Omnicom and the Interpublic Group has probably streamlined the business approach and given some firms a little more option for economies of scale. However, each firm, with its unique area of expertise in their respective practice, still maintains a good part of its autonomy.

In recent years, many firms with entertainment backgrounds have also started to edge themselves into the sports world, especially on the athlete representation and event side. Very successful entertainment firms like Dan Klores Associates in New York are doing sports-related work on a regional and national basis, leveraging the long-time success that they have had in the entertainment industry as the model for luring sports-related business.

Some of the key areas where firms work with clients on the sports side include:

- maintaining business and cultivating new opportunities
- specific project implementation and development
- crisis management, media training, and counsel
- strategic placement and positioning
- industry expertise.

Agencies also vary on how they drive revenue. Depending on the size and scope of the project, and the agency structure, there could be billing on a project basis, hourly, weekly, or monthly. The entity could have a firm on a retainer basis for specific counsel or projects as well. Depending on the size and scope of the work, agency rates can vary from a monthly fee in the low thousands to multimillion-dollar, multi-year accounts. Also the ownership structure of the firm can also affect billable time. Public agencies tend to have very strict billing practices, while also having very wide practice areas. Smaller, privately held agencies can tend to be more flexible in billing, although they may not have anywhere near the level of expertise that a major agency can have for a client.

One of the biggest issues with selecting an agency really is personal preference. This after all is a people business, and making you as the client feel comfortable and that your needs will be taken care of, is the biggest issue.

Let's take a look at each group and find some examples of how an agency works in that setting.

Large public relations and marketing agencies that deal with a myriad of sports and non-sports properties and find ways to marry them together

One of the buzzwords here is convergence. You have large companies who have pieces of business in different segments—the consumer side where they are trying to reach customers or bring in new business; they are trying to find added value for their employees; they are trying to show their backers and stockholders the value that is coming from their investment, and they are trying to find the company that can marry these opportunities together.

Many will take the easy route and find a large agency that can service all these needs, and in many instances can do it with global or national arms and legs under their umbrella.

Matter Edelman Public Relations

One of the first to see this need and still carry through with it today is Matter Edelman, with their sports practice based in New York, where it has been since 1984. They have been able to deal with large, sometimes unwieldy sports properties like the USTA, the New York Roadrunners Club, and the NFL and the Olympics business, as well as well-respected brands looking to grow their sports business like Unilever, Claritin, Barilla, Wrigleys, and Astra Zeneca. In many cases, the sports marketing division will cross with other groups within the firm to produce value for clients. Consumer, Crisis, Diversity, Healthcare, and Corporate Reputation, for example, can bring a client to the sports group such as Wrigley's and the sports group will be able to use its expertise to find a partner like the Williams Sisters for a promotion. It is that ability which makes the large firm very appealing to major companies. Spending the top dollar to pull in the top resources.

Ketchum Public Relations

Another major firm that has invested in a sports practice on a worldwide basis is Ketchum. Like Edelman, Ketchum has formed a sports practice designed to link all parts of its business together, and it has resulted in successful partnerships with the NFL, college football, NASCAR, Major League Baseball, Major League Soccer, and the PGA among others.

Ketchum's worldwide offices have put a concentration more on the grassroots level of sports sponsorship activation over the years, developing very effective bottom line campaigns that show solid return on investment per dollar spent for clients. Developing internal communications programs and employee incentives, creating compelling media guides and collateral materials, and then driving those aspects to high level media attention are what have made their work so successful over the years.

Hill & Knowlton

Perhaps the leader in growth internationally in sports marketing and sponsorship is Hill & Knowlton. With a large push in Europe and the Far East, especially with the Olympics on the horizon, they have used all their international branding as a way to really bring what were once thought of as "Western" ideals in sports public relations and marketing and shown how they can work amidst the diverse culture of the Far East. They have also began to take that success and re-brand their North American partnerships in a variety of ways, especially on the branding and crisis management side. The Hill & Knowlton sports practice is based in Chicago, but has had recent success helping moribund franchises like the Tampa Bay Rays and Pittsburgh Pirates begin their turnaround with solid messaging and strong public relations efforts in the community and brand building efforts across the board.

The sports-specific agencies that concentrate more on the public relations side and touch on the other aspects of agency business

There are boutique agencies that will specialize in any variety of topics—celebrity, healthcare, fashion and beauty, etc.—sports is no different. However, with sports becoming a larger business and the crossover into mainstream consumer marketing, PR and brand activation even more important these days, the sports-specific agency has emerged.

Many of these agencies are local, and deal with local properties. Many can also be considered start-ups or very small shops that are great places to start careers and learn about the public relations business. In many cases they are agencies that are being run by very savvy sports professionals who have been at teams or in larger agencies and have decided to take their business on their own for whatever reason. Some of them are even segmented into smaller areas, like just sports apparel or sports television work taking the bulk of their time. Some concentrate on a particular sport like boxing. Also, with the need for certain "economies of scale," some of these smaller agencies are combining their administrative needs to work together under the same roof and provide a slightly broader area of service to potential clients.

The sports-specific agency is also rarely the "agency of record" for large businesses. Because their expertise is usually for a particular niche or a project, that role will fall to a bigger or more diverse agency. Many times these agencies are small to mid-sized as well, and if they are able to take on a long-term or larger scale client for a project like the Olympics, they will add consultants to balance out their team.

We will take a look at three sports-specific agencies that have set the standard for this model.

Catalyst

A division of Taylor (which was founded over 25 years ago by Alan Taylor and Howard Dolgin), this New York-based agency (with an office in Charlotte as well) has become a leader for sports-specific PR firms. The agency has grown with a core business that spread with referrals, and with a solid core of young professionals that were willing to grow the business as one.

The original agency really took a strong leap forward when they acquired Mike Cohen Communications in the late 1980s after the company founder and industry trailblazer Mike Cohen (the former head of PR for NBC Sports) passed away very suddenly. The company's philosophy is simple: hard work and passion underscore creativity, strategic thinking, and service. It is also a company that has not steered too far away from its core business of sports marketing, PR and sponsorship from where it started.

One of the reasons for Catalyst's success is that the company uses a different business model than larger agencies. Billing is done by established rates for the project or the event (exclusive of expenses), so billable hours do not become a factor. The company is also still very much a midsized agency, so the hands-on approach the clients get from senior staff is balanced with junior staff members as well.

Brener Zwikel Associates

Unlike Catalyst, Brener Zwikel, based in Los Angeles and with an office in New York now, has taken the opposite approach when it comes to sports publicity success. The firm, founded by former Los Angeles Dodgers publicity professionals Steve Brener and Toby Zwikel, has focused almost all its efforts on the event and strategic placement side of publicity. They began in 1990 with work picked up from the Dodgers relationships, and quickly used their strong sports ties to add events like being the agency of record for the Super Bowl and other NFL projects. Their relationships with the sports agency IMG led them to strong Southern California ties in golf and tennis, which led to a long-standing relationship promoting *Showtime*'s boxing events.

The firm has grown from 4 to 25 people since its inception, all with sports clients, handling publicity, event management, and credentialing with a long-standing tradition of strong media relations, solid pitching and placement, and hands-on planning. The size of their firm also has a great deal to do with the reason for their long-standing relationships—both Brener and Zwikel still manage each account, an oddity in today's ever-growing sports publicity world.

Coyne PR

Coyne is a specialized group of public relations professionals who possess creativity, experience, and passion to impact your business. The sports roster consists of veteran sports specialists combined with the industry's top consumer public relations professionals, whose united strategies create winning game plans for our industry-leading clients, including Chunky soup and the NFL, the United States Tennis Association, the Harlem Globetrotters, Bull's-Eye Barbecue Sauce and NASCAR, and Campbell Soup Company and the United States Olympic Committee, among others.

Small groups or individual consultants who will work chiefly in one sport or in one aspect of the sports and entertainment world, like the sports television business

At the time of the original writing of this book, being a consultant is not something I would have envisioned. However as we move through 2012, it is where I have ended up, and I can say I have enjoyed much of the work.

The most effective consultants usually have a wide expanse of senior leadership with strong ties to their industry leadership. They can provide counsel, strategy or just old-fashioned pitching on various levels, and are usually brought in by an entity looking for particular expertise.

Some of those leaders in various areas have included former head of NBC Sports publicity and White House education spokesman Kevin Sullivan, former White House press secretary Ari Fleischer, and others.

This has become one of the key niches in the sports public relations and marketing world. The growth of segmented groups—be it die-hard tennis fans, the sports television industry or the world of poker—has seen a recent boom in small companies dedicated to serving just that core audience and the sponsors and media that are dedicated to that beat.

One of the best examples is the sports television trade world. Like industries like healthcare or mass communications, sports television is an industry unto itself. The growth or regional television, the digital cable world, the addition of online alternative and complementary programming, all have created magazine and newspapers "beats" that cover the industry, along with specific sponsors that need extra exposure for their brands to both the consumers who watch the shows and the industry insiders who will purchase their products. Sports television reviewers are prominent in most marketplaces as well, so the need to service those writers is also a particular area of expertise. In many cases these entities, like Comcast Sports Net, or Altitude TV in Colorado, or The Tennis Channel, or the Golf Channel, or CBS College will have an in-house publicity person to handle the day to day, and then will take on a firm or a consultant on the outside for both project work like launching a new show or moving into a new geographic area. The area of expertise of this outside group is very focused and can be very successful. The contacts they have are well cultivated and the media that is delivered is easily measured. Many times the firm or consultant will have such strong contacts that they are kept on retainer in order to keep them away from competition when they have similar needs. Reputation here is also key. Very rarely will these firms be found in a phone book or a directory. The amount of work they do will keep them very busy at key points of the year, and in these very tight markets success will breed success.

Vince Wladika Communications

One of the most well-respected and most quoted publicists in sports is former FOX Sports and Major League baseball publicist Vince Wladika. Vince recently set off doing his own small consulting business, and has concentrated on the sports television industry, where he does work for Comcast Sports, Altitude TV in Denver, the YES Network in New York and other entities. His goal is simple: find manageable clients that he knows he can work with and use his vast contacts to form strategic partnerships and create placement opportunities for them when they are needed. He sets his clients up on retainer so they know they are able to call on him when needed, or come in for advance planning sessions where he can use his 20 plus years of experience in television to their strategic advantage. His work has been nothing but successful, and his retainer work gives him a solid backdrop against which to choose other business. He is a one-man shop, but a very effective and successful one.

Agencies or groups that represent a specific athlete and all of his/her business interests

This is another area of growth as athletes, especially high profile athletes reach maturity and try to find new ways to build themselves as "brands."

For the most part, agency representation for an athlete lasts as long as his or her playing career. The agency business, largely based on commission, revolves around the "flavor of the month"—who is doing best with his or her on-field accomplishments at that time. The major agency representation firms will find ways to market their clients, especially their stars, during that window of opportunity that makes the most natural sense and try and drive maximum dollars for the agency and the client out of that relationship. Unfortunately as we all know, that window is very short, and the area for publicity for an athlete with his or her off-field ventures can be much longer lasting for those who care to look at themselves as brands.

More and more savvy athletes are learning from the success stories—Venus Williams, Tony Hawk, Michael Jordan, Cal Ripken—to find ways to grow themselves as "brands" and find elements both locally and nationally, to sustain themselves beyond their playing days. Sometimes it is a consortium of local athletes who are able to find ways to grow their presence as brands and find PR elements to make themselves more appealing. Sometimes it is an athlete who sees the end of his playing days ahead and diversifies his interests for the next stage of his life.

This person also involves him or herself in activities like charity foundations, websites, and other areas where the agent may not be able to get maximum exposure for activities. It is usually a person with a strong familiarity with the athlete throughout his career. It used to be that these tasks fell on a family friend or long-time confidant, and in some cases that still does happen. However, many times now the savvy athlete is looking around at those who both help others grow or those who have had a series of successful opportunities in the sports and entertainment world, and goes to that person or those people for the growth of their next careers. The detail that goes into this form of "agency" PR is usually very detailed and very personal. Hence, initially it is the person who can spend a great deal of one-on-one time with the athlete, developing interests, setting up meetings, and knowing where and what to pitch. It also takes a great deal of coordination with player sponsors, sometimes team and community activities, to make sure that it is all a positive experience for the athlete.

Two examples follow: one of a lesser known athlete building a brand and using publicity, the second of a well-known athlete and the company that arose from the relationship.

Example 1

Jerome Williams had a very successful NBA playing career with the Detroit Pistons, Chicago Bulls, Toronto Raptors, and finally the New York Knicks. The Georgetown graduate was never a star player in any of those markets, but he was always the publicity darling because of the way he played and the way he carried himself. During his career, Jerome created the "Junk Yard Dog" persona and made that into the offshoot for a series of opportunities both in business and in sports and entertainment that will continue well beyond his playing career. Jerome used a solid PR team, and one seasoned professional to help launch these ventures and get him exposure outside of being thought as of just Jerome Williams, basketball player. The opportunities for publicity included pieces in places from *Women's Wear Daily* (for a clothing line) to the *Wall Street Journal* (for his car detailing company) among others. He was not "Brand Jordan," but he is an interesting businessperson who used sports PR to launch a new career.

Example 2

Cal Ripken is perhaps one of America's most iconic baseball stars of the past 20 years. Still, as his career was ending in Baltimore, he realized that he had all these new business interests in and out of the sport, as well as his motivational techniques, that he needed to tell people about. He had to find ways to build his brand beyond the sports pages and into the business world, not just in Baltimore but around the world and outside the sports pages. He enlisted the help of Orioles publicity man John Maroon for ideas while he was winding down his career, and the off-sports stories began to grow. However, once his career ended, those ties to Maroon would have to end on a full-time basis, as John had other specific needs that his full-time job with the Orioles would require. However, Ripken created a position for John to run all his publicity and marketing needs through the auspices of "Ripken baseball." He saw the need to have a savvy publicist grow that aspect of his new life, and found the right person to do it. Subsequently as those businesses matured, John was able to start his own company and market his successes to other areas of sports and entertainment with new clients ("Maroon PR") all the while keeping the Cal Ripken brand as a key part of business. The result has been a growth of a very powerful baseball "name" into a strong regional and national "brand" through the use of positive and strategic public publicity.

The entertainment representation agencies which have now started to grow into the sports area

This is another area of growth, although it involves almost the opposite of the post-career player "branding" opportunity. This area has now become popular with athletes who are looking to expand their "brand" while they are still in the public eye every day. These publicists, like a Dan Klores in New York, will look to find media opportunities for athletes through film, movie, and television above what their normal media attention is. The goal here is to expose athletes to potential opportunities that will make them more mainstream and open doors for them with the media that will lead to bigger opportunities for them in areas like TV, perhaps fashion, or the restaurant industry. It gives the athlete both exposure and the opportunity to network outside of what their normal circle is.

This "glamour" area of publicity has given rise to more business in the mainstream of sports for these agencies. It exposes them to the marketing and publicity teams at teams, solidifies their contacts with agents, and also gives them an opportunity to create sports partnerships with some of their clients who have never had a sports presence.

Example

Klores was a long-time agency for one of New York's City's greatest restaurants, Junior's, which is based in Brooklyn. As Junior's sought to expand its brand outside of its location in a main and well trafficked part of the city, it had the agency do outreach to former new Yorkers to tell their "Junior's" story. Another hallmark part of the Junior's tradition was cheesecake. Junior's cheesecakes are legendary for their size, shape, and quality, and the stories about them being shipped around the world to ex-Brooklynites was well known. However, the Philadelphia 76ers in 1992 drafted a seven-foot-six rookie center named Shawn Bradley, out of Brigham Young University. Bradley was very athletic but was a beanpole, and had trouble keeping weight on his very tall frame through the rigors of an NBA workout. The team tried all sorts of plans, brought in Mr Universe Lee Haney, solicited opinions from some of the world's great doctors, to try and find ways to have Bradley bulk up so he could be a force in the NBA as a center. The Klores publicity staff read about Bradley's problems and went to their client, Junior's, to present Bradley with a year's supply of cheesecake in hopes of getting exposure and helping him bulk up. The team presented the opportunity to Bradley, who was amenable to the idea, and the presentation took place in front of a large throng of TV in Philadelphia prior to a practice. Klores then sent the media updates throughout the course of the next few months, along with Bradley's thoughts on the cheesecakes. Unfortunately, his weight did not increase and he went on to have a very mediocre career, but the Junior's brand was introduced to a new audience and it exposed the Klores staff to more sports media than before. Since that point the company has built a larger sports practice while still maintaining a heavy lifestyle presence, but the Junior's idea was a solid example of launching out and finding a connection to sports with a lifestyle firm.

The agency

Now that we have looked at some agency examples and what the goals are, let's take a look at the qualities needed to work in the agency setting.

Now pitching

The ability to pitch stories to media is probably the biggest piece that the agency will look for those up-and-comers. Recognizing a story, knowing the media, finding your angle, and then communicating it clearly and effectively is the biggest challenge.

The other part of the pitch on the agency level is familiarity with a client. Because you may have several different clients, it is important to be a quick study and know which areas of media will best work for the client. Remember that the client is looking to the agency as the expert in many cases. Therefore you being able to identify the media outlets and then deliver is key.

The network

It remains a staple of the agency business to grow contacts and do a great deal of networking. Staying fresh, knowing trends through constant research, and going to your solid sources to know what long-lead pitches are out there are all keys to agency success. Maintaining a solid, broad-based media rolodex and constantly updating and checking it will help make the agency experience a valuable one.

So what's new?

Another staple of the agency business is simply finding business. There is usually a good amount of "churn"—turnover—in the publicity business. Big reasons for churn usually have to do with budgets and expectations. The larger scale projects require larger budgets, and many times clients are not understanding or willing to invest the large money over extended periods in order to deliver effective results. The educated clients will, and the ones who realize the amount of services delivered can be solid partners. However, in the agency world there is always a distinct knowledge by the client of what the competition is doing or has gotten, and sometimes that "jealousy" will also cause churn.

Also in this environment some clients come in on a project basis, and the time for the project simply runs out. Once that client is off the payroll of incoming money, it is time to start over again, and usually in sports there is no secret as to when the cyclical period begins and ends. It goes with the season, or with the announced results of a campaign for a sponsor. As soon as that campaign ends, the agency review usually begins and the process to get new business or secure the old one begins again.

Also adding to churn is the idea that clients tend to always look to see "what else is out there." Much like buying a car, when it comes time to get a new one most clients will do their homework and sample the field. The hope is to either reassure the client they have made a good choice, to find an untapped gem to start with, or to simply provide competition to lower costs without decreasing return on investment. The third issue is always the toughest for the agency, because the more equity you build in a client the more you may be able to spend against it. Once the agency loses that book of business, the equity goes too. Constant maintenance with the client, and the ability to sign multi-year deals are what gives agencies security. That is possible with many mid to larger agencies that have a growing or diverse practice. However, for the small guys that is difficult to secure.

Play many positions

Versatility at an agency is also key for the up and comer. Be able to pitch and learn about multiple clients, a strong writing background, the ability to participate actively in brainstorm sessions, the understanding of budgets, and even speaking a second language are all areas that make the agency staffer valuable. It is also important to know what you don't know, and be able to change that. The education curve at an agency can be swift and steep, and being able to ask the right questions and solve problems, especially with a client or in a pitch, are extremely valuable.

You may not get rich digging a ditch

For those starting out at the agency level, entry level is just that. The entry of the front door, or the clip file, or the mailroom may be where it starts. However in today's sports PR world, the move up can be very quickly for those who are versatile. The need for new creative thought, especially from young people who are out there understanding trends like social media, gaming, or strategic video as a communications tool and even how to download songs onto an iPod, can all be critical to the right agency pitch. Once again the more exposure you can get, the better opportunity you will have to move and grow. Start fast and work cheap are two slogans to use as you get rolling.

On up the ladder

As you move and gain more experience, the barriers to entry for the mid-level move may be strong. It is important to look at the growth when you are looking at the agency level. These days many small to mid-size firms have seen the turnover at larger firms and are investing in the young people with classes, bringing in industry leaders to show how opportunities for growth exist. On the average, those rising in the industry change jobs every two to three years.

Don't just know sports

Again, firms look for diversity. Even the smaller firms that are very niche into sports areas will look to acquire different types of clients from time to time in order to stay fresh. The more you know about the front page of the newspaper, along with the gossip and business sections, the more valuable you become. There may also be the day where you don't want to work in sports any more. The worse thing to do is to pigeonhole yourself as a "sports" person. Even in working with teams, leagues, or athletes, think of them as sports brands, and categorize them that way. It makes you more diverse and gives you an opportunity to grow your base.

Be professional, not a fan

One of the easiest things to do if you are working at an agency that has a solid sports roster is to get caught up in the on-field success of the athlete or the team. Just like working for a team in their front office, it is important to be able to divest yourself from the emotional attachment and treat it as a solid, professional opportunity. Especially at the agency level, the team is another client. Wins and losses in the PR area are much more important than how the team does on the field.

Come early, stay late

Just like those you know who succeed in sales and other opportunities, being able to identify business trends and applying them to what you do is essential in sports publicity. It sounds silly, but the easiest way to do it is by just plain hard work. The web gives us the ability to do huge amounts of research on newspapers sites on our own before or after the workday. Search engines give us the ability to do quick backgrounders on a potential client. The more you can do on your own to show how to grow the business, the more valuable you become.

Don't take it personally

It is sports. It is what you love. It is your passion. However, it is a business and those clients may get even more emotional about what's in the paper—or what's not—than most. Hence the turnover on the client side for agencies may be higher than on the corporate side. With those changes come adjustments in staff and assignments. The important thing is to work hard and be fair for the client, and not worry about what we do not have control over.

Last but not least …

Expect for the unexpected

As a member of an agency team, you must always be prepared for anything to go wrong. When planning events, have a contingency plan for poor weather or for a sudden news story to change the coverage of your client's best efforts. If working with an athlete, expect him or her to sometimes be late or have car trouble. Don't be surprised to see the product you are working with have some unexpected twists and turns along the way as well. Here are a couple of examples.

Example 1

How to make it stop? Long-time publicist Ira Silverman has worked for a host of big names in sports over the years with his company SMMG, including athletes like Jim Kelly, Hakeem Olajuwon, "Rowdy" Roddy Piper, and many others. One of his staple events each year was handling the publicity for the International Auto Show at the Jacob Javits Center in New York City.

One year, the organizers gave SMMG the charge of finding some new angles to draw attention to the show, and the idea of honoring all the regional Soap Box Derby winners from around the country came up. Soap Box Derby are miniature cars made out of wood without engines that are raced in competition around the country by young teens. They are downhill races, usually on a track. They assembled a "race of Champions" in New York the Sunday prior to the opening of the Auto show, the first time that these regional champions had even competed. The media coverage was outstanding as the race day approached. Former Mayor Rudy Giuliani showed up to start the race, which was to take place on the downhill slope from 34th Street to 42nd Street on 11th Avenue in New York City. The streets were blocked off and a crowd assembled along the race route, with the winners to end on 42nd Street. Moments before the race was to begin, Silverman looked north along the route and saw a very clear problem. These cars are propelled by gravity at high speeds and do not turn and at the end of the route was traffic running east and west along a very busy 42nd Street. The details of assembling the race and clearing the streets and garnering publicity were set. What was not figured out was how to make these cars stop without running through heavy traffic.

A potential disaster was now at hand. Visions of teenagers in wooden cars meeting their demise on 42nd Street raced through Silverman's head as he thought about ways to solve the problem. At that moment, a New York City mounted police officer saw the issue, and informed Silverman that the police horse barn, containing bales of hay, was only a few blocks away. The officer worked with Silverman to delay the race for an unknown reason, while the hay bales were set up at the end of the race route.

The race then went off without a hitch, with no fatalities, a new champion, and an unknowing problem avoided.

Example 2

A prominent sunglass designer worked with a publicity agency to have a mass unveiling of its latest version of sport sunglasses at a prominent location—the speedway in Homestead, Florida on an Indy Car Race Day. Close to 100,000 people would received these new sunglasses with a very sporty shade, and the image of all these pairs gleaming in the Florida sun as the race begins would be a visual to remember.

The agency worked with the governing body, CART at the time, to arrange for the passing out of the sunglasses, reflective midnight black frames with black lenses, to everyone as they entered. They would come in a black pouch with the sponsor name on them, and an announcement would be made prior to the beginning of the race to all in attendance to take out their new shades and be part of this historical unveiling. The company also worked through PR to have the broadcaster, ABC, be aware of the promotion to get even more national attention. Every detail had been thought out. Notes would be placed in papers; media would receive the sunglasses too, so no one would be left out of this moment.

The only problem was in the packaging. The sunglasses had a special protection that turned them very dark in direct sunlight. The effect looked terrific, but the design limited some visual aspects for the person wearing them. It was discovered as they were being handed out that a small removable label had been placed by the manufacturer on the corner of each lens to give them some liability. The wording was never noticed by the publicity team or the marketing group of the sponsor until that minute.

The phrase said "DO NOT WEAR WHILE DRIVING." This was obviously an issue if they are being given out at an auto race. Luckily the publicity head of the promotion was able to get to the distribution team before the race began and held up the passing out of the glasses. Instead, the fans received vouchers to pick up a pair upon leaving the raceway. Although the publicity effect was lost for the day with the visual, the embarrassment to the sponsor was corrected, and the crisis management that would have had to follow was averted.

In summary, the agency side of the sports publicity business has grown in leaps and bounds over the past 10 years. The need to show effective return on investment for sponsors, leagues, and even athletes has made this area very critical in the growth of the business, and has made the opportunity for success in sports publicity very diverse. However, diversity does remain the key. For those getting involved in the business, the agency side will give you a good slice of what it is like to have professionalism in sports. It is right out of the corporate world. It teaches you how to work in a business setting, account for your time, and how to effectively pitch and sell.

Also like the corporate world in other areas, it is totally results based. The return that comes in and the fact that the customer or client is always right weigh heavily on your ability to advance. The security factor in other areas of sports publicity is not always there, but the ability to experience the business world while still being involved in sports is there, and is what makes it a worthwhile entry and growth point for many people.

Sports media publicity

The next area to be addressed here is the sports media publicity area, specifically television and the magazine area, which now will include the online version of sports sites, sports television, and the publicity opportunities that come from this fast-growing area. Some of the great publicists have emerged from the sports television area, especially at the network level. People like Mike Cohen, who was mentioned early on in the book, pioneered the idea of taking the personalities behind the camera such as producers and directors, and telling the audience their story, which sometimes was as compelling as what went on in front of the camera. Using that style, television industry giants like Roone Arledge at ABC, Chet Forte, Dick Ebersol, and Michael Weisman at NBC, all became known in the mainstream. With that growth in interest in television came a whole genre of sports writing to pitch ideas to. They were the sports television writers. Men and women who once covered regular sports beats like college football, basketball, and baseball now took on their own beat, the sports television industry. With that came the need for a larger publicity push as niche channels branched out and became fullfledged television networks, such as ESPN, Fox Sports, and most recently the national networks of Comcast-NBC Sports, CBS, and Fox, along with all the regional networks, college conference specific, sports specific networks (MLB Network, NHL Network, NBATV), and the broadcast networks themselves.

The magazine and digital publicity side is similar to the television side, with the key difference being the regular routine of the printing business versus the immediacy of the television business. The television side is more event based, the print side is more feature based, which gives the publicist a little more time to plan his or her pitches.

The concepts here have been discussed throughout the book and remain the same. They include the ability to recognize a good story, the ability to successfully pitch the story to the right media, and the ability to build a consensus amongst those internally for what the best stories are.

The difference here is that those media that specifically cover the television and print industry are also part of the pitch plan, which makes the TV and print side a bit more broader from a business to business perspective. The print and television areas are industries unto themselves. Therefore finding effective ways to pitch behind the scenes stories of a broadcast to publications like *Multichannel News* or *Variety* add to the opportunities available to these publicists.

In many newspapers like the *New York Post*, the *Boston Globe*, and *USA Today* there are also a steady group of influential media writers who also cover sports business now, and these writers can now create mainstream publicity opportunities for publications that did not exist before. The topics will include increased circulation and ratings, new sponsor innovations, changes in reader or viewer interest in general, new technology in the marketplace, and how the media covers news stories, especially controversial ones like crimes.

These writers, such as Bob Raissman in the *Daily News*, Barry Jackson in the *Miami Herald*, Michael Hiestand in *USA Today*, and Richard Sandomir in the *New York Times* cover the business side of the business of sports in addition to serving as watchdogs for how print and television both create new mediums and opportunities for the viewers and readers to get their news and information. The difference with these writers is that rarely will they accept the traditional pitch. They try and present their stories as unbiased and in the view of the fan or the consumer. Therefore working with them from a publicist side requires the ability to come up with a unique exclusive in terms of access or building a compelling story through raw data.

Example 1

Giving a media writer access to the behind-the-scenes working of a television production, especially a live television event. One of the better examples of successful publicity with this concept has been done in recent years by the New York-based YES Network. Their publicity team has worked with a writer like Richard Sandomir to set up access with their executives, like executive producer John Filipelli, to give the fan an exclusive view into how a production comes together, why certain technology and camera angles are used, and how the business is run. By providing that inside access, the publicists are able to humanize and create story lines that are told in print, thus giving the fans more inside information about the broadcast than ever before. It also gives YES a better entrée to the media who cover the business, and when opportunities arise to cover topics in sports media, their executives may be the first to be called upon. So if there is a story the *New York Times* may be working on about the changes in *Monday Night Football* coverage, or how podcasts are changing viewer patterns, a YES Network opinion will probably have a better chance of being included. There is no real spin to the pitch to these writers in this case, but it is an example of how access in this unique environment leads to more coverage and better awareness of a brand.

Example 2

On the print side, the use of publicity to promote a brand usually deals more with the granting of exclusives or excerpts.

Ironically, an area where these two media areas have been working together recently has been forged through the use of interactive partnerships. In some cases, like the example of the print of *Sports Illustrated* and the television power of CNN, or on the ESPN side where the writers for *ESPN the Magazine* also appear on the ESPN network, the ability to promote innovations and breaking news across platforms is best shown. The publicists for print publications can use the visual medium to both tease a story and draw attention to what will appear in an upcoming issue.

Example 3

The subject of the Duke University alleged rape case was a prime story for coverage in 2006. ESPN had both the print side working on coverage as well as the broadcast side. While the day-to-day details were played out in the real-time television and online world, the dedicated reporters who were assigned to cover the bigger long-term picture from the print side had their own goals and detailed objectives. This turned into a great cross-promotional opportunity for both groups. The publicists on the TV side were able to call upon the in-depth magazine coverage and use the writers as sources on opinions when key moments occurred in the trail, which drove interest in print for the detailed coverage. The print publicists were able to use the television side to get their writers daily visibility on a very large platform. Therefore both brands got increased exposure in two different mediums.

Similar situations will occur with polling done by media. CNN and *Sports Illustrated* will work together to garner public opinion on a sports topic, such as the Barry Bonds steroid issue. They will be able to draw from a large audience that watches television and gets news and sports from online, and then use the magazine to summarize all the poll information in a print format, with much greater detail than both the website or television can offer.

It is the publicist's job in this case to extract the data and then find additional media to drive interest in the story as well. Using the data from the final poll and offering that up to an *Associated Press* for example, as evidence of what the public is thinking on this issue shows the larger scope that publicists for media organizations can present.

Now there will always be the traditional publicity roles for these groups as well. They will include the weekly updating or telling of unique stories in their entity to the general public, such as when there is a new program or story or issue that the entity is unveiling. The publicist here will also get to work with the subjects and their media outlets to tell the story and raise awareness. For example, if *Runner's World* is doing a story on the business of the New York City Marathon, or a feature on a runner from Charlotte, North Carolina, they would work with the marathon group or the hometown media to drive coverage. Or if Comcast Sports Net in Philadelphia is doing an in-depth profile on Donovan McNabb, they will work with the Eagles to make sure that there is greater awareness through their media and through the NFL to make sure that the piece gets greater coverage in a variety of outlets, ranging from beat writer notes columns to online stories.

Example 1

Convergence at its best: ESPN

While the print, digital, and broadcast media continue to scramble to find partners, the best example of convergence on all fronts with regard to communications is ESPN. For all of its pieces, the Disney-owned "Worldwide Leader in Sport" was still operating in communications silos—print, broadcast, news, company-specific, etc.—for most of its existence into the early part of 2009.

However at that point, the communications team, led by industry veteran Chris LaPlaca, began a transformation to what is now considered "360 Communications." In short, what that means is that the global ESPN communications team now works in lock step with every part of the company to make sure stories are brought forth that service everything from internal news to their television networks to their mobile offerings and their magazine and all places in between. Although primarily based out of company headquarters in Bristol, Connecticut, ESPN as a brand and as a media company makes sure that all areas of the business are included in the thought process when pitching or placing stories.

Putting three communications websites, internal, media-specific, and external, gives ESPN the unique ability to effectively communicate to all both in and out of the company, making for a much more effective way of bringing all interested in the ESPN brand up to speed. By being all-encompassing communicators and not just publicists, the ESPN staff is better positioned to deal with crisis and with positive news than many large scale companies. The request is that communicators stay in communication with each other, and also make sure that communication both internally and externally is vibrant.

How does one make communication vibrant? That is another key factor in ESPN's growth as a communications staff. The staff represents a wide swath of expertise—media relations, digital development, social media, crisis management—each of which brings a different expertise and a different mindset to the table. The result is a more shared knowledge of all aspects of effective twenty-first-century communications, from social media to video to traditional pitching and placing, that makes sure that every aspect of a story is being effectively told in multiple mediums to the audience that uses that form of media. What does that mean? When covering a product launch or a press conference, an ESPN publicist may be adept in Twitter to provide up-to-date news to an audience following him or her, or he or she may be able to use video and drop that video onto a platform where business or tech media may want to get a little different perspective or background on an event going on. There may be a unique photo op that comes up with talent, and by being proficient in digital photography that communications staff member can post behind the scenes pictures both internally and externally to best tell a story.

Individually, the ideas are not unique. However, what makes them unique is that the media company as a whole recognizes their special place in the communications business as one that both makes news and reports news, and by servicing so many areas of the business with one streamlined department, ESPN is able to tell their story best, both internally and externally, to a very wide and interested global audience.

Example 2

Comcast/NBC promotes across platforms

While not exactly the same as ESPN, the merger between Comcast and NBC Universal also presented a unique opportunity for cross promotion and communication for another sports behemoth.

In the middle of the last decade there was talk that NBC Sports, like the sports division at ABC, would be downsized. The ABC/ESPN combo had given ESPN a traditional national broadcast platform, which made ABC Sports as a stand-alone unneeded. With the Olympics in question, there was some thought that the same could happen to NBC, which would be folded into an all-sports play combined with regional sports.

However, the merger went in the opposite direction, as the NBC Sports brand increased in stature and became the lead, the exact opposite of what happened to ABC. The Comcast merger brought in new outlets under the NBC umbrella—regional sports, a second national cable network (Versus) and other properties which were not part of the NBC family prior, as well as a growing digital platform. The push was also bolstered by strong partnerships with the NHL, the addition of Major League Soccer, and most importantly, a renewed long-term deal with the International Olympic Committee to keep NBC Sports as the Olympic home, now not just on one network but across the family of Comcast NBC platforms in the United States.

However, with all these new properties came the need for consistent messaging and combining efforts. Leading that charge for new president Mark Lazarus was sports communication veteran Greg Hughes. Hughes had spent many years running communications for Turner Sports, and his expertise in understanding both the television landscape and the need to know how to merge efforts from various divisions would be invaluable.

Without a print play like ESPN, NBC Sports' communication strength relies heavily on promoting shows and events the network has paid for, as well as promoting all the other programming that is now under the NBC umbrella. Finding economies of scale with rights holders like MLS to promote is key. With limited personnel, a staff of less than half of ESPN, NBC Sports communications has to find the best way to promote to many platforms while keeping a line of consultants and third party publicists in line with the messaging and style of NBC Universal.

The other key communications point for the new, larger NBC Sports entity is internal. Because some of the properties are so large, they will cross over into traditional entertainment, an asset that an ESPN does not have as a direct connection. Yes ESPN and ABC do cross over, but the ties from entertainment to sports for NBC is much stronger. So establishing effective cross promotions with a news division and an entertainment group and even with local stations is very important to the success of NBC Sports. Some divisions may not be as focused or interested 24/7 in what is going on in the sports world, but it is Hughes' team that is responsible in making sure all opportunities for cross promotion are brought to the forefront and managed and messaged correctly and effectively for the best interests of the powerful NBC brand.

Example 3

Sports Illustrated

Unlike Comcast NBC and ESPN, *Sports Illustrated* remains a stand-alone entity with amazing print and digital content, but no broadcast outlet. And while in a time of multi-media and five screens needed to deliver a complete event package, *Sports Illustrated* benefits from having great writing talent who can deliver a story to any broadcast outlet at any given time, because they are not tied to just one broadcaster.

Sports Illustrated remains the gold standard of weekly sports publications in print. Their edit schedule runs from Wednesday until the magazine goes to print Monday night, and it hits newsstands and mailboxes around the globe less than 48 hours later, almost every week of the year.

Like many other print publications, *SI* has adapted in recent years to deliver not just the magazine itself, but great volumes of additional content through every additional platform, from web to mobile to tablets. Their social media play, all coordinated through head of communications Scott Novak, is a robust addendum to what fans will read in the magazine, with as many as 50–75 writers all active in the social space. *SI* also enhances their magazine coverage with podcasts, compelling video, and events and special issues, all designed to make sure that subscriber and advertiser are getting the best experience possible. *Sports Illustrated* was one of the pioneers in offering free content to its online offering, when in 2008 it opened the vast archive of the *SI Vault*, much of which showcased the amazing writing and photography seen and read throughout the history of the publication. The vault was a great draw for longtime readers as well as a new generation that wanted to be engaged to some classic stories but preferred the digital space to consume media.

From a communications standpoint, the 24/7 world we live in has changed the face of even a weekly print publication. Novak and his team will continue to pitch the conventional stories and specials that appear in the magazine, but like their broadcast counterparts have to also deal with the news of the day and how that is being accessed through any of the digital platforms that *SI* feeds. Some days a breaking tweet or Facebook post may bring as many accolades as a full-length feature, and the magazine communications staff has to be aware, engaged and ready to proactively pitch a story or react to whatever news is breaking with their team of editorial experts.

It is a business that is much more fluid than ever before, even though the chief means of communication to brands and the public is a weekly magazine, albeit one with lots of additions that now lives in the digital space.

Conclusion

In closing, the agency side of the sports publicity business has grown in leaps and bounds over the last ten years. The need to show effective return on investment for sponsors, leagues, and even athletes has made this area very critical in the growth of the business, and has made the opportunity for success in sports publicity very diverse. However, diversity does remain the key. For those getting involved in the business, the agency side will give you a good slice of what it is like to have professionalism in sports. It is right out of the corporate world. It teaches you how to work in a business setting, account for your time, and how to effectively pitch and sell. In the same way, the ability to work and pitch for media properties has also created new avenues for publicists. Although the traditional story telling does exist there as well, the opportunities to learn business and publishing and television press publicity makes those positions both unique and worthwhile, and are probably two of the biggest areas for future growth in the industry.

14

WOMEN'S SPORT PROMOTION

They've come a long way, baby

In this chapter we will look at the subject of women's sports and how there are unique challenges and opportunities both on the team and individual levels. We will also look at the differences in publicity in women's sports outside of the United States and how these issues can be addressed.

Now, some of the suggestions in this chapter may seem repetitive or generic to promoting any sports entity, regardless of whether the sport is co-ed, men, or women. However, it is the experience of those working in entities that involve women's sports that these thoughts bear repeating or establishing with clear examples geared to women's athletics. The reason is this is still very much a growth area and is a prime entry point for those entering the sports publicity field. The social acceptance of women as athletes has grown in light-years since the 1980s, and with it the participation in athletics as socially acceptable has also risen dramatically. That growth has begun to take a foothold in developing countries as well, and that area of growth will also be an area for the emerging publicist. The establishment of women's athletics in the mainstream is growing, but is not at the point of across the board acceptance in what has traditionally been a male dominated field. This chapter will look at the specificities of women's sports from a publicity vantage point.

From the advent of Title IX to the growing discretionary spending of women and girls and the continuing emerging of marketing to a female audience, the opportunities appear endless. The success of the WNBA as a league, along with the strong continued force of women's athletics in gymnastics, figure skating, tennis, and golf, appear to have the opportunities for publicity at an all-time high, especially in the United States.

Still, there are the many failures when the element of sports is brought to the marketplace. Leagues like the ABL, WUSA, WPS, even the AVP (where elite female volleyball players were the real stars) and others have tried and failed to crack the mainstream. The name recognition in the male-dominated sports world, especially outside the United States, is lacking behind male athletes, and in doing so the sponsor dollar also lags behind. Although that is not great for the dollar value in women's sports, it is not a terrible thing for the publicity side at this time. As women's athletics continue to establish a foothold, the driving force behind the growth has been the publicity angle. We will take a look at some case studies in the chapter of some of the successes in crossover publicity on the collegiate and professional level, but before here is a look at the differences and challenges in publicizing women, or women and men together as opposed to a male athlete focused sport or event.

It may be a game, but there are differences in the way it's played and pitched

One of the great pitfalls into which publicists can plunge is the "Battle of the Sexes" concept. Now in the first boomtime of women's sports in the 1970s, the Philip Morris-owned Virginia Slims Tour made tremendous strides in taking its brand slogan "You've Come A Long Way, Baby," and tying it to the ever-growing sport of women's professional tennis. This came to a head with the famous Billie Jean King–Bobby Riggs "Battle of the Sexes" match in 1973 at the Houston Astrodome, which King beat Riggs and effectively gave women's athletics a landmark leap forward. This was the grandest, and most effective, male vs. female publicity stunt before or since, and it still resonates with many of the millions who saw it on TV or heard about it since. It was a crowning day for women's sports to be sure, and it opened a great door.

However, in some ways it opened a door for competition that is not very realistic in many ways, and created a problem for women's sports in gaining a place to stand alone as an entity. The publicity idea of men vs. women for the most part has not gone well. There is so much more that the female athlete can offer as a stand-alone, the idea of competing with men on the same playing field can sometimes slow growth and exposure as opposed to broadening it. Tennis and golf are the two sports where this has been tried out the most, and perhaps there are parts of tennis where the level of competition could be comparable among names as in the King vs. Riggs match. This was the most respected but not the only time the Battle of the Sexes has been tried.

Billie Jean King breaks down the barriers

By Melissa Murphy

Billie Jean King remembers what sports publicity was like before the digital age. King, the eventual winner of 39 Grand Slam titles, and Gladys Heldman, the publisher of Tennis World magazine, helped found the precursor to the WTA Tour.

King and eight other players formed the "Original 9," who broke away from the tennis establishment and signed $1 contracts with Heldman to start a women's professional tour in 1970. King said the men were starting their own tour and the leaders of what's now called the US Tennis

Association refused to form a women's tour. King said men were often getting paid 10 times as much as the women in prize money.

Hellman reached out her friend Joe Cullman, the chairman at Philip Morris, to sponsor the Virginia Slims Tour. King said the first year matches were not on TV, and relied heavily on PR, mostly through newspaper and magazine ads and TV shows.

"We had 16 players and six staff of people from Philip Morris at every tournament," King said. "They were a huge help, getting the stories out. They had the best agencies in New York to figure out how to market us."

Players spent more time on publicity and media training because the tour was so new. They arrived several days ahead of a tournament and would "do sponsor parties and pro-ams, like golf does," King said.

"We thought that it was very important they saw the whites of our eyes," she said. "We never stopped doing PR."

"The great thing with a magazine, the publisher brought all the advertisers in to wine and dine them for a week—play golf, do business and dinners," King said. "All the big wigs from the companies were there."

King said there are so many different ways to reach the public these days—not just newspapers and TV but websites and social media. But every league still needs stars.

King starred along with the "Original 9" at a reunion to celebrate the 40th anniversary of the Family Circle Cup in April, 2012, in Charleston, S.C. It's the longest running women's tournament on the schedule. Rosie Casals won the first tournament and picked up a $30,000 check from the unprecedented $100,000 total prize money. Champion Serena Williams won $115,000 among the nearly $750,000 in prize money at the 2012 tournament.

At the 40th anniversary of the Family Cup, there was a dinner to honor the Original 9 and a World Team Tennis format exhibition featuring Martina Navratilova, Chris Evert, John McEnroe, and Virginia Wade. Bringing back the former stars gave added entertainment value to the event.

While joint ATP and WTA tour events are not uncommon during the season, the stop in New Haven, Conn., transitioned to women-only in 2011. After Pilot Pen ended its 15-year relationship, Yale University stepped in to sponsor the New Haven Open at Yale in the 15,000-seat Connecticut Tennis Center.

The tournament is the last on the schedule before the US Open, but still manages to get players in the top 10. The event is televised in over 100 countries, which allows Yale to project a positive image around the globe.

The tournament also provides local youth with tennis lessons, free rackets, and a block party held in the inner city.

At the end of the day having a twenty something superstar in her prime beat a fifty something former champion in today's world of sports would seem more silly than competitive. The key in promotion of women's sports is its uniqueness, and the audience it appeals to.

In publicizing a women's-specific sport, as it is with any opportunity, it is always important to work from your position of strength. What are the story angles, the high level of competition, the newness of these athletes and the games they play that exists in this event and and sets it apart from similar sports and events?

It is important to always think of these athletes and these events not in the eye of a *woman's* sport. Do any men's sports ever use the word men on the professional level? Never. In college athletics yes, because the advent of Title IX has created gender equity. However, many colleges have also now gone to generic names as opposed to names for men and women.

Another key area where this has been adopted has come from the names and logos that teams in the WNBA selected for their teams. In previous women's sports incarnations, there were names like the Gems and the Peaches selected as team nicknames. The advent of women's pro soccer and basketball showed that these new brands could have strong recognition in athletics without having to be portrayed as just sweet or cute. They could be representative of what the game and the athlete actually are and should be thought of, and that should be reflected in the public relations pitch.

Now the differences in the two can be the positive in the publicity play. In some instances the style with which women play a game is actually more similar to the way the average person plays and can relate to a sport. For example:

- Men's professional tennis is largely a big serve game, while women's tennis for the most part has remained a serve and volley game. Talking up the nuances of the game and the athlete makes it much more understandable and less intimidating than the men's side.
- Women's golf is also more about the short game and the way the course is handled, as opposed to the long drive of the PGA Tour.
- Women's basketball is much more geared around the team concept, and around shooting and passing than the NBA or the NCAA men's game, which has evolved into much more flash than fundamentals.

The other big advantage in many women's sports is the accessibility to athletes, and their willingness to listen to and work harder to implement a publicity plan in many cases. Now in the top pro professional leagues and in many top collegiate programs, the media demand may actually exceed or be comparable to the men's. Venus Williams, Michelle Wie, or the University of Connecticut women's basketball team will garner as much publicity as most male counterparts. With that comes the same ability to balance media request time and prioritize opportunities. However for the most part, the female athlete is much more accessible and open to ideas from a publicity side to make both her and her sport more successful. The important thing is to listen to their wants and needs for publicity, communicate well, and find the best ways possible to achieve the level of public relations activity everyone needs to be successful.

Another good and bad news story here is the fact that women's athletics is not funded on the professional level the way men's athletics is. The positive side is that women athletes may be more interested in doing the small endorsement or PR opportunity to bring in some extra money for themselves and their career. The negative side is that many of these athletes will go overseas, or play in lucrative and unregulated exhibitions, to get more money in their offseason. For example, many WNBA stars will go to Europe or the Asia to play during the winter, and many will not return until the WNBA season is about to begin, which will limit the PR window. In tennis, the few months of downtime provide for promoters to come in and have players participate in exhibition matches in cities where pro tennis does not reach, and that conflict can create a smaller window of opportunity for publicity as well.

The trick here is to again use those instances of exposure as a positive for the sport. Although the manager or team or league official may view these things as an annoyance in the short term, the publicist must view this as a chance to extend compelling story lines, support the athlete, and open up new areas of media contact that may not exist on a regular basis.

Having the glass half full here will make you the champion of the cause and the sport.

Sensitivity training

So we have now established that the nuances of the areas of women's sport that are promotable, and where opportunities may lie.

It's not what you say, it's how you say it

One lesson learned in the politically sensitive world we now live in is exactly how women athletes are referred to and how this Affects the public perception.

Example 1

In the basketball world on the men's side, those involved with the game will constantly refer to the guards as "smalls" and the forwards as "bigs." In one incident, a publicist was referring to a very impactful female guard in the WNBA as a "small," and a very imposing and athletic female forward as a "big." It was with a female writer who was being pitched for a sports feature on the two teammates. The writer, a long-time advocate of women's sports who was more than happy to hear the pitch, took great offense to the terms as demeaning to the physical presence of both players, and actually had a hard time dealing with what she thought was an "insensitive" male publicist again. In turn, the head coach of the team also spoke to the publicist, who again went back to calling (at their choice) the players guards and forwards. It was an innocent mistake and the lesson was learned, but it was one that this very savvy publicist had never dealt with in men's sports.

Example 2

In 1992, the WTA Tour was looking for a title sponsor, and was represented in the marketplace by their long-time media and business partner, IMG. Also in the marketplace competing for a sponsor was IMG's largest rival at the time, Advantage International, which is now part of Octagon, itself one of the largest and most successful sports media and marketing companies in the world. The title sponsorship of a tour or an event is the most lucrative and all-encompassing branding statement a company can make. It bonds that brand with the sport or the entity for the period of time designated, usually a period of several years. In that time the brand name through publicity and marketing will become synonymous with the sport or event, and either solidify the brand with the marketplace it is trying to reach or grow the brand name into new areas. The best title sponsorships can accomplish both.

As the sport was just regaining its foothold in the public sector after a downtime in the 1980s, and competing for worldwide sponsor dollars, there was not a great deal of choices. However, one of the companies to step up to the plate and put up the money the Tour was looking for was Johnson & Johnson, the maker of women's hygiene product Tampax. Johnson & Johnson was looking for the right vehicle to grow their brand and reach their core audience, and the demo of women's tennis fit them exactly.

The deal never happened, and it was largely because of the PR perception. The feeling of the CEO of the women's tour, Anne Worcester, after counsel from her players and board, felt that the PR issues that would be created in a Tampax titled tour, especially outside the United States where the media would be less accepting, far outweighed the benefits of exposure and dollar value. (The Tour eventually landed software sponsor Corel as its title sponsor, and has had various incarnations over the years, including Sony Ericcsson as the latest.)

Now in today's marketplace, with pharmaceuticals being the rage and Viagra and Cialis becoming much more mainstream, the idea of Tampax sponsoring a women's sports league may be more acceptable to the general public. But in the 1990s, the stereotype and negative PR possibilities outweighed the positive.

Example 3

Sexual diversity. Women's sports have come a long way in both addressing the issue of sexual diversity and tolerance in the workplace, but the issue remains a PR topic with many women's sports when they try to enter the mainstream, which can still be a very homophobic atmosphere. The issue of the Los Angeles Sparks or the Dina Shore LPGA event marketing to a gay audience has been a public relations issue for many years, and has affected publicity plans both positively such as exposing the events to mainstream media coverage, and creating niche publicity opportunities with sponsors, and negatively such as the sports media backlash and off-color stories, and protests from conservative groups. However, the gay bias as a PR concern when working with women's sports has to be considered and factored in, but not be the main focus. It is not important to overcompensate with stories of married, attractive females with their kids and boyfriends. It is important to have balance and be sensitive to the needs of the athlete and the sport.

Example 4

Locker room space. Another male/female issue that all publicists should consider and be ready to deal with is the issue of female reporters and publicists in a men's locker room. While we have come a long way from the famous Lisa Olson story with the New England Patriots in 1990 (Olson, a reporter for the *Boston Herald*—and now the *New York Daily News*—was sexually harassed by three players in the Patriots locker room following a game and the incident was confirmed by the commissioners office), there are still many issues that have to be addressed, considered, and eventually overcome for the non-athlete in the male athletic environment. In the United States, virtually all locker rooms are open for media following a cooling off period, and generally athletes nowadays do use a bigger sense of decorum with regard to robes and towels. Many teams actually institute a "woman in the locker room" heads up to stay even more on top of things. While this sometimes is not taken well by female journalists, who feel like they are being singled out, it is most times meant as a courtesy for both the athlete and the journalist. From a publicity side, the female SID or team PR staffer has to deal with these athletes every day, and most will pick their spots entering the locker room. Again it may present some problems with regard to watching interviews or making sure media get what they need in terms of access and publicity in a locker room setting, but the idea of having male assistants around to help out in what is sometimes an uncomfortable situation is very helpful, and can help speed the process.

Women reporters in the men's locker room: rugged terrain

Randi Druzin, womensportsfoundation.org

Cub reporter Paola Boivin entered the St. Louis Cardinals clubhouse with her male colleagues after a game in 1987. While searching for infielder Terry Pendleton, one of his teammates approached her. "Are you here to interview somebody or to look at a bunch of guys (deleted)?" No sooner had he spat out the words then a jockstrap landed on Boivin's head. She fled the clubhouse and later interviewed a sympathetic Pendleton in the hallway.

Subsequent locker room visits were less problematic for Boivin, a former president of the Association for Women in Sports Media (AWSM), but she was surprised again a few years ago. During a post-game interview with then-Arizona Diamondbacks infielder Tony Womack, Boivin felt someone tugging on the hem of her jacket. The *Arizona Republic* reporter looked down to meet the son of then-Diamondbacks outfielder Steve Finley. "Miss, miss," the little boy said. "You can't be in here. This place is only for boys."

The lot of the female sports reporter is much better today than it was two decades ago, when women took their first steps into the locker room, tiptoeing through a minefield of jockstraps and naked men. Nonetheless, the female sports reporter is still not competing on a level playing field. She still encounters obstacles and frustrations her male colleagues do not.

A decade before Boivin's unfortunate encounter with a sweat-drenched bit of men's athletic apparel, *Sports Illustrated* reporter Melissa Ludtke had a run-in of her own. When Major League Baseball Commissioner Bowie Kuhn prohibited Ludtke from interviewing players in the locker room during the 1977 World Series, *SI* publisher Time Inc. filed a lawsuit. The following year, a US federal judge ruled that male and female reporters should have equal access to the locker room.

Players howled in protest "We're not a nudist colony putting on an exhibition," insisted NBA rookie Toby Knight, "and the locker room did not change overnight."

Indeed, in 1979, the Fort Myers News-Press battled the NFL's Tampa Bay Buccaneers to win equal access for sports reporter Michele Himmelberg. Later in the season, before a game in Minnesota, Himmelberg arrived in the press box to learn that all reporters would be banned from the Vikings locker room because of one woman reporter.

After the game, reporters were herded into a designated interview area. "We stood there for a long time and no players arrived," recalls Himmelberg, a co-founder of the Association for Women in Sports Media (AWSM) now with *The Orange County Register*. As deadlines neared, reporters began checking their watches anxiously and grumbling aloud. Himmelberg found herself cornered by two radio reporters. "What are you doing here anyway?" they demanded. "You're just a pervert trying to get a look at these guys." Himmelberg left the interview area, got some quotes in the Buccaneers' locker room and filed her stories. She then returned to her hotel room and burst into tears.

"Let's face it. I'm an outsider in the players' domain."

Her job became less difficult over time. By the mid-1980s, all four major professional sports leagues (NFL, NHL, NBA, Major League Baseball) had adopted policies in compliance with the US court ruling on equal access, and female sports reporters had become more commonplace in the locker room.

Nonetheless, several of these women learned that, while they were allowed into the locker room, they were not welcomed there. "Changing the rules doesn't necessarily alter attitudes," Ludtke observed.

No one learned that lesson better than Lisa Olson, a reporter for the *Boston Herald*. While conducting interviews in the New England Patriots' locker room following an NFL game in 1990, a group of Patriots surrounded the reporter and made aggressive, vulgar comments. The players were later fined and the team's general manager was fired for trying to cover up the incident.

When the incident sparked a national debate, Olson began receiving death threats. Vandals burglarized her apartment and painted an ominous message on a wall in her home: "Leave Boston or die." She received another note when the tires of her car were slashed: "Next time it will be your throat." Olson later recalled that she received mail that "would make you physically ill—depictions of rape scenes and horrible, horrible things."

Olson fled to Australia, where she covered cricket and rugby for five years. She returned to take a writing job at *The New York Daily News* hoping to put the past behind her. Nonetheless, she started receiving threatening phone calls and letters again, when two famous athletes spoke out against female reporters in the locker room.

In a 1999 *Wall Street Journal* article, retired NFL defensive end Reggie White wrote that he couldn't see a legitimate reason "for forcing male athletes to walk around naked in front of women who aren't their wives." White claimed to have seen female reporters "ogling guys in the locker room," and encouraged players to fight against equal access for female reporters.

Within a few days, New York Knicks guard Charlie Ward was distributing copies of the article to his teammates. The basketball player claimed having women in the locker room violated the sanctity of marriage.

Madison Square Garden president and chief executive officer Dave Checketts condemned Ward's actions and warned him not to use the locker room as a pulpit. No surprise to Rachel Bachman, a sports reporter at *The Oregonian* who covered the NBA's Portland Trail Blazers during the 1998–99 season and has covered them in post-season play since then. "Today, when a woman is harassed or there are access problems, there is an immediate response and a general understanding that the reporter has the right to be there," she says. "That was not necessarily the case just 10 years ago."

But some things haven't changed. Bachman confesses she is bothered by the current "blurring of boundaries" between professional male athletes and female reporters. "Female reporters suffer a lot of harassment because some men don't understand or respect that the women are in the locker room to do a job." Bachman says few women speak out because "they want to be defined by their work, not by their struggles."

"I have had athletes either ask me out or make inappropriate suggestions sexually. It's a horrible position to be in because you have to keep writing about these men after you have rebuffed them, and often they are not very understanding about the reason you say no."

Male athletes' problem with female reporters is rooted in "stereotypical, outmoded and confining images of women, not at all suited to the reality of their actual lives," suggests Ludtke.

"Let's face it," sports reporter Christine Brennan once wrote in the *Washington Post*. "I'm an outsider in the players' domain."

Now do the same issues exist for male journalists and PR staffers in the female sports world? Perhaps to some extent but not to the same degree because of the lack of both male publicists involved in female sports and the smaller amount of female sports regularly covered by a larger media contingent. Ironically in many cases for female sports, the locker room situation is different than for their male counterparts. Locker rooms for females are largely off limits to the media, with the exception of small media access areas. One of the biggest exceptions is at the US Open, where the female locker room is open to media to the same extent that the male locker room is open to females.

Example 5

The sex symbol issue. The quickest way to get into the male dominated area of sports with publicity is to play up the issue of physical attributes over athletic skill. Again, like the sexual diversity issue, this cannot be ignored in the public relations plan. The LPGA Tour has made the "sexiness" of their players a prime asset in their PR and marketing plans, as the WTA has for years. Women's fashion, recently Serena Williams' black "cat suit" at the US Open, is always a central part of the publicity plan at major tennis events for both apparel companies and athletes.

It is very rarely the case with men's sports. Indeed, when these issue shave come up as part of a publicity push in men's sports, the ideas are often shunned by mainstream sports media as "silly" or "uninteresting." Andre Aggasi's sex appeal is one of the bigger recent examples. Most sports writers chose to write little about Andre's physical persona, yet all physical attributes about his future wife, Steffi Graf, were easily the cause for debate, especially when she became pregnant.

The question in the publicity world becomes if the publicist can effectively play both sides of the fence. Can you pitch stories about physical beauty and sexiness like a Maria Sharapova and then expect a serious athlete who does not want that side of her persona to be the central focus to be taken seriously by the media? The answer is yes, but there must be a balance, and the athleticism must also be the main focus. Without the athleticism, the message is lost and that athlete usually becomes known just for her physical attributes and not her athletic ability.

Example 6

Respect for social tradition. Many times Americans living in a very liberal society forget that there are still traditions and cultures that are thousands of years old in other parts of the world that need to be factored into our decisions, even in the world of women's sports publicity. As women's sports grow around the globe and emerging nations realize that having young women participate in athletics is acceptable, new issues arise. Islamic culture has seen backlash in tennis and volleyball, where shorter skirts and bikinis which are common in some forms of competition, are not acceptable. Indian tennis player Sania Mirza actually received death threats several times for wearing skirts during tennis events while openly talking about her devotion to her heritage. Pro tennis and golf events in places like Dubai have seen great acceptance among larger populations, but players have had to be very careful and respectful when circulating in general population.

Publicists must be respectful of these issues and be able to deal with them in a crisis situation as women's sports grows. It will also affect the ability to effectively pitch such stories and athletes in an international sport setting as sports become more acceptable in emerging countries for women.

Do not work as an island

One of the common misconceptions in sports publicity for women's athletics is that each sport is going to be the trailblazer to get women's sports on equal ground with men's. Women's tennis, women's basketball, women's golf, women's softball, women's volleyball, collegiate women's sports, figure skating, women's soccer, gymnastics, even boxing, have all at one time or another proclaimed the breakthrough that will get their sport into the main male demographic with unique publicity ideas. All have tried, and many have worked for short periods of time (with tennis and golf being the obvious leaders), but in the end the wave rises and falls with little consistency.

Companies hungry to attach themselves to both the ever-growing female demo and the sports-minded male demo jump in eagerly hoping to ride the wave, Yet when the smoke clears they do not see always see the return they envisioned. Are there good publicity opportunities in the temporary intervals of mass popularity? Absolutely. The Women's World Cup will be one of the greatest case studies ever for strong initial publicity. Serena Williams and Maria Sharapova have created very unique and intriguing opportunities for the game of tennis. Annika Sorenstam and Michelle Wie have changed some of the perceptions about women's golf. Danica Patrick's presence in NASCAR has helped a rise in that sport. However, they are all short lived and on the publicity side many operate in a vacuum, or will copy off the other.

The perfect case study for this is women's tennis and golf on the individual side, and women's basketball and soccer on the team side. Here are some examples.

The WTA publicity machine of the mid 1990s and the WNBA

Arguably, both tennis and golf have produced the greatest individual sports publicity opportunities for women's sports. After Sally Jenkins famous' "Is Tennis Dead" story in *Sports Illustrated* during the late 1990s, the sport—especially the women's game—revamped itself to use the personalities of the game to sell the sport. The conscious effort was made to work with player agents, sneaker companies, and marketing agencies to combine efforts and find opportunities collectively to grow the game. Hence, the images of Martina Hingis as the first female athlete on the cover of *GQ*, to Conchita Martinez featured in *Wine Spectator* became the norm, because those publicists took the time to find out the interests of the athletes on and off the court and effectively manage the publicity opportunities both for the long and short term. The result was a boom over a five-year period in the interest of the sport, which resulted in growing prize money, the first-ever prime time exposure for a women's championship on television (the women's final of the US Open shown on a Saturday night), and more mainstream coverage of the sport.

The WNBA

The landmark move on the women's team front was David Stern's 1996 launch of the WNBA. The summer league began as a single entity opportunity to come off another strong Olympics and showcase the game of basketball year-round, using the strong and vibrant athletes that had flourished under Title IX at the collegiate level to grow basketball to a new year-round family audience. The league used its leverage with its NBA partners to launch the league to great fan-fare crowds, sponsor dollars, and television numbers, including a landmark deal with NBC. The personalities and the passion of the women's game was different from the NBA style, and had the support of the NBA behind it to push it solidly into the marketplace. WNBA faces and logos were seen everywhere in what was arguably the best start up from a publicity standpoint of any professional sports league. The WNBA—although in a slightly different format, many teams are individually owned now and in some non-NBA markets—continues to be the hallmark for women's sports leagues as it goes through its second decade.

Laurel Richie discusses WNBA success

By Melissa Murphy

WNBA President Laurel Richie discussed the importance of sports publicity and marketing for the league, players, and fans. Richie worked two decades in marketing at Ogilvy & Mather and was chief marketing officer for Girl Scouts of the USA before taking the helm at the WNBA in 2011. She's the first black woman named president of a US professional sports league.

LR: "It is very important for people to engage with the league or get into the arena or watch a game on TV. Marketing is important just to create awareness of the league and our teams. But marketing is also critical in terms of helping current and prospective fans and partners get to know our players. People don't necessarily follow a league, they follow a team that they love or their hometown team. Most importantly, they follow players, who they either like the style of play or like who they are as people or have some kind of connection to them.

Shine a light on the players and what makes those players unique. Diana Taurasi is a very different player and person than Cappie Pondexter or Tamika Catchings or Lauren Jackson. So the more we can get the stories of who they are as players and who they are as people, I believe the more we engage people in women's professional basketball."

a) How has marketing and PR changed since the days when you were at Ogilvy and Mather?

LR: "I think what's really changed is what's happening in the digital space. I've always believed that consumers and fans are the ones who own a brand for a league. I think that's even truer now that social media has made it so easy to have interaction with a brand or with the league and also to give immediate feedback. I think that has changed the landscape, the biggest change in the last 30 years."

b) What's been some of the most effective ways to promote the WNBA and reach fans?

LR: "It's a combination of very targeted initiatives and we are aware both on a league level and on a team-by-team basis. We have a pretty good handle on our fan base and the composition of our fan base, so it allows us to do some really good target-marketing initiatives. Reaching out, whether it's to the African-American market in Atlanta or the Hispanic market in San Antonio and Los Angeles. The Connecticut Sun's profile is an older audience and a bit more Caucasian and they're UConn fans. So when we know who we are, we can do our online and offline outreach to them in a very specific way."

c) TV is still important, for sponsors and eyeballs, and WNBA ratings and arena attendance were up in the 15th season in 2011. But there's also an online audience, and games are available on smart phones and mobile apps?

LR: "In 2011, it was the first year our fans were able to watch games on mobile devices and their ipads. Particularly for fans who don't have a team in their city or within driving distance, they're able to keep connected with them."

The WNBA television contract with ESPN runs through 2016 with a minimum total of 29 regular and post-season games broadcast during the four-month summer season. The 2007 contract extension provided the first rights fees paid to a women's pro sports league. Internationally, the WNBA All-Star games have been shown in as many as 168 countries around the globe.

The WNBA signed Boost Mobile as a league-wide sponsor in 2011 and its logo appears on a majority of the 12 teams' jerseys in what Sports Business Journal reported was an eight-figure deal.

Leaders of the WNBA consider the points of differentiation from other sports leagues in terms of affordability, access and community.

Tickets are as low as $10 per game, and team theme nights include honoring female business leaders, dads and daughters nights and dribble for diabetes. Players are available for autographs after the games.

Off the court, the WNBA focuses on key marketing pillars of "Inspiring Women" and "Health and Wellness." WNBA Fit programming partners with sponsor Jamba Juice for clinics to fight obesity in cities across the country. Richie says she's always looking to partner with other organizations such as the AAU or 100 Black Men or the Girl Scouts. Players go into schools in the offseason spread health, fitness and anti-bullying messages.

Richie says cause marketing is an important part of the DNA of the league— whether it involves heart and breast health or obesity—because of a strong commitment to serve the communities with WNBA teams and make a difference in the lives of fans.

Another way to publicize the league is to piggy-back on milestone events such as the Olympics, where all 12 of the 2012 US basketball team will feature WNBA players, and the 40th anniversary of Title IX. That's the US federal law that bans sex discrimination in any educational program or activity that receives federal financial assistance. Passed in 1972, it opened the doors to educational and athletic opportunities for women. The WNBA will feature two games on ESPN on June 23 and hold league-wide celebrations in its 12 cities, including thousands of youths at a "Believe in Girls" event at Liberty State Park in New York City.

Stars are always necessary to promote a team and league. Maya Moore went from a successful career at the University of Connecticut to become the No. 1 pick in the 2011 WNBA draft and earned Rookie of the Year honors while helping the Minnesota Lynx win their first title. Her skills and popularity made her the first female basketball player to sign an endorsement deal with the Jordan Brand, a division of Nike.

The Twin Cities feted the WNBA champions to a parade and 15,000 fans showed up in the fall of 2011. During the season, Lynx players dropped the puck at a Minnesota Wild hockey game, threw out the first pitch of a Twins game and attended Vikings games. Each pro men's team took turns buying up tickets for fans in the upper bowl to give away free to fans during radio call-in shows. Billboards, radio spots and social media are relatively inexpensive ways to promote the local team.

Certainly the image of the WNBA trophy with Minnesota's three stars—Moore, hometown girl Lindsay Whalen and Seimone Augustus—will be prominently displayed in all Lynx publicity material.

All of these were great efforts and have had their tremendous publicity opportunities in their lifetimes. What's the problem then? Consistency. Sport, as we know is cyclical, and for growing sports struggling to find the consistency, they need to *work* together to combine their facts, figures, and opportunities to maximize the good days and get through the rainy days. If you are a sports publicist working in a women's sport, take the time to study, contact, and work with *other* sports entities who are trying to find your niche.

Tennis and golf are the same story. A joint campaign by the governing bodies championing the efforts and ability of Annika Sorenstam and Serena Williams would have been groundbreaking and very telegenic. Numbers combining the two audiences would get each sport through its highs and lows. Instead the two work in their own silo, trying to each proclaim themselves "number one" in their media push at various times. As a result the short term is served and the long term suffers.

As a publicist, one should seek to unite to create *new* opportunities as opposed to constantly recreating the same ones. It would be trailblazing, and as a women's ports publicist, would set one ahead.

As an aside, there is one group that does use the cumulative to grow the women's sports picture for all. The Women's Sports Foundation, founded in 1974 by Billie Jean King, is a charitable educational organization dedicated to advancing the lives of girls and women through sports and physical activity. The Foundation's Participation, Education, Advocacy, Research, and Leadership programs are made possible by individual and corporate contributions, run by Dr. Donna Lopiano (http://www.womenssportsfoundation.org). The Foundation is the data collection and voice for all women's sports, and works the hardest to provide these services to the media and sponsors alike. It is a great resource for the publicist and is very underserved.

Find the advocates and make them your biggest voices

One of the biggest challenges for women's sports publicity to find the biggest advocates and make them yours. The sports editor of a specific paper may continue to be focused on his male demographic and subsequent stories, but there are the other angles to the paper, and the looks at columnists, to find who will be your voice as the entrée. If you are involved in women's sports publicity, the knowledge of those who have written and championed the causes (Christine Brennan, Sally Jenkins, Harvey Araton, Karen Crouse, Liz Clarke,

Rachel Nichols), voices that are very well heard in all sports, will be able to help you open doors.

The publicist today also has the great resource of the internet to locate those voices, an element which previous women's sports publicists have not had before. The ability to work as a consensus builder is key here too. Identifying those voices who have a passion for the cause will make your job easier.

ESPNW fills a void

By Melissa Murphy

The latest entry in the digital landscape is espnW.com, the website devoted to women's sports. ESPN launched the site in April 2011, featuring a variety of women's sports that's geared toward an active-lifestyle woman.

It's the newest sibling in the ESPN family that includes cable channels, radio, *ESPN the Magazine*, and ESPN3, which provides live online streaming of games. EspnW provides exposure of athletes through features and videos, roundtables and tweets, plus advertising opportunities for sponsors to reach a wider online female audience.

Although numerous websites cover men's sports, few provide a comprehensive roundup of women's sports in one spot. Sports magazines for women have been short-lived, even when backed by Sports Illustrated in the late 1990s, mostly because of low circulation and the magazine's changing emphasis from sports to fitness.

The espnW mission is to connect female fans to the sports they love. EspnW Vice President Laura Gentile says in addition to elevating women's sports, the site is about having a space for the female point of view and commentary on the sports world in general.

EspnW's content focuses on three areas: women's college and pro sports, recreational athletes and some men's professional sports. Women's basketball is prominently featured, with WNBA players such as Maya Moore and Tamika Catchings blogging on the site and cross-promoting the league.

Gentile expects the digital site will gain more visibility in the future, starting with its full coverage of the 2012 London Olympics. Content will be prominently displayed on various ESPN platforms, which will lead to greater awareness and more eyeballs in the years ahead.

So far, the most traffic has been generated by the Women's World Cup soccer and the NCAA women's basketball tournament. Clicks on pages for Olympic Sports, Commentary, Athlete's Life and More Sports provide revolving ads for Nike shoes, Gatorade, Secret, and Toyota.

"The Word" video tackles weekly topics discussed by a panel of women, generally espnW writers or former athletes. The main page also showcases "Athlete's Tweets" from Olympians such as swimmer Dara Torres, beach volleyball's Misty May Treanor and the WNBA's

Candace Parker. Race car driver Danica Patrick, skiing superstar Lindsey Vonn, track star Lolo Jones and former Olympic softball player Jennie Finch also tweet on the site.

The "Things to Do Near You" link allows readers to plug in their zip code and find athletic events in their area.

Two years of research before the espnW launch suggested women consume media differently from men. Former US Olympian and soccer star Julie Foudy, who blogs and provides commentary on espnW, suggests men are "ravenous about their sports," while women consume smaller portions of "soup and salad, a small dinner plate." They also prefer features for the back story on female athletes and how they achieved success.

A new group of "athlete moms" are becoming a bigger part of the audience. They are women who've grown up playing sports and are raising young kids. That's a segment that barely existed in the United States before the advent of Title IX in 1972. The law banned sex discrimination in any educational program or activity receiving Federal funds, opening the doors to more college degrees and sports opportunities.

The espnW advisory panel includes 41-year-old Foudy (2 kids) and a number of Olympians with young children. Many moms aren't just driving kids to practice, now they're coaching them as well.

Given that more youth are consuming their news, entertainment and sports online, it makes sense to try to reach viewers through the many platforms of the digital space, such as espnW.

Example

The sports editors of the *Philadelphia Daily News* have to serve their solid male consistency. However, there is also Mel Greenberg, the long-time voice of women's basketball for not just his paper, but in many instances for the nation as well. Mel has been covering women's basketball for over 20 years on a consistent basis, and his ability to help open doors and create interest in compelling stories is essential for any sports publicist.

There are also so many niche websites that can also assist in the effort as never before. Being able to identify, sometimes create, and grow demand through blogs, chats, and data will be essential in your efforts. You will also find that attention paid to these sites and online publications can come back to help you grow into other areas of publicity when there is peak demand for your sport or athlete. Many times this is where the mainstream sports publications will turn to for information, and the more familiar and accessible your efforts are with these easy online sources, the better chance you will have for wider coverage at the right time.

Also do not forget the use of Olympic sites, and national governing body help. Because so many women's sports have pique internet times around Olympic events, these places, and the publicists that work for the sport in general year-round, need to be your friends and key resources. Many times on the professional level these sources are not seen as allys (again the exclusion vs. inclusion problem), but as a publicist for a professional sport you need to strengthen, build, and pitch these key groups in both their quiet and active times.

If you are on the pro side of women's sports, never forget the college sites either. In many instances, these female athletes garnered their widest attention during their collegiate or high school years. The long-time allies of these athletes are more than willing to assist, do update stories, and help guide you to new streams of publicity. Inclusion vs. exclusion again.

Lastly on this subject, *make* new allies. Doing all the little "pitch" things we have talked about throughout the earlier chapters will help you create new allies with good, solid stories. Providing long-term lead ideas, constantly furnishing positive numbers, becoming an advocate for the sport in general as opposed to the athlete or league specific, all are very key to chipping away at the walls and making your female athlete publicity efforts strong, diverse, professional, and impactful.

The following information is provided to make sure that the appropriate facts and figures are used as background for working in women's athletics publicity and to provide a base as to where one can turn to for information.

Some facts and figures about women's sports (courtesy of the Women's Sports Foundation)

Participation opportunities for female athletes

Nationwide, more college women have more athletic teams available to them than ever before.

- 8.32 teams per school is the average offering for female athletes in 2004. The 2004 number of 8.32 is near the 2002 all-time high of 8.34 and far exceeds the 1972 (year Title IX was enacted) number of a little over two per school and the 1978 (mandatory compliance date for Title IX) number of 5.61 per school.
- The ten most frequently found college varsity sports for women are in rank order: basketball, volleyball, cross country, soccer, softball, tennis, track/field, golf, swimming, and lacrosse.
- Women represent 41 percent of coaches of collegiate women's sports, only 4 percent of coaches of men's sports, and 18.3 percent of athletic directors.
- Females have 1.3 million fewer high school and 56,110 fewer college sports participation opportunities than males and receive $148 million less in athletic scholarship funds each year.

- Women's sports are only 8 percent of all print and television sports media coverage (just exceeding horses, dogs, and fishing).
- Soccer exhibits the greatest growth of any sport in the last 27 years. It is now offered for women on 88.6 percent of the campuses while in 1977 it was only found on 2.8 percent of the campuses. Soccer has increased 40 fold since.

Individual pro sports vs. team pro sports

While women has been actively participating and involving in sport, the number of women who organize sports events has been gradually on the increase. Even women who make a career of sport have appeared: the birth of women's professional athletes. In women's professional sports, individual sports, such as golf, tennis, and bowling, have a much longer history than team sports. For example, one of the oldest history of women's professional sports in the United States is in golf. In 1950, the Ladies Professional Golf Association (LPGA) was established and it became an international organization in 1970s. This kind of organization sets up a standard whether or not the professional sport prospers. LPGA has stabilized under new leadership in 2010–2011, and is now again growing. Total prize money reached a high of over $60 million in 2008. It has been scaled back to $41.5 with less events in 2011. The WTA Tour was established in 1971 and offered over $70 million in prize money. In the case of bowling, The Professional Women's Bowling Association (PWBA) was established in 1959 and the Ladies Professional Bowlers Tour (LPBT) started in 1981. As of today, no current professional bowling circuit exists for women.

On the other hand, women's professional team sports have had a hard time to survive and stabilize, compared to individual sports. Some people argue that the masculine image of team sports has inhibited women from participating in them for a long time. It is quite a recent event that women's team sports began to develop and professional organizations of those sports emerged. The rest of this section briefly overviews the history of women's major professional team sports in the United States.

Women's hockey looks to ice a chance

By Melissa Murphy

Ice hockey for girls and women is making incremental strides on the sports landscape in the United States and internationally.

The top two states for high school girls hockey are Minnesota and Massachusetts, which have traditionally strong men's grassroots, college and professional hockey teams. Minnesota has about 130 girls high schools with programs and Massachusetts has more than 100.

However, only 15 states have sanctioned high school girls hockey programs, meaning girls in other states must consider playing on boys teams.

There are 8,200 high school girls playing hockey compared to 36,000 boys, according to the National Federation of State High School Associations.

The No. 1 girls sport is outdoor track, with 470,000 high school participants in 2009–10, followed by basketball (440,000), volleyball, softball, and soccer. Girls' hockey ranks No. 20 out of about 45 sports, according to NFHS.

Val Ackerman, the first president of the WNBA, is a consultant for the NHL. She's been researching the growth of girls and women's hockey in the US and abroad. She notes gains have been made in the last 20 years.

"The sport has growth potential," Ackerman said. "It needs more resources and visibility to get people paying attention. That might help provide resources."

Unless there's a men's team at a college, it's unlikely there will be a women's team. Even colleges that have strong men's programs, such as Michigan and Michigan State, don't field women's teams for a variety of reasons.

Unlike basketball, it's an expensive sport that requires plenty of equipment plus the need for a rink and ice time. The school athletic director and often the men's hockey coach need to back the addition of a women's team.

Penn State will have a men's and women's hockey team in 2013 thanks to the generosity of alum and Buffalo Sabres owner Terry Pegula, who donated $102 million to the school to build a hockey arena and provide scholarships for the Division I teams.

Most of the women's college teams are concentrated in the Northeast and Midwest, and neighbor Canada provides a strong showing in international competition because of the culture importance of the sport in that country. However, colleges in Canada don't offer scholarships in hockey, so many of the top players come to the US to play on university teams. The Canada Women's Hockey League runs from October to March, but offers unpaid competition, and features many players on the national team.

The University of Minnesota won the 2012 women's NCAA hockey championship. The Women's Frozen Four semifinal and final are held on the opening weekend of the NCAA basketball tournament and competes for exposure on a busy sports weekend. The NCAA men's hockey final is held after the basketball tournament.

The women's hockey championship is not shown on TV, which is a way for the sport to pick up momentum. It's available on streaming video on the NCAA website.

Ackerman says the NHL is paying attention and crafting a strategy to promote the sport. While it doesn't foresee a professional league in the near future, it can help with exposure on various TV and digital platforms.

She says the NBA saw the growth of girls and women's basketball during the 1980s and noticed the high television ratings when it was periodically shown on CBS and during the NCAA tournament.

"There were more girls playing and it was also on TV," Ackerman said. "The Final Four was pulling in great ratings and gave a sense there was interest in the women's game."

She says the NHL Network may show women's college hockey games in 2013. It could showcase women's hockey by featuring players and exhibitions during the NHL All-Star game and Winter Classic. The NCAA women's final may be shown, along with exhibitions between the USA and Canada before the 2014 Sochi Olympics.

Ackerman noted a yearlong USA women's basketball domestic tour leading up to the eventual gold medal at the 1996 Atlanta Olympics helped gain exposure for the WNBA, which formed in 1997. It competes in a 12-team summer league and draws the best players from various countries.

So far, the US and Canada have dominated the hockey world championships and Olympic competition. IOC President Jacques Rogge has said other nations need to catch up so the sport can remain on the program. Canada knocked off the Americans 5–4 in overtime at the 2012 World Championships in Vermont, while Switzerland upset Finland for the bronze. All of the finals have involved Canada and the US, with Canada holding a 10–4 record through 2012.

In the meantime, Ackerman says the growth of hockey starts at the grassroots level, with USA Hockey leading developmental programs for boys and girls hockey. The directors of amateur hockey for professional teams can get involved. The best practices of coaching, mentoring and player development in the US and Canada can be passed along to other countries, which don't have established infrastructure for the sport.

Women's baseball

Since many men were on the battlefield during the Second World War, the All-American Girl's Professional Baseball League (AAGBL), in place of Major League Baseball, was created in 1943 to provide entertainment of people exhausted by the war. It was such a success that the number of people who attended women's baseball games reached almost 1 million in 1948. Yet, when the war ended and Major League Baseball players came back home, female baseball players were obliged to fill the role of housewife at home. AAGBL lost its audience, struggled with finances, and ceased to exist in 1954. Forty years later, in 1994, a businessman in Atlanta struck a $3 million sponsorship deal with Coors and formed a women's professional baseball team called Colorado Silver Bullets. About 20 members were selected from 1,300 baseball players nationwide for this team. The Bullets played games with men's semiprofessional teams and regional teams. In 1997, when the Ladies League Baseball was born and included four teams, the Bullets fought with them. The Ladies League Baseball changed its name into the Ladies Pro Baseball and added two teams into the league in 1998. However, after the first month, the league was suspended, being faced with financial difficulties of its sponsors. The Bullets has not operated also since 1998 as Coors terminated its contract.

Women's volleyball

The Women's Professional Volleyball Association was established in 1986. The association organized professional 6-player indoor volleyball leagues and beach volleyball leagues, such as Budlight Pro Beach Volleyball League in 1997, in which four teams participated. The league dissolved in 1998, but with the help of superagent Leonard Armato, was resurrected as the Crocs AVP Tour in 2004. The league folded in 2010 and at this time is under restructuring.

Women's basketball

The first women's professional basketball league in the United States was created in 1976. The league consisted of eight teams. It was very popular, as the average attendance of 1,200 per game suggests, and the games were televised, too. The league did not survive the following year, however, since some teams faced with financial problems and the league lost its audience. Women's National Basketball Association (WNBA), which emerged in January 1997, remains the hallmark for women's professional sports. The WNBA consists of 14 teams, with seven Eastern Conference teams and seven Western Conference teams. There are many countries where women's professional basketball league exists besides the United States, such as Italy, Germany, Spain, and Brazil. Many Americans players went overseas and some WNBA players play basketball in foreign countries during WNBA's off-season.

Women's softball and soccer

The first women's professional softball league was established in 1976, but it only lasted for four years because of its financial reasons and failure in marketing. In 1994, the Women's Professional Fastpitch emerged to prepare a rebirth of the professional league, which came into existence with six teams in 1997. The teams were divided into two groups, had 66 games a year, and the winners of both groups did play-off. Several games were on the air. However, like its baseball counterpart, lack of funding forced the league to fold in 2001, with no current plans to revive it.

The 1999 Women's World Cup spawned the WUSA, the first women's professional soccer league, which launched in 2002. The league lasted only two seasons due to overspending and too much early growth. Women's Professional Soccer was relaunched in 2008 with a more cost controlled model, but it also only lasted three seasons and at the time of this printing no other women's professional league is in development.

Conclusion

In closing, women's sports publicity does have its challenges. However the opportunities as a growth area when one can be well researched, strategic, and informed about making a pitch can be very rewarding. The effect on pitching stories at the grassroots level and the subsequent breakthrough into the mainstream can be very rewarding, and will open many doors for the publicist in virtually every area.

15

LOOKING AHEAD

Who knows what the future holds? When we wrote this chapter in the original book, way back in 2007, tools like Facebook, Pinterest, and Twitter were barely on the radar screen. It was MySpace, CD-ROMS, and even fax machines, with a little text messaging thrown in. As you read this, will Pinterest be a thing of the past already? Maybe we will be back to rotary phones and dial up?

Well, hopefully not.

There has been an interesting yin and yang between hyper local and wide ranging in the past few years. The AOL-fueled rage for sites like Patch.com has come and started to wane, while mega media sites like *USA Today* scramble to combine the local assets they have through Gannett and Company in the United States with their national overlay. Large independent sites that have served as effective rollups—The Big Lead, Bleacher Report, SB Nation—have provided a great voice and many eyeballs for independent journalists, but as time goes on even these large traffic sites need to find partners to be viable on multiple screens.

The idea of that type of convergence and the use of multiple screens is what we believe will be the future of how we use media and how communications can best be used.

If you think about what aspect to use for effective communication going forward, think about convergence. What does that mean exactly? It certainly isn't a new concept, but what is different now is the rapidly changing environment that we have to adapt to.

Going forward. Much more than in the past, effective communicators will have to constantly be aware of how each screen, each device, each medium large and small can best tie together to tell the story, both to an internal audience or an external one. What are the best screens to complement your message? Are you using the right media to speak to one audience or the other? Are you taking hard news stories and effectively making sure that they are being distributed through social channels? Are those following you or your client the right followers to help communicate the message? Is your internal staff using social media effectively?

In short, how much water can you proactively drain from every communications stone? It can be fun and challenging and very effective if you always think about convergence of all platforms, and how they can best be used.

The great news is that the vehicles to merchandise and tell the stories through effective communication have never been vaster. The bad news is that the ability to tell stories and get information out has turned us into 24/7 communicators. The ability to shut off or shut down is less today than it ever has been, especially with the use of multiple means of messaging that can be shared around the world.

It is fun and it is challenging. So what are the areas of growth? In 2007 we talked about blogs, viral video, controlled media, and emerging sports. In 2012, the world is becoming more mobile, and through the use of social media good communicators, both to an internal audience (staff, corporate division, etc.) and to an external audience have an even better chance to manage the message and speak directly to the targeted audience.

The three areas we will look into the crystal ball, or the crystal tablet, at are:

- *Digital media.* The continued expansive use of all forms of social media, the mobile space, online publishing, webinars, and how all can be adapted to streamline communications.
- *Controlled media.* The process of breaking news by a followed news source that the party has control over, such as a Twitter or Facebook platform, limiting and tailoring media coverage, tailoring video and media access to breaking news.
- *Emerging opportunities.* Gaming integration, high school athletics, analytics as a communications tool, and where the jobs lie.

Many of these topics, although incorporated into different parts of the text thus far, are now becoming the areas of interest and expertise for the next era of publicist. However it is very important to look at these growth areas with the eye on the past, and incorporate all the ideas discussed in this text along with them. With all these emerging areas the need for good writing, strong pitching skills, knowledge of the market, and an intimate knowledge of your client remains tantamount. All those characteristics will continue to apply. They may just apply faster and in different formats than in the past.

Let's take a look at each one.

Digital media

In the past this area was tagged as "New Media," and developed over time. Now "new" can rise and fall in days or weeks, as a fickle public embraces technology, sees if it works, and then either continues to engage or throws it aside as the technology either adapts and finds its place or becomes swallowed up by whatever comes along next. Regardless of the outcome, it is tantamount for the effective communicator to have a vast understanding of what is being used now, and what is coming in the digital space.

That does not mean that every new app or platform is ripe for everyone. What it does mean is that any communicator should be curious enough to want to know what the public and the industry is embracing, and sees if there are aspects of new technology in media that can apply. Not everyone needs to launch a YouTube channel, or even be on platforms like Twitter or Facebook if they are not used properly. Those decisions have to be made effectively with the client—whether it is a brand, an athlete, a league, a product—in mind. "Cool" is nice. Effective is better.

Clearly the use of new technology and digital media has given the publicist new client streams and also publicity avenues. Those new client streams include website developers, online commerce companies, mobile carriers, and search engines all looking to use sports as the vehicle to reach their consumer. The new publicity areas for the traditional clients will see increased integration of mobile and social media into campaigns to tell their story, along with the use of broadband video and audio to provide real-time coverage for events and the growth of hyper-local stories that speak directly to a core audience interested in one small aspect of a campaign.

An important concept to keep in mind is the fact that many times traditional sports will lag behind popular culture in adapting to these new streams of publicity and opportunity. The traditional sports, especially in the United States, have a focus on two things: maintaining their fan base and running their events at hand. Only recently have traditional sports begun to fully embrace the advantages of digital media as a publicity and revenue source. This has been done by the savvy marketers and publicists who have come into sports from outside entities. You now see traditional sports teams who have struggled to hold on to market share on television and with younger audiences hire professionals from outside the traditional sports footprint to develop their digital platforms and create new streams of publicity and content for their fans.

Example 1

Bloomberg Sports. Launched in 2009, Bloomberg Sports is a vertical division of the financial business Bloomberg L.P., which for over 30 years has been the worldwide leader in data analytics. BSports came about when two employees, Bo Moon and Jay B. Lee, saw the need to better use analytics to help them grow their fantasy baseball play. They saw the parallels in data between business and sport and knew the engine was already built, and although they had never worked in sports, they were fans. The result was that Bloomberg took the power of analytics and developed various platforms and adapted them to any area where sports and analytics crossed paths. The entire business is based around digital media. There are fantasy products for consumers, tools for professional teams to better analyze player performance, tablet applications for players to better look at their own work on the field, and still other tools for broadcast to enhance their offerings to consumers, whether it is in a digital second screen or in broadcast. Bloomberg Sports' platform is offered on mobile, and on any other digital platform available, and is a great example of a company adapting existing technology to build a new business model. How does this apply to communications? It is all about communicating in the digital space. The business applies to consumers and industry leaders alike, and sends the message that analytics and information is king. At the time we are going to press, BSports is also forging a partnership with IMG to further enhance their global business and communicate their offerings to an even larger, more global audience now embracing digital media more than ever before.

Example 2

MLB.com. Perhaps one of the most traditional of all sports has been baseball. The ability to hold on to tradition is one of the keys to baseball's hold as the "National Pastime" in the United States. However, the lack of expanded leisure time to both watch games (which now take in excess of three hours) and to play the game past little league had begun to erode the fan base. Major League Baseball has sought to effectively address that issue by creating an expanded version of mlb.com, their official site. By adding so many areas of new content such as enhanced gaming options, statistics, video, talk shows, fantasy and rotisserie chats, the traditional sport has used the non-traditional means to grow. Furthermore, other entities like music and college basketball have seen mlb.com as a place to cultivate the key sports demographic, and are partnering with them to identify key online sports and entertainment fans to grow and introduce their products to as well.

For the publicist this is the next version of where opportunities will come from. The volume of fans and brands accessing digital media will continue to make the web must visit be locations for celebrities, athletes, and products the publicist is pitching, just like a stop on a local news show or a live meet and greet with fans has been in the past.

Audio

As much as we are aware of the moving image, the sound of the spoken word has never been more prominent or effective for communicating ideas and platforms. iTunes, podcasts, satellite radio, blogtalkradio, talk radio has made audio very important in communicating a story. At one point many people thought "radio" was obsolete. Yet today a plan that does not include a podcast, one that is effectively merchandised, is seen as lacking. It is also ironic that audio can be used as a communication tool because we are more and more non-verbal in our communication. Yet because we are so busy and are married to other devices, the ability to listen to a story and hear the inflection of the speaker, whether that is on a train or a bus or in an office or a car or walking in a park, will make audio as important going forward as it was when communication was all about radio in the 1940s and 1930s. The difference is this audio is customizable and will literally speak directly to the subject, as well as to the masses.

The written word

While some debate has been given as to the use of a blog as a media tool, the written word to speak directly to your followers is still very, very powerful. It is not a place any more to rant and give unfounded opinion. It is a tool to voice intimate and detailed thought, sometimes coupled with powerful and effective images, audio and video, that enhances a story, a pitch, and a platform. It is not something which is done haphazardly to be effective. It is the marathon of all forms of digital media in a 24/7 world. But cultivated correctly, the blog remains a key place to effectively and accurately tell a story and shape opinion and thoughts that cannot be included in traditional media because of time and space. Pitching media blog writers to include content about a story is becoming as accepted now as trying to get notes into a paper. The same thing holds for the client blog. The use of having a name athlete or celebrity doing a blog these days to carefully craft a company or individual messages for publicity is also a skill that is important in the publicity pitch.

Mobile

The use of higher quality video and still images by the publicist used to be a bonus, but is now essential. Having a strategy that now includes mobile as a way to engage and tell a story is critical, because more and more the world is becoming used to the hand-held device as the place where he or she consumes media. Understanding the mobile space and what can be delivered from a communications standpoint—size of images, quality of video, length of messaging—is key to making sure that use is effective. Another key area of mobile is understanding the value and penetration of each carrier in a different part of the world. For example, launching a mobile campaign for Indian Cricket on Apple phones may not work at the present time, as Apple's penetration with the iPhone in India is very small. So having a global understanding of the power of the hand-held device is critical.

Example

A glimpse into the future of the power of mobile occurred during the winter of 2011. Jeremy Lin burst on to the scene with the New York Knicks and suffered through his first poor game. For a brief time late at night an editor at ESPN dropped a headline "A Chink In The Armor," referring to Lin's setback on the court but also making a derogatory reference to his ethnicity (he is of Chinese Taipei ancestry). Despite the fact that this was only on ESPN's mobile offering and despite the fact that the headline was corrected after a short time, there was a huge uproar and great attention brought to the misstep. It was seen only by a few, but by the right few, who communicated the slur to the masses, created a big issue for ESPN overall and eventually cost an editor his job.

Tablets

Even with mobiles dominating the landscape, the effective integration of tablets into communications plans is going to be key as well. More and more brands are developing media opportunities sized and delivered to the tablet, starting with all versions of the iPad and going out from there. So making sure that any plan has an element that, like the mobile phone, speaks directly to a tablet application would also make great sense going forward. Media companies especially have developed content enrichment pieces that speak only to a tablet, so making sure that you have an understanding of the value of tablet technology and its implications is very important.

Video

At the time of this writing the launch of hyper-targeted video channels appears to be growing very quickly, with companies ranging from Google to YouTube to Netflix to Apple TV, Hulu and Vudu all developing customized streaming channels to offer video directly to a core audience. They are short, low-cost and sometimes high-quality video platforms that offer everything from high-lights to expanded interviews from behind the scenes of everything from high school sports to the UFC. Where all this will shake out in terms of value vs. cost and time is still to be determined. What does not have to be determined is the value of the moving image. It is compelling, it is human, and it draws crowds. That compelling video has to be factored into any campaign no matter what platform of the future is delivering it.

Social sites

Social media remains both the greatest advantage and the greatest issue with regard to communications. It is powerful and it is distracting. It is effective when done well; it is devastating when done poorly. It is all consuming and it is the cause of great worry. More than anything it has made us into a culture which cannot turn off, and that's probably not a good thing. There is probably not one chapter in this book that hasn't touched on an aspect of social media, so there is no need to rehash. Whatever the platform you are using today for social media—and I'm assuming that you are reading this and Facebook, Twitter and others still exist, although there are probably others now that make those maybe a bit archaic—the important thing to remember still is that social media platforms are *not* the only means of communication. They have to be integrated with traditional media such as video or audio, or the most effective communications programs will fall short. We will be more social in telling stories going forward, and we will speak directly to the audience we want to reach. That audience via the right social platform may be 20 people, or it may be 20 million, but using a social space to tell the story won't be going away. It will be enhanced.

Controlled media

Today more than ever entities have the ability to choose how to break news and focus their messaging. All the digital media platforms listed are means to doing so, and the effective use of controlled media is now being seen as more accepted by the mainstream than ever before. While the worlds of editorial and advertorial have become a bit more blurred, there is still a demarcation. Being accurate and telling the facts are one thing. Distorting the facts in a way to damage reputation is another. Being controlled on the time and place of dissemination of information is important, losing the faith and credibility of followers and the media by deception is not appropriate. Why has controlled media become more and more prominent? The ever-increasing scope of "citizen journalists" (which is basically anyone with a camera phone) in a 24/7 environment, along with the sometimes irresponsible actions of unconfirmed sources by some members of the media, have led to the client to look to more controlled ways of getting out the message.

> **Example**
>
> The New York Jets sign Tim Tebow in the winter of 2011. The choice of announcement? The Jets' Twitter feed. It spoke right to the fans and made the media follow their controlled platform as a source of hard news. The Jets' Twitter feed became the credible, undeniable news source for a major announcement.
>
> Juxtapose this to an incident in 2003, when the Toronto Maple Leafs chose to break a legitimate new story about the changing of a coach on their own news site, as opposed to letting the media know first in a traditional way. This was seen as a way to drive traffic and content for the site and its subscribers, and was viewed with disdain by many of the media as packaging and censoring news. Now that practice is seen as mainstream rather than radical.

The other area of controlled media growth remains broadcast television. Once seen as radical, teams, leagues, and conferences have turned to the cable environment to control all aspects of their business by speaking directly to their core audience. In New York the Mets, Yankees, Rangers, and Knicks all have their own regional sports networks where they can essentially control programming and messaging to their fans. Leagues, from the NHL to the NBA to Major League Baseball, as well as major collegiate conferences have set up their owned programming outlets to best tell their stories, communicate news, and create and develop content. Regional high school networks have also popped up to service that area of sport in many parts of the United States. While the team or sports-specific broadcast network is still germane to the North America, there are opportunities to create such entities globally, the difference being that most of the rest of the sporting world is more attuned to the mobile environment of getting news and video than television. Regardless, the publicist in a team environment now has a controlled environment to tell stories and help manage a news process which was less controllable in the past.

With those controlled vehicles also comes the idea of tailoring and limiting coverage to events. The idea of preferential media treatment by publicists has always been part of the publicity game. As has been addressed in the text, the maintenance of relationships is key to success. However, in the effort to control messages and information, clients and entities can now seek to arbitrarily control physical access to events by members of the media. This game of favorites can be a dangerous one, with the backlash becoming a cut down of coverage amongst mainstream, large circulation media. However, some entities are seeing this as a potential boon to concentrated coverage to their controlled outlets like television, broadband, and general web traffic. The amount of places to take publicity these days does not just reside with the local newspaper or television station, and in controlling access the entity today now has the ability to create demand through its core base of followers that can drive mainstream media to adhere to the policies it sets forth.

Example

An NFL team does not like the editorial coverage that a local newspaper is giving it as it looks to expand its stadium or increase its ticket prices. Therefore that team decides to only allow two credentials to a weekly game, as opposed to the regular coverage of four writers. The result is that there is increased coverage on the team site with its own writers and messages, and the local newspaper gets less in terms of access to generate coverage. In time, the theory is that fans will go more to the website than to the local newspaper for its coverage, forcing the outlet to change its stance on how it deals with the team off the field. This is a hypothetical situation at this time, but could be an issue in the future as the issue of controlled media becomes more prevalent.

The other advantage into controlled media is the inclusion of key sponsor messages and names in stories without risk of deletion, as opposed to taking chances with the writer including the facts and figures important to the organization. In recent years, the use of edited footage and canned stories given to media outlets for inclusion in regular newscasts has been met with more disdain and less use by national outlets such as CNN and Fox News. Many have recently even gone to the extent of running information on the screen that this is not network-shot footage. The editorial side can also remove sponsor mentions and images when used on air. The controlled media route going right to the consumer eliminates that problem.

While the value of relationships between the publicist and the media is still the priority, the use of the controlled media stance will become more of a debate going forward.

Emerging opportunities

They have been called niche in the past, but these entities now reach a very concentrated core demographic that many sponsors and communicators look to connect with. In the recent past, some may not have even considered them "sport." Others, like competitive poker, may have risen and leveled off, and may have their future controlled by whatever government regulation in the United States has to say about online gambling regulation. Some others, like Mixed Martial Arts and the UFC, may hit a ceiling on the "professional" side because of their violent nature and the hard fixed costs of events. Thrill sports;

extreme skiing, bull riding, BMX, even competitive jousting, maybe even Quidditch, will thrive in a strong video-dominated environment and can hold a certain demographic category, but may not succeed in crossing over as a demo matures and the sport or event needs to adapt. The growing interest in mind sports—chess, checkers, bridge, even poker—may present opportunities for a healthy mind, healthy body audience. In the United States, high school sports can provide some very interesting opportunities on the local, regional and even national level if managed correctly. Mature global sports like cricket, rugby, and even soccer are still looking to continue to crack a more mainstream American market. On the other side, baseball and even golf in some areas are still hoping to further emerge globally.

However, all of these opportunities may pale in comparison to the gaming world, which will continue to be perhaps the best point of convergence and opportunity going forward. More on that in a few minutes ...

All these outlets mentioned present great opportunity for publicity. They will provide to the publicists and to the fan what traditional sports have provided in the past but, due to overexposure in the marketplace, may no longer be able to provide consistently. They provide strong grassroots stories, access to the fans, and a connection that is hard to establish with athletes who are known in the mainstream. The amount and success of these opportunities is to be determined. However, the use of technology has given these sports more staying power than previous incarnations.

In past years the establishment of the American Basketball Association to combat the NBA, or the United States Football League or a United Football League or even the XFL to go against the NFL, was just adding to an existing marketplace and fan base. These sports are using publicity as a prime tool to grow a fan base that uses these sports as both a lifestyle tool (the fans are participants in the activity) and as a spectator sport.

In addition to the outlets themselves, the publicity opportunities for products and equipment that both support the demographic and are used in the activity is also great. Brands like Red Bull or Monster Energy or the SHEETS Brand or Mission Athletecare or Coca Cola's Vitamin Water have used some of these opportunities to launch and gain market share, while the brands that speak directly to a niche space have used the sports to promote their product to an audience that is at the core of their marketing plans.

What this does for the sports publicist is to create campaigns to highlight these local athletes to a larger audience using these mediums, and also identify sponsor publicity opportunities for a core market and grow that base like never before. The concern over exploitation of young athletes here is always a potential issue, but the ability to tell quality stories as well as gain exposure in a professional way is a key to this growing publicity opportunity.

With regard to the gaming world, at the beginning of this chapter we talked about convergence, and there is perhaps no growing opportunity that speaks to convergence better than the gaming space. From professional competitive gamers, who travel the world in a circuit playing specific non-sports games like World of Warcraft, to large-scale game companies like EA Sports and their wildly popular offerings like Madden, gaming offers all sorts of opportunities.

Most recently the mix of gambling engagement for those of legal age, combined with both a fan experience and competitive gaming has also created new opportunities for brands to integrate into the online space. Companies like Cantor Fitzgerald have created large scale platforms in the gambling space, and if rules for online gambling in the United States change, there will be new streams of business with a host of brands who can engage fans in legal, regulated online activities that already exist in many parts of the world and would then also work in the United States. Those opportunities as of this writing in the spring of 2012 are still in the distance but would open new areas for effective and creative communications as well.

Why?

It is mobile, anyone can play anywhere on any device. A fan with an affinity for a game can play on hand-held, on a tablet, on a computer, on a TV. The platform matches the player.

Its integration into an online environment gives any brand or athlete or league the ability to integrate into a game at any point. You can have Carmelo Anthony engaged in your version of an NBA licensed game from wherever he is at whatever time.

It transcends language and culture barriers. You don't need to speak English to play a UFC game, and you don't need to speak Italian to play Serie A Soccer online.

Because it is online, advanced play can integrate any level of data or news. Now you can have advanced statistics, news as it happens, dropped directly into a real time video game feed, making the gaming environment as real as an actual physical game for the player. Alex Ovechkin scores a goal for the Washington Caps; that goal and that move can be directly integrated into the real time feed of the game.

It is an easy platform for sponsor and brand integration and affinity. Because so much data is trackable for online play, giving players access to products and promotions that they have an affinity for is easier and more cost efficient to do than in any other promotion. All the tools are virtual, so providing them to a player eliminates many hard costs.

It is social. The current feeling by the more mature audience is that a younger demo sits somewhere and it limits their social interaction. However, the game environment today is actually more social and more interactive than any environment on the planet. The ability to speak to one or interact with thousands in real time, and the ability for brands to communicate with that affinity group, makes gaming the ultimate convergence opportunity for the future.

Are there issues with gaming going forward? Yes. Access to personal data, access to minors, over-stimulation, some loss of a sense of reality, copyright laws, and most importantly a lack of real time spoken and physical connection, are all in the pipeline.

However for communicators the ability to grow, understand and activate against and in the gaming world is one that should be embraced and looked at very carefully going forward.

Marketing and PR

The increased return on investment for those involved with publicity will lead to more mainstreaming of sports and marketing as joint areas of growth, as opposed to past instances where the two entities operated in silos apart from each other. The savvy integrated marketing techniques used by all entities looking for growth will use more and more publicity vehicles as key elements to their campaigns.

On the team and collegiate level, marketing groups will use publicists more to uncover stories and unique elements about athletes that can be used in integrated campaigns. The dollar value assigned to all publicity that can be garnered by savvy publicists, long just the work of the agency, will now be realized more by groups on the team and collegiate level.

These key areas will be the subject of considerable growth and debate as the sports publicity industry continues to evolve in the coming years. Technology which was not available only a few months ago will now make the integrated and controlled approach to publicity even stronger than before. Factor in the growth of markets in sports outside North America, and the growth of women's athletics in the coming years, and it appears the industry's best years remain ahead.

As long as the publicists continue to integrate the new ideas and use the strong skills of writing, listening, strategic planning, and effective pitching, the industry will grow and remain where it is in the marketplace.

As it was said at the beginning, it is the appetizer for athletes, sponsors, leagues, business partners, and media ventures. Without that great first taste, the meal behind it will not be as savory.

APPENDIX 1

The press release

News Release

New York Knickerbockers
Public Relations
Two Pennsylvania Plaza
New York, NY 10121-0091
Tel (212) 465-6471
Fax (212) 465-6498

FOR IMMEDIATE RELEASE

CONTACT: Joe Favorito
(212) 465-6422
Dan Schoenberg
(212) 465-6367

KNICKERBOCKERS TO HONOR NEW YORK NATIONAL GUARD WITH FINAL EMIGRANT "CITY SPIRIT" AWARD FRIDAY

NEW YORK, April 10, 2003 – The New York Knicks will honor the New York City National Guard with the season's final Emigrant "City Spirit" Award during the second quarter of their game with the Philadelphia 76ers this Friday, April 11 at Madison Square Garden. The Emigrant City Spirit Award is presented by the Knicks and their partner, Emigrant Savings Bank, to members of the community who have made a difference in the lives of others. In addition to the on-court recognition, each group is presented with a donation for $5,000 to the charity of their choice. The program is finishing it's second season, and is one of the organization's most popular and most worthwhile programs.

"The Emigrant 'City Spirit' Award is a great way for the Knicks to truly honor New York's real heroes, the men and women who go above and beyond to make a positive impact in the lives of their fellow citizens," said Karin Buchholz, New York Knicks Vice President, Community and Fan Development. "This month's recipients have made a great personal sacrifice and have taken time away from their families, jobs and lives to keep New Yorkers safe in the subways, train stations and at all key points of entry throughout the city. We cannot think of a more fitting tribute to cap this very successful program for 2002-03."

The troops accepting the award this month represent the 14,000 New York National Guard members called up to support and defend the city, the state and the nation since September 11, 2001. There are currently over 4,000 New York National Guard members on active duty, carrying out their duties in places ranging from Brooklyn to Baghdad. The $5,000 donation will go to the New York National Guard and Naval Militia Society, which assists families of National Guardsman.

Other winners this year have included the New York Road Runners Foundation, the YCS Foundation and Baptist Church of Lillies of Newark, New Jersey, Providence House, the New York Firefighters Burn Center Foundation and Project A.L.S.

The NBA's New York Knickerbockers basketball team, in its 57th year of operation, is part of Madison Square Garden, L.P. Cablevision Systems Corporation owns a controlling interest in MSG L.P., which also includes the New York Rangers (NHL), the New York Liberty (WNBA), the MSG Network, FOX Sports Net and the Madison Square Garden arena complex, located in the heart of the New York metropolitan area.

United States Tennis Association
70 West Red Oak Lane
White Plains, NY 10604
tel 914.696.7000
fax 914.696.7167

PRESS RELEASE

2000 US OPEN NETS RECORD $420 MILLION IN ECONOMIC BENEFITS FOR NEW YORK

World's largest-attended annual sporting event contributes more to the local economy than any other annual event in any city in the U.S.

White Plains, NY, May 14, 2001- The United States Tennis Association (USTA) and New York City Comptroller Alan G. Hevesi today revealed the findings of a recent study of the Economic Impact of the 2000 US Open on the New York Metropolitan region. The study, conducted by Sport Management Research Institute (SMRI), found that the 2000 US Open generated just under $420 million in direct revenue for the tri-state area, more than any other annual sports or entertainment event in any city in the United States.

"The US Open and the USTA National Tennis Center, the world's largest public tennis facility, have generated more revenue, more jobs and more international media exposure for the City of New York than any other annual event," said Arlen Kantarian, Chief Executive, Professional Tennis. "We are proud to join the City of New York and the Comptroller's Office to show just how valuable this partnership is, for both the City and for the game of tennis."

"New York City has one of the best municipal stadium deals in the country with the USTA and the presence of the US Open in the City," said Hevesi. "The benefits go well beyond the prestige and enjoyment brought to the City by the tournament. The Open generates tremendous economic activity, including thousands of jobs and tax revenue. All this, and we receive a healthy rent and revenue share from the USTA. As an added bonus, the USTA-financed facility is open to the public 300 days a year."

The roughly $420 million of economic benefit represents a substantial increase of over 125% from the previous Economic Impact Study on the event, which was conducted by the Comptrollers office in November of 1996. That study showed a direct impact on the area of $159 million, and was done prior to the opening of Arthur Ashe Stadium and the refurbishment of the USTA National Tennis Center, which began in 1997 and was paid for by the USTA without direct taxpayer subsidy. The USTA National Tennis Center, in addition to hosting the US Open annually, is the world's largest public tennis facility.

A USTA EVENT

Some key facts include:

- The 2000 US Open economic impact is *3%* of the total economic impact of tourism for New York in the Millennium Year.
- The total number of full-time equivalent jobs created either directly or indirectly from the staging of the event, was 11,437.
- The total indirect business taxes generated for local, state and federal governments was $57.4 million.

Of those surveyed:

- 94.2% plan to re-visit the NYC Metro area in the next two years, the highest re-visitation response ever captured by SMRI research.
- 76.2% come to New York City solely to attend the US Open.
- 49.8% had a more favorable opinion of New York because of attending the US Open.
- 46.9% are from outside of the New York area.

The only U.S.-based event that had a larger impact on a geographic area was the 1996 Atlanta Olympics, which generated $2.5 billion for the economy during its run over three weeks in the summer of 1996.

This announcement is the latest in a series of recent initiatives that the USTA has undertaken to position the US Open as one of the world's top sports and entertainment events. Recent developments have also included the moving of the 2001 women's final to prime time on CBS for the first time in Grand Slam history, a landmark international television rights deal with SFX, a record prize money purse that will top again $15 million, record on-site attendance of over 606,000, record traffic on USOPEN.ORG and a host of on-site innovations at the USTA National Tennis Center, ranging from giant video boards to star-studded on-site entertainment.

The Sport Management Research Institute (SMRI) is a full-service market research company, in operation since 1989. They have been examining consumer trends at the US Open for the past five years and were the primary investigators for the Economic Impact of the 2000 US Open. SMRI has also been contracted to execute such "economic based" investigations as Super Bowls XXIX and XXXIII; 1997 World Series; 1998 Bob Hope Chrysler Golf Classic;1999 Inaugural Winston Cup Race at Homestead Motorsports Speedway; 2000 Orange Bowl and the 2001 Bowl Championship Series, as well as a host of other professional sports teams.

Comptroller Alan Hevesi was elected New York City's 41st Comptroller in 1993 and reelected in 1997. He has used his position as the City's chief financial officer and watchdog to make municipal operations run more efficiently, to fight waste and fraud, and to protect and advance the City's long-term economic health. Before becoming Comptroller, Mr. Hevesi spent 22 years in the State Assembly, authoring over 108 laws. His 1996 study of the economic benefits of the National Tennis Center contract and investment is among several such analyses of City investments and infrastructure, assessing their economic impact.

The United States Tennis Association owns and stages the US Open and selects the teams that compete in Davis Cup, Fed Cup and the Olympic Games. The USTA is the national governing body for the sport of tennis in America and is a non-profit organization with more than 620,000 members. It invests all its resources to promote and develop the growth of tennis, from the grass roots to the professional levels.

-30-

For more information contact:
Joe Favorito, USTA Director of Publicity and Media Relations
(914) 697-2327 or Favorito@usta.com

Cathie Levine, Director of Communications, NYC Comptroller's Office
(212) 669-3747 or pressofc@comptroller.nyc.gov

United States Tennis Association
70 West Red Oak Lane
White Plains, NY 10604
tel 914.696.7000
fax 914.696.7167

BY THE NUMBERS

1,680,000,000	Hits on the official 2000 US Open web site, powered by IBM
420,000,000	Dollars of direct economic impact the US Open had on the New York City metro area in 2000
15,762,300	Dollars in prize money to be paid during the 2001 US Open
11,774,192	Fans have attended the US Open in the Open Era (1968-present)
1,533,069	Dollars in rent the USTA paid New York City for the USTA National Tennis Center
850,000	Dollars to be won by both the men's and women's 2001 US Open singles champions
606,017	Fans attended the 2000 US Open fortnight
522,000	Dollars raised for charity during the 2000 Arthur Ashe Kids' Day
125,000	T-shirts sold during the 2000 US Open
71,352	Wilson tennis balls ordered for the US Open
54,992	Fans attended the US Open on Sept. 2, 2000, establishing the single-day tournament record
40,000	MetroCards given away on American Express Day, Sept. 4, 2000
30,926	Hours of 2000 US Open coverage on television worldwide
25,000	Atomizers given away on Evian Natural Spring Water Day, Sept. 3, 2000
23,000	Heineken hats given away on Heineken Day, Sept. 9, 2000
15,000	Sets of disposable binoculars given way on Prudential Securities Day, Sept. 8, 2000
14,699	Fans attended 2000 US Open qualifying (up to the final rounds)
14,580	Fans attended the 2000 edition of Arthur Ashe Kids' Day (incl. the final rounds of qualifying)
5,000	Lanyards given way on MassMutual Day, Sept. 5, 2000
4,231	Staff credentials issued for the 2000 US Open
3,521	Racquets strung during the 2000 US Open
1,652	Sets completed during the 2000 US Open
906	Matches to be played during the 2001 US Open
667	Players credentialed for the 2000 US Open
503	Coaches credentialed for the 2000 US Open
204	Corporate hospitality functions held during the 2000 US Open
165	Countries had televised broadcasts of the 2000 US Open
99	Points won by Venus Williams in her semifinal victory against Martina Hingis
97	Points won by Martina Hingis in her semifinal loss to Venus Williams
87	Women's singles matches decided by a third-set tie-break since the tie-break's first use in 1970
62	Different clients for whom corporate hospitality events were held
47	Dollars is the average price of a promenade ticket for the 2001 US Open
19	Consecutive years the US Open has drawn more fans than any other Grand Slam event
15	Night matches Pete Sampras has won at the US Open, while losing none
11	Number of times US Open attendance records were broken in 2000
3	Percentage of 2000 New York City tourism dollars from the US Open
2	Total number of U.S. presidents to attend the 2000 US Open (Jimmy Carter & Bill Clinton)
1	Automobile unveiled during the 2000 US Open: the 2002 Lincoln Blackwood

A USTA EVENT

APPENDIX 2

The media advisory

ATTENTION: DAYBOOK

* * * MEDIA ADVISORY * * *

INTERNATIONAL FIGHT LEAGUE ATHLETES
AVAILABLE DURING WEIGH-IN FRIDAY 9/22

Final Media Opportunity Prior to Saturday's 13-Bout Fight Card at The Mark in Moline

WHO: More than **25 Athletes and Coaches** from the new International Fight League (IFL), the first professional mixed martial arts league, including:
- **Pat Miletich**, Mixed Martial Arts Champion
- **Renzo Gracie,** World-Renowned Jiu-Jitsu Artist and MMA legend
- **Frank Shamrock**, five-time undefeated MMA middleweight champion
- Several Quad Cities-area professional mixed martial artists

Gareb Shamus, Kurt Otto, IFL Founders

WHAT: Official **Weigh-in/Party** and pre-event **media availability** for Saturday's IFL World Team Championship at The Mark

WHEN: <u>Friday, September 22</u>
5 p.m. weigh-in, photo opportunities
5:30 - 7 p.m. media availability with athletes

WHERE: Hooters Restaurant
110 E. Kimberly Rd., Davenport
319/388-9464

BACKGROUND: The International Fight League (IFL) is the only team-based professional mixed martial arts organization. The IFL World Team Championship quarterfinals are set for **Saturday, September 23, at The Mark of the Quad Cities in Moline**. The 13-bout card features many local athletes, highlighted by the Superfight between popular local star **Pat Miletich** and fellow legend **Renzo Gracie**. Miletich coaches the Silverbacks team, which trains in Bettendorf, and will battle Gracie's Pitbulls, based in New York. The Dragons (Toronto) and Razorclaws (San Jose) clash in the other matchup.

Founded in 2006 by Kurt Otto, a highly successful real estate investor and a life-long martial arts participant and Gareb Shamus, chairman of the comics empire Wizard Entertainment Group, the International Fight League™ (IFL) and Pure Sport™ were created to establish a centralized and structured organization that brings the power and influence of the mixed martial arts industry together. For more information and action, go to www.IFL.tv.

CONTACT: Jerry Milani
917/797-5663 (cell); *jm@ifl.tv*

APPENDIX 3

Game notes

Stack 'em up!

- Schick NBA Rookie of the Month for March.
- First Sixer to ever win Rookie of the Month.
- Leads all NBA guards in blocks.
- Fourth among all guards in free throws made.
- Sixth among all shooting guards in assists.
- Eighth among all NBA guards in points scored.
- Ninth among all NBA guards in minutes played.
- Leads all Rookies in scoring and free throws made and attempted.
- Third in Rookie assists and minutes.
- In the top five in free throw percentage, treys made and attempted by a Rookie.
- Already Sixers all-time leader for points, free throws, and treys made and attempted by a Rookie.
- Leads all Rookies with five games of 30 or more points.
- Has scored 20 or more points 35 times this season.

Jerry Stackhouse
Guard,
Philadelphia 76ers

1995-96 NBA Rookie of the Year candidate.

Game Information

Detroit Tigers Media Relations Department • Comerica Park • Phone (313) 471-2000 • Fax (313) 471-2138 • Detroit, MI 48201 • www.tigers.com

Detroit Tigers vs. Pittsburgh Pirates

Saturday, May 19, 2012
Comerica Park, Detroit, MI
Game Time – 4:05 p.m. EDT

TIGERS AT A GLANCE

Record: 19–20 / Streak: W1

Game #40 / Home #22

Home: 10–11 / Road: 9–9

Today's Scheduled Starters

LHP Drew Smyly vs. RHP A.J. Burnett

(1–0, 2.31)   (1–2, 5.12)

TV / Radio

FSD/AM 1270 & 97.1 FM

TIGERS VS. PIRATES

2012 Record: 1–0

2012 at Home: 1–0

2012 at Pittsburgh: 0–0

All-Time Record: 16–12

All-Time at Home: 9–4

All-Time at Comerica Park: 7–3

All-Time at Pittsburgh: 7–8

2012 Game Log

Date	Site	Result	Winner/Loser/Save
5/18	DET	W, 6–0	VERLANDER/Morton
5/19	DET		
5/20	DET		
6/22	PIT		
6/23	PIT		
6/24	PIT		

STREAKS

Last five games: 2–3

Last 10 games: 4–6

Last 15 games: 7–8

Last 20 games: 9–11

RECENT RESULTS: The Tigers blanked the Pirates 6–0 last night at Comerica Park. Justin Verlander (5–1) fanned 12 batters as he fired a one-hit shutout to earn the win for Detroit. Delmon Young led the Tigers with a double, home run and three RBI. The Tigers continue a five-game homestand with the second game of a three-game series versus Pittsburgh this afternoon. Following an off day on Monday, Detroit begins a 10-game road trip to Cleveland, Minnesota and Boston on Tuesday.

INTERLEAGUE HAPPENINGS: Today's contest against the Pirates is Detroit's second of the club's 18 games during interleague play in 2012. Since interleague play started in 1997, the Tigers have compiled a 142–124 record. The Tigers are 70–39 in interleague games at Comerica Park. Detroit has compiled a 1–0 record in 2012.

AMONG THE BEST SINCE 2006: The Tigers have compiled a 71–38 record, a .651 winning percentage, during interleague play since the start of the 2006 season. The .651 winning percentage during interleague action is second-best among major league clubs during that stretch. The Boston Red Sox have compiled a 73–36 record, a .670 winning percentage, during interleague action over that stretch.

HAPPY AT HOME: The Tigers have compiled a 163–101 record at Comerica Park since the beginning of the 2009 season, a .617 winning percentage. Detroit is third among all major league clubs with a .617 winning percentage at home during that stretch.

PRINCE PLAYS LONGBALL AGAINST PIRATES: Prince Fielder enters today's game with a home run once every 13.00 at-bats against Pittsburgh, third-best among all active major league players versus the club. He is hitting .282 (99x351) with 13 doubles, a triple, 27 home runs and 75 RBI in 99 games during his career against the Pirates.

STARTING WELL: The Tigers have posted 14 quality starts in the club's last 19 games. Club starters have posted a 2.99 ERA (117.1IP/39ER) and 112 strikeouts during the stretch dating back to April 28, while limiting opponents to a .226 batting average (100x442).

A LONG STRETCH WITHOUT BEING BLANKED: The Tigers scored six runs last night versus Pittsburgh, marking the 107th straight game dating back to July 17, 2011, in which the club has not been shut out. It is the second-longest such streak in Tigers history, trailing the franchise record of 110 consecutive games with at least one run scored established August 28, 1992–June 29, 1993. *(Source: STATS LLC)*

DIRKS HAS BEEN DANDY DURING MAY: Andy Dirks enters today's game having hit safely in 13 of his 16 games during May, batting .404 (23x57) with four doubles, three home runs and eight RBI. He is tops among all American League players with a .477 on-base percentage during the month, while he is second with a .404 batting average and seventh with a .632 slugging percentage.

MARTE'S REHAB TRANSFERRED TO TOLEDO: The Tigers yesterday transferred the injury rehabilitation assignment of Luis Marte from Single A Lakeland to Triple A Toledo. He is scheduled to pitch with Toledo on Monday versus Syracuse. Marte was assigned to Lakeland as part of an injury rehabilitation assignment on Thursday and he tossed two scoreless innings that night versus St. Lucie, fanning three batters and allowing one hit. He has been sidelined since April 4 with a left hamstring strain.

NOTES ON THE SKIPPER: Jim Leyland is in his seventh season as the manager of the Tigers, compiling a 538–474 record (.532).

– Leyland enters today's game with 1,607 wins during his major league managerial career, 16th-most all-time in major league history. He is 12 wins shy of matching Ralph Houk for 15th-most all-time in major league history with 1,619 wins. Leyland is tops among all active major league managers with 1,607 wins.

– Today's game marks the 3,215th game Leyland has managed during his career, placing him in 15th place all-time in major league history.

– Leyland is one of only five managers in Tigers history to register at least 500 victories with the club. Sparky Anderson (1,331 wins), Hughie Jennings (1,131 wins), Bucky Harris (516 wins) and Steve O'Neill (509 wins) are the four other managers in Tigers history with at least 500 wins with the club.

18TH ANNUAL NEGRO LEAGUES TRIBUTE GAME IS TODAY: The Tigers will don the uniform of the Detroit Stars from the Negro Leagues in the club's 18th Annual Negro Leagues Tribute Game this afternoon. The Pittsburgh Pirates will don the uniforms of the Pittsburgh Crawfords for the game.

INJURY UPDATE: RHP Al Alburquerque (right elbow surgery, 60-day DL on April 4), RHP Luis Marte (left hamstring strain, 15-day DL on April 4), C Victor Martinez (left knee surgery, 60-day DL on March 12), LHP Daniel Schlereth (left shoulder tendonitis, 15-day DL on April 21).

TIGERS UPCOMING GAME DETAILS

DATE	OPPONENT	GAME TIME	TIGERS PROBABLE PITCHER	OPPONENTS PROBABLE PITCHER	TV/RADIO
Sunday	vs. Pittsburgh	1:05 p.m.	RHP Max Scherzer (2–3, 6.26)	RHP Kevin Correia (1–4, 4.50)	FSD/1270 & 97.1
Monday	Off day				
Tuesday	at Cleveland	7:05 p.m.	RHP Rick Porcello (3–3, 5.12)	RHP Ubaldo Jimenez (4–3, 5.09)	FSD/1270 & 97.1
Wednesday	at Cleveland	7:05 p.m.	RHP Doug Fister (0–2, 1.59)	RHP Zach McAllister (1–1, 4.34)	FSD/1270 & 97.1
Thursday	at Cleveland	12:05 p.m.	RHP Justin Verlander (5–1, 2.14)	RHP Justin Masterson (1–3, 5.04)	FSD/1270 & 97.1

All times Eastern. Radio coverage on AM 1270 and 97.1 FM The Ticket, unless otherwise noted. Local TV coverage provided by FOX Sports Detroit (FSD) and FOX Sports Detroit Plus (FSD PLUS).

TIGERS AT A GLANCE IN 2012

vs. AL East: 6–3	Scoring five-or-more runs: 12–3	Lead after 6th/7th/8th inning: 13–5/15–5/17–3
vs. AL East: 8–7	Scoring four-or-less runs: 7–17	Trail after 6th/7th/8th inning: 2–13/2–14/2–14
vs. AL West: 4–10	Extra innings: 1–1	Tied after 6th/7th/8th inning: 4–2/2–1/0–3
vs. NL: 1–0	One-run games: 6–8	Tigers out hit opponent: 12–7
Tigers score first: 14–5	Tigers get quality start: 15–8	Opponent out hits Tigers: 4–12
Opponents score first: 5–15	Tigers starter work 6+ innings: 5–11	Tigers and opponent have equal hits: 3–1

© Detroit Tigers, 2012

World Series Champions   •   1935   •   1945   •   1968   •   1984

APPENDIX 4

Player biographies

PLAYER BIOS

#21	Trevor Ariza		Forward
Height: 6-8	Weight: 200		Birthdate: Jun 30, 1985
High School: Westchester (Los Angeles, CA)	College: UCLA '07		Years Pro: R

2004–05: Leads all rookies and is sixth overall in steals per minute (2.96)...has already had the biggest impact of a Knicks second round pick since Gerald Wilkins averaged 12.5 PPG in 1985–86...five or more rebounds three times...two games with five or more assists...*best stretch was a five game period from 11/3–13 when he shot 47% from the floor (18–38), averaged 8.6 PPG, 4.6 RPG and 1.6 SPG*...Scored 10 points, three rebounds and three steals in 16 minutes vs. Sacramento...Averaging 4.3 points, 2.5 rebounds, 1.4 assists and .86 steals.

Last five games: Averaging 4.6 points, 2.6 rebounds and 1.6 assists.

Opponent	Mins.	Points	Rebs.	Assts.
vs. Sacramento	16	10	3	0
vs. New Jersey	12	2	1	0
vs. Minnesota	17	2	3	0
@ Orlando	20	4	4	6
vs. Charlotte	18	5	2	2

Best game...

Game	Min	FGM-A	3PM-A	FTM-A	OFF	DEF	REB	AST	ST	BL	TO	PF	PTS
11/9 vs. Phila.	21	5–9	0–0	4–6	2	6	8	3	2	0	0	2	14

#42	Vin Baker		Forward/Center
Height: 6-11	Weight: 240		Birthdate: Nov 23, 1971
High School: Old Saybrook (CT)	College: Hartford '93		Years Pro: 11

2004–05: Did not play (coach's decision) vs. Sacramento...Averaging 1.3 points and 1.3 rebounds per game.

Last five games:

Opponent	Mins.	Points	Rebs.	Assts.
vs. Sacramento	DNP	CD		
vs. New Jersey	DNP	CD		
vs. Minnesota	DNP	CD		
@ Orlando	DNP	CD		
vs. Charlotte	DNP	CD		

Milestone in Sight: *Needs 4 assists for 1,500 career...Needs 211 points for 12,000 career.*

Best game...

Game	Min	FGM-A	3PM-A	FTM-A	OFF	DEF	REB	AST	ST	BL	TO	PF	PTS
12/10 @ Wash.	8	3–3	0–0	0–0	0	1	1	0	0	0	1	2	6

#2	Jamison Brewer		Guard
Height: 6-4	Weight: 195		Birthdate: Nov 19, 1980
High School: Tri-Cities (Eastpoint, GA)	College: Auburn '03		Years Pro: 4

2004–05: Placed on the injured list on January 1st with right big toe tendonitis...Activated from injured list on Dec 26th...Went on the injured list on December 7th due to right big toe tendonitis...Three points and two rebounds vs. Charlotte...Averaging 1.3 points, 0.5 assists and 2.0 rebounds...Activated from injured list on Nov 21st...Went on injured list Nov 1st with sprain of the right big toe...has missed a total of 16 games.

Last five games:

Opponent	Mins.	Points	Rebs.	Assts.
vs. Sacramento	Injured	List		
vs. New Jersey	Injured	List		
vs. Minnesota	DNP	CD		
@ Orlando	DNP	CD		
vs. Charlotte	Injured	List		

Best game...

Game	Min	FGM-A	3PM-A	FTM-A	OFF	DEF	REB	AST	ST	BL	TO	PF	PTS
11/23 vs. Hawks	12	1–1	0–0	0–2	0	5	5	1	0	0	1	0	2

#11	Jamal Crawford		Guard
Height: 6-5	Weight: 190		Birthdate: Mar 20, 1980
High School: Rainier Beach (Seattle, WA)	College: Michigan '03		Years Pro: 5

2004–05: Went on injured list with right turf toe on December 26, 2004...Has missed four games this season...*Best three game stretch was from 12/12–15, averaged 28.7 PPG, 46% FG (27–59) and 70% from three pt. range*...Nine games of five or more assists...Five games of at least five rebounds...50% or better from three pt. range seven times...**Knicks are 7–0 when he gets to the line at least seven times in a game**...Recorded first career four point play against Utah on 12/19...Has led team in scoring, 11 times and assists once...Has scored 20+ points, 13 times and 30+ points, four times including a season and Knick-high, 41 points vs. Charlotte on Dec 4th...Averaging 19.3 points, 3/7 assists, 2.7 rebounds and 1.46 steals. **Record 1,000th assist vs. New Orleans on Dec 8th.**

Last five games: Averaging 19.0 PPG (.413 FGA), 3.6 assists, 2.8 rebounds and 2.0 steals. (Prior to Injured List)

Opponent	Mins.	Points	Rebs.	Assts.
vs. Sacramento	Injured	List		
vs. New Jersey	Injured	List		
vs. Minnesota	Injured	List		
@ Orlando	Injured	List		
vs. Charlotte	Injured	List		

Best game...

Game	Min	FGM-A	3PM-A	FTM-A	OFF	DEF	REB	AST	ST	BL	TO	PF	PTS
11/27 vs. Toronto	46	11–22	3–7	5–6	2	5	7	3	0	1	1	2	30

#1	Anfenee Hardaway	Guard/Forward
Height: 6-7	Weight: 215	Birthdate: Jul 18, 1971
High School: Treadwell (Memphis, TN)	College: Memphis '94	Years Pro: 12

2004–05: Did not score in seven minutes vs. Sacramento…Activated from injured list on January 1, 2005…Placed on the injured list on Dec 7th due to strained right hamstring…Has missed a total of 15 games this season…Averaging 5.8 points, 1.9 assists and 2.5 rebounds.

Last five games:

Opponent	Mins.	Points	Rebs.	Assts.
vs. Sacramento	7	0	0	1
vs. New Jersey	13	0	1	0
vs. Minnesota	Injured	List		
@ Orlando	Injured	List		
vs. Charlotte	Injured	List		

Milestone in Sight: Needs 14 3PT FGM for 500 career.

Best game…

Game	Min	FGM-A	3PM-A	FTM-A	OFF	DEF	REB	AST	ST	BL	TO	PF	PTS
11/21 vs. Cleve.	24	5–6	0–0	1–1	0	3	3	5	0	0	1	3	11

#20	Allan Houston	Guard
Height: 6-6	Weight: 205	Birthdate: Apr 20, 1971
High School: Ballard (Louisville, KY)	College: Tennessee '93	Years Pro: 12

2004–05: Scored 21 points and dished four assists in 35 minutes vs. Sacramento…Averaging 10.9 PPG, 1.1 RPG and 2.0 assists this season…**Shooting .425 from three-point territory (17–40 3PT FGA)…became the second Knick ever to make 900 treys on 12/19 vs. Utah (leader is John Starks with 982)…13 assists away from 2,000 career**…Activated from injured list on Dec 7th… Went on injured list Nov 1st with left knee pain…Missed a total of 18 games this season.

Last five games: Averaging 13.4 PPG and 2.8 assists in 23.8 minutes.

Opponent	Mins.	Points	Rebs.	Assts.
vs. Sacramento	35	21	1	4
vs. New Jersey	32	8	1	3
vs. Minnesota	27	7	0	0
@ Orlando	30	15	0	2
vs. Charlotte	29	16	1	5

Milestones in sight: *Allan needs 76 3PT FG to beome the Knicks all-time franchise leader. He will replace John Starks who is currently leading with 982 threes.*

Best game…

Game	Min	FGM-A	3PM-A	FTM-A	OFF	DEF	REB	AST	ST	BL	TO	PF	PTS
¼ vs. Sacramento	35	6–14	4–8	7–8	0	1	1	4	0	0	1	2	21

#3	Stephon Marbury	Guard
Height: 6-2	Weight: 200	Birthdate: Feb 20, 1977
High School: Lincoln (Brooklyn, NY)	College: Georgia Tech '99	Years Pro: 9

2004–05: Led team with 26 points and seven assists in 42 minutes vs. Sacramento…**12 double-doubles this season**…Averaging 20.7 points, **8.5 assists (3rd in league)**, 3.1 rebounds and 1.51 steals per game…Has led team in scoring 13 times and assists in 30 out of 31 games…Has scored 20+ points in 14 games and 30+ points in five games…Surpassed 12,000 point plateau scoring a season-high 37 points (4–7 3PT-FGA) and nine assists vs. Indiana Pacers on 11/13. **50% or better from the floor in 15 games, including four of last five**…been to the line at least seven times in 13 games, with a high of 12–12 vs. Atlanta on 11/30…five or more boards six times, three or more steals seven times…50% or better from long range six times (best was 5–7 vs. Memphis on 12/1).

Last five games: Averaging 27.4 PPG, 7.8 assists and 4.4 rebounds.

Opponent	Mins.	Points	Rebs.	Assts.
vs. Sacramento	42	26	1	7
vs. New Jersey	41	31	4	8
vs. Minnesota	38	32	7	11
@ Orlando	43	34	2	7
vs. Charlotte	40	14	8	6

Best game…

Game	Min	FGM-A	3PM-A	FTM-A	OFF	DEF	REB	AST	ST	BL	TO	PF	PTS
12/29 vs. Minn.	38	12–19	1–3	7–7	1	6	7	11	2	0	3	3	32

#25	Moochie Norris	Guard
Height 6-1	Weight: 185	Birthdate: Jun 23, 1973
High School: Cardoza (Washington, DC)	College: West Florida '96	Years Pro: 8

2004–05: Scored two points in eight minutes vs. Sacramento…Activated from injured list on Dec 7th…Placed on injured list with left Achilles tendonitis on 11/21…Averaging 3.2 points, 1.6 rebounds and 1.0 assists in 10.5 minutes per game…four or more rebounds twice (high of six vs. Charlotte on 12/26)…Missed seven games due to injury this season.

Last five games: Averaging 3.2 PPG, 1.6 rebounds and 1.0 assists.

Opponent	Mins.	Points	Rebs.	Assts.
vs. Sacramento	8	2	0	0
vs. New Jersey	7	0	0	1
vs. Minnesota	12	6	1	2
@ Orlando	9	6	1	1
vs. Charlotte	16	2	6	1

Best game…

Game	Min	FGM-A	3PM-A	FTM-A	OFF	DEF	REB	AST	ST	BL	TO	PF	PTS
12/14 vs. NJ	20	1–3	0–1	2–2	1	3	4	5	2	0	2	2	4

#13	Nazr Mohammed	Center
Height: 6-10	Weight: 250	Birthdate: Sept 5, 1977
High School: Kenwood (Chicago, IL)	College: Kentucky '99	Years Pro: 7

2004–05: 22 points (8–13 FGA), 11 rebounds and two blocks 39 minutes vs. Sacramento…Averaging 13.0 points (.536 FGA, 3rd in NBA), 9.5 rebounds (14th in NBA) and 1.2 blocks. Ranks 3rd in NBA in offensive rebounds (3.8)…13 double-doubles this season (six last season)…Mohammed has led the Knicks in scoring once and rebounding 14 times and has recorded 14 games where he has grabbed 10+ rebounds…Six games of 20 or more points…Scored 20 points (8–16 FGA), 15 rebounds, four blocks and two steals vs. Indiana Pacers including a career-high 11 offensive boards on 11/13 – previous was 10 (Jan. 10, 2002 vs. Milwaukee)…best overall stretch was from 11/23–30, averaging 21 PPG, 13.3 RPG and 69% from the floor in the trio…**shooting 57% from the floor in the last six games**…four or more blocks three times (high of eight vs. Utah on 12/19)…shot 50% or better from the floor in six of the last eight…**second on team in free throws made and attempted.**
Last five games: Averaging 16.8 PPG (.549 FGA), 11.0 rebounds and 1.2 blocks.

Opponent	Mins.	Points	Rebs.	Assts.
vs. Sacramento	39	22	11	2
vs. New Jersey	35	18	13	2
vs. Minnesota	35	19	9	0
@ Orlando	21	5	8	0
vs. Charlotte	40	16	9	3

Best game…

Game	Min	FGM-A	3PM-A	FTM-A	OFF	DEF	REB	AST	ST	BL	TO	PF	PTS
11/13 vs. Atlanta	28	8–12	0–0	2–2	4	10	14	1	3	0	0	2	18

#14	Bruno Sandov	Center
Height: 7-2	Weight: 260	Birthdate: Feb 10, 1980
High School: Winchendon Prep (MA)	College: Split, Croatia	Years Pro: 7

2004–05: Did not score in six minutes vs. Sacramento…Scored a season high, seven points and two rebounds in eight minutes against Dallas at MSG on Dec 21st…Averaging 1.8 points and 1.3 rebounds per game…Went on injured list Nov 1st with right Achilles tendonitis…Missed a total of five games before being activated on Nov 16, 2004.

Opponent	Mins.	Points	Rebs.	Assts.
vs. Sacramento	6	0	0	0
vs. New Jersey	DNP	CD		
vs. Minnesota	DNP	CD		
@ Orlando	DNP	CD		
vs. Charlotte	DNP	CD		

Best game…

Game	Min	FGM-A	3PM-A	FTM-A	OFF	DEF	REB	AST	ST	BL	TO	PF	PTS
12/21 vs. Dallas	8	3–8	1–2	0–0	2	0	2	1	2	0	1	1	7

#50	Michael Sweetney	Forward
Height: 6-8	Weight: 270	Birthdate: Oct 25, 1982
High School: Oxon Hill (Oxon Hill, MD)	College: Georgetown '04	Years Pro: 1

2004–05: Scored on point and one rebound in three minutes before leaving game with a sprained right ankle…Averaging 7.3 points (.536 FGA) and 4.2 rebounds off the bench…led team in scoring once and rebounding once and has scored 10+ points on six occasions…seven or more boards in a game five times…*best four game stretch from 11/3–12, average 12.8 PPG, 5.8 RPG and 57% FG*…**Ranks #19 in the NBA in free-throws attempted per 48 minutes (9.02).**
Last five games: Averaging 6.4 PPG and 4.4 rebounds.

Opponent	Mins.	Points	Rebs.	Assts.
vs. Sacramento	3	1	1	1
vs. New Jersey	13	3	4	0
vs. Minnesota	20	6	5	0
@ Orlando	20	11	5	0
vs. Charlotte	16	6	4	0

Best game…

Game	Min	FGM-A	3PM-A	FTM-A	OFF	DEF	REB	AST	ST	BL	TO	PF	PTS
11/12 vs. Clippers	31	4–8	0–0	6–6	3	6	9	3	2	2	3	1	14

#40	Kurt Thomas	Forward
Height: 6-9	Weight: 235	Birthdate: Oct 4, 1972
High School: Hillcrest (Dallas, TX)	College: Texas Christian '95	Years Pro: 10

2004–05: Four points and seven rebounds vs. Sacramento...**11 double-doubles this season**...has had at least six rebounds in every game but one this season (4 @ Char. on 12/4)...Averaging 10.9 points, 10.0 rebounds (10th in NBA), 1.8 assists, 1.09 steals and .90 blocks...Ranks 6th in NBA in defensive rebounds (8.0)...Has led team in scoring once and rebounding 15 times. Has posted 14 games where he pulled down 10+ rebounds...**50% or better from the floor 17 times**...*best three game stretch was from 11/18–21, averaged 18.3 PPG and 56% from the floor*...averaged 12.6 RPG over seven game stretch from 12/8–19, including a season best 18 boards vs. Denver on 12/12...**Moved into 24th place in Knicks franchise scoring surpassing Walt Bellamy on Nov 13th vs. Indiana**...Also pulled down his 4,000th career rebound on Nov 13th.
Last five games: Averaging 9.6 PPG, 8.0 rebounds, 1.4 assists.

Opponent	Mins.	Points	Rebs.	Assts.
vs. Sacramento	20	4	7	4
vs. New Jersey	38	6	10	1
vs. Minnesota	37	14	6	1
@ Orlando	39	14	9	1
vs. Charlotte	38	10	8	0

Milestones in Sight: Needs **106** points for 5,459 with New York (passing Bernard King to move into 23rd place in Knicks franchise history).
Best game...

Game	Min	FGM-A	3PM-A	FTM-A	OFF	DEF	REB	AST	ST	BL	TO	PF	PTS
12/8@ Hornets	35	7–15	0–0	2–2	4	11	15	0	0	3	2	3	16

#5	Tim Thomas	Forward
Height: 6-10	Weight: 240	Birthdate: Feb 26, 1977
High School: Paterson Catholic (Paterson, NJ)	College: Villanova '00	Years Pro: 8

2004–05: Scored 11 points, eight rebounds and one assist in 36 minutes vs. Sacramento...**over last 21 games, has averaged 11.5 PPG, .45 PCT FG (89–196), .42 PCT from three (22–52)**...prior to that was averaging 7.6 PPG, .31 FG and .25 from three pt. range...overall averaging 10.5 PPG, 3.5 rebounds and 1.2 assists in 27.2 minutes...Led team in scoring once and rebounds once...*best three game stretch to date was from 12/22–27, averaged 18 PPG and 53% from the floor*...Hit a four-point play (3rd of his career) with 5:38 remaining in 4th vs. Spurs on 11/16 when he was fouled by Brent Barry...Thomas converted four point plays as a Milwaukee Buck on March 13, 2001 at Toronto and in the Playoffs on May 1, 2003 vs. NJ...It was the **17th** regular season four-point play in Knicks history (first since Sprewell at Sacramento on April 7, 2002).
Last five games: Averaging 14.4 PPG (.501 FGA), 4.6 rebounds and 2.4 assists.

Opponent	Mins.	Points	Rebs.	Assts.
vs. Sacramento	36	11	8	1
vs. New Jersey	37	14	4	2
vs. Minnesota	38	10	6	1
@ Orlando	40	15	4	6
vs. Charlotte	35	20	3	4

Best game...

Game	Min	FGM-A	3PM-A	FTM-A	OFF	DEF	REB	AST	ST	BL	TO	PF	PTS
12/26 vs. Charlotte	35	7–11	1–2	5–6	3	3	3	4	2	0	3	1	20

#31	Jerome Williams	Forward
Height: 6-9	Weight: 240	Birthdate: May 10, 1973
High School: Magruder, (Germantown, MD)	College: Georgetown '96	Years Pro: 9

2004–05: One point, one assist and four rebounds in 28 minutes off the bench vs. Sacramento...**five or more boards nine times** (high of nine on 12/7)...scored in double figures four times, with a high of 15@ Orl. on 12/27...averaging 4.8 points and 3.5 rebounds in 15.1 minutes off the bench.
Last five games: Averaging 5.4 PPG (.636 FGA) and 1.8 rebounds.

Opponent	Mins.	Points	Rebs.	Assts.
vs. Sacramento	28	1	4	1
vs. New Jersey	12	5	1	0
vs. Minnesota	16	4	2	2
@ Orlando	18	15	2	3
vs. Charlotte	8	2	0	0

Best game...

Game	Min	FGM-A	3PM-A	FTM-A	OFF	DEF	REB	AST	ST	BL	TO	PF	PTS
12/17 @ Phila.	23	6–7	0–0	1–1	3	6	9	2	4	0	1	3	13

APPENDIX 5

Unique and special event publicity

PRESS RELEASE
DETROIT TIGERS

Detroit Tigers Media Relations Department • Comerica Park • Phone (313) 471-2000 • Fax (313) 471-2138 • www.tigers.com

FOR IMMEDIATE RELEASE
SATURDAY, APRIL 7, 2012

CONTACT: COMMUNICATIONS
313-471-2000 / tigers.com
@Tigers / @TigresdeDetroit
facebook.com/tigers

HOP ON DOWN TO COMERICA PARK TOMORROW FOR KIDS OPENING DAY AT 1:05 P.M.

DETROIT – Join us tomorrow for Kids Opening Day as the Tigers wrap up their Opening Weekend series against the Boston Red Sox at 1:05 p.m. All kids 14-and-younger will receive an "Every Kid, Every Sunday" Building Block Calendar, compliments of Little Caesars. Twenty-three Kids Opening Day contest winners who were selected from an essay contest will participate in Kids Opening Day in a variety of roles including honorary starting lineup announcer, honorary radio broadcast announcer and honorary groundskeeper. Additionally, the Easter Bunny will be hop, hop, hopping around Comerica Park in celebration of Easter Sunday and the first 200 kids will get a free photo with him!

Kids Opening Day marks the first Sunday Kids Day promotion of the season. All Sunday home games are Kids Days at Comerica Park. All kids 14-and-younger will receive a free promotional item as part of the "Every Kid, Every Sunday" giveaway guarantee, can enjoy free rides courtesy of Kroger on the Comerica Bank Carousel or the Fly Ball Ferris Wheel, can take part in free face painting, have the chance to win a bicycle and are invited down to the field for Kids Run the Bases courtesy of Aquafina and Meijer following the game.

SUPER SPRING TICKET DEAL: For games versus Tampa Bay (April 10-12), Mezzanine seats are just $10 (regularly priced $16) and Upper Box Infield seats are only $12 (regularly priced $24).

GET YOUR TICKETS NOW: Tickets for Opening Week are available at the Comerica Park Box Office, online at tigers.com and by phone at (866) 66-TIGER (84437). For complete ticket information including single game, season, group and suites visit tigers.com/tickets or call 313-471-BALL (2255).

--TIGERS--

Thursday, May 5 – New York Yankees @ 1:05 p.m. (Gates open at 11:30 a.m.)

PAWS' Super Sweet 16 Birthday Celebration: Join Detroit's favorite mascot, PAWS, to celebrate his **Super Sweet 16 Birthday** prior to Thursday's game! Special events to mark the celebration include:

- A **large birthday cake float** on Witherell Street, near Gate A, displayed by The Parade Company.
- The opportunity to win a **Super Sweet 16 prize pack**, which includes tickets to a Tigers game, AMP live tickets, autographed merchandise and a few other surprises (AMP Radio will be set up to register fans on the Main Concourse).
- The chance to leave PAWS a **special birthday video greeting** at the Big Cat Court near section 119 and to sign his **Sweet 16 Birthday card**, on the Main Concourse.
- Everyone is also invited to meet sixteen (16) of PAWS' special mascot friends who will make the trip all the way to Comerica Park to celebrate with PAWS: **PAWS' Father, The Parrot of the Pittsburgh Pirates, Southpaw of the Chicago White Sox, Gapper of the Cincinnati Reds, Sparty of Michigan State University, Grizzly of Oakland University, Mudonna and Muddy of the Toledo Mudhens, Big Lug of the Lansing Lugnuts, Crash the River Rascal of the West Michigan Whitecaps, Belle Tire from Belle Tire, Remote from Comcast, Clownie of The Parade Company, Caesar Man from Little Caesars Pizza, Red Robin from Red Robin Restaurants, Mr. Pop from National Coney Island and Hooper of Detroit Pistons.**

In honor of PAWS' Super Sweet 16, a Michigan State Police booth will be placed on the main concourse for fans to learn more about safe teen driving. A **special pre-game ceremony** will be held on the field for Paws and all his special mascot guests for a **surprise birthday reveal and performance**. It will be the birthday celebration of a lifetime, so don't miss out!!!

TIGERS VALUE OFFERS AT COMERICA PARK

- **$5 Ticket** – Available for regular season Tigers home games, subject to availability
- **$5 Adult Meals** – Hot dog, chips and a soda, available at the Big League Grill
- **$5 Kids Meal** – Hot dog, chips and a juice box, available at the Big League Grill
- **$5 Parking** – Lots off of Columbia St. between Cass Ave. and Grand River Ave.
- **$5 Tigers Magazine** every game – Includes a scorecard and game notes.
- Group tickets, including suites and indoor and outdoor picnics, offer reduced ticket prices in certain seating sections on specific days for groups of 15-or-more.

THE FIERCEST

BLAZE

IN AMERICA

IS

FORDHAM ALL-AMERICA LINEBACKER

★MARK BLAZEJEWSKI★

"BLAZE'S" CREDENTIALS

- *Honorable Mention all-America by The Sports Network.*
- *First team ECAC all-star for the second straight year.*
- *LED the Patriot League in tackles for the third season (13.0).*
- *Team high three interceptions, including a 44yd. TD @ Villanova.*
- *Patriot League Defensive Player of the Week for Sept 19 and Nov 7.*
- *Featured on ESPN's "Thursday Night College Football."*
- *Keyed a defense that was FIFTH in 1-AA against the run.*

HIS CAREER

- 1992 Patriot League preseason Defensive Player of the Year as selected by *The Sporting News*, League Coaches and Sports Information Directors.
- 1992 Second team preseason all-America, *The Sports Network*.
- 1992 Second team preseason all-America, *Street and Smith's College Football Yearbook*.
- 1992 preseason all-America, *Don Heinrich's Football Annual*.
- 1992 preseason all-America, *Dan Shonka's College Football Annual*.
- 1991 First team all-Patriot League.
- 1991 First team all-Eastern Collegiate Athletic Conference (ECAC) pick.
- 1991 Second team all-America by the *Associated Press*.
- 1991 Honorable Mention all-America by the *Football Gazette*.
- Bounced back after missing the entire 1990 season with total reconstructive surgery of the left knee.
- 1990 Second team all-America by the *Sports Network*.
- Three time team captain.

CAREER STATS

SEASON	G/GS	UT	AT	TT	AVG
1992	10/10	40	53	93	13.0
1991	10/10	72	73	145	14.5
1990	INJURED, DID NOT PLAY				
1989	8/7	56	68	124	15.5
1988	10/0	7	3	10	1.0
TOTALS	38/27	175	197	372	10.6

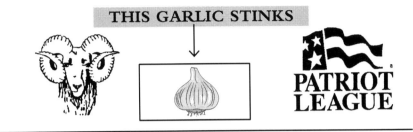

THIS GARLIC STINKS

THIS ONE DOESN'T

FORDHAM ALL-AMERICA RECEIVER

TOM GARLICK

THE "SWEET" NUMBERS:

THE 1992 SEASON*

– 6.7 catches per game (**FOURTH in 1-AA**)
– 130.3 all-purpose yards per game (**26th in 1-AA**)
– 89.3 receiving yards per game (**16th in 1-AA**)
– **FOUR** games of 100 yards or more receiving
– **LEADS** Patriot League in catches (47), touchdown catches (6), and catches per game (6.7)
– **FOURTH** in kickoff return average (20.5 avg)
– **SIXTH** in scoring (5.1 pg)
– 80 yard touchdown reception @ Hofstra, Rams **LONGEST** at the 1-AA level

CAREER MARKS

GARLICK IS FORDHAM'S
ALL-TIME LEADER IN*:
– RECEPTIONS (157)
– KICKOFF RETURN YARDS (898)
– RECEIVING YARDS (2,210)
– RECEIVING TOUCHDOWNS (19)
– MOST 100 YARD RECEIVING GAMES (10)

SEASON MARKS
– TIED FOR MOST TOUCHDOWN CATCHES (8)
– THREE OF TOP FOUR BEST SEASONS IN RECEIVING YARDS AND RECEPTIONS
– MOST KICKOFF RETURNS IN A SEASON

* Numbers as of 10/24/92

APPENDIX 6

Media seating charts

TO BROADCAST BOOOTHS

ERNIE HARWELL MEDIA CENTER
SEATING CHART
JUNE 1-3, 2012

FIELD VIEW

Left	#	Middle	#	Right	#
				Windsor Star	26
		Yankees PR	50	Jon Morosi	25
		NY Post	49	Detroit F-P	24
Television Stats	70	NY Post	48	Detroit F-P	23
Visiting Media	69	NY Times	47	Detroit F-P	22
Visiting Media	68	NY Daily News	46	Detroit F-P	21
Visiting Media	67	Bergen Record	45	Detroit F-P	20
Visiting Media	66	Journal News	44	Detroit F-P	19
Visiting Media	65	ESPNNY.com	43	FSDetroit.com	18
Visiting Media	64	Star Ledger	42	Associated Press	17
Visiting Media	63	Wall Street Journal	41	Associated Press	16
Visiting Media	62	WFAN	40	Oakland Press	15
Sports Xchange	61	Newsday	39	Oakland Press	14
Telegram News	60	Kyodo News	38	Booth News	13
Huron Daily Tribune	59	Jiji Press	37	Booth News	12
Crain's Detroit	58	Sports Nippon	36	Offical Scorer	11
24-7 Baseball	57	Visiting Media	35	Detroit News	10
Latino Press	56	Visiting Media	34	Detroit News	9
Detroit Monitor	55	MLBAM Scoring	33	Detroit News	8
Michigan Chronicle	54	MLB.com	32	Detroit News	7
Toledo Blade	53	MLB.com	31	Detroit News	6
Detroit Tigers	52	STATS Inc.	30	Detroit News	5
Detroit Tigers	51	Associated Press	29	Tigers PR	4
		Tigers PR	28	Tigers PR	3
		Tigers PR	27	Tigers PR	2
				Tigers PR	1

STAIRS

2005/2006
NY KNICKS VS. NJ Nets
SEATING CHART
DATE: October 28, 2005   TIME: 7:30 PM

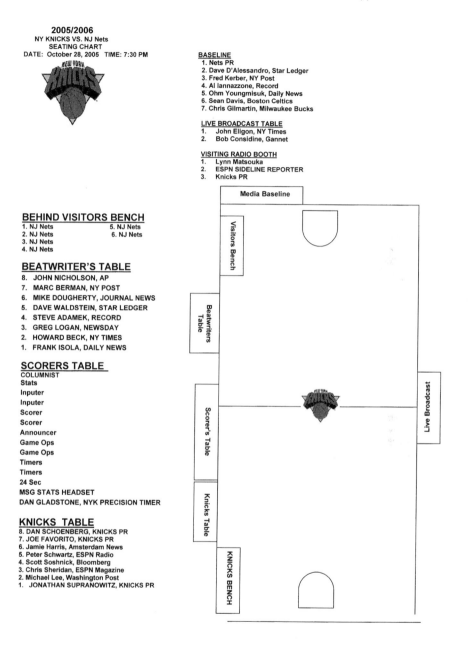

BASELINE
1. Nets PR
2. Dave D'Alessandro, Star Ledger
3. Fred Kerber, NY Post
4. Al Iannazzone, Record
5. Ohm Youngmisuk, Daily News
6. Sean Davis, Boston Celtics
7. Chris Gilmartin, Milwaukee Bucks

LIVE BROADCAST TABLE
1.   John Eligon, NY Times
2.   Bob Considine, Gannet

VISITING RADIO BOOTH
1.   Lynn Matsouka
2.   ESPN SIDELINE REPORTER
3.   Knicks PR

Media Baseline

Visitors Bench

Beatwriters Table

Scorer's Table

Knicks Table

Live Broadcast

KNICKS BENCH

BEHIND VISITORS BENCH
1. NJ Nets	5. NJ Nets
2. NJ Nets	6. NJ Nets
3. NJ Nets	
4. NJ Nets	

BEATWRITER'S TABLE
8.   JOHN NICHOLSON, AP

7.   MARC BERMAN, NY POST

6.   MIKE DOUGHERTY, JOURNAL NEWS

5.   DAVE WALDSTEIN, STAR LEDGER

4.   STEVE ADAMEK, RECORD

3.   GREG LOGAN, NEWSDAY

2.   HOWARD BECK, NY TIMES

1.   FRANK ISOLA, DAILY NEWS

SCORERS TABLE
COLUMNIST
Stats
Inputer
Inputer
Scorer
Scorer
Announcer
Game Ops
Game Ops
Timers
Timers
24 Sec
MSG STATS HEADSET
DAN GLADSTONE, NYK PRECISION TIMER

KNICKS TABLE
8. DAN SCHOENBERG, KNICKS PR
7. JOE FAVORITO, KNICKS PR
6. Jamie Harris, Amsterdam News
5. Peter Schwartz, ESPN Radio
4. Scott Soshnick, Bloomberg
3. Chris Sheridan, ESPN Magazine
2. Michael Lee, Washington Post
1.   JONATHAN SUPRANOWITZ, KNICKS PR

Gate 64 Press Box Seating - pg 2

**NY KNICKERBOCKERS VS NJ NETS
SEATING CHART**

GATE 64 PRESS BOX

Row A (bottom of Ramp – Seats l to r)
1. Jim Sann, Houston Rockets
2. Wes Unseld, Jr., Washington Wizards
3. Jimmy Powell, Indiana Pacers
4. Mike Wilhelm, Cleveland Cavs

5. Jerry Powell, Charlotte Bobcats
6. Bratskeir Guest
7. Anne Bratskeir, Newsday
8. Fran Fraschilla, ESPN

Row B (Seats l to r)
1. Tom Kertes, Basetball Digest
2. Robbie Kass
3. Constantino Viloria, El Diario
4. Knicks PR
5. Al Coqueran, Bronx Times

6. Howie Karpin, CBS Radio
7. Trevor Kearney, Inside Stuff
8. Willard Ogan, CBS Newspath
9. Rich Coutinho, AP Radio
10. Knicks PR

ROW C (seats l to r)
1. Sebastian Bednarski, Poland
2. Kaoru Sanada, Japan
3. Daisuke Suguira, Japan
4. Massimo Lopes, La Gazette dello Sport
5. Al Marchfeld, Knicks

6. Wanda Mann, NY Sportscene
7. Mike Mancuso, WFAN
8. Pascal Giberne, France
9. David Corral, Spain
10. Arik Henig, Israel

33rd UPPER PRESS BOX
(Directly below Sections 421 thru 425)

21. Scott Mandel, Sports Reporters.com
22. Jeff Lenchiner, Inside Hoops
23. Frank Rivera, Black Reign
24. Bob Trainor, Trainor Comm.
25. Robert Elkin, VOICE of NY
26. Lloyd Carroll, Queens Chronicle
27. Stepahnie Stepp, WHCR
28. WFUV
29. Alex Labidou, Basketball News
30. Tom Beer, Basketball News
31. WFAN
32. KNICKS PR

35. Reserved
36. Reserved
37. Reserved
38. Reserved
39. Sportsticker
40. AP SPORTLINE
41. Reserved
42. Reserved
43 Reserved

[BREAK]
44. Reserved
45. Reserved
46. Reserved
47. Reserved
48. Reserved

49. Reserved
50. Reserved
51. Reserved
52. Reserved
53. Reserved
54. Reserved
55. Reserved
56. Reserved
57. Reserved
58. Reserved
59. Reserved

31st UPPER PRESS BOX
(Directly below Sections 404 thru 407)

1. Reserved
2. Reserved
3. Reserved
4. Reserved
5. Reserved
6. WADO SPANISH RADIO
7. WADO SPANISH RADIO
8. WADO SPANISH RADIO
9. WADO SPANISH RADIO
10. WADO SPANISH RADIO

**PHOTO POSITIONS
NY KNICKS VS NJ NETS**

KNICKS BENCH (8TH Avenue Baseline)

8th Avenue & 31st St. Quadrant (far corner from Knicks bench)
12. NEWSDAY (extreme corner)
11.　ASSOCIATED PRESS
9.　 NEW YORK TIMES
8.　 REUTERS
7.　 BERGEN RECORD
6.　 JOURNAL NEWS
5.　 STAR LEDGER
4.　 NBA Photos
3.　 DAILY NEWS
2.　 NEW YORK POST
(ESCAPE LANE)
1.　 TV HAND HELD CAMERA

BASKET

8th Avenue & 33rd St. Quadrant (next to Knicks bench)

1.　 TV HAND HELD CAMERA
(ESCAPE LANE)
2.　 GEORGE KALINSKY
3.　 RESERVED
4.　 RESERVED
5.　 RESERVED
6.　 RESERVED
7.　 RESERVED
8.　 RESERVED

VISITORS BENCH (7TH Avenue Baseline)

7th Avenue & 31st St. Quadrant (far corner from Visitors Bench)
10. NBA ENG Crew
9.　 Star Ledger
8.　 New York Times
7.　 NBA PHOTOS
6.　 Newsday
5.　 AP
4.　 Reuters
3.　 Daily News
2.　 New York Post
(ESCAPE LANE)
1.　 TV HAND HELD CAMERA

BASKET

(7th Avenue & 33rd St. Quadrant – next to visitors bench)

1. TV-HAND HELD
(ESCAPE LANE)
2. NBA PHOTOS
3. MSG PHOTOS
4. Matthias Krause, Basketball, Germany
5. Chie Suzuki, HOOP
6. NY Sportscene

2006 IFL WORLD TEAM CHAMPIONSHIP – MOLINE
MEDIA SEATING CHART

Courtside Press Seating

1. Quad City Times
2. Quad City Times
3. Sherdog.com
4. Dispatch/Rock Island Argus
5. MMA Weekly
6. MMANews.com
7. IFL Media Staff
8. IFL Media Staff

9. Grappling
10. MMA Fighting
11. Full Contact Fighter
12. Hola America
13. Fearless Radio
14. Fearless Radio
15. IFL Media Staff
16. IFL Media Staff

(all other print media to be seated in auxiliary media seating, **Section 102, Rows 6-10**, unassigned)

Courtside Photo Positions

Northeast Corner
NE-1. IFL
NE-2. Sherdog.com
NE-3. MMA Fighting
NE-4. MMA Weekly
NE-5. ROTATING

Southwest Corner
SW-1. ROTATING
SW-2. Quad City Times
SW-3. Dispatch/RI ARgus
SW-4. CBS/60 Minutes
SW-5. IFL

Photographers not listed may utilize "ROTATING" photo positions for one match, then please allow other photographers to use for succeeding matches. Auxiliary photo area located at **top of section 103, 105**, aside main television camera location.

INDEX